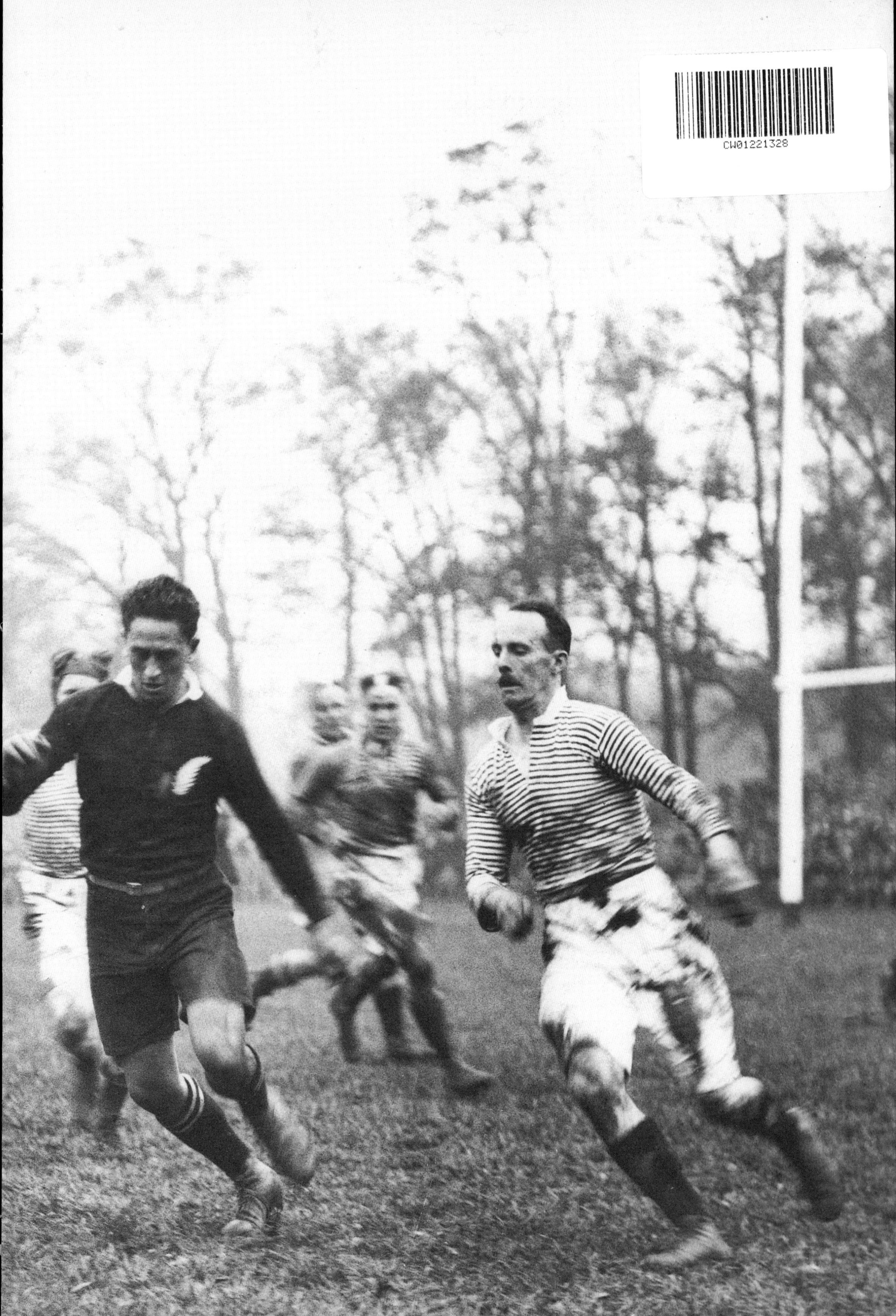

THE POWER BEHIND THE ALL BLACKS

THE POWER BEHIND THE ALL BLACKS

THE UNTOLD STORY OF THE MEN WHO COACHED THE ALL BLACKS

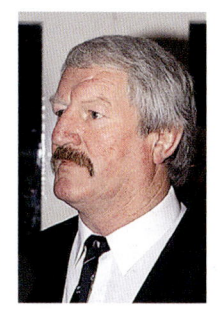

PAUL VERDON

PENGUIN BOOKS

CONTENTS

Foreword, by Sir Terry McLean *9*

Introduction *10*
'There never was a poor All Black team'

The Early Days *12*
Forerunners to the All Blacks and their coaches

1 / **Tom Ellison** 1893 *18*
First of the few truly great contributors

2 / **Jimmy Duncan** 1904, 1905-06 *22*
Father of All Black coaches had an inauspicious end

3 / **David Gallaher** 1908 *28*
Legacy handed down to future coaches and captains

4 / **George Mason** 1913 *32*
Missionary George may have helped kill the game

5 / **Billy Stead** 1921 *35*
Undefeated All Black lost one test as coach

6 / **George Nicholson** 1908, 1921 *39*
Gave long service to the game

7 / **Cliff Porter** 1924-30 *43*
Guiding hand through much of a fabulous decade

8 / **Maurice Brownlie** 1928 *53*
Series share with Boks was to prove benchmark for 68 years

9 / **Norm McKenzie** 1930, 1947, 1949 *60*
Great influence on All Blacks over three decades

10 / **Ted McKenzie** 1925, 1930 *66*
The only sole selector in New Zealand rugby history

11 / **Billy Wallace** 1932, 1937 *71*
'Carbine' was a great player and much more

12 / **Vince Meredith** 1910, 1935-36 *76*
Vinny was an autocratic All Black Coach

13 / **Jim Burrows** 1937 *82*
Great leader of men could not halt Bok juggernaut

14 / **Alex McDonald** 1921, 1938, 1949 *91*
Fabulous career darkened by blackest days of All Black history

15 / **Tom Morrison** 1950, 1952, 1955-56 *99*
Never lost a series in seven years

16 / **Len Clode** 1951 *108*
Len was the right man in the right place at the right time

17 / **Arthur Marslin** 1953-54 *111*
Cavanagh's treatment opened the door

18 / **Bob Stuart** 1956 *116*
A mastermind of the 'greatest series win in history'

19 / **Dick Everest** 1957 *122*
Could have bestrode the All Blacks' 'Everest'

20 / Jack Sullivan 1958-60   *126*
Craven's revenge awaited Sullivan and Whineray

21 / Ron Bush 1962   *134*
Helped throw off 'chains' of the 1950s

22 / Neil McPhail 1961-65   *137*
Outstanding record in combination with great captain

23 / Fred Allen 1966-68   *144*
'The Needle' had what others strive for — the perfect record

24 / Ivan Vodanovich 1969-71   *150*
Fine servant of game but coaching record unenviable

25 / Bob Duff 1972-73   *154*
History should not judge 'Duffer' unfairly

26 / John ('J.J.') Stewart 1973-76   *160*
JJ was rugby's gentleman revolutionary

27 / Jack Gleeson 1972, 1976-82   *167*
All Blacks' first Grand Slam didn't tell whole story

28 / Eric Watson 1979-80   *172*
Eric plotted ruin of the Welsh centenary party

29 / Peter Burke 1981-82   *178*
Regained 'world crown' from beseiged Boks

30 / Bryce Rope 1983-84   *184*
The full range of highs and lows

31 / Brian Lochore 1985-87   *189*
All Blacks' guide to victory in first World Cup

32 / Alex Wyllie 1988-91   *196*
Grizz had more wins than any other All Black coach

33 / Laurie Mains 1992-95   *205*
Poisoned chalice robbed Mains of glory he earned

34 / John Hart 1987, 1991 (co-coach), 1996-   *154*
First professional coach fashions record to match

Conclusion   *225*

Selectors and Managers   *232*

Bibliography   *236*

Index   *238*

PENGUIN BOOKS
Penguin Books (NZ) Ltd, cnr Airborne and Rosedale Roads, Albany,
Auckland 1310, New Zealand
Penguin Books Ltd, 27 Wrights Lane, London W8 5TZ, England
Penguin Putnam Inc, 375 Hudson Street, New York, NY 10014, United States
Penguin Books Australia Ltd, 487 Maroondah Highway, Ringwood, Australia 3134
Penguin Books Canada Ltd, 10 Alcorn Avenue, Toronto, Ontario, Canada M4V 3B2
Penguin Books (South Africa) Pty Ltd, 5 Watkins Street, Denver Ext 4, 2094, South Africa
Penguin Books India (P) Ltd, 11, Community Centre, Panchsheel Park,
New Delhi 110 017, India

Penguin Books Ltd, Registered Offices: Harmondsworth, Middlesex, England

First published by Penguin Books (NZ) Ltd, 1999

10 9 8 7 6 5 4 3 2 1

Copyright © Paul Verdon 1999

The right of Paul Verdon to be identified as the author of this work in terms of section 96 of
the Copyright Act 1994 is hereby asserted.

Designed by Penguin Books and Seven Visual Communications
Film by Wyatt & Wilson Print, Christchurch
Printed in Hong Kong by Everbest Printing

All rights reserved. Without limiting the rights under copyright reserved above,
no part of this publication may be reproduced, stored in or introduced
into a retrieval system, or transmitted, in any form or by any means
(electronic, mechanical, photocopying, recording or otherwise), without
the prior written permission of both the copyright owner and
the above publisher of this book.

ISBN 0-14-028913-5 (trade edition)
ISBN 0670-88952-0 (deluxe edition)

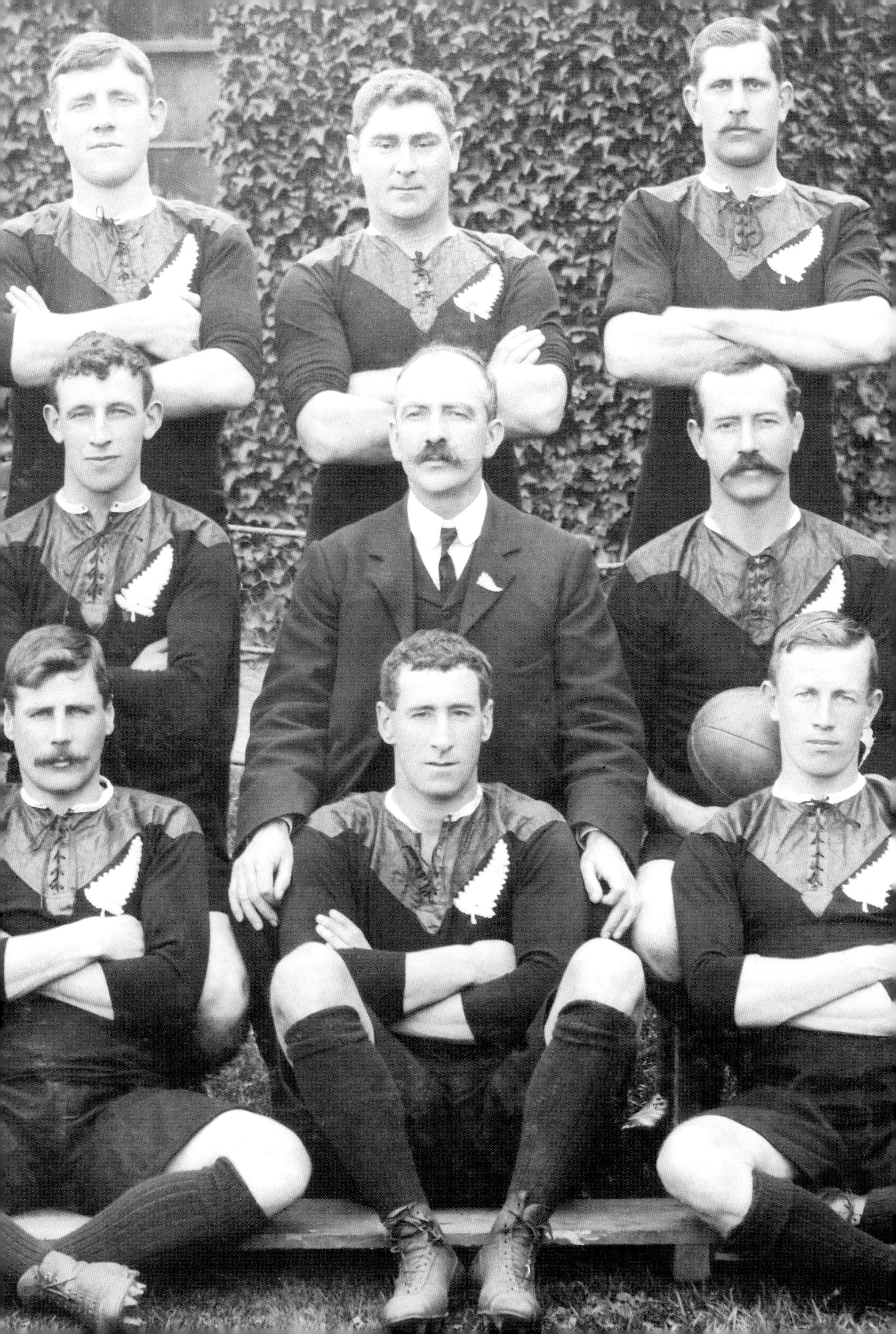

ACKNOWLEDGEMENTS

In the researching and writing of this history the author acknowledges the great support he has enjoyed from surviving All Black coaches and from the families of coaches past. In addition he has been assisted by a host of New Zealand rugby personalities. Without their cooperation and courtesy this book would not have been possible. The author owes a debt of gratitude to the following:

Helen Adams and Fionna Hill; Neil Bond; Joanna Buchanan; Dick Cavanagh; Brent Edwards; Bruce Hawkins; Lindsay Knight; Bob Luxford, curator, New Zealand Rugby Museum; Reg Maskell; Dave McLaren; Sylvia and Grant Morrison; Jim McKenzie; Sir Terry McLean; Neville McMillan; Colin Meads; Michael O'Donnell; Ron Palenski; the Ropati brothers; Charlie Saxton; J. J. Stewart; Bob Stuart; Mary Sullivan; Russ Thomas; Wilson Whineray, and anyone else who assisted.

The author and publishers are grateful to the following for permission to use the illustrations appearing in this book. Note abbreviations: ATL (Alexander Turnbull Library), NZRM (NZ Rugby Museum), PS (Photosport):

Front jacket: NZRM, PS; **back jacket:** NZRM; **front and back endpapers:** NZRM; **page 13** NZRM; **14-15** ATL; **17-67** NZRM; **68-69** Jim McKenzie Collection; **72-77** NZRM; **78** *NZ Herald*; **80-81** ATL; **83-97** NZRM; **100-102** Grant Morrison Collection; **103-109** NZRM; **110** NZRM; Len Clode Collection; **112-128** NZRM; **131** *The Dominion*; **135** Australian Photo Agency; **138-139** NZRM; **140-141** NZ Newspapers; **144-147** Fred Allen Collection; **148-151** NZRM; **155** PS; **157** Bob Duff Collection; **158** *The Dominion*; **160-169** NZRM; **171** PS; **172** NZRM; **175-177** PS; **179** Peter Burke Collection; **180** *Evening Post*; **182-186** NZRM; **187** PS; **190** (top) NZRM; **190** (bottom) PS; **192-194** PS; **197-198** NZRM; **199** PS; **201** *The Dominion*; **202-223** PS.

The author acknowledges the permission of various copyright holders to use extracts from their books.

FOREWORD

ODD AS IT MAY SEEM, I CANNOT RECALL A moment of what I would call my waking life in rugby football when I have not been aware of coaching as part of the game.

Having been born in Wanganui, to which my grandfather had migrated from Co. Roscommon in Ireland in 1860, I was about seven (and the seventh in a family of five girls and four boys), when as a family we transferred to Hastings. A defining moment occurred a year or so later when Jack, my father, was recalled to his native city to receive life memberships badges from, I think, both the Wanganui union and the Kaierau club. These had been awarded because of his services as a player and, later, as a coach. He was deeply (and rightly) proud of the miniature gold rugby ball the union awarded him.

In no time, he was coaching the senior team of the Hastings club, for which, among others, Maurice Brownlie was a leading player. He also chose, and coached, the Hastings rep. team which beat Napier sub-union in a titanic contest. Famous not least because of the two young Maori boys, George Nepia and Lui Paewai, whom Dad had placed in the five-eighths line.

Later, our family moved to Wellington, then New Plymouth and back to Wellington. As a junior member, I tagged along; and always, rugby was the sport and coaching was an integral part of it.

It so happened that an older brother by six years, Hugh, was an extremely gifted flank-forward of pace, superb hands and the kind of "seeing eye" which distinguishes, in particular, great midfield backs. Through Hugh, I learned to look closely at the great player-captain-coach of the 1920s, Cliff Porter, whose loss to New Zealand rugby because of his 'spat' with the manager of the 1924 All Blacks, Stan Dean, cost New Zealand a coach of exceptional quality and high standing.

So, as Time marched on, I became aware of coaches all about the country — the McKenzies of Hawke's Bay and Wairarapa, Meredith of Auckland, Millard of Wellington, 'Old Vic' of Otago, and a great many more. All had their skills and successes; and for the most part, did their jobs quietly and without the fanfare which has embraced the greater coaches in the New Zealand game since World War II.

In my experience, which I take leave to say has been fairly considerable, the Big Three of this large team were 'Young Vic' Cavanagh of Otago, Dick Everest of Waikato, and Fred Allen of Auckland. I bow the knee to such as Charlie Saxton, Neil McPhail, Jack Sullivan, perhaps the greatest forward coach of them all Bob Stuart, J.J. Stewart, Jack Gleeson, and many more.

Not being capable of easily accepting the notion that rugby has done itself a great service by becoming professional, I prefer not to discuss the qualities of John Hart, even though his record in 1996-97 was so exceptional. Somehow, rugby has despoiled itself by allowing players to be switched from the sideline to the game at the will of the coach. The game has become extremely fast, the physical fitness astonishing, the goal-kicking unbelievable. And the coach is supreme.

But is it REALLY rugby? I wonder.

Nevertheless, in spite of my old-fashioned views, I appreciate the industry of Paul Verdon in writing his work about coaches of New Zealand teams. I have known a good many of them personally, toured with a number and, in spirit, have suffered with them in their inevitable trials and tribulations.

The book will, I do hope, achieve its purpose of acquainting Kiwi lovers of rugby with the great deeds and great love of the game which animated so many of these men. Without them, New Zealand rugby would never have achieved its sustained high eminence.

Sir Terry McLean

INTRODUCTION

'You never meet a poor All Black team'

IT IS MORE THAN A CENTURY SINCE THE FIRST New Zealand representative rugby players nervously laced up their boots and inhaled the smell of liniment, team talk buzzing in their ears, in preparation to do battle in the international arena.

From its beginning the tiny pioneer nation, both settler and native, embraced the new game. Its growth throughout New Zealand, in a few short years, was phenomenal. The feats of the national team, called the All Blacks from 1905 onwards, reflected the fledgling country's aspirations and psyche. The game, and stars at club, provincial and international level had a huge following on and off the paddock.

The populace quickly came to have the highest expectations of the All Blacks. New Zealand's confidence plumbed the depths when calamity occasionally struck.

The All Blacks, year in and year out, decade after decade, forged an international record that none — excepting South Africa — could match. Unlike other national sides, considered poor travellers, the All Blacks, if anything, frequently proved stronger on tour, thousands of miles from home, often for many months. The challenge seemed to increase the cohesiveness and homogeneity of the New Zealanders.

Styles and personnel might change through the seasons, but consistency was such that opposition coaches were unanimous that 'You never meet a poor All Black team'.

At the beginning of 1999, the All Blacks' test match success rate was 71.6 per cent — far ahead of closest rivals South Africa (65 per cent), England (50 per cent), and Australia (47.5 per cent).

But the achievements of the All Black teams cannot be laid solely at the feet of the hundreds of fine players who have put on the black jersey. Behind every successful side has been at least one organiser — a man or men who have taken the brilliance of 15 individuals and moulded them into a team. Tour, practice and game plans have been laid and the downfall of each upcoming opposition carefully plotted.

Let us look back for a moment to that magic time of 1905 and the Originals, or Incomparables. In fact, apart from Wales, the game in Britain was found to be 20 years behind the New Zealand standard. 'Most British sides were baffled and bewildered by the systematic, machine-like rugby of these Antipodeans with an infinite variety of brilliant tactics and copybook moves,' wrote rugby historian Morrie Mackenzie.

'The scientific system of play whose foundations had been laid in primitive tin sheds at night and out at Tahuna Park on Sundays fifteen and twenty years before had proved its surpassing merit in the very home of the rugby game itself.'[1]

But not too many conservative British rugby folk were going to admit to a superiority of organisation and philosophy among colonials. This peculiar and jaundiced outlook ascribed some fantastic reasons to the All Black successes. One was that the leather strengthening the black jerseys was for the purpose of foiling the opposition from getting a good grip on them. The famous physical culturist Eugene Sandow hailed the All Blacks as triumphs of his methods and obligingly offered to train a British side to beat them, guaranteeing success with his system. Expatriate New Zealanders even joined in the publicity, some with fanciful stories couched in terms of 'the secrets of the New Zealanders'.

In truth, few of the arts of the 2-3-2 scrum, the wing

THE POWER BEHIND THE ALL BLACKS

forward or the five-eighth system of setting a back line had reached the British Isles, while New Zealand coaches had been developing the possibilities for years.

Strong opposition to the coach as an official part of rugby persisted in Britain for many decades. Coaching hinted of professionalism, and of course the British game had gone through its schism — the breakaway of the northern clubs to form the Northern Union, or rugby league — in 1895. At all levels of British rugby, the captain was expected to organise the minimal coaching that was deemed required.

The benefits of coaching a team sport — despite the corresponding downside of sometimes curbing the individuality of a brilliant player in the interests of overall team performance — were quickly accepted in New Zealand. But this development was not without its controversies, a classic irony of the early period being the appointment of the now legendary Jimmy Duncan as official coach of the 1905 All Blacks amid senior-player opposition that stripped him of all but the most elementary coaching role on that great tour. There was irony, too, that the now equally legendary Dave Gallaher, who captained the 1905 team to their glories and deprived Duncan of the coaching duties, should, within a few years, expect All Black teams to co-operate with his coaching philosophies.

Some readers may believe it is only in recent decades that the cult of the coach has become a powerful, even leading, part of international rugby and media coverage. The controversy which raged over the respective merits of Messrs Wyllie, Mains and Hart through the early 1990s, and virtually split the country, certainly reflects a high level of contemporary interest in 'the power behind the All Blacks'. But such rows are not new. The Vic Cavanagh–Alex McDonald furore which led to the 1949 whitewashing of the All Blacks by the Springboks — then the lowest point in All Black history — is another. Problems have beset other All Black coaches too.

Rugby and the art of rugby coaching, especially at international level, have evolved over time. The modern game did not arise overnight. What John Hart employs today is often built on foundations sunk in the mists of time, perhaps by Duncan and Gallaher.

All Black captains, from Duncan and Gallaher, through Cliff Porter, Maurice Brownlie, Fred Allen, Bob Stuart, Wilson Whineray, Brian Lochore, Andy Leslie, Graham Mourie, Andy Dalton, Wayne Shelford, to Sean Fitzpatrick, have deservedly received their plaudits. Autobiographies and rugby histories have recorded and publicised their achievements. In stark contrast, the All Black coaches have never collectively received their dues or been analysed in any great depth. Yet the new professional game owes much to their services.

For the first time, therefore, in this book, an attempt is made to understand what drove the men who selected and coached All Blacks teams to countless victories and a growing national pride; who worked with their respective captains at home and overseas; and who sometimes had their problems with fellow selectors, the national union, players, media and public.

Paul Verdon

Metric and imperial measurements
Readers should note that in the interests of historical context, rugby field measurements and statistics such as a player's height and weight have been kept in the style of popular use of their times. Imperial measures are maintained up until the Alex Wylie chapter (1988-91), after which they are metric.

References
1. J. M. Mackenzie, *All Blacks in Chains*, Truth, 1960.

THE EARLY DAYS

*Forerunners to the All Blacks
and their coaches*

THOUGH IT WAS NOT UNTIL 1904 THAT THE FIRST official coach of a New Zealand rugby team was appointed, the rapid growth of rugby from its introduction in 1870 made the formation of a national side inevitable.

The game spread like a bushfire throughout the land, hundreds of clubs coming into existence within a very few years. Combinations of clubs for tours, then unions, swiftly followed. Serious competition from other Victorian games was quickly extinguished as rugby's popularity enveloped all classes and both European and Maori races.

A combination of Auckland clubs made the first national tour, in September 1875. They lost to a team drawn from Dunedin clubs, 9½ to ½ point, before 3000 spectators, and lost all their other tour matches, to Wellington, Christchurch, Nelson–Picton and Taranaki clubs. Three weeks later New Zealand's provincial government system would fall, but its provincial rugby system would carry on to become perhaps the finest in the world over the next 120 years.

However, it was the arrival of the first overseas team, the New South Wales side which toured New Zealand in 1882, playing provinces and losing to Auckland and Otago, which showed the potential for a national team. The first New Zealand side was formed in 1884, to reciprocate the Australians' visit. It won its eight matches in New South Wales comfortably, including three 'tests'.

A New Zealand union had not yet been formed, and the tour was organised by a Dunedin businessman, Samuel Sleigh, who became the team manager, and William Milton, secretary of the Canterbury union and the team's captain. Milton, a barrister and outstanding cricketer and rugby player, had captained his province since 1878. He was to die of typhoid, aged 27, three years later.

The New Zealand team was made up of nominations from the Auckland, Wellington, Canterbury and Otago unions. Players wore a dark-blue jersey with a gold fern. One of the stars of the team was Otago's Jack Tairoa. The side 'overmatched', as the *Sydney Morning Herald* wrote, its opponents in every game. The New Zealand team's good organisation, discipline, unselfishness, modesty in victory and forbearance of umpires' decisions were noted.

But it was to be half a decade before another New Zealand team was organised, perhaps because the promoters of the 1884 side had been left out of pocket. New South Wales toured in 1886, and in 1888 a British team gave the New Zealand game a boost. Andrew Stoddard, an English international cricketer and fine rugby three-quarter, took over the captaincy when Robert Seddon was drowned in Australia. Stoddard's team won 13 of 19 matches in New Zealand but did not meet a New Zealand combination.

THE POWER BEHIND THE ALL BLACKS

FORERUNNERS: This is the way footballers used to look. It's the Otago University team of the 1880s. Otago was New Zealand's rugby powerhouse then. It had thrashed Auckland in 1875 and beat the first overseas touring team, New South Wales, in 1882.

It was in 1888–89 that Thomas Eyton organised what was the first tour to Britain by any rugby team from New Zealand. This was the New Zealand Natives team, whose exploits have taken on a mystical nature, especially the accomplishment of playing 107 matches over 14 months, an average of three games per week.

As is convincingly argued by Greg Ryan in his analytical and deeply researched book on the Natives, many of their games were against far stronger opponents than the 1905–06 All Black Originals or the 1924 Invincibles were to encounter. The British game had not yet been split by the 1895 decision of many northern English clubs to leave the Rugby Football Union, because of the dispute over 'broken time' payments, and start the Northern Union (later rugby league) game.

In 1893, the union had 481 affiliated clubs, including 150 from Yorkshire and many from Lancashire. By 1903 there were only 244 clubs. It was not until 1925 that the numbers were recovered. Yorkshire won seven of the first eight English county championships up to 1895, Lancashire taking the other. Yorkshire would not win another until 1926, and Lancashire until 1935. England's playing strength was in the north until 1895. The England national team dominated through the 1870s and 1880s, but in the 18 years between 1892 and 1910 England never won the Triple Crown.

Evidence of the horrendous effect the schism had on

THE EARLY DAYS

English rugby can be seen in the long list of powerful club opponents the Natives met but were absent from the 1905 All Blacks' itinerary. The Natives played at least 40 of their 78 British matches against clubs, or combinations of clubs, which would soon turn professional. But the 1905 All Blacks played only four games against northern clubs, scoring 150 points with three against, including a 40–0 win over Yorkshire, while the England team, beaten 15–0, did not contain any players from the former heartland.

Originally to be a New Zealand Maori team, the side was renamed the Natives when Pakeha players were included because not enough Maori players could be persuaded to join the party. Of the 26 members, five were full Maori, 14 were definitely born of Pakeha fathers and Maori mothers and another possibly so, and five were full Pakeha, including the star, Otago's Pat Keogh, one of two players born overseas (and therefore not 'native'). Thus, the racial make-up of the team was almost half Maori, half Pakeha.

The Natives were sometimes controversial. They were described as professionals (their tour was a privately promoted one) and gamblers. They got 'offside' with the Rugby Football Union over excessively vigorous play, and especially when three players walked off the field in the test against England in protest at unreasonable refereeing decisions.

Yet they were also a pioneering and inventive team who won 78 games, drew six and lost 23. Their many fine performances included a win over Ireland and narrow losses to Wales (0–5) and England (0–7). They steadily improved their skills and combinations, witnesses stating they were unrecognisable from the side which had left New Zealand when they returned home to beat the finest provinces (except Auckland) at the end of their marathon tour.

Though their brushes with English rugby authority would damage the reputation of the Native team for posterity and stifle future privately promoted tours, thereby hastening the formation of the NZRFU, the team should occupy a position of honour in New Zealand's rugby history.

The Natives team was to produce two future New Zealand captains, Tom Ellison and Davey Gage. Ellison

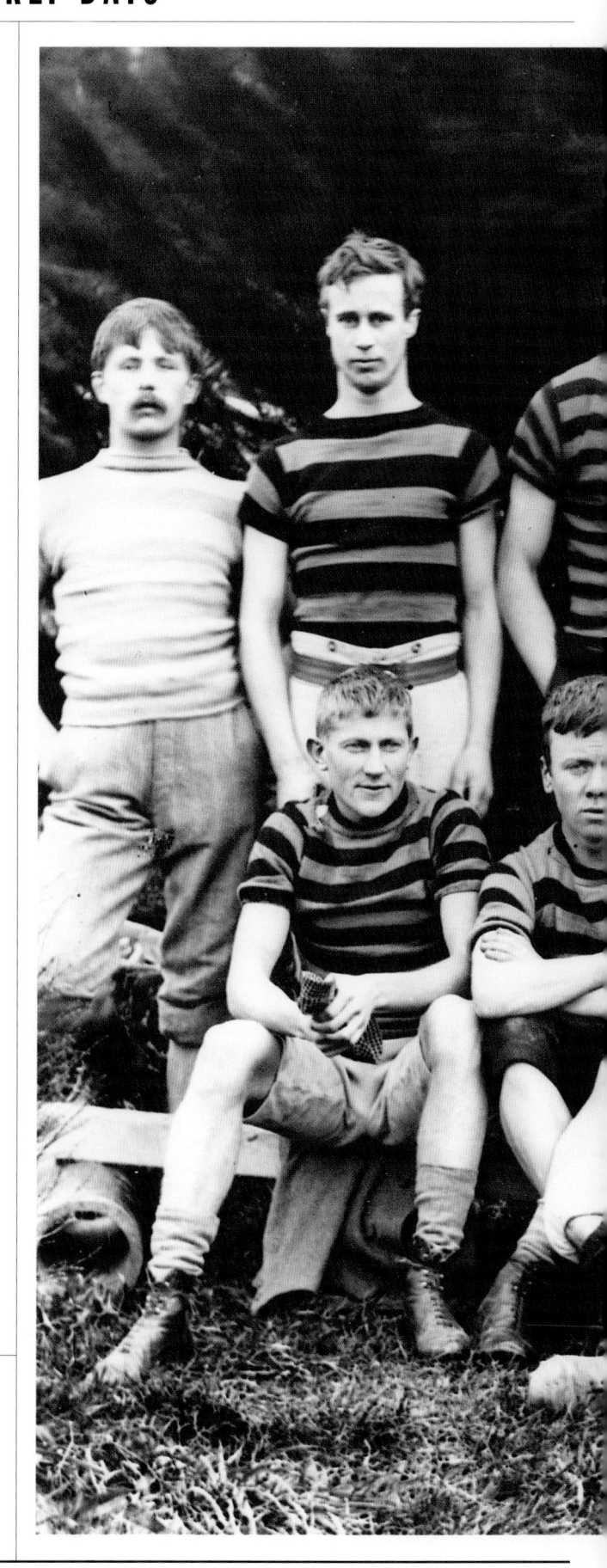

BUSH FIRE: Rugby spread like bush fires throughout New Zealand after being introduced in 1870. Hundreds of clubs sprang up, many of them one-team organisations. Rugby's popularity swiftly enveloped all classes and both European and Maori races. This is the Government Insurance club of Wellington in 1890.

THE POWER BEHIND THE ALL BLACKS

THE EARLY DAYS

learnt many of the finer points of coaching and strategy on the Natives tour, and would invent the wing-forward position and its application to the 2–3–2 scrum, which would characterise New Zealand rugby's style up to the early 1930s. He would also write an excellent instructional book, *The Art of Rugby Football*, and contribute much as an administrator, including helping lay the foundation of the NZRFU itself. The Natives were thus to have a profound effect on the development of the New Zealand game.

The New Zealand union was founded in 1892, but the 1893 national team which toured Australia contained no players from Canterbury, Otago or Southland as these unions stubbornly remained unaffiliated. Led by Tom Ellison, the side won 10 of its 11 matches, beating New South Wales and Queensland twice each, but also losing a third match to New South Wales 3–25.

In the series decider against New South Wales, the New Zealand forward Bill 'Offside Mac' McKenzie was ordered off by the referee, Ted McCausland, who had settled in Australia after being on the Natives' tour four years earlier.

New Zealand's first home game, in 1894, was lost 6–8 at Lancaster Park to New South Wales, after the tourists had lost the first six games of their 12-match tour.

This match provides rugby students with some of the first evidence of the effect coaching might have at national level. The press of the day blamed lack of adequate preparation for the defeat. One report claimed the first time the New Zealanders packed a scrum down was in the dressing room before taking the field. Another stated the New South Welshmen had played as a team, whereas the New Zealanders, the forwards in particular, had played as individuals.

Otago was admitted to the NZRFU, and Southland readmitted, in 1895. All unions were now affiliated, but it was not to be smooth sailing. Queensland toured in 1896, losing to Auckland in its first match and then to Wellington 7–49, the capital's players scoring 14 tries. But the New Zealand selectors announced they regretted the unavailability of the southern star Jimmy Duncan, when they chose their test team. The Otago union and the NZRFU were in dispute over financial terms for the Queensland–Otago match. The game was cancelled and the tourists played a second match against Canterbury. The Otago union then refused to allow its players to play for the national team. Davey Gage captained New Zealand to a 9–0 win in Wellington.

Duncan, who was to become New Zealand's first national team coach, was in the side which toured Australia in 1897. The team was again captained by Taranaki's versatile Alf Bayly. Features of the tour included the improved standard of the opposition and crowds as large as 25,000. Again it took until the third match against New South Wales for the series to be decided, honours going to New Zealand.

New South Wales toured once more in 1901. Duncan, now 31 and playing wing forward, was virtual player-coach for New Zealand. In magnificent form, he scored two tries, and his team won 20–3. Played in Wellington, the test drew a record crowd of 8000 and a record gate of £420.

Duncan led another team to Australia in 1903, playing as a five-eighth. Brilliant football produced record scores and 63 tries in 10 matches. Large crowds, as many as 35,000, loved the New Zealanders' style. George Nicholson, who was to tour with the Originals in 1905 and become an All Black selector and coach, was to describe the 1903 team, many years later, as 'the greatest ever'.

Duncan, superb in combination with Morrie Wood in the five-eighths, would retire after this tour and become New Zealand's first coach against the touring Great Britain team the following year.

The 1903 test in Sydney, won 22–3, was New Zealand's first full-scale test, although 13 'intercolonial' matches had been played against New South Wales between 1884 and 1901, for 10 wins and three losses, and seven against Queensland, all New Zealand victories. Australia had played internationals against Britain in 1899.

SOUTHERN MEN: The Southern Club's team of the 1880s. Rugby in Dunedin, New Zealand's largest city until about 1900, was perhaps the strongest in the land. Dunedin clubs had walloped touring Auckland in 1875; Otago had beaten the first overseas touring team, New South Wales, in 1882; and the first New Zealand team, in 1884, was Otago-organised and wore the colours of dark blue and gold. Sound familiar?

CHAPTER 1

FIRST NZRFU TEAM CAPTAIN 1893

TOM ELLISON

First of the few truly great contributors

NO BOOK ON THE EVOLUTION OF THE ALL BLACK coaches could ignore the various contributions made to New Zealand rugby by Tom Ellison.

Of the few truly great men to have guided the development of the game, Ellison was the first and contributed perhaps the most.

Described as 'a magnificent forward' by a contemporary writer, Ellison is credited with inventing the 2-3-2 scrum and its accompanying wing-forward position, but undoubtedly brought many other new features to the New Zealand game after touring Britain as a 21-year-old with the New Zealand Natives team in 1888–89. He would later captain and coach the Poneke, Wellington and New Zealand teams and transform the rugby game from what New Zealanders had played pre-1888.

Ellison successfully proposed, at the first annual meeting of the New Zealand Rugby Football Union in 1893, that New Zealand wear a black jersey with silver fern, white knickerbockers and black stockings. Fittingly, he became the first captain to wear the colours later that year on a successful tour of Australia.

A Wellington management official and selector through much of the 1890s, Ellison wrote perhaps the first coaching book on the New Zealand game, *The Art of Rugby Football*, in 1902, two years before his death at the age of only 36.

'The mana of Ellison the footballer was strengthened by events in the life of Ellison the man,' wrote Terry McLean. Of Ellison's 2-3-2 scrum/wing-forward invention, he declared this 'so suited the New Zealand temperament that the players of his and subsequent times became the most adventurous and, often enough, the ablest in the world'.[1]

Ellison was a visionary. Having endured hardships with the Natives beyond the imagination of modern-day footballing tourists, he would write, after a tour to Britain by a New Zealand representative team had been proposed, of the lack of realism in expecting a team and their players to embark on a long tour without adequate out-of-pocket expenses. It would take almost a century before the rugby authorities would fully acquiesce to this line of thinking.

'I see one difficulty only and that is getting the best men away without giving them some allowance over and above their actual hotel and travelling expenses — a difficulty due to the stringency of the laws as to professionalism,' wrote Ellison.[2]

Ellison wanted to see players being compensated for relinquishing their salaries by between two and four pounds a week. Terry McLean contacted the governor of the Bank of New Zealand while writing *New Zealand Rugby Legends* to inquire what the value of those

THE POWER BEHIND THE ALL BLACKS

FIRST STRIKE: Tom Ellison and the first New Zealand team under NZRFU auspices. It won 10 of 11 games in Australia. Top Row: F. Murray, S. Cockroft, J. Lambie; Third Row: A. D'Arcy, G. Speight, T. McKenzie, W. McKenzie, G. F. C. Campbell (manager), C. N. McIntosh, W. Watson, P. Webb, R. Gray, W. T. Wynyard; Second Row: W. Pringle, H. Butland, H. C. Butland, H. C. Wilson, A. Bayly, T. R. Ellison, A. Good, G. Shannon, F. H. Jarvis; Front Row: A. Stuart, Hiroa Tiopira, D. Gage, R. Oliphant, J. Mowlem, J. H. Gardiner, G. Harper, M. Herrold.

amounts would have been in 1987. He was informed that two pounds in 1897 was the equivalent of $178.52 and four pounds was worth $357.04 in 1987 terms. Ellison's views must have been breathtaking at the time, particularly since the members of the Rugby Football Union (of England) had banned all broken-time payments five years earlier, causing the horrendous schism of 1895 and the formation of Northern Union (later rugby league).

It is not surprising, then, that his ideas on this point came to naught. The All Black Originals of 1905 received three shillings a day in expenses; by 1924 it had gone up slightly; and by 1953–54 Bob Stuart's All Blacks were receiving just 10 shillings a day. Common was the players' grievance that while vast sums of money were brought through the turnstiles on the great tours, the 'entertainers' were paid a starvation rate.

He fared better with other innovations. In a *Wellington R.F.U. Annual*, he is to be found asking: "Where would our football have been had we not met the English team of 1888, or had not the Native team toured to England in the same year? I suspect we would have been where we were in 1887 — glorying in the old-fashioned 15 minute scrums of those days, and trying to please the spectators by showing how well we could play without the assistance of our comrades. The present up-to-date and educated game would still have been unknown."[3]

In his book Ellison wrote: 'Prior to 1888, back play was not generally the order of the day, and when it occurred it was not the result of systematic play. This state of things . . . was due to our strict interpretation of the laws, considering heeling out illegal because the process left the pack forwards offside. After the visit of the English . . . who were allowed to heel back . . . we immediately developed back passing.

'It was said, shortly after we started the passing

19

TOM ELLISON

game, that we had learnt the whole art from the English; but I never agreed with this opinion. I challenge anyone to tell me what else they taught us.'

Some history books claim it was the 1905 All Black Originals who introduced specialised scrummaging to the British. The Blackheath RFC of London, one of the oldest clubs in the world, still claims it introduced scrummaging positions to the game, in 1905. But such claims cannot be correct.

In Ellison's book, published three years before that tour, we can still read how 'in the scrum [the Natives] invariably beat the best English packs, not through having better men, but through our more scientific system of packing the scrum, and having specialists in each position, instead of merely fine all-round men; the result being that our two front-rankers, for instance, simply buried the two Jack-of-all-trades who happened to be pitted against them in the different scrums'. So it is reasonable to assume New Zealand clubs were employing scrum specialists many years before 1905, and perhaps before 1888.

Ellison was a leading player on the Natives' tour of Britain, Australia and New Zealand. He scored 113 points, including 43 tries, and played in the 'internationals' against England, Wales and Ireland. He is reputed to have played in 86 of the 107 matches. *(See The Early Days)*

However much was learned and imported back to New Zealand by the Natives, they unfortunately gained a reputation for rough play and bad sportsmanship. Neither charge stands the test of time nor close scrutiny. The claim of over-vigorous play was not upheld by the fact that dozens of north England clubs happily hosted the Natives, sometimes more than once, and loved to play the game in a similar muscular manner. The claim of poor sportsmanship arose from an incident in the match against England, when three New Zealand players, utterly frustrated with the quality of the refereeing, marched off the field. They later returned.

'The England team . . . should never have won the game against us so easily, but for three early and distinctly erroneous and depressing decisions of the referee, Mr Rowland Hill,' wrote Ellison. He then detailed two incidents, the description of which is foreign to the modern rugby follower, that led, unreasonably, to tries by England. The third came when an England player was tackled by Ellison himself, but left only his shorts in the New Zealander's clutches.

'He dashed along, and the crowd roared; then, suddenly discovering what was the matter, he stopped, threw down the ball, and in an instant we had the vulgar gaze shut off by forming the usual ring around him, stopping play, of course, for the purpose.

'While we were thus engaged, Evershed [an English player], probably seeing a splendid opening for a try, seized the opportunity and ball, and flew for the goal line . . . We, of course, disputed the try . . .'

Ellison, again way ahead of his time, wrote that Rowland Hill, who was 'the most important official in the English union [he was a secretary] . . . and the father of the team pitted against us', should never have been refereeing the match.

The Natives were subjected to severe criticism (and forced to apologise to the union) for not meekly abiding by the referee's decision and being unable to take a licking.

'I have always been inclined to make large allowances for the frailties of referees . . . [but] I shall always consider myself entitled to raise my voice against any wrong decision, by any referee, whoever he may be, that goes beyond the bounds of a reasonable or excusable mistake,' wrote Ellison. It was asking too much of human nature to expect footballers to passively submit to all and any kinds of decisions, particularly if they were palpably wrong, he said.

Within two or three years of the Natives' tour, Ellison would devise and then perfect, through his Poneke and Wellington teams, the wing-forward position. He had been frustrated by the offside interferences of players around the scrum, so he pulled a man out of the scrum and brought up one of the halves, using them as shields for his halfback. The results were brilliant. This innovation would soon be modified further, with one of the shields becoming the wing forward, putting the ball into the scrum and becoming a marauder in his own right.

'As the New Zealand game developed from Ellison's invention, it produced the fastest, finest, most exciting rugby that has ever been played,' wrote McLean. 'Of necessity, the back lines at a scrum were compelled to stand some distance to the rear of their halfbacks because the uncertainty of possession made essential a steps-and-stairs formation which would compel speed from men racing to take their passes. For about 40 years . . . the game, because of the backs, initially, had the room to manoeuvre, was adventurous, fast-flowing and enterprising.'[4]

Ellison's 1893 New Zealand team played the wing-forward game on its 10-match Australian tour and carried all before it, bar one of three games against New South

Tom Ellison.

Wales. In the side were such early stars as Alf Bayley, Doss Jervis, Davey Gage (a Natives team-mate who would later captain New Zealand) and Sammy Cockroft.

Charles Marter would write of Ellison that he 'could not only plan out deep, wily schemes, but personally carry them through to triumphant execution'. A man could learn more in a half-hour's talk and exhibition in the gymnasium with Ellison than he would pick up otherwise in years.[5]

Ellison worked as a solicitor from 1891 and was admitted to the Bar in 1902, one of the first Maori to do so. He had been appointed an interpreter in the Native Land Court in 1886 and stood three times, unsuccessfully, for the Southern Maori seat in Parliament. He was hospitalised at Porirua Lunatic Asylum, where he died on 2 October 1904, at the age of only 36.

BIOGRAPHICAL DETAILS

Thomas Rangiwahia Ellison

Born: Otakou, Otago Peninsula, 11 November 1867
Died: Wellington, 2 October 1904
Position: Forward
Represented NZ: 1893 (7 matches)
Points for NZ: 20
Provincial record: Wellington 1885–89, 1891–92 (Poneke club)
Selector/coach: Wellington 1892, 1897–98, 1902
NZ coach: 1893 (while captain)
Other service: Wellington RFU management committee 1892, 1894, 1898; leading role in formation of NZRFU 1892
Other: Cousin Jack Tairoa represented NZ 1884
Occupation: Solicitor

NEW ZEALAND COACHING RECORD

1893: Tour to Australia: played 11, won 10, lost 1; beat NSW twice, lost once; beat Queensland twice; no tests played

REFERENCES

1. Terry McLean, *New Zealand Rugby Legends*, Moa, 1987.
2. Tom Ellison, *The Art of Rugby Football*, Geddis and Blomfield, 1902.
3. *The Art of Rugby Football*.
4. *New Zealand Rugby Legends*.
5. *New Zealand Free Lance*.

CHAPTER 2

NEW ZEALAND COACH 1904, 1905-06

JIMMY DUNCAN

Father of All Black coaches had an inauspicious end

JIMMY DUNCAN SHOULD HAVE BEEN SEEN as the father of All Black coaches. He has gone down in history as one of the New Zealand game's pioneers and innovators, and as captain of New Zealand in its first officially recognised test match.

But the first officially appointed coach of a New Zealand team — he coached New Zealand to beat Great Britain, 9-3, in Wellington on 13 August 1904 — had an inauspicious end to his time with the All Blacks.

Amidst controversy, Duncan was appointed to coach the 1905-06 team on its tour of Britain and France — a team which transformed the game in both hemispheres and became known for ever more as the All Blacks. But he was not given rein by senior players to coach the side as he wanted.

Recognised as a brilliant tactician, Duncan had played in 50 matches for Otago over 14 seasons — a huge number considering the provincial set-up was just evolving and three matches a season was the average for a union. He captained Otago for six seasons and led the South Island in the inaugural interisland match in 1897. He is credited with inventing the two-five-eighths system of back line alignment. He played at wing forward and later at first five-eighth.

Duncan toured Australia in 1897, captained New Zealand in 1901 and led the 1903 team on their tour to Australia. This team won all of its 10 matches, including the first officially recognised test match between the two countries, 22-3. Scoring 276 points with only 13 against, it was hailed as the 'greatest ever'. Historians of the era argued it was better than the 1905 team, especially in the forwards, which included a great lock in Bernie Fanning (Canterbury) and the powerful wing forward Dave Gallaher (Auckland), who would go on to lead the more famous 1905 team.

Billy Wallace scored 85 points at fullback, while Opai Asher, the 'India Rubber Man' from Auckland, dotted down 17 times to set an imposing benchmark for All Blacks of future generations to chase. Duncan McGregor scored 11 tries. The team played before large crowds, including 32,000 in Sydney.

Duncan retired in 1903 at the age of 34, by which time Otago had built an enviable record. But provincial rivalries abounded, perhaps exacerbated by Otago — the country's most prosperous and influential area, owing to the gold rushes of the late 1800s — being the last province to accept the formation of the national union. Before long, Duncan would fall victim to such antagonism.

Duncan was asked to coach the 1904 New Zealand side which played the touring Great Britain team at Athletic Park. Aged 35 at the time, he remains one of the youngest men to be appointed coach of the New Zealand

THE POWER BEHIND THE ALL BLACKS

OPINIONS DIVIDED: Ernest 'General' Booth (left), Jimmy Duncan, Steve Casey, Bill 'Massa' Johnston and Alex McDonald (seated) pose as the Otago contingent in the 1905 All Black 'Originals'. Letters home to Dunedin from players provide evidence of a division in the team. Duncan, the officially-appointed coach, was pushed aside.

team. Only Vince Meredith and Jim Burrows were younger.

The team was announced a week before the arrival of the British, who had completed an unbeaten 13-match Australian tour, including three tests. The match aroused tremendous interest, with the governor-general, the prime minister and most of the ministers of the crown present among the 20,000 crowd. New Zealand won 9-3, with the help of two tries from Duncan McGregor, one of the stars of the Originals tour the following year. The Wellington winger was carried shoulder high from the ground when spectators invaded the playing area after the final whistle.

Interviewed before the test Duncan explained why he thought his team would win: 'I have given them my directions. It's man for man all the time, and I bet Gallaher a new hat that he can't catch Bush [Percy Bush, the uncapped Welshman who had emerged as a star of the back line on tour]. Bush has never been collared in Australia but he'll get it today. We are going to stick to our own 2-3-2 scrum formation and I think we can win.'

Duncan was appointed coach of the 1905 team amid much controversy. Senior members complained the 26 players chosen were insufficient, especially as only one halfback, Freddy Roberts, was among them. They said a coach, instead of an extra player, was an expensive and unnecessary luxury. The NZRFU, whose chairman, George Dixon, had been appointed the team manager, relented, and Bill Cunningham (Auckland), a burly lock, was added and became one of the major successes of the tour. Duncan was retained as coach.

However, historians are in general agreement that Dave Gallaher, the captain, and Billy Stead (Southland), the vice-captain, quickly informed Duncan they would be running the forwards and backs, respectively. Perhaps they had not appreciated Duncan's input the year before.

Correspondence from team members fuelled rumours that Otago's favourite son was being sorely treated by 'the Auckland members of the side'. A Dunedin newspaper said: 'It was definitely known here on Saturday that the relations between certain sections of the New Zealand football team were very much strained. This can easily be gathered from the contents of a number of letters received by the last mail by friends of the Otago members. The trouble had apparently risen out of the old sore feeling over the appointment of Jimmy Duncan as coach.

'The letters indicate that from the first the Auckland members set themselves up in sharp opposition to Duncan and then to the Otago members in general. A number of others, including Stead, had sided with the Auckland contingent. The general result had been that every attempt by Duncan to assert authority had been met with open hostility at meetings of the team, while on the field he had been simply ignored.'

Morrie Mackenzie, who reported on the New Zealand game for many decades and accumulated a tremendous amount of knowledge in the process, wrote in 1969 that Duncan had been told, gently but firmly, right from the start of the tour, that his services would not be required. He was to relax and enjoy the tour as a first-class passenger at the union's expense.

'George Dixon did make some effort to carry out the behest of the NZRFU, but soon gave it up as a bad job. However, Duncan had a wonderful time. He became a sort of P.R.O. for the team, sounding off about this and that for the benefit of all and sundry,' continued Mackenzie.

'He delighted prejudiced U.K. scribes with his fulminations about the wing forward. He had been a hot number in that position himself, but saw the light and became a five-eighth — one of the greatest. Maybe his own situation in respect to Gallaher's captaincy had something to do with it, but only a very patient captain would have tolerated the astonishing newspaper attack Duncan made towards the end of the tour on the wing-forward position.'[1]

If there was a serious dispute in the team, it was not apparent to outsiders. After his return home Duncan was quoted as saying the utmost harmony prevailed and the rumour that ill-feeling existed between the players was untrue. But was he just putting his new-found PR skills to use?

The reaction to Duncan as coach should perhaps not surprise. In Britain, coaches were to remain persona non grata for many generations to come. The captain was king. This was still the era in which the amateur ethic was strong among New Zealand sportsmen and officialdom — although that ethic would be tested just two years later with the formation of the All Golds Northern Union (i.e. rugby league) professional team. Rugby players of pioneer stock or living off the land were an independent bunch, still unfettered by the cult of the coach and encouraged to show individuality, originality and initiative at every turn.

But if, as some historians are sure, Duncan had an anonymous role on the 1905 tour, it seems strange that the team adopted, with great success, the dual five-eighths system of alignment, which Duncan has been

THE POWER BEHIND THE ALL BLACKS

'THE GREATEST EVER': The 1903 All Black team which played New South Wales with Jimmy Duncan (wearing hat, middle row, fourth from left) as its captain. The team was unbeaten on its tour of Australia. Billy Wallace (right, in front row) was the side's leading scorer. But was it a better team than the 1905 All Blacks as some have claimed?

credited with inventing in the early-1890s. A possible explanation is that Stead, being a Southlander, was familiar with it and recommended it to his team-mates in his role of vice-captain.

Duncan, who had begun as a forward, was converted into a back. He later specialised at five-eighth, but could play well anywhere. He was especially well built for the era, weighing over 13st and standing 5ft 9in tall.

His courage was renowned. It sometimes needed to be. The famed 'Battle of Solway' Ranfurly Shield match at Masterton in 1927 between Wairarapa and Hawke's Bay was said to be a Sunday-school romp compared to the infamous 'Butchers' Match', in which he participated in 1897 when Wellington beat Otago at Carisbrook 10-6.

The match was the first test of two newly developed styles of play — Otago's, with its two-five-eighths system, and Wellington's using two wing forwards to develop what was then called the wing game. The over-vigorous tactics of the northerners caused the crowd to go wild. The Wellington wing forward William McKenzie, nicknamed Offside Mac, and the older brother of two All Black coaches-to-be, kneed Tommy Wood and closed the Otago man's eye. Other players from both sides were injured.

The then-teenaged Billy Wallace was in the Wellington team, and later recalled for author Morrie Mackenzie that Otago's extra five-eighth had caused him to face overlaps in the first half.

'The first time Jimmy Duncan got the ball in the second half Mac launched himself like a battering ram. He not only skittled him ball and all, but split his scalp as well. Things got a bit lively after that . . . The crowd took to us as we left the field. I was the smallest in the team, but that didn't stop me getting a crack over the head from a woman's umbrella.

'The crowd, in an ugly mood, shouted "Dirty butchers, Wellington slaughtermen", this being an

JIMMY DUNCAN

allusion to the fact that McKenzie and several other players worked for the Gear Meat Company in Petone.'[2]

And Duncan and McKenzie had been New Zealand team-mates in Australia only two months earlier!

To get some idea of Duncan's style of play, we can turn to New Zealand rugby historians, the late Rod Chester and Neville McMillan. They related how, in 1901, Duncan, then 31, was chosen for New Zealand at wing forward, scoring three tries in two matches against Wellington and New South Wales. He scored from the kick-off in the second game. 'Duncan put in a strong run as the New South Welshman held off, waiting for the pass which did not eventuate; and the New Zealand captain ran through to score behind the posts.' Eyewitnesses of the day reported Duncan was 'a master schemer. From the time he took the field, he never stopped thinking of ways to put off his man, or the whole of the opposing side, by some shrewd move no one could have guessed at.'[3]

A saddler by trade, Duncan took up refereeing after the 1905 tour and in 1908 he refereed the first test between New Zealand and the Anglo-Welsh at Carisbrook. He also coached teams at Otago Boys' High School during the 1920s and 1930s, having a great influence on many young players, including Charlie Saxton, whom he immediately recognised as a natural scrum half.

. . . .

JIMMY'S STYLE NEVER CRAMPED

Jimmy Duncan, as team photos show, wore a woollen cap on the playing field, especially later in his long career from 1889-1903. It was to hide his baldness.

It is said he had a reputation for using his cap to fool the opposition into thinking he had passed the ball to a team-mate. Playing for Otago against Auckland just

TRANSTASMAN FOES: There was already an intense Transtasman rivalry when the New Zealand and Australian teams met in the 1903 test in Sydney. New Zealand beat Australia 22-3.

before the turn of the century, he tricked his opponents into chasing and tackling a man with the cap rather than the one with the ball.

Duncan's baldness did not appear to cramp his style with the ladies. The Llanelli Rugby Club's visitors' book remains witness to a visit by the 1905 All Blacks. Skipper Dave Gallaher wrote of 'good beer, better girls, good times'. Duncan's comment: 'Also the numbers of young ladies and old widows who are desirous of taking me into partnership, as a sleeping partner only.'

. . . .

THE FIRST FIVE-EIGHTH

The basis of the concept introduced to British rugby by the 1905 All Blacks was the 2-3-2 scrum, the wing forward and the five-eighths system of pivoting attack and defence in the centre of the field.

The British played a more deeply positioned line of four three-quarters and packed down eight forwards in a 'first up, first down' system, with forward positions not nearly as specialised as the All Blacks and no particular halfback to feed the ball into the scrum.

In comparison, the All Blacks employed each forward in a specialised position in the scrum; they had a wing forward who stood off the scrum and acted both as a protector of the halfback and as a link between forwards and backs; and they used the five-eighth system. The three arrangements were complementary, and of limited value without each other. Used together, and honed into a smooth combination during the historic tour, they opened up the game. Previously, the game had been aptly described as 'just a pushing affair'.

Jimmy Duncan has been credited by some historians with originating the five-eighth system of back play with his club, Kaikorai, in Dunedin. He appears to have introduced the system of two five-eighths but a year or two after the powerful rival Otago club, Alhambra, had begun to use one five-eighth with two wing forwards in a 2-3-2 scrum in the 1890 season.

There has been more than a century of debate about where and by whom the wing forward was invented.

BIOGRAPHICAL DETAILS

Jimmy Duncan

Born: Dunedin, 12 November 1869

Died: Dunedin, 19 October 1953

Represented NZ: 1897, 1901 (captain), 1903 (captain) 10 matches (one international)

Points for NZ: 9 pts (3 tries)

Provincial record: Otago 1889-1903 (Kaikorai club), also South Island 1897

NZ coach: 1904, 1905-06

International referee: NZ v. Anglo-Welsh 1908

NEW ZEALAND COACHING RECORD

1904: beat Great Britain 9-3

1905-06: beat Scotland 12-7; beat Ireland 15-0; beat England 15-0; lost to Wales 0-3, beat France 38-8

REFERENCES

1. J. M. Mackenzie, *Black, Black, Black*, Minerva, 1969.
2. J. M. Mackenzie, *All Blacks in Chains*, Truth, 1960.
3. R. H. Chester and N. A. C. McMillan, *Centenary: 100 Years of All Black Rugby*, Moa, 1984.

CHAPTER 3

NEW ZEALAND COACH 1908

DAVID GALLAHER

A legacy handed down to future coaches and captains

DAVE GALLAHER, WHO COACHED THE 1908 ALL Blacks against the touring Anglo-Welsh, packed many important rugby activities into a tragically short life.

Best known as the captain of the ground-breaking 1905-06 All Blacks — a team which set standards and records which will for ever secure its place in history — Gallaher had many other strings to his rugby bow. He was co-author, with fellow 1905 All Black Billy Stead, of an influential rugby coaching book, *The Complete Rugby Footballer*, written near the end of the great tour. He was also Auckland's sole selector/coach for 11 years and a New Zealand selector for eight years.

Gallaher was 29 when first selected for New Zealand, on the unbeaten tour of Australia in 1903. He began the tour as a hooker and ended it as a wing forward. He went on to play against the 1904 British team.

On the 1905-06 tour Gallaher was to receive much criticism for his performance at wing forward, with frequent complaints that he was offside or obstructing play.

Given the opportunity to defend himself by an English journalist, he said the Welsh had 'adopted the wing-forward game in all its nakedness, as they have already modified their back and scrum formation in keeping with ours — perhaps the greatest compliment the New Zealanders have received during their tour'.[1]

His team dazzled its opposition and played before huge crowds. Gallaher was highly regarded as a leader, although he was not originally a popular choice. On the ship on the way to Britain he is said to have offered to resign as captain, and only a vote among the players saw him happy to continue (although the poll was apparently only 17 to 12 in his favour).

The team's officially appointed coach was Jimmy Duncan, one of the most influential players of the decade to 1903, and the first official coach of a New Zealand team (against the touring British in 1904). It appears senior players, especially Gallaher and Stead, quickly consigned him to a minor role.

Gallaher's captaincy style, honed from time spent in the Boer War, was effective. He knew how to psych his team up, and on match days would ask each man to spend an hour on his own to 'rest and contemplate the game ahead'. He insisted the team be totally disciplined and pay attention to detail, both on and off the field — very much a forerunner of the captains who were to follow.

The team worked to a strict pattern, using code names for moves, employing extra men in the backline and making use of skip passes, decoys, scissor passes and other ruses. A hooker or wing forward threw the ball in at lineouts. The forwards were adept at close passing, slipping the pass as a player went to ground and supporting the ball-carrier.

LEADERSHIP SKILLS: The manager of the All Black 'Originals', George Dixon (pictured with the walking sticks, with Dave Gallaher on his right) was appalled at the way British journalists attacked Gallaher's wing-forward style. He said so in the book he wrote on the tour. But although he attempted to persuade Gallaher and the team to accept the official coach, Jimmy Duncan, early on in the tour, he made no mention of the problem in his book.

It was only the controversial loss to Wales which prevented the Originals from completing a 35-match unbeaten record. Incredibly, the team scored 830 points, including 205 tries, with 39 points against, on the British section of the tour.

A member of the team, Ernest 'General' Booth (who, in the 1920s, became New Zealand's first professional coach, in Southland) was to write: 'Dave was a man of sterling worth . . . girded by great self-determination and self-control he was a valuable friend, and could be, I think, a remorseless foe. To us All Blacks his words would often be "Give nothing away: take no chances." As a skipper he was something of a disciplinarian.'[2]

Gallaher's team is immortalised as much as anything for the Bob Deans non-try, which, if awarded, could have saved New Zealand from its only defeat on the tour. In the event it lost to Wales 0-3. Deans, the youngest member of the team, was so adamant he'd scored he wrote a telegram to the *Daily Mail* stating he'd grounded the ball over the line but had been pulled back by Welsh players. As he lay on his deathbed in September 1908, aged only 24, following complications from an appendicitis operation just a few weeks after playing for the All Blacks against the Anglo-Welsh, he reputedly repeated his claim.

Sir Vincent Meredith, manager-coach of the 1910 All Blacks in Australia and the 1935 All Blacks who toured Britain, recalled meeting Judge John Dallas, the former Scottish international who had refereed the 1905 Wales-All Black test, on the 1935 tour. Dallas had been 27 at the time of the game.

'I couldn't resist on one occasion telling Dallas that story about what Deans said,' wrote Meredith in his biography. 'The reply I got was, "If he did say that, then he went to meet his Maker with a lie on his lips!"'[3]

Gallaher retired immediately after the 1905-06 tour and became a New Zealand selector in 1907. He was in good company. Also on the panel in the years preceding the 1914-18 war were men like 'Old' Vic Cavanagh, who would invent the ruck and second-phase play and lead many Otago teams to great riches; Meredith, who would coach the All Blacks in 1910 and 1935; and Jimmy Lynskey, a famous Wellington schoolmaster.

In 1908, when the Anglo-Welsh toured New Zealand, Gallaher coached the All Blacks with his old Original team-mate George Nicholson. With Billy Stead captaining the side at first five-eighth, outside Freddy Roberts, the All Blacks hammered the visitors 32-5 in the first test at Carisbrook.

In the second test at Athletic Park, the selectors decided to blood a number of new players, including the Canterbury inside-back pairing of Paddy Burns and Doddy Gray. Billy Wallace, now nearly 30, was brought back after injury to play what would be his final test. In a sea of slush, the Anglo-Welsh held their hosts to a 3-all draw and were unlucky not to win.

The All Blacks spent the following week training hard under Gallaher and took the field in great shape for the third test at Potter's Park, Auckland. Roberts and Stead had been recalled, as had Bob Deans. These three, plus Jimmy Hunter, had made up one of the successful combinations of the Originals tour. With the great Frank Mitchinson scoring three tries from the wing, the All Blacks won 29-0.

Although he would remain a national selector until 1914, that was to be the last time Gallaher played a direct role in the All Blacks' preparation. No other tests were played in Auckland until after the war.

From 1905 to 1913 Auckland held the Ranfurly Shield. In those nine seasons it made 23 successful defences. Gallaher was Auckland's sole selector/coach from 1906 to 1916, and was therefore responsible for most of the preparation during the province's shield tenure. Such a long tenure seems a grand achievement when compared with later eras, but the shield in those days was yet to develop the magnificent aura it has come to possess. It was already — sometimes — a great money-spinner, but officials tended to regard it as a nuisance and an embarrassment. Much of the reason for this was the rules that came with it. The challenger could not claim any of the gate monies, and the shield could not be taken on tour. Smaller unions could not afford to challenge, and from 1909 to 1911 challenges were a rarity.

Gallaher had enjoyed quick success as a coach. In his first season, 1906, he could call on nine All Blacks, many of whom had played under his captaincy and thus knew his philosophy and tactical approach well. The basis of Auckland's rampant form was its powerful, well-drilled forward pack.

Gallaher's teams continued their merry way right

MIGHTY MEMORABILIA: All Black 'Originals' captain and vice-captain Dave Gallaher and Billy Stead, were featured on collector cards like this one with other members of the fabulous 1905-06 team which enthralled Britain.

THE POWER BEHIND THE ALL BLACKS

RIVALRY AND ENMITY: The golden reputation of Dave Gallaher has lost little lustre through the years even though he usurped his officially-appointed coach, Jimmy Duncan, as captain of the 1905-06 All Black 'Originals'. Gallaher had played under Duncan, captain of the outstanding 1903 New Zealand team and official coach of the 1904 New Zealand side which beat Great Britain.

through to 1912, when age and familiarity inevitably began to catch up with them.

In 1913, after a 6-5 cliffhanger against Wellington, Auckland lost to Taranaki 14-11.

Already a veteran of one major war, Gallaher enlisted for further service in 1916. He died of wounds at Passchendaele, Belgium, in 1917. He was 26 days short of his 44th birthday.

BIOGRAPHICAL DETAILS

David Gallaher

Born: Ramelton, County Donegal, Ireland, 3 October 1873

Died: Passchendaele, Belgium, 4 October 1917

Position: Wing forward

Represented NZ: 1903-06
36 matches (6 internationals)

Points for NZ: 14 (4 tries, 1 conversion)

Provincial record: Auckland 1896-97, 1899, 1900, 1903-05, 1909 (Ponsonby club); North Island 1903, 1905

Selector/coach: Auckland 1906-16

NZ selector: 1907-14

NZ coach: 1908, with George Nicholson

Other: Emigrated to New Zealand with his family in 1878, aged 5, when his father took up land at Katikati. Moved to Auckland in 1893 and played junior rugby for the Parnell club before transferring to Ponsonby. Served in the Boer War as a corporal in the 6th Contingent NZ Mounted Rifles 1901, later joining the 10th Contingent with the rank of Squadron Sergeant-Major. In 1922, the Auckland RFU presented the Gallaher Shield in his memory. It remains the premier interclub trophy to this day.

Occupation: Foreman at the Auckland Farmers' Freezing Works

NEW ZEALAND COACHING RECORD

1908: beat Anglo-Welsh 32-5; drew with Anglo-Welsh 3-all, beat Anglo-Welsh 29-0

REFERENCES

1. J. A. Buttery *Daily Mail*.
2. Ernest Booth, *The Encyclopedia of New Zealand Rugby*.
3. Sir Vincent Meredith, *A Long Brief*.

CHAPTER 4

NEW ZEALAND COACH 1913

GEORGE MASON

Missionary George may have helped kill the game in North America

BON VOYAGE: Pictured on board ship, George Mason (fourth from left, second row) guided this powerful All Black team through North America in 1913, winning all 16 matches and scoring 610 points with only six against. But it was an error of judgement by the NZRFU to send a full All Black team and probably helped 'kill' the game there.

THE POWER BEHIND THE ALL BLACKS

GEORGE MASON WAS MANAGER AND COACH OF the All Blacks who made the ground-breaking tour of North America in 1913.

Although All Black teams have customarily stopped off in America to play one or two games on their way to or from a major tour of Britain and Europe, the 1913 team is unique for the fact that it made a full-scale tour there. It played 16 matches on the Pacific Coast, winning all of them easily. The questions that arise almost 90 years later are a) why did the All Blacks make such a tour?, and b) why did the game not take off in America after that missionary expedition?

Rugby had been played in the United States and Canada since the 1870s, the same time it was introduced to other parts of the world, the British Empire in particular. But the American universities gradually modified the rules until the game of American football evolved, and this new code was adopted throughout the United States and Canada.

By the turn of the century, however, American football had become extremely dangerous to play. A statistician claimed that in 1904 there were more deaths from injuries in the game than there had been in the biggest naval engagement of the Spanish-American War six years earlier! Consequently, the American game began to wane in popularity. In California, the state governor banned it, and universities and high schools began to adopt rugby again.

An American Universities rugby team had toured New Zealand and Australia in 1910. Although the visitors had suffered four losses and secured only one draw in their five games in New Zealand, the draw, 13 all, had been with Auckland, the long-time Ranfurly Shield holder. The Americans had also come to New Zealand to learn. They spent a week under the tuition of Dave Gallaher, captain of the 1905 All Black Originals, former All Black coach and, in 1910, in the midst of a long tenure as Auckland's sole selector-coach.[1]

The Australians sent a fully representative team to the Pacific Coast in 1912, and sometimes struggled. They lost two games to university sides and just managed to despatch a California representative team called All America.

The California Rugby Union then invited New Zealand to tour. In light of what occurred, it would have been better for the future of the game in America if New Zealand had sent a universities or an age-restricted team. Instead, because of the Australians' experience, a fully representative All Black team was sent.

New Zealand had not played international rugby since 1910, so the 1913 side had a new look. However, the captain, Alex McDonald, was no newcomer. He had been a leading member of the Originals and was to go on to coach the All Blacks in 1921, 1938 and 1949. Only three others had been All Blacks — Frank Mitchinson, Doddie Gray and Leonard ('Jack') Stohr. But Mitchinson, the Wellington five-eighth who could play anywhere in the back-line, had played 11 tests between 1907 and 1913. His 10 tries in those games, including three on his debut, made him the New Zealand record-holder for almost 65 years, until Ian Kirkpatrick came along.

The unbeaten All Blacks romped through California and British Columbia, scoring 610 points while conceding just six. In many of the games they had to pull the reins in. American and Canadian pride was hurt, the result being the game in those parts was damaged rather than stimulated. Of the university teams the All Blacks met, Southern California reverted to American football in 1914, California, Nevada and St Mary's did the same in 1915, and Stanford and Santa Clara followed in 1918.[2]

One All Black, Jim Wylie, did not accompany the team from California to Canada. He remained to study geology at Stanford University, where he was appointed professional rugby coach in 1917. However, he held the position for only one year before American football was restored.

Despite the trend back to American football, the United States, represented by players from the Californian universities, would win the rugby championship at the Olympic Games of 1920 and 1924, beating France in both finals, 8–0 and 17–3 (although no other major rugby nations were represented).

Manager/coach Mason almost missed the trip from California to British Columbia. Immediately after the game against All America at Berkeley — in which the home team was chosen from only one state and its players wore the national uniform — there was a mad rush to the ship taking the visitors to Canada. Mason arrived as the vessel was pulling out, but hired a motorboat and was taken aboard before the steamer left the harbour. The NZRFU had granted the All America game test-match status, it was watched by 10,000 spectators and the All Blacks won 51-3.

The Canadians, with British expatriates to call upon, offered sterner, more knowledgeable opposition than the Americans. Their game was already well established and would continue to flourish.

Mason had a gift for coaching boys at a formative stage. All Black halfback Bill Dalley, of the 1924 Invincibles and the team that toured South Africa in 1928, tying the series two-all, was coached by him at Christchurch Boys' High School.

Dalley played in the school first XV under Mason in

GEORGE MASON

1917-19, as halfback and first five-eighth. In 1919 he had Curly Page at halfback and Sid Carleton outside him. All three would become All Blacks.

'He taught us the arts of rugby, and he taught us how to think,' said Dalley. 'Every lunch hour we practised sidestepping until it became automatic, and when we made a tackle we had to put every ounce into it.[3]

Mason's emphasis was on the running game — the sidestep to spark an attack and the tackle to halt one.

Mason coached the University club to the Christchurch club championship in 1928. In the key fixture of the season, played on 21 July 1928, University beat High School Old Boys before a crowd of 9000. It was University's first title, and the team went unbeaten that year.[4]

. . . .

'NO MORE COACHES, PLEASE!'

Bill Dalley was the centre of a rumpus on the eve of the 1960 All Black tour to South Africa when he persuaded the Canterbury union to pass a unanimous motion that the team shouldn't have a coach.

Dalley had been a halfback on the 1924 Invincibles tour to Britain and France and the 1928 tour to South Africa. Neither of these teams had had an appointed coach. Instead, the coaching had been left to the captains, Cliff Porter in 1924 and Maurice Brownlie in 1928.

In 1959, when preparations for the 1960 tour were being made, Dalley, who became a longtime Canterbury administrator and was by then a former chairman of the union, called for the All Blacks to tour without a coach. He was backed up, among others, by fellow Invincible Read Masters, and the result was a request to the NZRFU that only the captain and vice-captain be responsible for coaching.

The move drew a blank, and Jack Sullivan, convenor of the national selectors, got the job. But it caused a major debate, with many critics, officials and the rugby public backing Dalley's opinion.

'I feel selectors should pick the team and leave the rest to the captain. Surely a captain who has played for a few years knows more about the game than some of our selector-coaches?' said an unrepentant Dalley in 1965 when, at age 64, he was interviewed by Max Smith. 'Players should be able to show initiative, and their game on the field should be left to themselves.

'Winning is important, but not that important. The game is the thing, and wins should be based on decent football. The blasted coaches have a stranglehold on our rugby.

'The coach says, "That's the way it's going to be, boys," and that's the way it is! We get statistics, records and wins, but we don't get enough open rugby . . . The first thing to do is to give the captains more say.'

Dalley pointed to the 1905, 1924 and 1928 All Black touring sides as examples of teams in which the captains coached successfully. He claimed Vin Meredith, the manager of the 1935 All Blacks in Britain, had started the coaching trend, and that national teams had been under the coach's yoke ever since.

A product of the 1920s, when New Zealand's back play with the 2-3-2 scrum was at its finest, Dalley saw his fears about the 1960 All Blacks in South Africa borne out. The team, under Sullivan, played a very tight, forward-oriented, riskless style. It was to take until the late 1960s, and new rules, for Dalley's beloved back movements to reappear with any frequency. How delighted he would have been with the modern trend — again, the result of rule changes which have allowed the emergence of a multifaceted game.

REFERENCES
1. Chester and McMillan, *Centenary*.
2. *Centenary*.
3. Max Smith, *Game As You Like*.
4. Larry Saunders, *Canterbury Rugby History 1979*.

BIOGRAPHICAL DETAILS

George Harry Mason

Born: England, 1863

Died: Wellington, 19 October 1934

Selector/coach: Canterbury University coach 1928

NZ coach: 1913

Other service: Canterbury RFU management committee 1890, 1892–93, 1895, vice-president 1896–1909, president 1910; NZRFU president 1913, 1915

Occupation: Accountant, Registrar of Canterbury University College 1908–19

NEW ZEALAND COACHING RECORD

1913: beat All America 51–3

CHAPTER 5

NEW ZEALAND CO-COACH 1921

BILLY STEAD

Undefeated All Black lost one test as coach

IT WAS A GREAT PITY THAT BILLY STEAD'S extraordinary playing record for the All Blacks did not carry over to his coaching duties with New Zealand.

Stead, New Zealand's first captain in a home test match in 1904, vice-captain of the All Black Originals in 1905–06 and captain against the Anglo-Welsh in 1908, played 42 times for New Zealand — and was never in a beaten side.

But when Alex McDonald and Stead, from the Originals team, assisted by another 1905 veteran, George Nicholson, took over the coaching of the 1921 All Blacks to play the touring Springboks, Stead's playing record counted for little.

The All Blacks took the first test, in Dunedin, comfortably enough, winning 13-5. But the national selectors, who included Nicholson in their number but not Stead or McDonald, made three changes to a winning team. South Africa won the second test, in Auckland, 9-5.

There has been historical uncertainty over whether this group actually took the All Blacks for the third test. Terry McLean has written that the trio "were summarily dumped for the third test, the New Zealand union itself assuming all responsibilities" for the match, but interviewed in June, 1997, by the author, McLean said he was unable to recall where he had acquired that information.

Research at NZRFU headquarters in Wellington uncovered the minutes of meetings in 1921. These state that Nicholson, Don Stuart and A. J. Griffiths were appointed the national selectors early in the year. A later meeting agreed Don Stuart would coach the All Blacks in the three tests. A later meeting still decided that for the third test Griffiths would be the manager and Messrs Nicholson and Stuart "be invited to assist Mr Griffiths".

The author then called on the Auckland Research Centre in an attempt to unravel the mystery. Stead and McDonald (but not Nicholson) are pictured with the team, as the coaches, in Auckland, in a photograph published in the 1 September 1921 edition of the *New Zealand Sporting & Dramatic Review*. A search through the microfilmed copies of the *New Zealand Herald* at the centre also failed to unearth any clues to a possible dumping by the NZRFU, an action which would have presumably caused controversy.

On the contrary, the *Herald* of 14 September 1921 reported, in the lead-up to the third test, that 'the All Blacks are doing their training under the public eye at Day's Bay', across the harbour from Wellington City, and that the work was proceeding well.

'Mr McDonald is also rendering good service in the coaching work. Mr George Nicholson, famous as a forward in the 1905 touring team, and now one of the New Zealand selectors, joined up yesterday, and will remain with the team, in company with the other

BILLY STEAD

selectors, Messrs A. J. Griffiths and Donald Stewart, until the side is chosen on Friday night,' the article stated.

There is no mention of Stead in this article. Part Maori, he coached the New Zealand Maori team which played the Springboks at Napier 10 days before the third test. In a match in which no quarter was given by either side, the visitors won 9-8. 'To counter the strong Springbok pack, the two Maori hookers put their hard heads together and charged on to the shoulders of two rather than three South Africans. The Springboks did not appreciate this . . . The match turned into a general dust-up . . .'[1]

However, there was more of a dust-up after the match, when a South African pressman's story was leaked from the telegraph room of the Napier Post Office. The story deplored the 'racist, anti-white antagonism' of the largely white crowd against the all-white South Africans. It was published in the New Zealand press and led to an international incident. Questions were asked in Parliament and four post office workers were sacked over the affair, although three were later reinstated.

The national selectors caused a sensation when they dropped the All Black captain, George Aitken, for the third test. Aitken would later become one of the great all-Oxford University quartet of the Scottish team's three-quarters. The selectors also reshuffled the back line to allow a place for the famous Karl Ifwersen, a New Zealand rugby league representative who had been reinstated a few weeks earlier.

The game was played in atrocious conditions on an Athletic Park largely covered in water. It ended in a nil-all draw that meant the first series between the great rugby nations was shared.

Years later, Stead was to write that, 'The strongest feature of the South Africans' play was their lineout play. It was quite illegal. The favourite method was for "Baby" Michau (17st) and "Boy" Morkel (16st) to force an opening through the opponents' lineout, drag one of their own comrades [who had possession of the ball] through behind

SETTING THE PACE: Many future New Zealand leaders would emerge from this 1904 team which beat touring Great Britain, 9-3, at Wellington. It was captained by Billy Stead and coached by Jimmy Duncan (who is not in the photo). George Nicholson, Dave Gallaher, Stead, Duncan and Billy Wallace would all go on to play coaching roles with the All Blacks during the next three decades. The team was: Back Row: W. Glenn, C. Seeling, G. Nicholson, D. Gallagher, B. Fanning, P. McMinn; Middle Row: E. Harper, T. Cross, M. Wood, W. Stead (captain), G. Tyler, W. Wallace, W. Coffey (manager); Front Row: R. McGregor, P. Gerrard, P. Harvey, D. McGregor, J. Hunter.

THE POWER BEHIND THE ALL BLACKS

STEADFAST AND TRUE: The great southern rivalry between Otago and Southland was already strong when this 1905 photo of the great All Black captain and coach Billy Stead (fielding ball for Southland) was taken.

them and then deftly send the ball to one of the giants who had got clear.[2]

As a player and leading contributor to tactics, Stead was a master of his time. A Southland representative who made an outstanding debut with two tries against archfoes Otago in 1896, he had become a well-rounded footballer by the time he got the national call in 1903.

He played in four back-line positions on the 1903 tour of Australia, New Zealand's first full-scale tour, although he did not play in the test, since Jimmy Duncan was the captain and five-eighths.

Duncan then retired and was coach of the New Zealand team which met Darkie Bedell-Sivwright's British team in 1904, and Stead captained it to a 9-3 win in the only test, in Wellington. Public interest in the match against the mother country was exceptional. The New Zealand team went into camp in Day's Bay for a week, and the Premier, Richard Seddon, called Stead by telephone to wish the side good luck.

A first five-eighths on the Originals tour in 1905–06, Stead linked superbly with his halfback, Freddie Roberts, to send their back line away on numerous movements. Their outsides set scoring records which no other All Black side has come near to equalling. The team scored 204 tries, 164 from the backs. Stead played 29 matches on the great tour, second only to Freddie Roberts' 30 games.

Team-mates on the tour were to state that Stead's absence from the Welsh test, the only game lost on the tour, was crucial to the outcome. Reports of the day explained Stead was ill, but writing in Dunedin's *Sports Special*, Stead himself said: 'When I stood down for "Simon" Mynott, I was sure I was giving way to a fresher man, one that the Welsh had seen little of and whose form in the Cheshire match just beforehand had been brilliant. Perhaps that 'Land of My Fathers' from the 40,000 throats had unsettled him, as it did others, but he never rose to the heights he was capable of.'

He went on to say that even though Bob Deans had fairly scored his 'non-try', the All Blacks had missed opportunities early in the game and 'on the day we did not deserve to win'.[3]

Stead did not play on the 1907 tour of Australia, but he captained the All Blacks in the first and third tests against the 1908 Anglo-Welsh tourists. After the first test win, 32-5, at Carisbrook, where Duncan was the referee, the national selectors took out the injured Stead and brought in a number of young players. But the match, played in a sea of mud on Athletic Park and drawn 3-all, was a moral victory for the tourists, who scored the only try.

The inclusion of Freddy Roberts, Stead, Jimmy Hunter and Bob Deans in the back line for the third test at Potter's Park, Auckland, gave the All Blacks the back combination that had proved so successful in 1905. They had spent a hard week of training under Dave Gallaher and George Nicholson, and scored nine tries to win 29-0.

It was to be Stead's last international playing year. He had played 52 times for Southland, a massive tally considering the very limited fixture lists in provincial rugby of the time. He was persuaded to lead the New Zealand Maori team on its 19-match inaugural tour of Australia and New Zealand in 1910, and played in 13 matches. He continued to be involved in the game in one capacity or another, and was a legendary identity in Southland rugby until his death at 81 in 1958.

Stead was described by critic R. A. Stone as 'fast . . . quick to see an opening, his defence was par excellence'.[4] In an obituary in 1959 he was described as 'one of the "immortals" . . . a key man in the New Zealand scoring machine, steadiness itself, a good tactical kicker, superb handler and of unruffled temperament'.[5]

At the end of the 1905–06 tour, as the players were looking forward to three weeks' holiday before catching the boat home, Gallaher approached Stead about collaborating on a rugby coaching book. He had been asked by a British publisher, Henry Leach, for a standard work on rugby. The payment was to be £100 (worth about £4500 today). The pair got to work, but quickly found they could make no progress. Gallaher, according to Stead, wanted to give the project up.

Stead, who would later become a perceptive and prolific rugby writer, decided to go ahead on his own. In less than a week, writing longhand, he had completed 80,000 words. Gallaher, meanwhile, organised the photographs and the outstanding diagrams of tactical ploys the All Blacks had used against their British counterparts. *The Complete Rugby Footballer* was an extraordinary achievement, and one which should have revolutionised the British game had its contents been fully assimilated by the hosts.

The *Daily Mail* reviewer stated, 'To players of the present, it is indispensable; and in its 300 pages, practically every phase of the game is touched.'

REFERENCES
1. Terry McLean, *New Zealand Rugby Legends*, Moa, 1987.
2. *Southland Times*.
3. *Sports Special*.
4. R. A. Stone, *Rugby Players That Made New Zealand Famous*, Scott & Scott Ltd.
5. *New Zealand Rugby Almanac*, Sporting Publications.

BIOGRAPHICAL DETAILS

John William Stead

Born: Invercargill, 18 September 1877

Died: Bluff, 21 July 1958

Position: Five-eighths

Represented NZ: 1903–06, 1908
42 matches (7 internationals)

Points for NZ: 36 (12 tries)

Provincial record: Southland 1896–1908 (Star club); South Island 1903, 1905; Otago–Southland 1904–05; NZ Maoris 1910

NZ coach: Co-coach 1921

Other: Co-author, with Dave Gallaher, of *The Complete Rugby Footballer* (Methuen, 1906); rugby columnist for Truth; brother Norman played for Southland and NZ Maoris

Occupation: Bootmaker

NEW ZEALAND COACHING RECORD

1921: beat South Africa 13-5; lost to South Africa 5-9; drew with South Africa nil-all

CHAPTER 6

NEW ZEALAND COACH 1908, 1921

GEORGE NICHOLSON

Gave long service to the game

GEORGE NICHOLSON, WHO HAD A LONG CAREER as a player, selector and coach of Auckland and the All Blacks, always reckoned the 1903 All Black team which toured Australia was the finest he ever saw or played with.

Nicholson coached the 1908 All Blacks, with Dave Gallaher, against the touring Anglo-Welsh. The series was won when the All Blacks scored nine tries to demolish the visitors 29-0 in the third test at Potter's Park, Auckland, after winning the first but drawing the second. He served an additional short stint as co-coach of the 1921 All Blacks with Billy Stead and Alex McDonald *(see chapters 5 and 14)*. But his influence on rugby at a national level went far beyond his coaching endeavours.

Nicholson was a New Zealand selector in three distinctly critical periods of the game — in 1920–21, 1929–30 and 1936–37. The defining occasions of these periods were, respectively, when the Springboks first toured, in 1921, and the series was shared; when the great All Black players of the 1920s had their final sally by beating the touring Great Britain team in 1930; and when the Springboks returned with their greatest of all teams to take the 1937 series.

Nicholson was all things to rugby:
- As a loose forward, he represented Auckland over nine years, 1901–09, and New Zealand in 1903, 1904, 1905 and 1907.
- As a referee, from 1912 to 1915, he controlled four Ranfurly Shield matches and three internationals.
- As a coach he helped guide not only the All Blacks and Auckland, but also his beloved Ponsonby (for many, many years) and at different stages, Auckland Grammar, Sacred Heart College, the Grafton club and Morrinsville and Matamata clubs.
- As a selector he also chose the Auckland teams of 1916–19, 1921–22, 1925 and 1930–31.
- As an administrator he served on the Auckland RFU management committee for 14 years.
- He was conferred life membership of the ARU, the Auckland Rugby Referees' Association, the Barbarians club and Ponsonby.
- As a spectator, in his later years, he was a 'wet or fine' man, present at Eden Park for every international, provincial, club and school fixture.

Known as Long Nick because of his build — he stood 6ft 3in and weighed 13st 10lb — he played his early rugby as a three-quarter but developed into a fine loose forward.

After playing in New Zealand's first official test, in Sydney in 1903, and against the touring British in 1904, Nicholson could not manage to win selection in any of the five tests on the Originals 1905–06 tour. But he did win glory for his try against Cardiff, following up to recover a

QUICK AS LIGHTNING: The speed and overall team mobility of the 1905-06 All Black 'Originals' was a feature which shocked their British hosts, especially after the opening-game 55-4 walloping of English county champion Exeter. Note the 'spiked' running shoes they wore for speed training. George Smith (at left of the pair in front), who scored 19 tries on tour, was quickest. He had set an unofficial world record of 58.5 sec. over the 440 yards in 1904, had won the 1902 British AAA title over 120 yard hurdles and had held 13 New Zealand national titles in sprints and hurdles between 1898-1904.

miskick by the international, Percy Bush, and scoring to help give the All Blacks a 10-8 victory.

While on holiday in Australia in 1907 he was called into the touring All Black team because of injury and won two more test caps. But he always maintained the 1903 All Blacks were 'the greatest'.

'That's the best team I ever saw or ever played with — and it also had the best five-eighth combination of the lot,' he told Max Smith.[1] He was 87 at the time and would live to be 90. His lifelong love of the game was still strong, for he gladly posed for Smith wearing his 1905–06 All Black jersey.

'Otago's Jimmy Duncan at first-five and Wellington's Morrie Wood at second were the perfect pair,' he continued. 'They were the champions in an unbeaten team that put on 276 points to 13 against in 10 matches.

'On that tour, we said we'd never force the ball behind our goal line for a drop-out 25, and we never did, either. We ran with it.'

But it was as one of the pathfinding All Black Originals of 1905 that Nicholson obviously held fond memories. The team rocked the pride and complacency of British rugby, losing only one of 32 matches, and not even the invincibility of their 1924 successors could dull their achievements.

'Just the hard, manual workmen lasted the distance,' chuckled Nicholson to Smith about the fact that he, Billy Wallace, Bunny Abbott and Alex McDonald were then the only survivors of the 27 players in the 1905 side. 'We were typical of the fellows in that team — hard, outspoken, tough working chaps. There was no old-school-tie stuff, and we were a bit unwelcome among some of the toffy-noses we ran into in Britain.'

One of the fastest forwards in the team, Nicholson played 18 matches and scored the first and last tries on British soil. He was plagued by boils on tour, missing some big matches, and blamed the drinking water.

He resumed service with the All Blacks in 1907 in an unusual way. He was holidaying in Australia, planning to watch a few of the All Blacks' tour games. But the team was badly hit by injuries, and after two matches the management sent him an SOS. He didn't miss another game.

After retiring in 1909, Nicholson took up refereeing. He controlled a test match between New Zealand and

GEORGE NICHOLSON

A sketch of George Nicholson from the times.

BIOGRAPHICAL DETAILS

George William Nicholson

Born: Auckland, 3 August 1878

Died: Auckland, 13 September 1968

Position: Loose forward

Represented NZ: 1903–07 39 matches (4 internationals)

Points for NZ: 24 (9 tries)

Provincial record: Auckland 1901–04, 1906 (City club), 1907–09 (Ponsonby club); North Island 1902–03

Selector/coach: Auckland selector 1916–19, 1921–24, 1930–31

NZ selector: 1920–21, 1929–30, 1936–37

Other: Refereed 3rd NZ v. Australia test 1913; life member Ponsonby RFC, and the Auckland RFU and RRA

Occupation: Bootmaker

NEW ZEALAND COACHING RECORD

1908: beat Anglo-Welsh 32-5, drew with Anglo-Welsh 3-3, beat Anglo-Welsh 29-0

1921: beat South Africa 13-5, lost to South Africa 5-9, drew with South Africa 0-0

Australia, in 1913, but was just as happy taking the schoolboys' grades.

'As a matter of fact, I took the opportunity to keep an eye out for promising material and tip off Ponsonby,' he told Smith. 'I spotted Fred Lucas in a Remuera school team, and that's how Ponies ended up with one of New Zealand's greatest wingers.'

Stead and Nicholson were both bootmakers by trade. The pair used to fix the sprigs on the All Blacks' boots before games on the 1905–06 tour. A Blackheath player, seeing the pair at work, fetched his boots from his locker. 'My man,' he said. 'Get these boots in order.'

'Never in your life,' said the All Blacks. 'Who do you take us for?'

In a rage, the player departed to find the club's secretary and complain at the insolence of the bootmakers. His rage abated when he learned the facts; and the pair fixed his boots for him anyway.[2]

REFERENCES

1. Maxwell Smith, *Game as You Like*.
2. Terry McLean, *New Zealand Rugby Legends*, Moa, 1987.

CHAPTER 7

NEW ZEALAND COACH 1924-30

CLIFF PORTER

*Guiding hand through much
of a fabulous decade*

CLIFF PORTER WAS NEW ZEALAND RUGBY'S most influential leader through the 1920s. So it was ironic he played such a small on-field role in its finest moments of the decade, did not feature at all on its most challenging tour, and was completely lost to the game once he retired.

Porter captained and coached the All Black Invincibles in 1924 but played in only one of the home-union test matches. He missed selection for New Zealand's first tour of South Africa four years later, when his calm direction on the field and care of his men off it were sorely missed.

If the events of those two major tours were a personal disappointment for Porter, the fact he came to dislike the 1924 touring manager, Stan Dean, so intensely he would have as little as possible to do with the man in future was to prove a disaster for New Zealand rugby in the long term.

Dean, as NZRFU chairman from 1922 to 1947, would go on to run the New Zealand game for almost the next quarter-century, while Porter, whose wise coaching and administrative counsel would have been invaluable during the tough times of the 1930s and 1940s, fell from sight.

Porter's qualities were such that he came to be revered by his players. His leadership style was consensus driven. He was only 24 when he captained the 1924 All Blacks, but he already had an invaluable insight into the demands of several positions, so could coach and encourage players and talk tactics.

Concern for his players was probably Porter's major legacy to All Black captaincy and coaching. One of his old team-mates from so many of those hard campaigns, George Nepia, was to say of him: 'His first and last thought was for us.'

Porter was never a dictator, even at the end of his career. Merv Corner, the Auckland halfback who became an All Black selector in the early 1950s, recalled coming in for Jimmy Mill in the 1930 series against Great Britain. He was impressed by Porter's invitation to participate. 'He built up my confidence. He was a marvel at getting the best out of each of us.'

'We never set out to go through unbeaten,' said Porter many years later. 'We were primarily concerned with avenging the defeat by Wales in 1905. Once it became apparent halfway through the tour, however, that we could get through unbeaten, this became our main desire.

'But I'd never advise any team to try it. It was a terrible burden, knowing we had to win every match. To achieve it, we played our best team every match, midweek and Saturday.' This meant that George Nepia, only 19, played in all 30 tour matches, but seven of the team made less than 10 appearances.

'It speaks volumes for the spirit of these men that they continued to train and were as keen as the rest of us for an unbeaten record to be achieved.'

CLIFF PORTER

But what made the Invincibles such a great team? 'Fitness was probably our greatest attribute, and the fact that each man knew what he had to do.'

Porter recalled the game against Newport as an illustration of this. Newport had scored to lead 10-8 a few minutes before the end of time and after the All Blacks had been defending for most of the second spell. Down but not quite out, Porter called on his men to make one last valiant effort with a move they had planned for just such an emergency, from the kick-off. The high kick was fielded by the Newport fullback near his posts, but virtually all of the All Black 15 converged on him. He froze with the ball and the New Zealanders caught him, forced a ruck and got the ball back for winger Svenson to flash over for the winning try.

It was appropriate the side should thrash Wales 19-0, for New Zealand had waited 19 years to take revenge for the controversial 3-0 loss of 1905.

'At the dinner after our win, I talked to the man who tackled Bob Deans, whose try had been disallowed in 1905,' said Porter. '"How about writing something on my menu for me to take back to Billy Wallace [fullback and goal-kicker of the 1905 team]" I asked him. He did. He wrote: "To Carbine" — that was Billy's nickname — "Dean did score. Teddy Morgan."

'And Teddy told me exactly what happened. He said the referee was still back near halfway when Dean dived across the line and grounded the ball in Morgan's tackle. By the time the ref arrived, Teddy had pulled Dean back 15 inches from the line.'

Porter was injured early in the great 1924 tour. But the All Blacks became even stronger with his replacement, Jim Parker, in the test team. Porter was not considered for the Irish test, but had thrown off the injury and was available for the Welsh and English internationals. However, Parker was playing so magnificently the selection committee could not leave him out.

The vice-captain, Jock Richardson, who captained the Invincibles in their three tests on the British leg of the tour (they did not play Scotland), spoke years later about the agonising of the committee over the two men.

'It was a terribly hard decision,' said Richardson. 'I don't know what we would have done if Cliff had not got injured. He was a terrific player, but then Jim was something special too.

'The trouble was that Cliff got hurt early and lost his form and fitness. I felt, and so did Stan Dean, the manager, that Parker was the superior wing forward with Cliff struggling. We chose Jim for all the tests in Britain and naturally Cliff didn't like it much. He felt he'd become a figurehead captain, which I suppose he had. But he never let on to the rest of the team how he felt, which was a mark of the man.'

To fully understand the reasoning behind the choice of Parker over Porter in those big matches we need to look at Parker. His was an incredible talent. Standing 6ft and 12st 7lb, he played a different style of wing forward game from Porter's, and because the All Blacks were winning so handsomely, probably had more to offer the team.

Parker's game was more like the classical no. 8 game of the future, offering support on attack and a deeper cover defender's style. When he put the ball into the scrum he would immediately retire to join the back line for the resultant attack.

The chunkier Porter's game was a spoiling, combative, close-quarters style. A crunching tackler standing only 5ft 8in tall and weighing up to 13st, his main objective in any match was to make life hell for the halfback and five-eighths.

Parker had astounding speed. He was the Canterbury

ALLROUND SKILLS: Porter brought the skills of a five-eighth to the wing forward position when chosen to captain the 1924 All Blacks who would return as the Invincibles.

THE POWER BEHIND THE ALL BLACKS

SIDELINED AGAIN: Cliff Porter (in hat at right) gave way to the in-form Jim Parker again for the international against Ireland.

100 and 200 yards champion and could beat all the other 1924 All Blacks over 50 yards with ease. That included speedsters like Fred Lucas, Alan Robilliard, Gus Hart, Snow Svenson and Jack Steel, the New Zealand 100 yards champion!

On the 1924 tour Parker played in 21 games and scored 18 tries, including five tries in one game. When Cyril Brownlie was ordered off early in the test against England, and, later, Steel was injured, the All Blacks were one and then two men down. Parker played in four different positions during the remainder of the game!

An anomaly about Parker was that while he joined the All Black elite, his first-class career was very short. It consisted of only 35 games, including the 21 tour matches and a few for Canterbury in 1920 and 1923. The reason was illness. He had contracted malaria while serving in Palestine in World War I. Together with the demands of setting up as a Canterbury farmer, it caused him to miss the 1921 and 1922 seasons, hastened his retirement and troubled him throughout his long life (he died in 1980 aged 83). He retired after the tour and later pursued a successful business career, becoming chairman of the New Zealand Apple and Pear Marketing Board. He served on the NZRFU executive from 1935-1956 and in 1949 was manager of the ill-fated All Blacks who were whitewashed 4-0 in South Africa.

Years later, Porter said he had wanted Parker to play on the wing against England.

'I reckoned England, who wanted to break our run of successes, would play rugged football and that's where I would have been in my element, giving our backs the chance to feed Parker, an unstoppable wing on the day,' said Porter. 'But Jock Richardson didn't see it that way, and rather than cause a rumpus in an entirely happy team, I conceded the point.'

Near the end of the 1924 tour Porter thrust his name firmly back into the selectors' minds with a return to form and replaced Parker for the French international. He finished the tour with 17 matches from the 32 played, scoring nine tries.

But Porter came to dislike the team manager, Stan

CLIFF PORTER

Dean, intensely. On the tour, Dean was often away from the team, socialising or dealing with officials or dignitaries. Such hobnobbing, at the expense of time and attention for the players, seemed to rankle most with Porter, though the tourists' unbeaten record has meant little evidence of any discord has been left for posterity. But Porter, as the captain and coach, became the person the players usually turned to with their problems as the tour progressed.

Bert Cooke was to recall that 'Dean had taken up with the nobs. He talked of "Viscount This" and "Lord That". Porter managed the team.'

George Nepia reported years later how, at the first practice run of the tour at Newton Abbot, Porter had reminded the players he was responsible for everything on the field and Dean for everything off it.

By contrast Mark Nicholls was to write how Dean was 'chairman of our selection committee and of all our team talks, to which he contributed as much as the players. He co-ordinated the ideas expounded at the team talks into a set pattern of play [mainly defensive] and we were fortunate to have him at the head of the team.'[1]

Another team member, Read Masters, who wrote a book on the tour, stated the success was due 'not only to our speed, weight combination and teamwork, but to the good fellowship that existed between us all both on and off the field. There was never any back-biting or chipping during the progress of the play'[2]

Terry McLean described a chance meeting about 60 years ago, when he was a young reporter on the *Taranaki Daily News*, with the great captain. Porter told McLean, whose brother Hugh had played with Porter for Wellington and the All Blacks, that while Dean remained in office he would indeed have nothing to do with the game.[3]

The team weren't just hellbent on achieving their famous record though. The players knew how to enjoy themselves. After the formal dinner following the victory over England, some of the All Blacks took bicycles off the street into the hotel and had races through the foyer. They used a fire extinguisher to prop open a door and it 'suddenly' burst into action just as Dean was walking past.[4]

Porter, when chosen as captain of the 1924 team, was confronted with a situation that would have daunted even a man of greater age and experience. Ces Badeley, who had led the All Blacks against the 1921 Springboks, was expected to be captain. He had led the side on its 1924 preliminary tour of Australia, and had captained the side which was convincingly beaten by Auckland on its return. He was still in the seat of honour at the

SERIOUS STUFF: The All Blacks' kiwi mascot and supporters in front of a section of the huge crowd that witnessed Swansea's 39-3 defeat.

parliamentary farewell for the big tour, replying to the distinguished tributes to his side. He was still there, at the top table, at the NZRFU farewell the same evening.

Then it was announced that Porter, who'd been outstanding in Australia, would be the captain. This meant that, as a comparative tyro, he would have to lead a side containing at least two former captains and many players far more experienced than him.

Badeley supposed, in later years, that the knee injury he had sustained in Australia had been the reason he'd been dropped as captain. But it has been claimed a clique of senior players decided on Porter during the voyage back to New Zealand. Mark Nicholls was said to be a key mover in such deliberations. Like Badeley, he was a five-eighth. He was also very confident, and had no doubts he should play the major games on the big tour. Badeley, who'd played 15 matches for the All Blacks between 1920 and 1924, got only two matches on tour, the eighth and tenth of the 32 games, despite clearly being fit to play. He virtually became the team's back coach.

When the tour did not begin as well as its predecessor had, Porter took the drastic action of calling

THE POWER BEHIND THE ALL BLACKS

CRUNCHING BLOWS: Porter narrowly prevents this Swansea player from moving the ball in the 39-3 tour victory. But the powerfully-built Porter often made life miserable for inside backs.

the players together and putting the position squarely before them. He told them they must draw up rules of conduct if they wanted to succeed. He said the team must manage themselves, since their manager would often be busy with issues at international level. He was well supported by the dominant members of the team. They drew up rules about practices, exemptions, curfews for those playing the next game and other matters. The outlook of the tour changed immediately when the team destroyed the first Welsh club, Swansea.

Porter said later he had got a lot of practical assistance from the old hands coaching the team, especially Alf West, who'd been an All Black since 1920. Looking back, three-quarters of a century after the fact, the achievement of Porter's Invincibles in becoming the first All Black team to be unbeaten on a tour of Britain and France remains remarkable. It was to take a half-century for the feat to be, arguably, surpassed.

Comparing the greatness of teams from different eras is futile. But it should be noted that, as with the 1905 All Blacks, who had struck British rugby when it had not recovered from the mass exodus of many northern English clubs to form rugby league, the 1924 All Blacks met a game severely weakened by the deprivations of war and the Depression.

The 1924 All Blacks did not play in Scotland, but that country had lost 31 international players to World War I. The other home unions had been similarly devastated, far more so even than New Zealand. Meanwhile the Depression of the 1920s hit Wales, where the game was dominated by the working class, hardest. The industrial Rhondda Valley, for instance, lost 20 per cent of its population between 1921 and 1931 to emigration.

Rugby clubs by the dozen passed into oblivion. The Welsh national teams of the decade had their poorest results on record. They were not helped by infamously poor selection methods, with players seldom being given a second chance, and there was no coaching for them. Many forget that while the All Blacks beat Wales, 19-0 in November 1924, the Welsh had suffered their most ignominious defeat in February of that year when the Scots routed them 35-10 (22-0 at half-time).

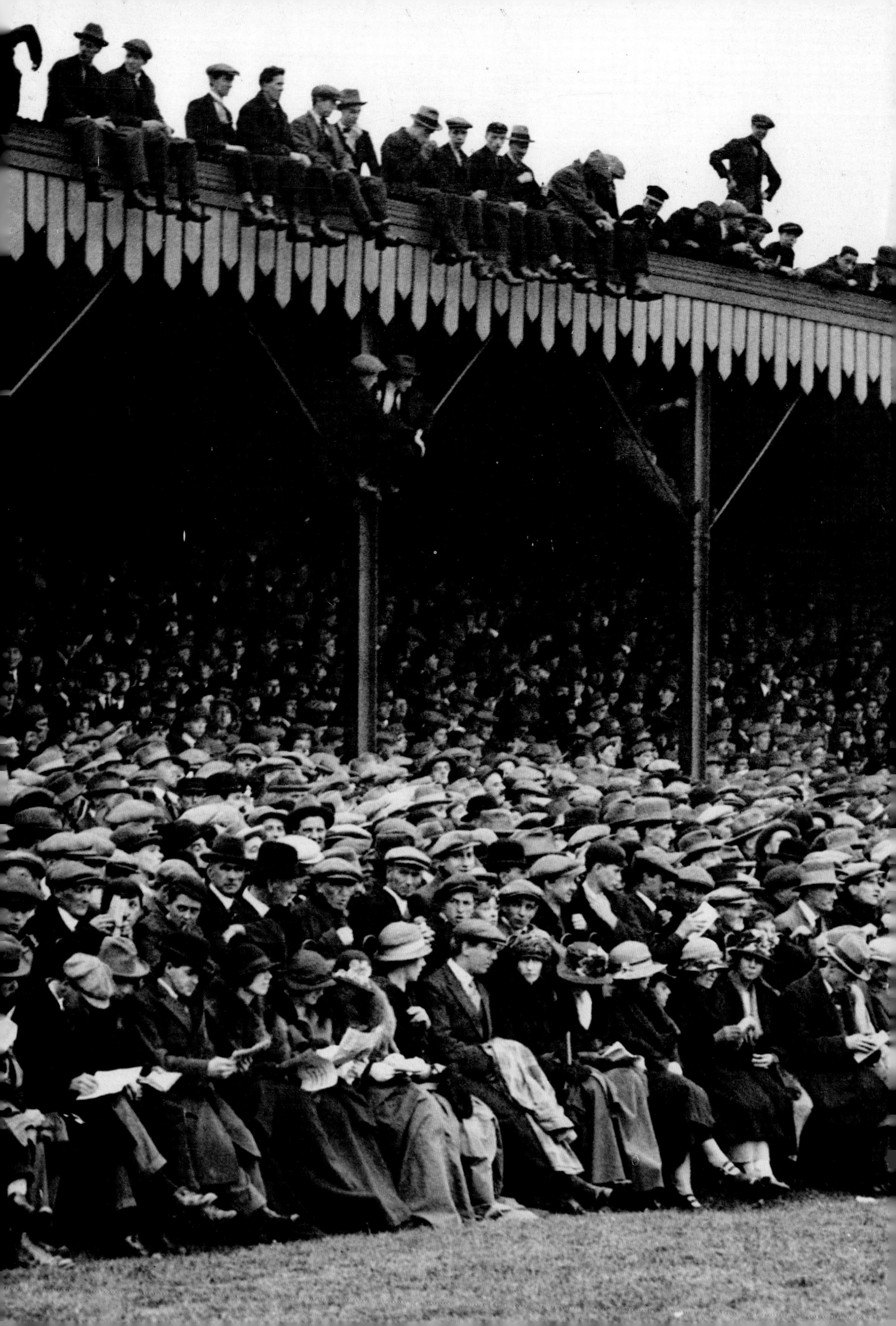

THE POWER BEHIND THE ALL BLACKS

Part of the reason for Porter's success as a wing forward was his experience as a five-eighth and three-quarter in his early rugby. It was not until 1923, the year before he led the Invincibles, that he made the switch to wing forward.

In 1923 he was brought into the All Blacks for the final test against the touring New South Wales team, which New Zealand won 38-11. He replaced the well-performing Moke Belliss.

After the great tour, Porter was to continue a long All Black career, interrupted only by the strange decision not to choose him for the 1928 tour of South Africa (although he was one of the reserves).

He led New Zealand to a 36-10 win over New South Wales in Auckland in 1925 and then took the All Blacks to Australia in 1926. Though the team included 13 of the Invincibles, it was affected by illness and injury at the start of the tour. Porter, assisted by Mark Nicholls with the backs, had to work hard to knock his multi-talented team into winning shape after it lost to Wellington before departure and to New South Wales in the opening 'test' of the three-match series. The All Blacks then took the other two 11-6 and 14-0.

While the All Blacks completed their South African tour in 1928, New South Wales toured New Zealand. Porter led a second national team to two very narrow victories in the first two tests, 15-12 and 16-14, but lost the third in Christchurch 8-11.

On the 1929 tour of Australia, Porter did not play until the second test and only participated in the final four games of the 10-match tour. The tour was remarkable for several reasons: it was the first time Australia had played in full internationals since 1914; the Wallabies won the series 3-0, an historic milestone; and it was the first time an All Black team had lost all the tests in a series.

A number of leading players, including back-line kingpins Mark Nicholls, Bert Cooke and Freddy Lucas, were unavailable to tour. A large number of injuries affected the team, and at one point before the final test, Porter flew from Brisbane to Sydney to arrange treatment for the injured, while the team travelled south by train.

The Wallabies fielded a powerful team, including many stars of the era, such as Alex Ross, Tom Lawton, Syd Malcolm, Eddie Bonis and 'Wild' Bill Cerutti. The captain, Lawton, who had played for New South Wales against the touring All Blacks of 1920, had been an Oxford blue in 1921-23 and a reserve for England against the Invincibles in 1924. A huge first five-eighth, he had led the Waratahs on their 1927-28 tour of Britain and was still good enough to captain Australia against the All Blacks in 1932.

For the first test, with Porter injured before leaving New Zealand and still not fit, the Auckland three-quarter Lew Hook, only 10st, was chosen to play in his position. In the absence of Porter and Bill Dalley, halfback and vice-captain, who was injured out of the tour before the first test, Herb Lilburne, the Canterbury first five-eighth, captained the team. Only 21 at the time, Lilburne remains the youngest player to have led the All Blacks in an international.

New Zealand lost the opening test 8-9 and could not hold the Wallabies in the second half of the second test in Brisbane. After being tied at 3-all at the interval, Australia swept to a series win in convincing fashion, 17-8.

Though they gave a much improved performance, in spite of a reorganised back-line, New Zealand was pipped 15-13 in the final test. But Porter had a champion's game. 'No one who saw the match will forget the New Zealand captain's heroic, inspiring effort. He was a rover, on hand in nearly every movement, back on defence as often as he was hurling himself into the attack. His great tackling and his speed in short, sharp bursts were wonderful,' wrote one reporter.

Porter's greatest triumph in the last chapter of his career came when he led the All Blacks to a 3-1 series win over a very competitive Great Britain in 1930. The visitors pipped the All Blacks 3-6 at Carisbrook in a game played in the most miserable conditions — snow, sleet, rain and wind. With the teams locked at 3-all and New Zealand pressing the opposition line, the All Blacks won a scrum. But loose forward Ivor Jones intercepted a sluggish pass from Jimmy Mill, ran strongly and, faced only with George Nepia as the last line of defence, passed to winger Jack Morley before halfway. The Welshman ran down the sideline with Bert Cooke gaining on him and crossed in the corner for the winning try in the closing seconds of the game.

New Zealand took the second test at Lancaster Park 13-10, with tries shared two each. The British could have won. Their brilliant centre, Carl Aarvold, who scored two superb tries, was guilty of squandering another when he ignored Morley outside him with the line begging, tried to score himself, and was flattened in a great tackle by Nepia. New Zealand's tries, by the wingers Gus Hart and Don Oliver, were also well executed.

A New Zealand record crowd of 40,000 watched the third test at Eden Park and did not go away disappointed, even though the All Blacks packed a scrum a stone a man

WELSH FERVOUR: Part of the capacity crowd at Newport, where Porter's team came close to defeat, finally scraping home 13-10.

CLIFF PORTER

OLD CHUMS: Porter's 1924 All Blacks pose with Oxford before putting their opposition to the sword.

TWO-THREE-TWO: The speedy scrum delivery of the 1924 All Blacks is demonstrated as halfback Bill Dalley probes and readies to get his backs away. The All Blacks beat Lancashire, 23-0, in this game at Manchester.

lighter than the British. Hugh McLean, a loose forward having his first test, celebrated with two tries, but it was the experience of players such as Porter, Cooke, Lucas and, particularly, Nicholls which enabled the All Blacks to win. Nicholls was outstanding, as a general, an opportunist, a tactician and a goal-kicker. As they had done in the two previous tests, the New Zealand forwards took a firm grip on the game in the second half and this time were well rewarded.

But the British were in the game throughout and could never be discounted, so in Porter's home town, Wellington, the crowds again turned out in huge numbers for the fourth test — almost another 40,000 of them. This time the All Blacks made it a no-contest, scoring six tries to one, with Porter and Cooke claiming two each. It was said to be Porter's finest match.

It was a brilliant way to bow out for a number of All Black stars of the previous decade. The series ended the test careers of Nepia, Cooke, Lucas, Nicholls, Stewart, Finlayson, Mill, Irvine and Porter.

But Porter was still crossing swords in 1930 with his old adversary Stan Dean. When the NZRFU tried to cut back the All Blacks' traditional supply of match tickets for the fourth test, because of the great public demand for tickets, Porter threatened to lead a team mutiny. Dean backed down and the team got its allocation.

Porter was by then a towering personality of the game and looked capable of beginning an administrative or selection/coaching career at national level. But, according to the veteran rugby journalist Morrie Mackenzie, 'the Hierarchy had no place in their calculations for outstanding personalities or outspoken types who wouldn't toe the party line, even if they came from Wellington'.

In 1932 'they refused him a hearing at the annual meeting . . . Porter was fighting for the very existence of the New Zealand system of play . . . when ruled out of order. He was trying to demonstrate how a recent rule amendment made the 3-2-3 scrum a better proposition than ever'.

'Worse still, when the election of the management committee came up, the Hierarchy ganged up on Cliff, who was beaten by one vote for a seat on the committee. I never asked Cliff about this, but I can only assume that after these rebuffs he washed his hands forever of rugby administration, as did other great figures before and since, rather than submit meekly to victimisation and intrigue.'[5]

MARK NICHOLLS — TACTICIAN

Mark Nicholls deserves a prominent place in any book about the evolution of the All Black coaches. Not only was he a faithful lieutenant to the two great All Black captain-coaches of the 1920s, Cliff Porter and Maurice Brownlie, but he was also an outstanding contributor as both goal-kicker and tactician.

Nicholls became a Wellington selector-coach within three years of retiring from playing and in 1936–37 was a member of the New Zealand selection panel. He was still influential at national level more than a decade later, for he was a North Island selector in 1948.

Nicholls was a great All Black. He represented New Zealand in 51 matches between 1921 and 1930, playing in 10 tests. A first or second five-eighth, he became renowned for his clear-headed leadership, judgement and development of attacks, as well as his all-round abilities as a runner, passer and kicker. In that time he scored 284 points.

An outstanding schoolboy player, Nicholls made a spectacular debut for Wellington in his first season out of college in 1920. He scored in four different ways against Taranaki, with a try, a conversion, a penalty and a goal from a mark taken by another player.

In 1921 Nicholls played all three tests against the Springboks. He led the point-scorers on the tour of New South Wales in 1922. On the Invincibles' tour of 1924–25 he played in all four tests and was the leading scorer, with 103 points. He kicked six conversions against New South Wales in 1925, and was the leading scorer, with 41 points, on the 1926 Australian tour.

The controversy about Nicholls' mysterious omission from the first three tests of the 1928 series in South Africa is covered more fully in Chapter 1, on Maurice Brownlie. He was chosen for the fourth test and guided the All Blacks to a convincing victory to tie the series. The test was won 13-5, with Nicholls playing brilliantly and kicking 10 points.

Nicholls played in the second and third tests against the British Lions of 1930, but was unavailable for the fourth. His career ended in 1931, when he played the last of five matches for the North Island.

Although renowned in his heyday as an outstanding tactical kicker, especially at provincial level, where he did not always have the running backs he could let loose at international level, Nicholls said in 1967, then aged 66,

CLIFF PORTER

Mark Nicholls.

BIOGRAPHICAL DETAILS

Clifford Glen Porter

Born: Edinburgh, Scotland, 5 May 1899

Died: Wellington, 12 November 1976

Position: Wing forward

Represented NZ: 1923–26, 1928–30

Points for NZ: 41 matches (7 internationals)

Provincial record: Wellington 1917–18 (Wellington College OB), 1923, 1925–30 (Athletic); Horowhenua 1921–22 (Hui Mai); North Island 1924–26, 1928–29; Wellington–Manawatu 1923; Wellington–Manawatu–Horowhenua 1925

NZ coach: 1924–26, 1928–30

Occupation: Partner in paper-bag manufacturing business, Hutt Valley

NEW ZEALAND COACHING RECORD

1924–25: beat Ireland 6-0; beat Wales 19-0; beat England 17-11; beat France 30-6

1926: lost to NSW 20-26; beat NSW 11-6, 14-0

1928: beat NSW 15-12, 16-14; lost to NSW 8-11

1929: lost to Australia 8-9, 9-17, 13-15

1930: lost to Great Britain 3-6; beat Great Britain 13-10, 15-10, 22-8

that his era 'did not have the kicking complex of the players of today'.

'We were encouraged to run with the ball. If we couldn't, we would be kicked out of the team,' he said. 'What was the good of having great three-quarters like Bert Cooke and Jack Steel if you never gave them the ball?'

He summed up rugby of the 1950s and 1960s as 'a game where four men [the wingers] are trained to throw the ball in for 26 to kick it out'.

He also criticised the 'over-organisation' of the game. 'In our day the coach didn't decide the tactics. He chose the players and left it to them. The forward leader decided what the forwards would do and the back leader called the back-line moves. The coach would indicate at halftime where we were going wrong and suggest we try such-and-such a move.'

Two of Mark Nicholls' brothers — 'Ginger' and 'Doc' — also played for the All Blacks, while another brother — Guy — played for North Auckland. The brothers' father, Syd, had played for Wellington, something Mark's son also did over half a century later.

REFERENCES
1. Terry McLean, *New Zealand Rugby Legends*.
2. *Sydney Sun*.
3. Keith Quinn, *The Encyclopedia of World Rugby*.
4. Morrie Mackenzie, *Black, Black, Black*.
5. *Black, Black, Black*.

CHAPTER 8

CAPTAIN & COACH 1928

MAURICE BROWNLIE

Series share with Boks was to prove benchmark for 68 years

MAURICE BROWNLIE HAD ALREADY FORGED A reputation as perhaps the greatest forward New Zealand had produced when he was given the task of leading the All Blacks on their first tour of South Africa.

Depending on the source, the 1928 tour is said to have been a playing and diplomatic disaster, or a happy trip on which much was learned and the honours equally shared.

Certainly, to have won two of the four tests and tied the rubber is a feat that puts Brownlie's team above their successors, the humiliated 1949 team and the 1960, 1970 and 1976 touring sides. But it took time for respect for the team's effort to grow, as each succeeding attempt failed. In 1928, New Zealand rugby enthusiasts had thought they had a team to match the Invincibles of four years earlier, so were bitterly disappointed when the All Blacks suffered five losses and a draw on the gruelling tour. The critics had a field day.

Bill Hornig, a Wellington men's outfitter and member of the NZRFU management committee, had won the manager's job over three other candidates, including Norman and Ted McKenzie, two of the finest thinkers in the New Zealand game and both destined to coach the All Blacks and be long-time national selectors. In retrospect, either McKenzie, but especially Norman, who had been Brownlie's mentor throughout his career, could have played a crucial part in allowing the captain to lead on-field while they prepared the team.

Questions were asked in some quarters about Brownlie's leadership qualities as he became increasingly withdrawn and totally hostile to the media.

Preparations for the tour had been thorough at the New Zealand end, but South Africa's racial laws had prevented the selection of a number of talented players, most notably, George Nepia. A star of the Invincibles tour when aged only 19, Nepia was at the peak of his powers by 1928 and would play for the All Blacks until 1930 and at a lower level in both league and rugby for much longer. His long, spiralling touch-finders, in the rarified air of the high veldt, might have countered Bennie Osler's probing kicks.

Although named in the reserves, Cliff Porter's omission, considering his proven leadership ability and his influence on All Black rugby both before and after the tour, seems a strange decision. Perhaps the selectors wanted Brownlie to be free to put his own stamp on the team.

Yet another setback was the withdrawal, after the team had been chosen, of Bert Cooke on business grounds. A freakish midfield back, Cooke would become the first New Zealand player to score 100 tries in first-class rugby. He would finish his 131-game career with

MAURICE BROWNLIE

121 tries, a remarkable strike rate considering he was often very heavily marked. The 1928 All Blacks scored only three tries in this series against the Boks' five. Cooke's ingenuity was clearly missed.

'If we'd had Nepia and Cooke, we wouldn't have lost a match,' Brownlie was to state, somewhat wishfully, after the tour.

The great differences in weather and ground conditions between sea level and high veldt, the difficulties with the rarified air at altitude, the huge distances to be travelled by train between match venues — these were just some of the problems New Zealand rugby administrators had been warned about by Charlie Brown, captain of the New Zealand Army team which had toured South Africa in 1919, warnings which were ignored in accepting the itinerary and tour arrangements.

Troubles began before the team even touched South African soil. The ship took exactly a month to transport the All Blacks from Sydney to Durban. It was to have taken them on to Cape Town but sprung a leak and needed repairs, so the team continued by train. Leaving Durban on the Friday night, they travelled via Johannesburg, arriving in Cape Town on Monday morning. They had to play their first match two days later.

Vice-captain Mark Nicholls, as famous in his heyday as Brownlie, wrote a book on the tour and made many perceptive observations on South African rugby in general and the tour in particular. He pinpointed the All Blacks' scrum weaknesses as a major obstacle that was never truly overcome. After experimenting, with some promise, with the 3-4-1 scrum being used so devastatingly by all their South African opponents, the All Blacks reverted to their old methods after the loss to Transvaal in the fourth game because the new formation 'was not congenial to the forwards'.

Nicholls told of a conversation he had with George Devenish, a South African selector, who said

BIG BRUSH-OFF: This hapless Swansea opponent is about to get the famous 'Brownlie brush-off' as the 1924 All Blacks swamp the Welsh side 39-3. Alf West and Quentin Donald are in close support.

THE POWER BEHIND THE ALL BLACKS

HAKA TIME: The 1928 All Blacks give their haka on the first tour of South Africa. Captain-coach Maurice Brownlie is fourth from left. Ironically, George Nepia and Jimmy Mill were among a number of Maori players who might have aided New Zealand's efforts but were barred from playing by South Africa's racial laws.

that when he saw the All Blacks line up for their first game they were, physically, the finest set of forwards he had ever seen, and that his spirits fell. But after watching them lose to Transvaal he said, 'They cannot scrum and they will be beaten time and again by ordinary provincial teams.'

Nicholls said his long experience had taught him the 2-3-2 scrum had never managed to gain equal share of possession and he recommended change. Unfortunately, although the IRB would force the 2-3-2 scrum from the game in the early 1930s, New Zealanders' acceptance and mastery of the 3-4-1 scrum would still not be up to standard when the All Blacks next toured South Africa, in 1949.

New Zealand's wing-forward game and a failure to master the six- and eight-panelled balls of South Africa were other reasons for the All Blacks' difficulties, according to Nicholls.

'We did well, considering all things, to come out "all square" at the end of the tour. We went there grossly overrated. In the first 10 games we did not find our feet, but from then on we improved and played, at times, really good football. Our record, although disappointing to New Zealanders, is one which any team can feel proud of against such worthy antagonists.'[1]

Nicholls never alluded anywhere to the fact he played in only the last of the four tests, although he was a member of the tour selection panel. This anomaly has fascinated rugby historians ever since Nicholls, whose brilliance had helped the All Blacks to victory many times in the years, kicked the team to victory in that test and the question will always be asked if he could have done the same in one or more of the others.

Unlike on all the later All Black tours of South Africa, there were no complaints about the refereeing in the test series. Knoppie Neser, selected by the touring team, controlled all four tests and did a very fair job. He was a former Oxford rugby and cricket blue and became a Supreme Court judge.

According to Terry McLean, the 1928 tour raised many issues about Brownlie: 'His own form, which a leading South African critic considered indifferent until the last three weeks; his hostility to the newspapermen, not forgetting the two New Zealanders, Graham Beamish and Syd Nicholls, a brother of Mark, who were with the team throughout; his having to put up with a manager who was so unthinking that at a formal dinner in Pretoria he casually remarked: "You know the last time I was in this town was when we were fighting you blokes in the Boer War"; incompetence in the back line, magnified by the loss of [Frank] Kilby; an anti-Mark Nicholls clique in the selection committee, two members of which, Neil McGregor and Ron Stewart, harboured grudges from the '24 tour; and, not least, Brownlie's qualities of captaincy.'[2]

The major question is whether Brownlie, given all these difficulties and taking account of his own determination to do all things well, was wanting in compassion for his fellow players or lacked the man-management skills that other great All Black coaches

MAURICE BROWNLIE

CAPE TOWN RACERS: Winger Bert Grenside throws into the lineout on the 1928 All Blacks' tour of South Africa. The opposition is Cape Town Clubs, who gave New Zealand its first tour loss, 3-7. The All Blacks suffered five losses and a draw on the gruelling tour, but tied the series, 2-all.

and captains have displayed. There is evidence, from some players who toured, that he approached the leadership as aggressively as he played every game.

But his leadership and example were not found wanting towards the end of the tour. It is at this point that many rugby tours, the All Blacks' included, have faltered. But Brownlie seems to have found new energy in his own play for the final hurdles and transmitted that power and inspiration to his fellow players.

Midway through the tour, when the party moved north to play Rhodesia, Brownlie ordered a week of rest before the game. No training was held and the team, thoroughly refreshed, turned in easily its biggest score of the tour, 44-8. It then won its next game, the second test, in Johannesburg. In the lead-up to the fourth and deciding test, after losing to Western Province, Brownlie again ordered a week of complete rest.

On the morning after the Province match Brownlie assembled the team. 'These are my orders for the week, gentlemen,' he said. 'They are few, and simple. Each of you will go for a walk of about an hour. You will go to bed at a reasonable hour. For the rest, you will do what you like with this proviso: Under no circumstances whatever is any one of you so much as to touch a rugby ball until we play the Springboks in the last test.'[3]

Against predictions, New Zealand went on to score a magnificent 13-5 victory. The All Black forward pack dominated the game, and Mark Nicholls, playing at second five-eighths, kicked two penalties and a dropped goal. It was the first time South Africa had been beaten on Newlands for 37 years.

'Probably no greater shock has ever come to the Springboks,' wrote Nicholls. 'Their grand pack, which had overwhelmed us well and truly at Durban, here wilted and faded under the titanic pressure of the All Black vanguard.'[4]

Brownlie himself concluded: 'Our improved form was due to the week's rest. We had become tired and jaded, because of all the travelling, to which we are not accustomed. So we did very little training and brightened up as the week progressed, with the result we were able to put all our energy into the game.

'In all our matches we have found South Africans most worthy foemen, and we shall carry with us most pleasant recollections of the many hard matches we have enjoyed.'[5]

Maurice was one of three brothers who played for the All Blacks. The youngest, Laurence, was the first to win national honours, in 1921, but a knee injury forced him to retire. Cyril, the oldest, 6ft 3in tall and weighing in at 15st, was a huge forward for the era. He played 90 first-class matches over a nine-year career and toured Britain and France in 1924 and South Africa in 1928 with the All Blacks. He earned the dubious distinction of becoming the first All Black to be ordered off in an international, in the England test.

Maurice and Cyril Brownlie went off to war as young men, being posted to the 2nd Mounted Rifles. They fought in Palestine and took part in the long chase of the Turks to Damascus. The brothers came home to the family farm at Puketitiri, near Hastings, and to rugby.

It was the selection of Laurence, to play for the All Blacks against New South Wales in 1921, which was the spur for Maurice and Cyril. Their father, James, urged them to get fit and try to emulate their little brother.

Maurice played in the Hawke's Bay – Poverty Bay team which held the 1921 Springboks to 8-14. Within a year he was an All Black, touring Australia, where his robust style had the critics in raptures. From this point he would go on to become one of New Zealand's greatest forwards, talked about for many decades with the same reverence as was Colin Meads 30 years later.

He was a loose forward whose greatest attributes were courage and legendary strength — perhaps setting the mould for tight-loose players like Meads and others after him. He was 6ft tall and weighed little more than 14st, but played, as the saying goes, well above that weight.

Work on the farm had made Maurice and Cyril tremendously strong. Stories abound, in the same vein as those about the Meads brothers, of Maurice carrying a sheep under each arm, dragging the family car out of a river and hefting 70lb bales of hay high all summer's day.

We are indebted to Norman McKenzie, the great rugby coach, selector and administrator, who became Maurice Brownlie's mentor, for the most intimate pen portrait of the player. He said Brownlie was 'the greatest man I have ever seen as a siderow forward: great because he was great in every aspect of forward play.

'He could handle the ball like a back, he could take the ball in a lineout and burst clear, he could stimulate movements, and, greatest of all, he had the ability to lead his forwards out of a tight corner, yard by yard, along the touchline.

'For sheer tenacity I have seen no one to equal Maurice Brownlie. His outstanding qualities were

FOUR FAMOUS CAPTAINS: Maurice Brownlie (second from left) is photographed with three former Springbok captains during the 1928 All Black tour of South Africa. From left, they are Billy Millar (1912 Springbok captain), Theo Pienaar (1921) and Paul Roos (1906).

strength and resolution. He was in every respect a remarkable man and one of the finest specimens of manhood I have ever seen.

'He always took the field physically fit, and I don't know that he did a great deal of training – that is, training as we regard it today. He constantly invigorated his friends with his offensive spirit. He was a hard, but never a tough player, and although he was often a marked man and set upon, he never complained, but got on with his game.'[6]

McKenzie, who was to become an All Black coach and serve as a national selector for many years, was, incredibly, the Hawke's Bay coach from 1916 to 1946. With Maurice Brownlie as his captain, he guided the Bay through its most famous Ranfurly Shield era, when it repulsed 24 challenges between 1922 and 1927, and nurtured great players such as George Nepia, 'Bull' Irvine, Jimmy Mill, Lui Paewai, Jack Ormond, Bert Cooke (who moved there from Auckland) as well as the Brownlie brothers.

'In 1921, at their father's urging, Maurice and Cyril made the 40-mile journey from the farm to Hastings each Saturday to play. A couple of looks at them were enough for me and I put them in the Hawke's Bay team. Maurice had his first game against Manawatu as a lock, but never again did he fill that position for Hawke's Bay. He was too valuable to bury in the scrum,' said McKenzie.[7]

Maurice and Norman were to form a unique partnership as they forged the Bay team, from a previously weak, widespread country union, into the best New Zealand had seen. Whether they put the shield up at home or took it on tour throughout New Zealand, the Bay was to develop into an invincible unit, racking up record scores from brilliant, running displays against the strongest provincial rivals. *(See Chapter 9)*

Before the great shield matches, Brownlie would arrive in Napier from the farm on the Friday evening and head straight for McKenzie's house. The pair would discuss the opposing side and then scheme out the type of game they intended to play.

'Once we had decided on a plan, the rest was over to him. So it went on through his wonderful career. I never heard him speak disparagingly of another player. His motto was 'deeds, not words', and what deeds they were!'[8]

At the end of the shield era Brownlie was to gain a little notoriety when he and fellow Invincible Quentin Donald were ordered off in the infamous Battle of Solway, the controversial shield match between Wairarapa, the new holder, and Hawke's Bay, in 1927. The opposing coach was Norman McKenzie's brother Ted, while the referee was another brother, Bert.

There have been few players able or willing to turn on the sheer consistency of Brownlie through such a long career. His determination was the key to his ability to focus on a team's task in match after match. On the Invincibles tour, for instance, he played in 25 matches and scored 11 tries. In the Hawke's Bay shield era he played in 19 games and scored ten tries.

The Invincibles tour, in 1924-25, was possibly the high point of Brownlie's career. In the company of other great forwards such as Cliff Porter, Jock Richardson, Jim Parker, 'Bull' Irvine and his brother Cyril, he stood out as exceptional. Observers rated the England test, after Cyril had been ordered off the field unfairly, as Maurice and the other All Blacks felt, as his (Maurice's) finest performance. He played like a man possessed and helped inspire New Zealand to a 17-11 victory.

The try Brownlie scored that day was described by Wavell Wakefield, the English captain: 'I could see him going straight down the touchline, though it seemed impossible for him to score. Somehow he went on, giving me the impression of a moving tree-trunk, so solid did he appear to be and so little effect did various attempted tackles have on him. He crashed through without swerving to right or left and went over for one of the most surprising tries I have ever seen.'[9]

Brownlie had team-mate Jim Parker alongside but is reputed to have said to him, 'I wouldn't have passed it out for 100 pounds.'

Maurice Brownlie continued to be New Zealand's most outstanding forward through the 1920s and to lead the All Blacks on their ground-breaking tour of South Africa in 1928. He retired from big football after that, although he did play for Hawke's Bay against Great Britain in 1930. He played a total of 119 first-class games, including 61 for the All Blacks, which was to remain a record until broken by Kevin Skinner 28 years later.

Brownlie was also a boxer of some renown, in an era when the sport was strong and attracted large numbers of participants and followers. He was beaten in the 1921 New Zealand amateur championship heavyweight final by Brian McCleary, who turned professional in 1922 after an unbeaten amateur career of 32 bouts and became the New Zealand heavyweight and light-heavyweight champion that year. McCleary, also a

THE POWER BEHIND THE ALL BLACKS

GOLDEN ERA: It is 1923, the second year of Hawke's Bay's unprecedented six-year tenure of the Ranfurly Shield. The Magpies repulsed five challenges in 1923, and six of its players were All Blacks that year. Maurice Brownlie (third row, fifth from left) and Norm McKenzie (second row, far right) provided the leadership.

front-row forward from Canterbury, joined Brownlie as a member of the 1924-25 All Black Invincibles.

REFERENCES
1. M. F. Nicholls, *With the All Blacks in Springbokland*, L. F. Watkins, 1928
2. Terry McLean, *New Zealand Rugby Legends*, Moa, 1987.
3. *New Zealand Rugby Legends*.
4. *With the All Blacks in Springbokland*.
5. *New Zealand Rugby Legends*.
6-8. Arthur Carman, *On with the Game*, Reed, 1960.
9. W. W. Wakefield, *Rugger*.

NEW ZEALAND COACHING RECORD

1928: lost to South Africa 0-17; beat South Africa 7-6; lost to South Africa 6-11; beat South Africa 13-5

BIOGRAPHICAL DETAILS

Maurice John Brownlie

Born: Wanganui, 10 August 1897

Died: Gisborne, 21 January 1957

Position: Loose forward

Represented NZ: 1922-26, 1928
61 matches (8 internationals)

Points for NZ: 63 (21 tries)

Provincial record: Hawke's Bay 1921-27, 1929-30 (Hastings club); Hawke's Bay – Poverty Bay 1921; Hawke's Bay – Poverty Bay, East Coast 1923; North Island 1922-25, 1927

NZ coach: 1928 (while captain)

Occupation: Farmer

CHAPTER 9

NEW ZEALAND COACH 1930, 1947, 1949

NORM McKENZIE

Great influence on All Blacks over three decades

NORM McKENZIE BESTRODE THE NEW ZEALAND rugby scene like a colossus over many decades — not only as a coach of the All Blacks, but far more influentially as a national selector and the force behind the amazing rise to power of the record-breaking Hawke's Bay Ranfurly Shield team.

McKenzie, as sole selector-coach, built Hawke's Bay from a weak side to one which consistently ripped apart the reputations of New Zealand's traditionally powerful provinces, especially in the 1920s, and supplied a ready group of outstanding players to the All Blacks each year. He held the Bay reins for 31 unbroken years, from 1916 to 1946.

'Big Norm' was an All Black selector from 1924 to 1930 (while still the Bay coach) and from 1947 to 1949 — a total of 10 years. He was also on the NZRFU council, attended the International Rugby Conference as the NZRFU representative and was a life member of the NZRFU. He was still involved in big rugby in 1956, as liaison officer to the touring Springboks, whose manager, Dr Danie Craven, laid an official complaint about the referees at one stage of the tour.

McKenzie played five seasons in the backs for Wairarapa, before being transferred by the post office to Napier in 1912. He then represented Hawke's Bay for three seasons.

Norm's activities as a coach became part of rugby legend, while the McKenzie family ties with the game must be unique. Norm was one of five rugby-playing brothers. The other four were New Zealand and Wellington wing forward and famous identity William 'Offside Mac' McKenzie; fellow New Zealand selector and coach, Wairarapa coach and international referee Ted; international referee Bert; and Wairarapa representative (1899–1903) Jack.

The New Zealand rugby historian Arthur Carman wrote and edited McKenzie's biography. McKenzie had begun preparing it himself but had a massive heart attack at the 1959 NZRFU annual conference. Carman recorded the ailing man's reminiscences on tape and completed the book after McKenzie died in April 1960.

In the foreword, Carman wrote that McKenzie 'was one of the greatest personalities New Zealand rugby has produced during the past half-century. As player, selector, referee, coach, tactician, administrator and writer he touched the game at every point and his views always commanded respect.

'Becoming known from North Cape to the Bluff during five years in the 1920s as selector-coach of the all-victorious Hawke's Bay Ranfurly Shield team, he remained a national figure for the rest of his life.

'Because he had been one himself, he was a great champion of the "country" player and had a great deal to do with the ultimate honours gained by many a back-country lad.

'He knew the game intimately and expressed his

THE POWER BEHIND THE ALL BLACKS

KEEP IT IN THE FAMILY: Norm (left), Bert and Ted, three of the five famous McKenzie brothers. They were household names in the 1920s and 1930s in particular. Oldest brother William, known as 'Offside Mac', was a great New Zealand wing-forward late in the 19th Century. Another brother, Jack, was a Wairarapa representative. In this 1927 photo Norm is the Hawke's Bay coach, Ted the Wairarapa coach and Bert is about to referee the famous 'Battle of Solway' Ranfurly Shield match between them.

opinions in a forthright manner. He was a sound judge of a player and an astute tactician, able to pin-point a weakness and devise the means to victory.

'He brought wisdom and sound judgement to the council table, and contributed greatly to the government of the game.'[1]

Winston McCarthy, the great radio commentator, wrote that 'Norman could be a martinet or a diplomat as the occasion demanded — one minute he would be tearing a strip off a reporter or official, the next he would be cajoling another official into granting him something that wasn't what others would want him to have.

'He had a memory a yard long which, allied to his gift as a raconteur and his sense of humour, made him a delightful and interesting companion.

'With the players he was a psychologist supreme and could, consequently, get more out of a mediocre player than the majority. He knew all the tricks of the trade and was never hesitant about exploiting them if he felt the occasion demanded.'[2]

McCarthy recalled such an incident in 1933, when a strong Wellington team, containing Fred Fuller, one of the game's greatest goal-kickers, played Hawke's Bay at Napier. McKenzie, sitting in the grandstand with Wellington officials, predicted Fuller would have an off day with his boot. So it was to be. McKenzie had apparently taken measures to have the match balls overblown so Fuller's longer kicks ballooned away harmlessly.

Four years later, in 1937, with the Springboks set to play the Bay, McKenzie received a call from the Boks' captain, Philip Nel, asking him to drop round the three match balls. McKenzie took the balls, realising someone in Wellington had been telling tales. Ace goal-kicker Gerry Brand rejected one of them. Norman promised to see to it, climbed aboard his bike, rode back home and had a cup of tea. Then he went back to the Boks' hotel and again Brand rejected the ball.

'Off rode Norm again, this time around to the Club where he spent half an hour or so chatting to the members. Back again to the hotel where he said to Brand, "Now, Gerry, if it's too tight for you this time I suggest you blow it up yourself to your satisfaction." Gerry prodded the ball a few times with his thumb, then signed his name across the lace.'

Next day the Boks won the game 21-12 (one of the closest of the Boks' provincial matches on that tour), but Brand's long-range attempts were all unsuccessful.[3]

McKenzie's record-breaking Ranfurly Shield tenure from 1922 to 1927 was almost nipped in the bud. He did not include Maurice Brownlie in the first defence, and long before the match was over he was regretting that decision. Challenger Bay of Plenty scored by the posts with two minutes to go, to make the score 16–17. But under the pressure of taking the winning kick, the Bay of Plenty missed the simple conversion.

In 1923 the Magpies repulsed five challenges, including a 9-8 win over Canterbury. Names such as Nepia, Paewai and Mill had come onto the team lists. Grenside, Mill, Gemmell, Irvine and Maurice Brownlie played for the North Island. Paewai, Brownlie, Mill, Gemmell, Irvine and Ormond became All Blacks in 1923.

In 1924 Hawke's Bay won all five challenges comfortably. Six Bay players made the 1924 All Black Invincibles — Maurice and Cyril Brownlie, Paewai, Nepia, Mill and Irvine.

THUMPING TIME: Norm McKenzie's 1947 All Blacks have returned from a triumphant tour of Australia and are about to face Auckland at Eden Park before a mid-week crowd of 25,000. With both All Black hookers injured, Arthur Hughes, an Auckland Grammar Club player, has been asked to fill in, and would later play six tests for New Zealand. But as it has done several times, Auckland thumped the All Blacks, 14-3. The team is: Fred Allen (captain), Roy White, Keith Arnold, Johnny Simpson, Ray Dalton, Lachie Grant, Charlie Willocks, Nev Thornton, Tim Mason, Arthur Hughes, Tom Webster, Jim Kearney, Johnny Smith, Percey Tetzlaff, Morrie Goddard.

In 1925 seven challenges were accepted and won. Four more Bay players gained the black jersey — Jack Blake, Tom Corkill, Alex Kirkpatrick and Jack McNab. The Bay took the shield to Wellington to defend it at Athletic Park. By then they had repulsed 18 challenges. The Bay kept the shield that day, 20-11, after a most sensational opening try by Albert Falwasser.

The next year, 1926, was the Bay's vintage year. In five matches it aggregated 229 points — an average of 46 a game. By then the little genius Bert Cooke had migrated from Auckland. The Bay opened its campaign against arch-rival Wairarapa, a powerful side, including Fred Fuller and a good number of All Blacks past and future. The Bay scored 17 tries to win 77–14.

Then came Wellington's turn. It fielded six All Blacks in Mark and Ginger Nicholls, Snowy Svenson, Cliff Porter, Jim Moffitt and Les Thomas, with Ned Barry to become one. The score was 58–8. Auckland fared little better. It had nine players who were or were to become All Blacks. It lost 11-41.

The Bay then took the shield to Christchurch in its final defence of the season. Ten of Canterbury's side were present or future All Blacks. The Bay led 11-3 at half-time, but Canterbury fought back to 15-17 and right on top. In the final minutes Canterbury was awarded a penalty straight out in front. Syd Carleton, an imperturbable player, took the kick but missed. So ended 1926, after 24 defences.

It was to be the Bay's last success. During the off-season six Bay All Blacks were lost — Nepia went farming near Ruatoria, Lance Johnson was transferred by his employers, Irvine and Cooke migrated to Wairarapa, Paewai went to Auckland and Jimmy Mill moved away.

The first 1927 challenge was against Wairarapa, which had 10 current or future All Blacks against the Bay's seven. Rawi Cundy kicked Wairarapa to a 15-11 win. However, McKenzie's heroes were not finished. They had a regular home-and-away fixture with Wairarapa, and it was agreed it would be for the shield. The match was played at the Solway Showgrounds in Masterton and has forever afterwards been known as the Battle of Solway. Hawke's Bay defeated Wairarapa 21-10 and, so they believed, regained the shield.

These two shield games were remarkable for several reasons. One was that two brothers coached the opposing teams — Norm's opposite number was Ted McKenzie, almost as legendary a figure as he was. More remarkable was that a third brother, Bert, refereed both matches. Bert didn't let anyone down that day at Solway either — when matters got very willing at the start of the game he ordered off both captains, the All Blacks Maurice Brownlie and Quentin Donald.

But the Solway game had other strange twists. The Bay played Wattie Barclay, who had been in Auckland earlier in the season but had returned to his home in the Bay in time to qualify on residential grounds. The rules of both unions stipulated a period of 14 days.

However, after the match, the NZRFU chairman, Stan Dean, who'd been a spectator, told Wairarapa officials that the residential qualification for shield matches was in fact 21 days and if they protested, they would undoubtedly win. Wairarapa protested accordingly, and eventually won the decision. But during the time the question was in dispute both teams played matches, and Wairarapa lost 16-18 to Manawhenua, which was thus awarded the shield.

Both Norm and Ted spoke at the protest hearing. When Hawke's Bay unsuccessfully appealed the decision, Norm threatened Supreme Court action. The Bay refused to part with the shield for some time. Meanwhile, Bert, as a matter of principle, resigned as secretary of the Wairarapa Referees' Association when the unions of Wairarapa and Hawke's Bay decided to take no further action against Donald or Brownlie.

Norm was to say of the incident: 'It has always been my contention that if that official, who had been in Masterton long enough, did not see fit to mention the fact to representatives of both unions beforehand, he should have forever held his tongue.'[4]

George Nepia recalled how he'd returned from the triumphant 1924-25 All Black Invincibles tour, on which he'd played every game at fullback, to be placed in the midfield for Hawke's Bay by McKenzie. The great coach had used Nepia, then only 19, as five-eighth before the tour and never a fullback.

'. . . like any other man he had his foibles and I think my field placing . . . was one of these. The fact was that just as Norman could never forgive me later for turning to league, so he could never quite forgive himself for having failed to recognise, though he knew my abilities better than anyone, that I had possibilities as a fullback.

"Add to this that in the days I am talking about he could be very sharp-tempered and that he was all pins and needles before and during a big game and you have some idea of his moods and their complexity."[5]

In his book, McKenzie reminisced back to 1897, the

63

NORM McKENZIE

year his brother William — known universally as Offside Mac — was captain of Wellington.

'I was the youngest of five brothers, all of whom played rugby. William, of course, was my hero because four times he had gained a place on the New Zealand side.

'Meal table discussions were on rugby more often than not, and, as the youngest, I was allowed to listen, no more! I learned a lot. Later, William was stricken with rheumatism. His rugby career was cut short, but during the two years that he was ill he used to recite to me his exploits on the field and tell me about the players with whom he associated. He always stressed the value of the tactical side of rugby. He used to plan how rugby matches would be played. He had an apt listener in me.

'Those were the "horse and cart days" of rugby and it was common for players to ride all day to get to a match. The telephone was almost non-existent in country districts. Though a team might travel 10 or 12 miles to play a game, the villagers had to await the team's return to learn the result. Ten o'clock closing made the hotels an

CULTURAL BLEND: Norm McKenzie coached Hawke's Bay for 31 unbroken years. This 1923 photo at Rotorua before the Bay of Plenty game shows McKenzie (far right) with the team. McKenzie was able to blend the Maori and Pakeha talents into many wonderful combinations.

attraction. So if one wanted to know the result of a game, one had to wait until about midnight for the team's return'.[6]

The first of Norm McKenzie's three periods as an All Black coach or assistant coach came at the end of his first stint as a national selector. He helped his brother Ted, the chairman of selectors, to coach the All Blacks to a 3-1 series win over a very competitive Great Britain in 1930.

The great coach returned to the national selection panel 17 years later, a year after he finally retired from coaching his beloved Hawke's Bay for 31 straight seasons. McKenzie stayed on the panel for three years (1947–49). In the first year he coached the All Blacks in Australia, a team captained by Fred Allen. This side won its two tests comfortably, but narrowly lost an early match to New South Wales, 9-12, and was well beaten by Auckland, 3-14, on its return. It had to borrow a local player, hooker Arthur Hughes, to make up the numbers against Auckland, and tried to play a running game, to please the large crowd, on a waterlogged, rainswept Eden Park.

Interviewed in 1997, Allen, who is remembered as perhaps the greatest All Black coach after an unbeaten record over three years, said Norman McKenzie was a very astute coach.

'By that stage of his career, Norm was getting on. He used to stand on the sideline and leave the running of the practices to me. But he would give very powerful team talks and had a wonderful knowledge of the game and what tactics suited every situation,' he said.

Bob Stuart, another All Black coach of the future, was Norm McKenzie's vice-captain and forward leader when the All Blacks played Australia in two tests in 1949. He also recalled that McKenzie had left a lot of the organisation at practices to the team leaders.

The 1947 tour had an encouraging effect on the All Blacks' prospects for South Africa, with the team to be chosen the year after. But success on this occasion was not to be. McKenzie was involved in the selection of the two 1949 All Black teams which together lost their six tests that year.

He coached the team which lost both official tests to the touring Wallabies. On the day of the third test in South Africa, it played the first test in Wellington, losing 6-11. Although regarded in some quarters as a third-string side, it contained much talent. Three Maori backs, Johnny Smith, Ben Couch and Vince Bevan, would almost certainly have been on the South African tour but for South Africa's racial policy.

After such a long and distinguished career, it seemed a sad way for McKenzie to go out. The NZRFU appointed a completely new selection panel in 1950.

REFERENCES
1. Arthur Carman, *On with the Game*, Reed, 1960.
2. Winston McCarthy, *Haka! The All Blacks Story*, Pelham Books, 1968.
3, 4. *On With The Game*.
5. Terry McLean, *I George Nepia*.
6. *On with the Game*.

BIOGRAPHICAL DETAILS

Norman Alfred McKenzie

Born: Carterton, 24 May 1888

Died: Napier, 28 March 1960

Provincial record: Wairarapa 1907–11 (Carterton Rovers and Carterton clubs); Hawke's Bay 1912, 1914 (Marist club)

Selector/coach: Hawke's Bay 1916–46

NZ selector: 1924–30, 1947–49

NZ coach: 1930, 1947, 1949

Other service: NZRFU council 1949, life member 1950; representative at international Rugby Conference, Scotland, 1954

Other: Had four rugby-playing brothers — NZ and Wellington wing forward William 'Offside Mac', fellow selector and coach, Wairarapa coach and international referee Ted, international referee Bert, Wairarapa representative (1899–1903) Jack; founded Napier Athletics and Cycling Club and Hawke's Bay–Poverty Bay Athletics Centre; NZAAA president 1948–49; Napier city councillor; president Napier division of Order of St John; Napier Patriotic Committee, World War II; Napier Welfare Committee for aftercare of World War II servicemen; organiser Napier centenary celebrations 1940; returning officer Napier municipal elections

Other: OBE

Occupation: Post Office employee

NEW ZEALAND COACHING RECORD

1930: lost to Britain 3-6; beat Britain 13-10, 15-10, 22-8

1947: beat Australia 13-5, 27-14

1949: lost to Australia 6-11, 9-16

CHAPTER 10

NEW ZEALAND COACH 1925, 1930

TED McKENZIE

The only sole selector in New Zealand rugby history

TED MCKENZIE, ONE OF THE REMARKABLE McKenzie brothers of the most influential family in the long history of New Zealand rugby, might have pulled off the coaching coup of the century in 1925 — if he had been allowed.

McKenzie, not to be confused with his younger brother and fellow New Zealand selector and All Black coach Norman, guided the 1925 All Black team on their tour of Australia. In those days, with significant rugby not being played in Queensland, it was New South Wales which represented Australia at home and abroad. McKenzie's team won both their 'tests'.

But McKenzie's suggestion — that his team then be pitted against members of the previous year's All Blacks, the 1924–25 Invincibles — was not taken up by the NZRFU, perhaps mindful that the Invincibles had lost to Auckland in a warm-up game just before departing for Britain. So the chance to lock horns with perhaps the greatest players New Zealand had produced in its first half-century of the game, plus the public relations and monetary windfalls that would have emerged, was lost.

McKenzie's 1925 team was largely young and inexperienced. Many members had not previously played for New Zealand. They performed well on tour, although they had the misfortune to play on grounds heavy from Sydney's wettest winter in a quarter-century. The forwards were too strong for their opponents, while the backs gave several brilliant displays. However, only six of the 23 players were to play for New Zealand again, and the reason is simple — this was a golden period in New Zealand rugby and the provinces abounded with fine players.

New South Wales toured New Zealand later that same year and, after winning eight of its nine lead-up matches, was pitted against the All Blacks. But this time the national selectors, who included Ted and Norman, had chosen a team which included 13 of the Invincibles, plus Micky Lomas and Bunny Finlayson, who had toured under McKenzie.

Led by Cliff Porter and including Nepia, Lucas, Robilliard, Swenson, Cooke, Mark Nicholls, Mill, Richardson, Masters, Maurice Brownlie, Irvine and others, the team is remembered as the strongest combination New Zealand had ever put onto a rugby field at home. The All Blacks won 36–10, scoring eight tries.

Ted McKenzie had an outstanding career in many areas and at many levels of rugby, and probably equalled his brother Norman in the variety of posts he held, the length of time he was involved and his influence over such a long period. He was on the New Zealand selection panel from 1924 to 1937, a period which included the selection of the Invincibles, the 1928

McKENZIE COUNTRY: This 1909 photo of the Carterton Druids seven-a-side team contains three of the five remarkable McKenzie brothers – in the front row, from left are Norm McKenzie, Bert McKenzie and Ted McKenzie.

team to South Africa, all the other great teams of the 1920s through to the 1930 tour by Great Britain, the 1935-36 All Blacks to Britain, and the All Black team of 1937 which faced the touring Springboks, 'the greatest team ever to leave New Zealand'.

Ted McKenzie was sole New Zealand selector in 1938 and 1939, the only time in New Zealand's rugby history when one person has been entrusted with the job. In 1939 he chose the All Black team which would have toured South Africa in 1940 if World War II had not intervened. He never announced the team he had chosen. He was also a test-match referee, having officiated in the first test between the All Blacks and Springboks in 1921, was secretary of the Wairarapa union for almost 20 years, was on the New Zealand union's management committee for eight years and coached the Wairarapa team during one of its finest periods.

Ted McKenzie was one of five brothers prominent in rugby *(See Chapter 13 for more details)*.

In 1924, with the All Black tour to Britain and France looming on the horizon, the NZRFU held a special meeting, at which the entire 1923 national selection panel was voted out of office. Eventually, a seven-man panel was elected, with Ted McKenzie as its chairman. Norman was also elected to the panel. Either one or the other, sometimes both, was to be on every All Black selection panel for the next quarter-century.

There were eight trials, and Ted McKenzie said when the 1924 team was selected that his panel 'has travelled from the northern to the southern extremities of the Dominion, and has seen the cream of the rugby players presented to them'.

After a warm-up tour of four matches in Australia and a very rough trip home across the Tasman, when most of the players were cot cases, the team arrived to discover the NZRFU had acceded to a request from the Auckland union that it play Auckland. So just 14 hours after landing on terra firma, the All Blacks played, and lost 14-3.

TED McKENZIE

BROTHERLY LOVE: Ted McKenzie (front row, fifth from left) coached Wairarapa in an era when it was among New Zealand's most powerful provinces. This is the 1922 team. His brother Norman McKenzie's Hawke's Bay team held the Ranfurly Shield from 1922-27, when Wairarapa lifted it, 15-11. Soon after followed the famous 'Battle of Solway' challenge, when the Bay, as it thought, regained the shield 21-10 in a match laiden with All Blacks and refereed by a third McKenzie brother, Bert. However, Wairarapa protested and the parties went to a special and bitter NZRFU hearing.

Two days later the deputy prime minister, Gordon Coates, announced in a press statement that he had been requested by "certain gentlemen" to convey to the NZRFU that the Auckland team wanted the All Black team altered. It wished an Auckland player, Don Wright, to be included and said it would pay all expenses. Coates said in his statement that he, personally, held strong views against political interference or control in sport.

Norman McKenzie was to state it was he whom Gordon Coates had approached. 'Pressure was brought to bear on the selectors to revise the team. The selectors stood firm. They were prepared to stand or fall by their selection, but there was one area in New Zealand that considered it was hard done by and it sought political assistance. I was the unfortunate selector whom this politician approached.

'It was done over the telephone. He asked me could we not do something to alter the team to bring it up to New Zealand standard. After listening to him carefully, I replied that we thought the team was up to New Zealand standard. Furthermore, we did not presume to interfere in politics and we would be very pleased if politicians didn't interfere in rugby. He retired very gracefully.[1]

The team was not altered and went on to complete a glorious unbeaten record.

But that was not the first or last time one of the McKenzie brothers was involved in controversy at the highest level.

In 1930, the year in which Great Britain toured, and the farewell year for so many of the All Black greats of the 1920s, Ted McKenzie was involved in an incident that would embarrass the NZRFU at IRB level.

Manager of the British team, the first with players from four home unions since 1904, was James 'Bim' Baxter, of the (English) Rugby Football Union. The Brits were to lose six matches on tour, including three tests and provincial games against Wellington, Canterbury and Auckland.

Baxter did not mince matters when, early on, he attacked the wing forward of New Zealand rugby. He said it was contrary to the spirit of the game. Later in the tour, at the official dinner after the All Blacks' third test win in Auckland, Ted McKenzie, manager-coach of the team and chairman of selectors, rose in reply to speeches (which had not raised the touchy subject) by Baxter and British captain on the day Carl Aarvold. Seizing on the subject of the wing forward (All Black captain Cliff Porter filled the position in all four test of the series), McKenzie said Baxter had previously called the player of such a position a cheat.

'I appreciate Mr Baxter's remarks, particularly as they were made by a man so high in the game. And I feel I might reply by criticising certain aspects of the British side's play.'

He then went on to talk about obstruction — or shepherding as it was called in New Zealand.

'Shepherding the player with the ball so that he can't be tackled has been common with the British team,' he said. 'I hope it is not intentional, but it appears to have been deliberately studied.

'Jersey-holding — pulling the jersey of an opponent after he has released the ball — is also common and an offence against the rules of the game,' he added.

There were gasps from dinner guests at this point, and Aarvold attempted an interjection.

'I am speaking now, Mr Aarvold, not you,' said McKenzie. After the embarrassed silence that followed, he added he felt it was the right time to bring these matters forward, to get them out in the open.[2]

The chairman of the NZRFU, Stan Dean, expressed regret over the incident. Ted McKenzie was voted off the NZRFU management committee the following year, having served on it since 1923. He refused ever again to be nominated for a place. But he did not lose his place among the New Zealand selectors, remaining on that panel until 1940.

As for Bim Baxter, though his team was well and often beaten, he also triumphed. At the end of the tour, he was to state that rugby's rules were 'laid down by the International Board. We don't intend to alter them one jot. Those who don't want to play under them can stay outside.'[3]

The IRB in 1930 was to announce that, in future, all matches in member countries were to be played under a uniform code of rules. Previously, the board had functioned to settle rules for international matches only. It was also clear the IRB was unhappy with New Zealand's 2–3–2 scrum formation and the wing-forward position.

Additionally, New Zealand, Australia and South Africa had long attempted to be represented as full members on the IRB. At this time all three came under the umbrella of the English union, which put any concerns to their IRB on its behalf. New Zealand needed to conform, Baxter is believed to have told NZRFU officials, if it wanted to become a full member of the board. So it did. In 1932 out went the old scrum, the wing forward and the kick-into-touch dispensation. But

GREAT MINDS: Ted McKenzie and Billy Wallace 'in conference'. Both gave an extraordinary amount to New Zealand rugby over half a century. Both played as fullbacks. Wallace's exploits are legendary. McKenzie had once kicked a 67-yard goal from a mark in a Wairarapa-Canterbury match. McKenzie, a huge man of 19 st, selected All Black teams from 1924-39, often as convenor. Wallace, a 1905 All Black 'Original', was never a national selector. But both experienced highs and lows as All Black coach.

TED McKENZIE

the NZRFU was to wait until 1948 for full membership of the IRB.

Ted McKenzie's All Blacks played sublime rugby in the 1930 series, after losing the opening test 3–6 at Carisbrook.

After 13–10 and 15–10 victories in the second and third tests, they opened up in the final test at Wellington, Porter and Bert Cooke scoring two tries each in a resounding six-tries-to-one, 22–8 win.

Winston McCarthy, the famed rugby commentator of the 1950s and rugby author, played at halfback under Ted McKenzie for Wairarapa. He wrote that McKenzie "was an introspective man, saying little, thinking deeply. He would tell you what he thought you should be told, no more no less.

'He was inscrutable, a hard man to get next to, but his integrity was never in question. And a kindly man.' During the Depression McKenzie had once selected McCarthy, who had just obtained a rural job and had no hope of being available to play. McCarthy had telephoned the selector, explaining his predicament, and was pleasantly surprised to see his name included in future selections that year, even though he could not play.[4]

As the sole selector in 1938 and 1939 Ted McKenzie had the responsibility of picking an All Black team to beat the Springboks for the first time on South African soil. When war was declared in September 1939, McKenzie was told by the NZRFU to submit his team to the union by December 31 — if the war was over by then. So the team was never submitted and McKenzie did not divulge to anyone the names of the players he chose. Some have wished there had been more than one selector, since the chances of the team leaking out would have been greater.

According to McCarthy, there was only one occasion when Ted McKenzie bent on the subject of the 1940 team. In 1946, in poor health and with only a few months to live, he used to visit Wellington for medical treatment. On one such visit he raised the matter with Tom Morrison, a new NZRFU executive member that year and later to become chairman of the union.

'I suppose you have wondered, like many others, whether you were in the team to go to South Africa in 1940? Well, you were — and so was your friend Charlie Saxton; in fact I was going to recommend him as captain.'

Tom Morrison, naturally elated, said, 'Thanks, Mr McKenzie. Who else did you . . .'

BIOGRAPHICAL DETAILS

Edward McKenzie

Born: Greytown, 26 May 1878

Died: Carterton, 7 September 1946

Position: Fullback

Provincial record: Wairarapa 1898, 1900–07 (Carterton club) — 35 matches; North Island 1902

Selector/coach: Wairarapa

NZ selector/coach: 1925

NZ selector: 1924–39. (Sole selector 1938 and 1939 — team to tour South Africa in 1940 not announced.)

Other service: Founder of Wairarapa Rugby Referees' Association, life member; refereed first NZ–South Africa test 1921; Wairarapa RFU secretary 1922–29, life member; NZRFU management committee 1923–30, life member 1942, president 1946 (died in office)

Other: Four brothers also prominent in rugby: New Zealand representative William 'Offside Mac'; New Zealand and Hawke's Bay selector/coach Norman; international referee Bert; Wairarapa representative Jack

Occupation: Public secretary

NEW ZEALAND COACHING RECORD

1925: beat NSW 4–0, 11–3

1930: beat Great Britain 6–3, 13–10, 15–10, 22–8

But before he had finished the question he was interrupted with, 'That's all you're entitled to know, Tom,' and that was that.[5]

REFERENCES
1. Norman McKenzie with Arthur Carman, *On with the Game*.
2. *On with the Game*.
3. *On with the Game*.
4. Winston McCarthy, *Haka: The All Blacks' Story*.
5. *Haka: The All Blacks' Story*.

CHAPTER 11

NEW ZEALAND COACH 1932, 1937

BILLY WALLACE

A great player and much more

BILLY 'CARBINE' WALLACE IS RENOWNED AS A player of almost legendary feats — among them being that he once scored a try for the All Blacks wearing a sunhat.

He was undoubtedly one of the greatest players ever to don the black jersey, and it seems certain that, unlike some, had he been born into the modern era, he would easily have climbed to the dizzy heights in professional rugby. However, it was the years he put back into the game, as a member of the New Zealand management committee and executive council in the 1930s, and coach of the All Blacks at home and away during the same decade, which made his contribution greater still. He eventually became the oldest former All Black and was revered when he died in 1972, at the grand old age of 93.

Wallace's 379 points for the All Blacks remained a record for 50 years, until Don Clarke bettered the mark. Other records stood for almost as long and some still do. His statistics were given as 5ft 8in and 12st.

Nicknamed after the Auckland racehorse which had won the Melbourne Cup in 1890 by two lengths while bearing the enormous weight of 10st 5lb, and was later bought by the Duke of Portland and shipped to stud in England, Carbine was known to generations of New Zealanders up until at least World War II as the supreme rugby player.

He was first chosen for the New Zealand team on the 1903 tour of Australia, a side led by Jimmy Duncan, who was to be the ill-treated coach of the 1905 team. Wallace scored 85 points on the tour, including 13 in winning the first official test between the two rivals.

Wallace struck more than one telling blow for rugby on that tour. Two teams of Australian rules footballers from Victoria were staying at the New Zealanders' hotel in Sydney, and the conversation at the bar inevitably got to which code had the better kickers.

'Come to our match tomorrow,' said Duncan. 'We have a player who will show you.'

During the game, after New Zealand claimed a mark, Duncan whistled up Wallace to take the kick at goal. Wallace thought the distance too far but agreed to try for it. He retreated 11 yards beyond halfway to place the ball, then, as the saying has it, he let 'er go. The ball flew dead-centre and carried over the dead-ball line. 'It was the finest goal I ever kicked,' recalled Wallace. 'The Victorians seemed satisfied.'[1]

Wallace played on the wing against the touring British in 1904, and in the five internationals of the 1905-06 tour played three at wing, one at fullback and one at centre. The 230 points he scored on the tour of Britain and France remains a record for any touring team to this day. In Australia in 1907, Wallace scored points in all three tests playing on the wing. His final match for the

BILLY WALLACE

All Blacks was against the Anglo-Welsh of 1908. Cartilage trouble ended his career.

But it was for his part in the 1905 tour that Wallace is so fondly remembered. The sunhat incident occurred in the opening match, when the New Zealanders demolished Devon, the champion county of 1904-05, by 55-4, a quite incredible scoreline according to English observers. Wallace scored three tries and kicked eight goals on that hot afternoon.

Massive scorelines were the order of the tour, apart from the Welsh section at the tailend. The All Blacks, as they first came to be called on the tour, scored 204 tries in 32 matches in Britain, 164 of them by the backs. The crowds were large, sometimes huge. The official attendance at the England international at the Crystal Palace was 45,000, but at least another 30,000 were said to have 'hopped the fence'. New Zealand won 15-0.

The Welsh reception for those 1905 All Blacks was to be the forerunner of a rivalry that has ebbed and flowed ever since.

The host team had quietly been laying its trap for weeks as the smooth-functioning New Zealand machine continued on its merry, winning way outside the principality. The Welsh took the visitors on at their own game — with a seven-man scrum and roving forward. Injuries and illness ruled out key All Blacks, notably Billy Stead, George Smith and Bill Cunningham. The Welsh team contained some of the great names in Welsh rugby — Teddy Morgan, Gwyn Nicholls, Bert Winfield, Willie Llewellyn, Dicky Owen, Charlie Pritchard and Arthur Harding. Owen was to win 35 caps for Wales, a record that stood until after World War II.

The less-experienced All Blacks were said to be rattled by the 'perfervid enthusiasm and singing of the Welsh crowd'. The match was mainly a forward slog, with the referee penalising wing forward Dave Gallaher mercilessly and the usual All Black teamwork failing to operate.

New Zealanders have been regaled ad nauseam

STYLE AND GRACE: Hec 'Moana' Thomson, Billy Wallace and Freddy Roberts make a stylish trio dressed in their 'number ones' during the All Blacks' 1905-06 tour of Britain. All backs, they scored 55 of the All Blacks' 205 tour tries between them.

with the details of the Bob Deans' try that would have saved the match but went unawarded. Of how Teddy Morgan confessed years later that it was a fair try. Of the unabashed Welshmen who can gleefully take a New Zealander to the spot where the try was scored. To old footballers, it was just one of those things.

Wallace had set the movement up, and could probably have scored the try himself. Morrie Mackenzie has described what happened:

'He had taken the ball from in front of a Welsh forward lineout rush and surprised the Welsh by racing for the open field, instead of finding touch. His dash cut clean across the Welsh forwards and then he straightened up on their inside backs.

'Alert to the danger, Gwynn Nicholls, the Napoleonic general of Wales, raced in to stop him. Wallace half-turned to meet the danger and then side-stepped Nicholls and tore down on the Welsh fullback Winfield.

'Hearing a cry from Deans, he drew the fullback and passed to his centre, who went on to score.

'But sensing that the referee, a quaint old-world figure in Norfolk jacket, knickerbockers and brown walking boots, was miles away, a couple of Welshmen adroitly dragged Deans back into the field of play, ball and all. When the character with the whistle arrived, he happily conceded them a scrum instead of a try for New Zealand.'[2]

The Welsh were confident of winning the four remaining games, for a depression had settled on the All Blacks. But Wallace was to take a stern revenge. 'Throughout all these games, while listless companions were losing the aura of invincibility right and left, the genius of Wallace blazed like a beacon in a dark sky,' states Mackenzie.

Wallace had an outstanding game in helping to beat Glamorgan 9-0. Against Newport, whom the All Blacks beat 6-3, he kicked a penalty from near halfway. A George Nicholson try was converted by Wallace to win the game against Cardiff 10-8. And in the last game in Britain, against Swansea, Wallace let fly with a left-footed drop kick to win the game 4-3, causing the usually sobersided Gallaher to give him a hug.

Wallace's first tenure in charge of the All Blacks, on the 1932 tour of Australia, came at a time of vast change at the top of New Zealand rugby. New Zealand's greatest era to that time, the 1920s, had come to a grinding halt with a mass exodus of All Blacks who had served the side for much of the decade. The 4-0

PRACTICE MAKES PERFECT: Even Billy Wallace had to practise kicking. He is pictured at West Ealing, London, on the 1905-06 All Black 'Originals' tour as the team goes through its paces. His 230 tour points remains a record. His 379 points for the All Blacks overall was a mark not surpassed until the great Don Clarke broke it 50 years later.

whitewash of the British team in 1930 had signalled the end for George Nepia, Fred Lucas, Bert Cooke, Mark Nicholls, Jimmy Mill, Cliff Porter, Bunny Finlayson, Ron Stewart and Bull Irvine.

Australian rugby in the 1930s was particularly strong and included true Wallaby greats in Alec Ross, Tommy Lawton and 'Wild' Bill Cerutti in the sides which opposed Wallace's young tourists.

Wallace's skipper was the Wellington halfback, Frank Kilby, who had made the 1928 All Black tour to South Africa but had been severely restricted with an ankle injury. Opinions were divided as to whether Kilby or the Aucklander Merv Corner was the better halfback. Both were chosen for the 1934 tour to Australia, with Kilby again captain, but Corner got the nod for the big 1935 tour to Britain, which Kilby missed.

Wallace's tour leadership enabled the All Blacks to make an impressive recovery from the early setback of a 17-22 loss to Australia in Sydney. They trounced Australia 21-3 at Brisbane, forcing its selectors to panic and drop its captain, Lawton. The All Blacks made certain of taking home the impressive new Bledisloe Cup — presented by

BILLY WALLACE

THE RIVAL CAPTAINS: Billy Wallace's 1932 All Black captain Frank Kilby shakes hands with the Wallabies' great Tommy Lawton before the first test match at the Sydney Cricket Ground.

the then governor-general of New Zealand for play between the two countries — by winning 21-13.

In 1937, after the All Blacks had won the opening test against the touring Springboks 13-7, at Athletic Park, Billy Wallace was brought in as assistant manager and back coach. Jim Burrows *(see Chapter 17)* was manager and coach in the first test, but needed to spend more time with the forwards.

None of the New Zealand backs had played test rugby before the first test, several stars of recent teams having been discarded in favour of the newcomers, but they had all played well in the trials. However, the Springboks improved as the tour continued, not least in their selection methods. Fullback Gerry Brand regained fitness; Danie Craven, after playing fly half in the first test, returned to scrum half, so making way for the brilliant Tony Harris; and the Boks' scrum was bolstered by captain Philip Nel and 'Boy' Louw, who joined his brother 'Fanie' and the great hooker Jan Lotz in the front row.

The Springboks won the second test at Lancaster Park 13-6, despite two tries by Jack Sullivan, who was to become the All Black coach in South Africa in 1960 and chairman of the NZRFU for a long period. They were even more dominant in the third and final test at Eden Park, winning 17-6. The All Blacks were outclassed, and for the first time a test rubber between the two countries was won outright. Years later observers still claimed the 1937 Springboks were the greatest of all — they had no weaknesses and played a superb style of rugby.

Wallace's long career in the game spanned many eras. He took part in the infamous 'Butcher's match' between Wellington and Otago at Carisbrook in 1897. The game got its name from the fact that several Wellington team members worked for a freezing works in Petone, and the Otago crowd claimed their men were 'butchered'.

In 1900, Wallace had a season with the Alhambra club in Dunedin, and played for Otago. He also played in the first Ranfurly Shield match, in 1904, against Auckland, which had been awarded the shield because of its record. In 1967, then aged 89, he recalled how Auckland had been unable to present the shield when Wellington had won the game:

'We sailed from Onehunga Wharf happy, but without

the shield,' said Wallace. 'Auckland had left the shield in the vault of a bank. They got it to us about a week later. I don't think it has ever been left behind since.

'The interest [in the shield] grew fast from that first game. The shield soon meant big gates and big interest. It meant a lot to rugby, because previously there were only ordinary provincial tours.'

One of the game's early great kickers, Wallace said Syd Nicholls, the father of the three Nicholls brothers who all played for the All Blacks in the 1920s, had taught him how to kick.

'I could kick long. I landed any amount from halfway,' he said. 'But in my day the opposition didn't have to remain passive while I was kicking. The defenders were allowed to stand on the mark and could charge the ball once the helper from his team, holding it slightly above the ground, had placed it. They used to say, "You haven't a show of landing this", and I quite often used to say, "Bet you a quid I can",' he reminisced.

Wallace believed modern goal-kickers usually took too long in their endeavours. 'I reckon they're saying the Lord's Prayer when they take all that time.'

In 1908, upon retirement from playing, Wallace was presented with a purse of 400 sovereigns, which assisted him in establishing his own iron foundry in Wellington. Compare the way the NZRFU turned a blind eye to the principles of amateurism for its hero to the treatment meted out to the great Welsh fullback, Arthur Gould. Thirteen years earlier, in 1895, Gould, who held the Welsh record of 27 caps, had had a testimonial game from which 600 pounds was raised, enabling the deeds of a house to be presented to him. All hell broke loose when the IRB discovered what had happened and Gould was labelled a professional. Neither Ireland nor Scotland would play Wales the following year, and the incident led to the tightening of the rules of amateurism — though not in lucky Billy's case!

BIOGRAPHICAL DETAILS

William Joseph Wallace

Born: Wellington, 2 August 1878

Died: Wellington, 2 March 1972

Position: Fullback or three-quarter

Represented NZ: 1903-08
51 matches (11 internationals)

Points for NZ: 379 (36 tries, 114 conversions, 9 penalties, 2 goals from marks, 2 drop goals)

Provincial record: Wellington 1897, 1899, 1901-04, 1906-08 (Poneke club); Otago 1900 (Alhambra club); North Island 1902, 1905, 1907-08

NZ coach: 1932 (manager/coach to Australia), 1937 (v. South Africa)

Other service: Life member Poneke club and Wellington RFU; NZRFU management committee 1931-36; NZRFU executive 1937-38; co-managed NZ Maoris on tour to Australia 1935

NEW ZEALAND COACHING RECORD

1932: lost to Australia 17-22; beat Australia 21-3, 21-13

1937: beat South Africa 13-7; lost to South Africa 6-13, 6-1

REFERENCES

1. F. H. D. Sewoll, *The Man's Game*.
2. Morrie Mackenzie, *All Blacks in Chains*.

CHAPTER 12

NEW ZEALAND COACH 1910, 1935-36

VINCE MEREDITH

Vinny was an autocratic All Black coach

VINCE (VINNY) MEREDITH'S AUTOCRATIC methods when he took the 1935-36 All Blacks to Britain would not have been tolerated by later generations of New Zealand players.

His selections — dropping key players from the final test match of the tour — almost certainly contributed to the biggest loss the All Blacks have ever suffered in Britain.

The team lost three matches and drew one on the 30-match tour — a record which compared unfavourably with its two predecessors and was the subject of much criticism at the time. In hindsight, it was a reasonable record in the circumstances. The 1935 team encountered stronger and better organised opposition than had the 1905 and 1924 teams.

Meredith had a long and influential career as a selector-coach. He twice led New Zealand teams overseas — with a quarter-century gap between the tours. Five years after the 1905 All Black Originals, Meredith managed and coached the All Blacks in Australia in 1910, when he was only 33 years of age. He is, with Jim Burrows, the youngest All Black coach in history, two years younger than was Jimmy Duncan in 1904 and Bob Stuart (a co-opted forward coach) in 1956, and three years younger than Tom Morrison in 1950.

Meredith was an Aucklander who moved to Wellington to work in the Customs Department and then studied law. A halfback, he represented Wellington for four seasons (1899-1902) and then became a Wellington selector and coach (1908-09, 1912-13). He was appointed Crown Prosecutor in Auckland in 1921 and was Auckland's sole selector-coach in 1923-24, 1927-29 and 1934. He was a New Zealand selector in 1910 and 1934-35.

The 1935 tour, it was said, had problems from the beginning. According to Terry McLean, Vince Meredith 'had acquired, during years of selecting and coaching club and provincial teams, an autocratic belief in the divinity of his selections'.

McLean contended that Frank Kilby, the Wellington and All Black captain during the early 1930s, should have been the captain of the 1935-36 All Blacks.

'Kilby had one disqualification. He knew his own mind. Since no assistant manager or coach was appointed, this quality was sufficient to make him unacceptable to Meredith.'[1]

Canterbury's Jack Manchester, who had been impressive as a flank forward on the 1934 tour to Australia, was appointed captain. He was an honest, hard-working player whose mind was too frank and open to compete with Meredith's subtle shifts and manoeuvres, according to McLean.

A problem throughout the tour was the All Blacks' scrummaging. The IRB had made the three-fronted scrum

76

THE POWER BEHIND THE ALL BLACKS

compulsory four years earlier. New Zealand's domestic game had been slow, indeed reluctant, to adapt. At international level the All Black forwards, nurtured on the 2-3-2 scrum, could hardly cope.

The experienced E. H. D. Sewell, who had witnessed the 1905 and 1924 tours, wrote that the 1935 All Blacks were trying to live up to an almost impossible tradition — that of practical invincibility.

'The present team is playing in the (for New Zealand) new formation of eight forwards and seven backs, to which we and not they, are accustomed. Remember that fact, and never forget it, when you are comparing notes . . . This vital difference does not suit their game . . .'[2]

According to newspaper reports the All Blacks did a good deal of training on the voyage to Britain aboard the Rangitikei, though in the tropics they found the heat trying. The team had a scrum machine aboard the ship. Rumour had it that there was more than one occasion when members of the team plotted to go up on deck at dead of night and feed it to the fishes.

But the machine gave the team a preview of what would be needed on tour. When the All Blacks packed a 3-2-3 scrum against it, they could hardly get it to move even an inch or two. But when they packed the 3-4-1 scrum, up went the measure considerably.

The usual shipboard programme was physical drills under Rusty Page for half an hour each morning, the drills 'increasing in severity' every few days. The forwards then practised on the scrum machine for half an hour and then did lineout drills.

Meredith hurt himself on the voyage, straining a tendon in his right leg. After it had almost healed, he aggravated the injury at the team's first practice on dry land at Newton Abbot. But this did not prevent him from taking a full part in the training of the team. According to reports, while the backs spent most of the time running and passing, the forwards, 'under the guidance of Mr Meredith, had a go at practically every department of forward play.

'Dribbling, hooking, lineout play, following up — the forwards went solidly at it for about two-and-a-half hours. It was tough work after a long sea voyage and three days of gaiety in London town.'[3]

Charlie Oliver, the vice captain, and Eric Tindill, another team member, were to praise Meredith when they wrote their tour book.

LONG LEAD-UP: Meredith's 1935-36 All Blacks met British opposition that was far stronger and better organised than their more famous predecessors had met. They played 19 matches as lead-up to the first test – far too many. The team was: Back Row: H. M. Brown, G. D. M. Gilbert, F. H. Vorrath, W. R. Collins, S. T. Reid, J. J. Best, N. A. Mitchell; Third Row: A. Lambourn, R. R. King, H. F. McLean, J. G. Wynyard, A. Mahoney, R. M. McKenzie, G. T. Adkins, C. S. Pepper; Seated: T. H. C. Caughey, W. E. Hadley, G. F. Hart, J. E. Manchester (captain), Mr V. R. S. Meredith (manager), C. J. Oliver (vice-captain), J. Hore, D. Dalton, D. Solomon; In Front: N. Ball, E. W. T. Tindill, B. S. Sadler, M. M. N. Corner, J. L. Griffiths, J. R. Page.

VINCE MEREDITH

DIVINE SELECTION: Vinny Meredith, the short man third from right in this photo of the 1935-36 All Blacks, had 'an autocratic belief in the divinity of his selections' and insisted all the players address him as 'Mr Meredith'.

'Mr Meredith cannot be given too much credit for the manner in which he successfully overcame this [scrumming] difficulty. He spent hours on end correcting the faults which were found to exist in the New Zealand method of play.

'It is true our 3-4-1 scrum turned out a success, but that was not until the latter part of the tour, after we'd learnt to pack low in front. When Bill Hadley wasn't playing, our opponents usually chose scrums instead of lineouts.'

By contrast, in 1997 a team member and future All Black captain, Jack Griffiths, then aged 85, told the author the All Blacks had seldom had the benefit of Meredith's expertise as a coach.

'He was so involved with official matters that the team did not often benefit from his knowledge at training sessions,' he said. 'Tactics were left to discussions by team members plus the experience of the captain and the vice captain.'

But Meredith was to play a part in the outcome of the team's final test, against England, although just how much of an influence he had has long been debated. Terry McLean claimed Meredith put a ban on three key players for disciplinary reasons. But other evidence points more strongly to the trio having been dropped solely because of form.[4]

Interviewed in 1997 by the author, McLean said his main source of information had been his late brother, Hugh, an All Black who was on the 1935 tour and died early in 1997.

According to the McLeans, the All Blacks retired to Porthcawl to prepare for the England test on January 4. The Porthcawlians put on a bang-up New Year's party, but Meredith laid down a curfew of midnight for the team to be back at their hotel and stayed up to see it was strictly observed. Though, it is said, other team members returned even later, Meredith caught halfback Joey Sadler, winger George Hart and first five-eighth Griffiths — who had all played in the previous three tests — returning late.

Hart had dominated the English wing, Russian émigré Prince Obolensky, in the game against Oxford, and the trio were all to go on to play major roles for the All Blacks in the future. But disciplinarian Meredith had to make an example. The back line stars were all dropped from the team to play England — with disastrous consequences. England, in front of 70,000 spectators, won 13-0, with Obolensky scoring two sensational tries.

'Hugh came home so late from that New Year's party in Porthcawl that Vinny Meredith had given up and gone to bed. Hugh played in the England game,' McLean told the author.

However, the rugby historians Chester and McMillan attributed the trio's absence from Twickenham solely to a loss of form.[5] Oliver and Tindill's account strongly supports this, and makes no mention of any incident like the one McLean described. But that might not be surprising, since the authors would not have wanted to rock the boat as concerned their own All Black futures, and were clearly at odds with other team members in their summing up of Meredith's strengths and weaknesses.

A vital piece of information they do supply, though, is that the team for the England test was chosen before New Year's Eve, so the players could not have been dropped as a result of missing a curfew. The team played London Counties on December 26, between the Wales and England tests. Griffiths and Hart played in that game, but Sadler did not. Instead, Merv Corner played halfback and captained the side and had his best game of the tour. Some critics rated this performance one of the tourists' best. Corner, Tindill and Ball played themselves into the test team, it was said.

Interviewed in 1997, Griffiths denied all knowledge of the curfew incident and said he had been dropped entirely on the basis of form.

Meredith was a stickler for formality, the All Blacks'

attendance at after-match functions and many other formal dinners and occasions being high on his list of obligations. He attended every function himself and expected the majority of the players to do so, although he did operate a roster system whereby a few of the team were excused each function. But Meredith's insistence that the All Blacks wear dinner jackets at formal functions caused derision, both among some of the team and, especially, in New Zealand. 'New Zealand was still climbing out of the Great Depression. Egalitarianism was all. Dinner suits were snooty,' said McLean.[6]

To be fair, Meredith also seemed keen that his young charges absorb as much of British life as possible. Outings were many, varied and often once-in-a-lifetime opportunities that would not be available to the average tourist.

Meredith also insisted the All Blacks call him 'Mr Meredith' at all times.

Mike Gilbert, a fullback on the tour, was to recall that when the team left Auckland on the boat, a team member brought along a case (12 bottles) of cough mixture, which had been donated for the team's use in Britain. Meredith had it off-loaded in Panama and returned to New Zealand unopened. He believed accepting the product would breach the principles of amateurism.

'Pat' Caughey, another team member who years later would become chairman of the Auckland department store Smith & Caughey and be knighted for services to the community, related to McLean how Meredith had treated Fred 'Did' Vorrath, the Otago forward, on the tour.

'Vinny had a snitcher on Vorrath, for some reason. He got few games, and once, when he saw his name on the team list on the notice board, Vorrath exclaimed, "The old bastard has chosen me!" Unfortunately, Meredith was standing behind him and immediately erased his name from the list as a punishment,' McLean told the author.

The 1935 All Blacks' results and success rate must be looked at in the context of the times. Tours to Britain are commonplace nowadays, but then there had not been a similar tour for 11 years. The public's expectations were high.

British rugby was much stronger and better organised than it had been when the All Blacks had made their earlier tours. It had taken two, even three decades for English rugby to recover from the disastrous split of its northern clubs to play Northern Union (later rugby league) in 1895. Most of the best players had been in the north, and numbers did not climb back until the 1930s. Conversely, Welsh rugby during the 1920s and 1930s was devastated by the Depression.

A probable influence on the results was that the 1935 All Blacks had played as many as 19 matches in the lead-up to their four tests. They beat Scotland and Ireland handsomely enough, but were then pipped by Wales, 12-13. The England débâcle followed. Their only other loss was to Swansea, 3-11, in their fifth match. They drew with Ulster.

Meredith was to state at the end of the tour that there had been a considerable advance in the standard of British rugby.

'Surprise may have been felt at the narrowness of some of the scores. We found that only on rare occasions did we meet weak sides . . . we packed three in the front row as the New Zealand union agreed to do and found we had a deal to learn about this method of packing,' he said.

'In the early stages we were badly pushed, and with the loss of Hadley in the first game we were unable to get much share of the ball from set scrums.'

A quarter-century before the 1935 tour, the 1910 All Blacks, managed and coached by Meredith, won the first test on their tour of New South Wales 6-0, but were well beaten, 11-0, in the second. The tour was originally scheduled to end at that point, but midway through, the New South Wales union had requested a third test. A rejuvenated All Black team scored eight tries in handing out a 28-13 hiding to Australia. All the tests were played in Sydney.

Outstanding in the backline were the 1905 veterans, halfback Freddy Roberts and first five-eighth Simon Mynott. It was the third tour they had been on together and their combination was excellent. They both retired from international football after the tour, Mynott, at 34, being the oldest back to play for New Zealand until Joe Stanley emerged in the 1980s and Frank Bunce in the 1990s.

Meredith's best coaching efforts came with Auckland, whom he coached over three short periods in the 1920s and 1930s. The Depression hurt activities throughout New Zealand, but Auckland rugby was also faced with the threat of rugby league. League was pulling in the crowds — and one of the reasons was the Auckland rugby team's six losses in 13 matches in the 1922 season. The union faced financial difficulties.

Meredith was appointed sole selector-coach for 1923. He 'discovered' an unknown 3rd-grade player called

Bert Cooke and put him among backs like Karl Ifwersen, Vic Badeley and Fred Lucas.

Auckland proceeded to thrash Southland, Taranaki, Wanganui, North Auckland, Otago and New South Wales, and beat Wellington 21-15. They lost to the great Norm McKenzie-coached Hawke's Bay team in a Ranfurly Shield challenge 5-21, but then beat the champions 17-9 in a return, nonshield game in Auckland that provided a fitting climax to a superb season. Auckland rugby was back in business.

Meredith was the brother of the prominent referee of the 1920s Bill Meredith. Bill must have been quite a character on the field. He was immortalised by a famous poem of the era, published after one of the great 1920s Hawke's Bay Ranfurly Shield defences against Southland.

It was a very robust match, and one of the Southland forwards, Bill Hazlett, who would become a famous All Black but was then only 19, was giving as good as he got. At one stage he became embroiled in a mêlée with the majesterial Maurice Brownlie. Mr Meredith stopped play and admonished Hazlett by saying: "Now then, Hazlett, you leave Mr Brownlie alone."

Bill Meredith officiated over many great provincial matches and apparently believed in keeping the crowd entertained. He was said to have "more hand gestures than a traffic cop directing traffic".

As the Crown Prosecutor in Auckland for 31 years, Meredith prosecuted in a long list of murder trials. The most famous of these were the trials of Marco, Bayly, McKay and Talbot, Pansy Haskell and Horry — the last generally considered to be (by then Sir Vincent) Meredith's greatest forensic feat. His autobiography, *A Long Brief*, relates many of the cases, but it also reminisces on his long career in rugby.[7]

It is fascinating to read that Meredith, born in 1877, was playing, as a youth, in the formative years of the game when there was little back play as we know it; was a leading player when the game took some of its first giant leaps forward; and was an influential coach and

BIGGEST LOSS: England has the All Blacks scrambling. Prince Obolensky's two brilliant tries helped England to a 13-0 victory in 1936, still the largest loss New Zealand has ever suffered in Britain.

selector through the first four decades of the 20th century. By 1964 he was a strong advocate for Maori being eligible to tour South Africa — which would be allowed, for the first time, in 1970.

Meredith played against the likes of Davey Gage and Jimmy Duncan, two of New Zealand's early great captains, and played with Billy Wallace and had William 'Offside Mac' McKenzie as his coach. He describes how, the week after playing for Wellington against Otago in 1899, Otago played Taranaki. The Otago and New Zealand winger, 'Barney' Armitt, attempted to jump over the tackle of the Taranaki and New Zealand wing, Alf Bayly, but landed on his head, broke his neck and died soon after. Bayly never played again because of the incident.

BIOGRAPHICAL DETAILS

Vincent Robert Sissons Meredith

Born: Whangarei, 31 March 1877

Died: Auckland, 15 January 1965

Position: Halfback

Provincial record: Wellington 1899-1902 (Wellington club)

Other service: Wellington RFU management committee 1909

Selector/coach: Wellington 1908-09, 1912-13; Auckland 1923, 1924, 1927-29, 1934

NZ selector: 1910, 1934-35

NZ coach: 1910, 1935-36

Occupation: Crown Prosecutor, Auckland; Crown Law Office; Customs Department

Other: Knight Batchelor; Queen's Counsel; brother Bill a rugby referee in 1920s

NEW ZEALAND COACHING RECORD

1910: beat Australia 6-0; lost to Australia 0-11; beat Australia 28-13

1935-36: beat Scotland 18-8; beat Ireland 17-9; lost to Wales 12-13; lost to England 0-13

REFERENCES

1. Terry McLean, *New Zealand Rugby Legends*, Moa, 1987.
2. H. D. Sewell, *The Man's Game*.
3. *The Man's Game*.
4. *New Zealand Rugby Legends*.
5. R. H. Chester and N. A. C. McMillan, *Centenary: 100 Years of All Black Rugby*, Moa, 1984.
6. *New Zealand Rugby Legends*.
7. Vincent Meredith, *A Long Brief*, 1966.

CHAPTER 13

NEW ZEALAND COACH 1937

JIM BURROWS

Great leader of men could not halt Bok juggernaut

ALTHOUGH HE WAS TO GO ON TO NUMEROUS triumphs as one of New Zealand's wartime leaders, Jim Burrows could not prevent the 1937 Springboks from becoming 'the greatest team ever to leave New Zealand'.

Burrows, a hooker in the 1928 All Black team which shared the test series with the Springboks in South Africa 2-all, and the first All Black hooker to play in a 3-4-1 scrum, was manager-coach of the All Blacks in 1937.

After winning the first test at Athletic Park 13-7, he was joined by Billy Wallace, the legendary fullback of the 1905 Originals. Wallace had coached the All Blacks earlier in the decade, and was made assistant manager and coach of the backs, all of whom were uncapped before the first test.

The move enabled Burrows to concentrate on moulding the forwards, but it was to no avail. The Springboks went from strength to strength as their tour progressed. They won the second test 13-6 at Lancaster Park. At Eden Park in the third test, the big Bok pack humbled the All Blacks in a one-sided exhibition, allowing Danie Craven to give one of his greatest displays in serving a fleet-footed back line. South Africa won 17-6 to rightly claim the fictitious world rugby crown.

As Burrows was to recall: 'They were the best team to visit New Zealand. For their all-round good football they deserved all the praise showered on them. They left us with a message that rang loud and clear throughout the land — you cannot score points in rugby unless you gain possession of the ball.

'We knew what we were up against in the scrums, but we didn't have the Springbok technique, nor did we have any front row men the size of the Springboks. We played the best front row available, and they were all excellent forwards, but they were much smaller than their opponents.'[1]

For the opening test of the series, after six trials and the interisland match, the cumbersome seven-man New Zealand panel of selectors chose a team that did not inspire much confidence among followers.

While the forwards included only one newcomer, none of the backs had played test football, several stars of recent times having been discarded after selections made on trial form. Jack Sullivan, Jack Hooper, Jack Taylor and Johnny Dick were all to tour Australia in 1938 and would surely have had long careers but for World War II. Sullivan, who had an outstanding test series against the Boks, was to become the All Black coach on the tour of South Africa in 1960 and chairman of the NZRFU for a long period.

'Brushy' Mitchell, the Southland winger, would probably have captained the first test team, but was injured after having to play in three trial games after a

82

brilliant display in the interisland match — the necessity of which was known only to the national selectors. All Black halfback Joey Sadler was also out injured and did not play again.

The South Africans pulled some shocks in their first-test selections too. Captain Philip Nel was not chosen, and Danie Craven, the vice captain, led the team from fly half. Gerry Brand, their great fullback, was injured, as was 'Boy' Louw, the powerful prop.

The game was won by the New Zealand forwards and the fine kicking of first five-eighth Dave Trevathan, who played outside his Southern club and Otago teammate Harry Simon throughout the series.

The Springboks selected a much stronger team for the second test. The great Gerry Brand was fit again and was to be remembered as the finest of all touring fullbacks for years to come. His 100 points in the series remained a record until Barry John of the 1971 Lions bettered it.

Craven went to halfback and the brilliant young Tony Harris was selected at fly half. To play cricket for South Africa 10 years later, Harris was rated with such all-time greats as 1950 Lion Jackie Kyle as a handler, runner and originator of scoring attacks. In the pack, Nel was included, as was 'Boy' Louw, who joined his brother 'Fanie' and the great hooker, Jan Lotz.

Sullivan, at centre, was New Zealand's hero of the day. With both teams scoring two tries, he got a pair. The All Blacks were defending desperately when he intercepted a pass between Harris and Louis Babrow. He found clear space ahead of him, but winger Dai Williams chased and drew level with him. With Williams and fullback Brand converging on him, Sullivan kicked over Brand's head. Williams and Sullivan ran neck and neck, with Sullivan just able to toe the ball onwards again. With inches to spare to the dead-ball line, Sullivan dived on it for the try. The 45,000 Lancaster Park crowd, who'd risen to Sullivan during the long chase, went wild with joy.

The All Blacks therefore led 6-0 at half-time. With the scent of a series victory in their nostrils, they began the second half with strong attack. But the Springbok forwards gradually began to take control. The referee, J. S. King (Wellington), had to read the riot act to both packs midway through the second half after play became

WE'RE ONE UP: Coaches Burrows and Wallace were quietly confident when this photo of the 1937 New Zealand team was taken before the second test at Lancaster Park, Christchurch. They were 1-up in the series. But the Boks turned a 0-6 halftime deficit into a deserved 13-6 victory and were poised to take a New Zealand – South Africa series outright for the first time.

overvigorous and Jack Rankin, 'Boy' Louw and W. E. Bastard received medical attention.

Late in the half Brand kicked a magnificent penalty from halfway to give his team the lead. Bastard, a flanker, scored when supporting a three-quarter movement. Brand's conversion made it 13-6 and the rubber tied up.

Nel, who had rallied his side with an inspired half-time team talk, said later he had told his team-mates: 'This is it. We're one test down already and if we lose this one the series will be lost. It's today or never. Just concentrate on getting possession.'

The third test fuelled unprecedented national interest. The crowd of 58,000 at Eden Park was a record. Thousands travelled from other parts of New Zealand and people slept outside the ground to ensure good positions on the terraces.

The match was more one-sided than the final score of 17-6 suggests to modern-day audiences. The All Blacks were reduced to 'a rabble', as one writer described the situation, their conceding five tries without scoring one themselves, being without precedent before or since. The Bok forwards gained complete domination and Craven had a brilliant game. His huge dive passes gave Harris, operating like an orchestra conductor, time and more to set his three-quarters in motion.

The Springboks, up 8-3 from two brilliant tries, made the perfect start after half-time. They used a ploy that had been practised in secret, planned around the reputation Craven had gained for the stupendous length of his dive pass. The move was called when the All Black fullback, Taylor, had found touch near halfway and the Boks chose to scrum. Craven waved his fly half out further than normal on the open-side, and then even further with a second flourish of his hand. It meant a wide gap between the scrum and Harris, whose marker, Trevathan, after hesitating, moved out to mark him.

But when South Africa won the scrum, it was Freddy Turner, the blind-side winger, who burst into the gap to take Craven's pass and run in behind the All Black back line. The Bok centre, Lochner, passed to his partner, Babrow, who raced in at the corner for a fabulously executed try.

New Zealand was unstinting in its praise for the South Africans, whom it called the greatest team ever to leave New Zealand. The All Blacks, it was agreed, had been beaten by a superior and very great side.

Analysis of the difference between the two countries' games revealed New Zealand's forward play was too loose, its knowledge of the 3-4-1 scrum still too sketchy and its players not big enough to handle the Bok scrummagers.

The year after he left school (1923), Burrows went straight into senior rugby with Old Boys and was picked for Canterbury that same year. It was a strong team and included Lew Peterson, Jocky Ford, Reid Masters, Jim Parker, Jack Harris, Curly Page and Bill Dalley — all All Blacks at some stage of their careers.

On tour, Canterbury played Hawke's Bay, which was just beginning to earn its reputation as one of the greatest provincial sides in rugby history. The Bay won 9-8, but it was the first time Burrows had played in the front row of a scrum, with its then 2-3-2 formation.

After a year off from rugby because of complications following an appendicitis operation, Burrows, now a teacher at St Andrew's College and part-time university student playing for Varsity, took part in the 1925 North-South match, off the back of the scrum. The occasion was a reunion of the great 1924-25 All Blacks, and spectators were overjoyed to witness them playing.

Afterwards, Burrows was informed that, at 13st, he was too light ever to become an All Black loose forward. 'Jim, you'll get no further unless you turn yourself into a front-row forward,' said Tom Milliken, a South Island selector.

The 1928 All Black team would be the first to tour South Africa. The tour was going to settle which country was the 'best in world rugby'. Burrows promised himself he would do everything possible to make the side. But fate intervened when he was offered a teaching position at his old school, Christchurch Boys' High. With extra school duties and university commitments, he did not play any rugby in 1926.

Canterbury's North Island tour was to include a challenge for the Ranfurly Shield with Hawke's Bay. Canterbury had never won the shield, in spite of 10 challenges made since 1904, so there was much disappointment when the Bay, which had been holders since 1922 and still looked invincible, lost to Wairarapa. But the shield then moved from Wairarapa to Manawhenua, so Canterbury's match at Palmerston North became a challenge. Canterbury fielded a team in which 12 players who had worn, or were about to wear, the silver fern — Harris, Robilliard, Carleton, Steel, Lilburne, McGregor, Dalley, Scrimshaw, Jackson, White, Godfrey, Pickering, Alley, Clark and Burrows.

'We won the match 17-6, and for the first time the Ranfurly Shield had a resting place in Canterbury,' said Burrows.

CRASHING THE PARTY: It's 1-all in the series as the 1937 All Blacks and Springboks line up for the deciding third test at Eden Park, Auckland. But the Boks turned on the greatest display ever seen in New Zealand by a touring team, scoring five tries to none to wallop the All Blacks 17-6.

The victory proved a lucky break for the Canterbury players. 'With the shield goes publicity, and it was not surprising that the Canterbury union nominated a good proportion of the team to take part in the extensive trials for South Africa.'

Burrows quickly realised that the road to All Blackdom was hard and lonely and that those who made progress owed a lot to Lady Luck. The 1927 interisland match, in superb conditions at Athletic Park, brought a 31-30 win to the South in what is regarded as one of the greatest of the now discontinued series. Final trials were held several days later.

The South Island players left Wellington on the ferry a few hours after the final trial. 'Completely and utterly exhausted, I was in bed as soon as we left the wharf. Geoff Alley occupied the other bunk in the cabin,' recalled Burrows.

'At about 11.00 p.m. the door burst open and a Canterbury supporter, knowing he was the bearer of vital news, shrieked, "You're both in the team!"

'I suppose we went to sleep again. I can't remember.'

Burrows, therefore, was part of the Maurice Brownlie-led All Blacks who undertook the first great trek of South Africa, in 1928, and shared the series 2-all — a superb feat when the circumstances under which the tour took place are analysed, but one which was not appreciated at the time or for many years to come. It was to take until 1996 for an All Black team to better the 1928 team's record in a full series.

That tour came only four years after the most famous of all All Black tours — the unbeaten tour of Britain and France by the 1924 Invincibles. New Zealand critics regarded the 1928 selection as potentially greater than Cliff Porter's 1924 team, so the results were traumatic for the nation.

The All Blacks, with Brownlie as both captain and coach, won 16 of their 22 matches, with five losses and a draw. 'The losses caused much head-shaking among the oldtimers in New Zealand,' said Burrows. 'No-one could understand why a team which had been proclaimed a great side when it left home should have lost even one game.

JIM BURROWS

'We were the first and there were lessons to learn about the conditions, the people and their rugby.'

The All Blacks found South Africans were as fanatically fond and as knowledgeable of rugby as New Zealanders, while no-one had really looked into the effects the interminable travel by train, across vast tracts of country, would have on the team.

In the second match of the tour the All Blacks struck disaster and defeat in the form of a Western Province Town scrum formation vastly superior to their own. New Zealand rugby still used its beloved 2-3-2 scrum, developed in New Zealand in the 1880s but not adopted by any other nation except Australia. New Zealanders believed it had been the springboard for much brilliant back play over the decades. It had been put under great pressure on the 1924 tour, but the results had seemed to vindicate its retention.

The 3-4-1 scrum formation, as used today by all rugby teams, was the reason behind South Africa's successes over many decades. It evolved from the traditional 3-2-3 scrum and was invented by South Africa's legendary A.F. 'Oubaas' Markotter. The effect of moving the two outside back row men up to push on the props instead of the locks was profound. It gave the scrum a wedge as the thrust came inwards and forwards simultaneously. With the breadth of the scrum increased it gave the halfback more protection, because marauders had to travel further. It also meant the birth of the modern flanker, who was closer to the opposing back line than previously.

In 1928 the All Blacks immediately found they could not win enough possession to be competitive. To its credit, their management made a bold but agonising decision — to use the South African formation in the next game. It was against Griqualand West, and the All Blacks won 19-10. Burrows therefore became the first All Black to hook in the middle of the three-man front row.

The next game was against Transvaal, with its huge and powerful forwards. Encouraged by their initial success with the new formation, the All Blacks continued the experiment. But the forwards chosen were not skilful at the new art of obtaining maximum cohesion in the eight-man push. The scrums often collapsed, and Burrows injured his ribs so badly he did not recover to play in any of the tests, though he played in six successive games up to the final test.

FLYING HIGH: Springbok flyhalf Tony Harris splits the All Black defence on one of his many runs in the third test of 1937. Served by the great halfback, Danie Craven, Harris helped South Africa to five tries and a 17-6 win to take the series.

THE POWER BEHIND THE ALL BLACKS

Transvaal won the match 6-0. The All Blacks immediately reverted to their old 2-3-2 formation, saying there was not enough time before the test series to master the 3-4-1 scrum techniques.

This was a crucial decision. If more serious thought had gone into the team selection against Transvaal and the game been won, the All Blacks would surely have kept the new formation, while New Zealand rugby might well have followed a different and more successful path over the next 30 years.

As it was, Brownlie's All Blacks lost the opening test to the Boks 0-17, the biggest hiding in All Black history right up to the present day. The New Zealand scrum was completely eclipsed, the South Africans choosing scrums instead of lineouts when the option was offered, as was allowed by the game's laws then.

The All Blacks fought back to win the second test in Johannesburg 7-6, their forwards having by far their best match. An Archie Strang drop goal, worth four points, made the difference. But the Springbok forwards proved too strong in the third test at Port Elizabeth. South Africa won 11-6, outscoring New Zealand by three tries to two. Against all expectations, however, the All Blacks ended their tour with a magnificent 13-5 victory in the fourth test in Cape Town, a match in which their forwards dominated and Mark Nicholls, having his first outing of the series, kicked the Boks out of the game.

'So ended a tour harder than any All Black tour New Zealand had undertaken before, but one which, in the long run, did our football much good,' wrote Burrows.

'We learnt much from the play of the Springboks, particularly their scrummaging techniques, though I must add it was typical of our conservative way of doing things that another four years elapsed before we adopted the three-fronted scrum and, in my opinion, about another 20 years before we could begin to say that we had mastered the techniques of this scrum.'

Burrows continued to play for Canterbury and the South Island and ended his career for Canterbury against the British Lions in 1930, a fast, open game, with play surging from one end of the field to the other before the home side won 14-8. He was only 26, but had married in 1929, had had his fair share of injuries in recent seasons, and reckoned that, since it was Depression times, the risk was too great to continue.

Burrows' coaching career got a kick-start when Canterbury won back the Ranfurly Shield from Wellington at the end of the 1931 season.

'I was fortunate to inherit a nucleus of outstanding players,' said Burrows. 'Beau Cottrell, George Hart and Charlie Oliver had played for New Zealand. Gordon Innes and Jack Manchester were to become All Blacks in the near future. Beau was one of the best captains I have known.'

Canterbury beat off another eight challenges in 1933, most of them tough. The closest call came against Taranaki. First five-eighth Buck Hazlehurst dropped the goal which levelled the scores 15 all and saved the shield. After the final shield match of that season Burrows informed the union that his two years as a selector were over and he would not be available the next year.

'Our audiences were coaches and players, but our real targets were the coaches. Coaching schools are common today, but were a novelty when we were operating.'

In 1936 Burrows, now a delegate on the Canterbury union, was nominated for one of the six national selector positions that would carry New Zealand through to the tour by the Springboks in 1937. He joined Ted McKenzie (Wairarapa), Mark Nicholls (Wellington), George Nicholson (Auckland), William Pearson (Otago) and Alan Adams (West Coast). Harold Masters (Taranaki) was co-opted onto the panel.

Although two tests were played against a touring Australian team in 1936, the main concern was to find the talent to pit against the Boks the following year.

'As soon as the New Zealand union had announced our players for the first test, it appointed me manager-coach of the team. This was a nice compliment, though considering the many experienced and successful coaches throughout the country, I was a little surprised. I wondered as well why no team manager was appointed to take over the administrative matters — there was enough for me to do if in one week's time I was to have the All Blacks physically ready and in the right frame of mind for a test match,' wrote Burrows.

Looking back on the series defeat that ensued — the first in the history of the All Blacks — Burrows concluded:

'I am sure we would have profited more from these harsh lessons if the war had not intervened. We did not duel with South Africa until 1949, 12 years later. Then we

THE EYES HAVE IT: The intensity of the occasion can be seen as All Black captain Ron King (in headgear, closest to ball) and Springbok rivals contest possession in the first test at Athletic Park, Wellington, in 1937. New Zealand won 13-7.

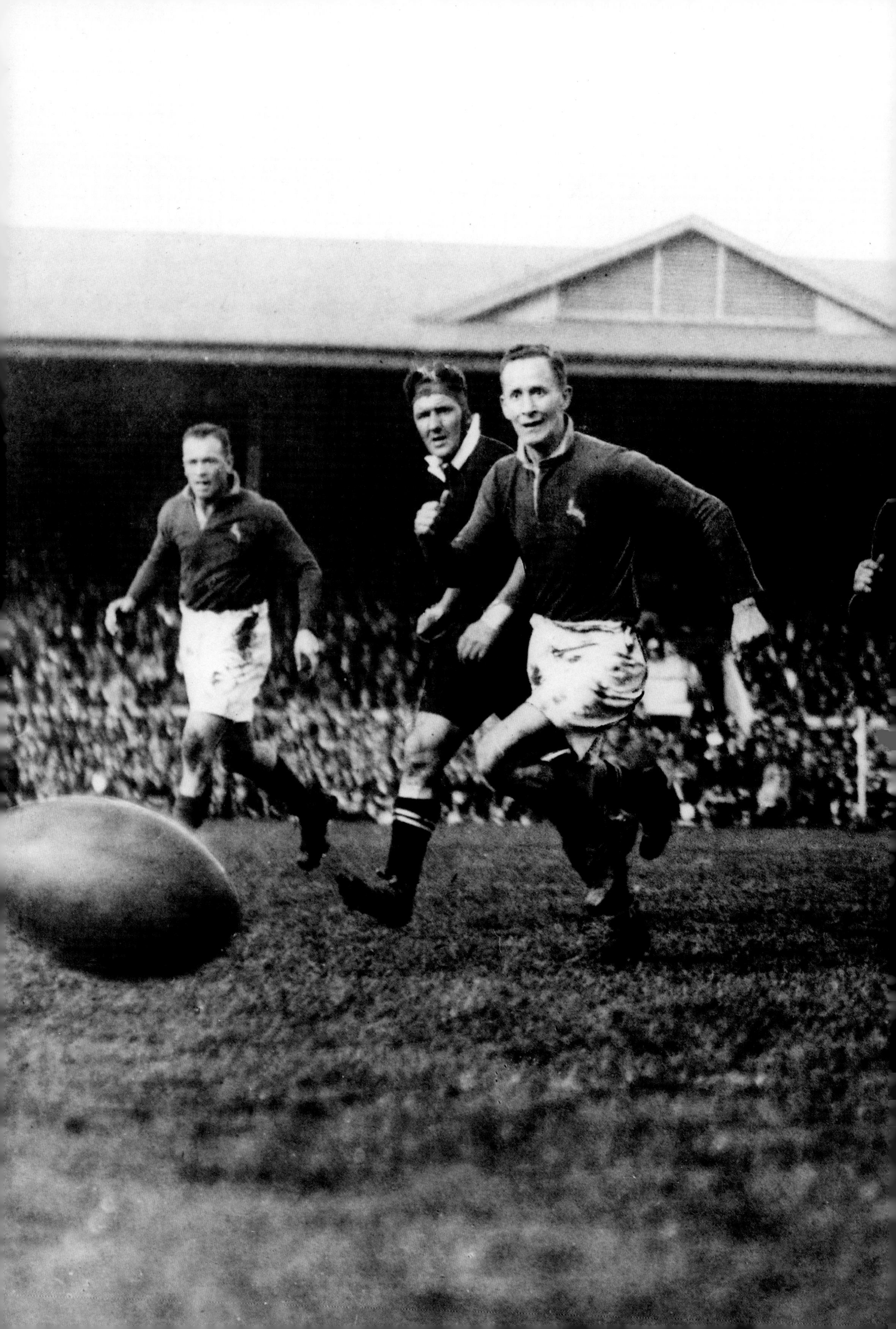

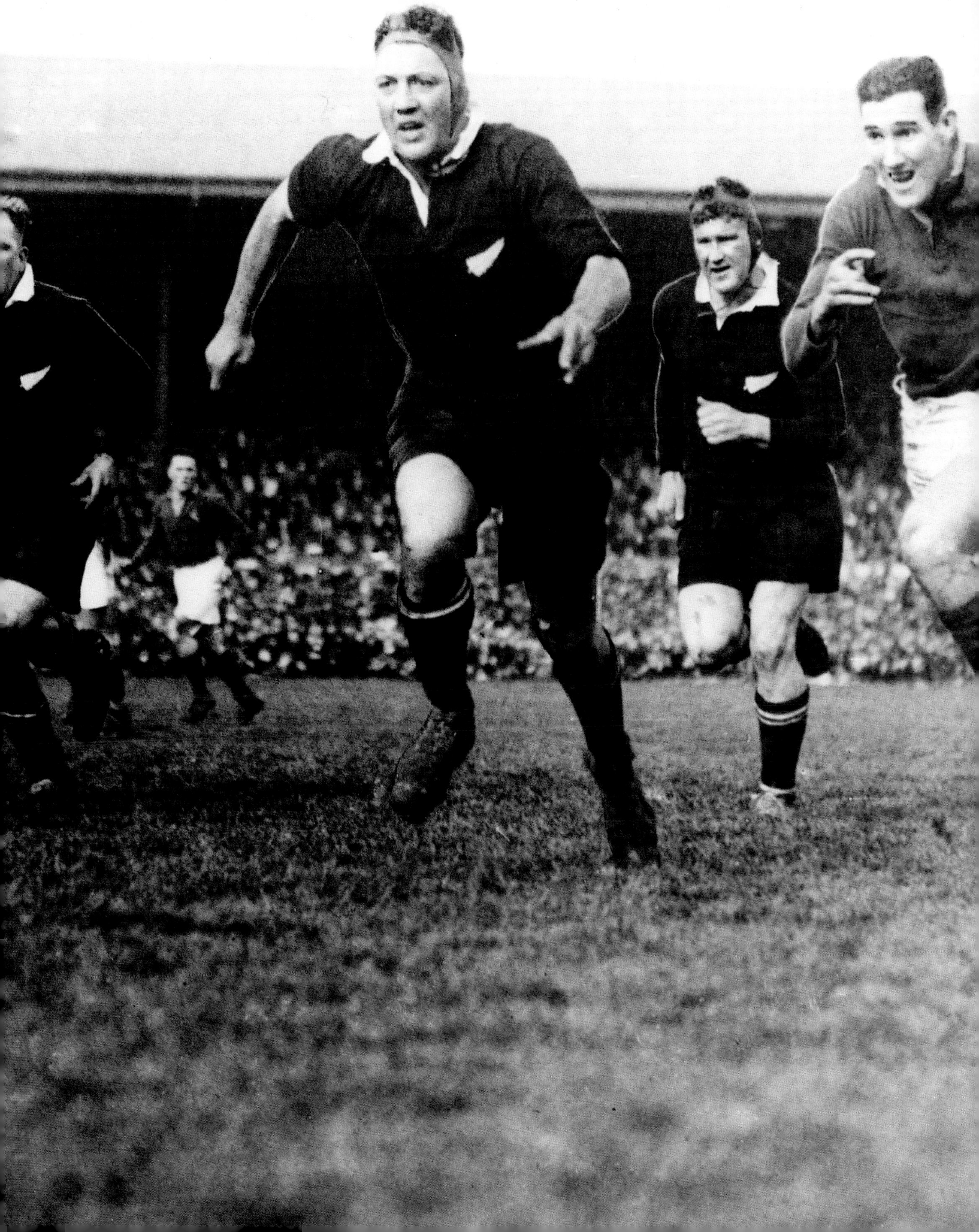

JIM BURROWS

were glad to accept some coaching from the South Africans on how they packed their scrums.

'I see nothing wrong with this. Good men lose nothing in stature by admitting they can learn from their opponents.'

Burrows' size, strength and superb physical conditioning had been honed years earlier when still at high school. In the summer holidays he would return to his family in Waiau, North Canterbury, and work on farms in the area. Because of the shortage of manpower in the immediate postwar period, boys could earn a man's wages in the harvest field. At 15, young Jim was earning two shillings an hour, the full harvest rate for a man.

'This work was hard for a growing boy not brought up on a farm and there were times during hot afternoons, with a Canterbury nor'wester blowing, when I was so tired only a dogged kind of pride and an idea that a good man never gives in kept me going.'

Burrows played for three years in each of the Christchurch Boys' High School first XV rugby and first XI cricket teams. The 1920 rugby team was exceptional because it won the interschools' championship easily, became the first winner of the Moascar Cup for competition among New Zealand secondary schools and was later to have five of its members make the All Blacks — Curly Page and Syd Carleton from the backs and Geoff Alley, Frank Clark and Burrows from the forwards. From the 1921 cricket team, Curly Page and Ian Cromb both went on to captain New Zealand, while Arthur Cox, Jack Powell and Burrows, a medium fast bowler, played for Canterbury.

Burrows must have been a born leader. At Boys' High he was head prefect, head boarder, captain of the first XV, captain of the first XI and senior cadet officer. Immediately on leaving school, while attending Canterbury University, he became a full-time high-school teacher and soon afterwards captain of his senior rugby team. He was only 28 when given charge, as coach, of the Canterbury rugby team, and 33 when he coached the All Blacks.

With war came more leadership. As a soldier he rose to be Brigadier Burrows, CBE, DSO and bar, Order of Valour (Greece). That is how the men of 20 Battalion and others who fought with him in Greece, Crete, North Africa and Italy remember him. As do those Papakura CMT conscripts in the early 1950s, the regular soldiers under his command with the Southern Military District in the late 1950s, and those who knew him as commander of New Zealand's K Force in Korea and Japan.

Burrows certainly had a varied, rich and exciting life.

BIOGRAPHICAL DETAILS

James Thomas Burrows

Born: Prebbleton, 14 July 1904
Died: Christchurch, 10 June, 1991
Position: Front-row forward
Represented NZ: 1928 (9 matches)
Points for NZ: 6 (2 tries)
Provincial record: Canterbury 1923 (High School Old Boys), 1925, 1927, 1929, 1930 (University); South Island 1925, 1927, 1929
Selector/coach: Canterbury 1932-33
Other: University boxing blues 1924-26; Canterbury medium-pace bowler 1926-34; commander 20th Battalion 2nd NFEF, later 4th and 5th Brigades; CBE, DSO and bar, Order of Valour (Greece); commander K Force, Korea; CBE
Occupation: Army brigadier; rector, Waitaki Boys' High; schoolmaster

NEW ZEALAND COACHING RECORD

1937: beat South Africa 13-7; lost to South Africa 6-13, lost to South Africa 6-17

References
1. This and subsequent Burrows quotes are from Jim Burrows, *Pathway Among Men*, Whitcombe and Tombs, 1974.

CHAPTER 14

NEW ZEALAND COACH 1921, 1938, 1949

ALEX McDONALD

Fabulous career darkened by blackest days of All Black history

MUCH HAS BEEN SAID AND WRITTEN OVER almost half a century about how and why Alex McDonald won the 1949 All Black coaching job over Vic Cavanagh.

McDonald was described by Terry McLean as 'one of the great gentlemen of New Zealand rugby who never recovered from the mortification of being ignored by the 1949 All Blacks he was appointed to coach through South Africa.'[1] But is that really the truth of the matter? We need to explore the backgrounds of both coaches to gain an insight into how and why McDonald got the job, and whether Cavanagh could have altered history and saved New Zealand rugby from its most humiliating hour.

McDonald had achieved a tremendous amount in a long rugby career. No other All Black coach compares for the length of time he was in charge — over three decades.

It is fascinating to trace his name through each of the decades of the first half of the 20th century:
- Plays in the All Black scrum in each of the four home union tests on the 1905 Originals tour.
- Captains the All Blacks on their ground-breaking tour of North America in 1913.
- Helps coach the All Blacks for the first time in 1921.
- Serves on the Otago union from 1921 until the early 1930s.
- An Otago-based New Zealand selector from 1929 to 1932.
- Moves to Wellington, headquarters of the game, and coaches Wellington College Old Boys to the club championship in 1933.
- Serves on the NZRFU management committee and the council through the 1930s and 1940s.
- Coaches the All Blacks on a triumphant, unbeaten Australian tour in 1938, helping the New Zealand rugby psyche recover from the damage inflicted the previous year by the Springboks.
- A New Zealand selector again from 1944 to 1948.
- As coach of Wellington in 1946, gives the great Kiwis their only defeat on a New Zealand tour following their return from Britain.
- Appointed to coach the All Blacks for a third tenure in 1948 — the ultimate challenge.

McDonald shared the coaching and management duties of the 1921 All Blacks, against the touring South Africans with two of his 1905 team-mates, Billy Stead and George Nicholson (who was a New Zealand selector). In the first true international series of the postwar period, and the first series between the countries, the All Blacks won the first test in Dunedin 13-5, and the Springboks the second in Auckland 9-5.

There has been historical uncertainty over whether this group actually took the All Blacks for the third test.

After excellent conditions during most of the week's

preparation, the weather deteriorated and the test was played in atrocious conditions — much of the playing area was covered in water — and the result was a 0-0 draw.

McDonald was recalled by the NZRFU to coach the All Blacks on their 1938 tour of Australia. It would not be an easy task because New Zealand rugby faced a number of problems, not the least being the intense state of depression brought on by the resounding series defeat by the Springboks the year before. South Africa had shown New Zealand forward play to be loose, unskilled with the 3-4-1 scrum formation and without front-row forwards big and powerful enough to seriously test the Springboks.

Australian rugby was powerful at this time. In 1937 New South Wales had beaten the Boks, and, in the two internationals at the Sydney Cricket Ground, South Africa only won by fairly narrow margins — 9-5 and 26-17. The Wallabies had a host of fine players.

But the tour proved a triumph for McDonald and his players. Nine matches were played and won, with 279 points scored and only 73 against. The Wallabies were beaten 26-9, 20-14 and 14-6.

The first-string back line was to prove as strong as any New Zealand had fielded. From Charlie Saxton at halfback, through Trevor Berghan, Jack Sullivan, 'Brushy' Mitchell, Tom Morrison, Bill Phillips and, at the back, Jack Taylor, it contained a fine balance of attacking and defensive qualities.

Saxton, whom Danie Craven had praised when the Springboks had met South Canterbury the year before as the finest halfback the South Africans had met on tour, was a godsend to New Zealand rugby. He had the speed of foot and delivery that had been lacking in his Otago team-mate Harry Simon against the Boks. It was a great pity that, like so many young All Blacks and potential All Blacks, his best rugby years were taken from him by Adolf Hitler.

In another of his books, Terry McLean stated that during the trials held in 1948[1] to choose the 1949 touring team, NZRFU chairman A. St C. 'Slip' Belcher promised the manager's job to his friend McDonald, who promptly sought out Cavanagh and invited him to become coach of the team. Young Vic was keen. But because they pledged to keep the matter secret, the arrangement became known to only a few.

Then Jim Parker, the man who had displaced his captain, Cliff Porter, in tests on the 1924 Invincibles tour, and an NZRFU executive member since 1939, expressed interest in the manager's job. Belcher 'resolved' the problem by backing Parker as manager and McDonald as coach. The appointments were made.[2]

McLean told the author in a 1997 interview that his sources for this information were Cavanagh, principally, and Mark Nicholls, the former All Black great who was a North Island selector in 1948, the year the 1949 team was chosen.

"McDonald asked Cavanagh to be the coach when the pair were in Christchurch,' said McLean. 'Parker had been away overseas. When he came back, he said he wanted the manager's job. I understand that Belcher and Parker were members of the Masonic Lodge, and McDonald may have been too."

Newspaper reports of the time certainly support McLean's theory that Belcher found himself in a sticky position and then extricated himself in a very questionable manner.

Newspaper reports stated that the Otago union, which had nominated both McDonald and Cavanagh for the two management positions, protested to the New Zealand union about its method of appointment. Otago had been led to believe there were two separate positions — and that the nominations were not interchangeable. The Otago president, R. W. S Botting, explained to a special meeting that his union's interest had been solely in the assistant manager's position.

'We were just awaiting Mr Cavanagh's decision [as to whether he would accept being put forward] before making his nomination,' he said. 'An approach was then made to the Otago union to nominate Mr McDonald for the position of manager. Coupled with this was the assurance of Mr Belcher that in making Mr McDonald's nomination, Otago would not be affecting Mr Cavanagh's position.'

Botting, a member of the NZRFU council, told the Otago meeting he found it hard to reconcile Belcher's statement then with his subsequent attitude at the council meeting. He considered Belcher's ruling, as chairman of the NZRFU, unconstitutional and distinctly arbitrary. However, newspaper reports confirmed Belcher had blandly announced the positions were interchangeable a fortnight before the vote was taken.

'We were the only union that had had experience of Messrs Cavanagh and McDonald — and bearing in mind our experience, we did not hesitate to support Mr Cavanagh', Mr Botting added.

To add to the debate was the fact the now-Wellington-domiciled McDonald sat on the NZRFU executive as the Otago representative. Speakers at the special Otago meeting said they could not understand how McDonald, knowing Otago's feelings on which man it preferred as the assistant manager/coach, could have allowed his name to

THE POWER BEHIND THE ALL BLACKS

STAYING POWER: The incredible longevity of Alex McDonald as a top-level coach is amply illustrated in the these two photos – of the (*above*) 1921 and (*below*) 1949 All Blacks – both coached by McDonald, almost 30 years apart.

93

go forward for the vote. According to Botting, McDonald had told him immediately before the meeting that he did not intend to stand as assistant manager.

Otago's fury and embarrassment at the way things had been handled in Wellington were magnified by the fact it had pressed Cavanagh to stand after he had initially said he would not be available.

Another school of thought has it that Cavanagh never seriously came into NZRFU calculations. Management of overseas rugby tours was a highly sought-after sinecure — even more so than today, when the specialist nature of the job is appreciated — and appointments were almost always given for services rendered. The way the two plum jobs fell to the council's own members illustrates this. So there is much irony in the fact that, long before the tour was completed, both Messrs Parker and McDonald would have cause to rue the day they had allowed their names to go into the hat.

The NZRFU compounded its appalling blunder the next year by dropping Cavanagh from the South Island selection panel. Reliable sources said not one councillor voted for Cavanagh. His Otago team had continued to win during 1949, despite having 11 members away with the All Blacks in South Africa. But someone had to pay for the ignominy of the 4-0 whitewash and, apparently, it was Cavanagh. He was to drop out of serious rugby coaching to pursue business interests from that time.

In 1950, in Dunedin's *Evening Star*, Cavanagh disclaimed arguments against Otago's style, which had been used by some to countenance the tour appointment. 'Figures — clear, indisputable figures — reinforce the story of Otago's constructive brightness and scoring ability. In the 17 matches played for the Ranfurly Shield in 1947, 1948 and 1949 Otago scored no fewer than 347 points, against the meagre total of 69 collected by all challengers.'

He concluded that 'this criticism must be regarded as incongruous, unbalanced and, quite needlessly, a little bitter'.[6]

By the time McDonald toured South Africa as coach of the Forty-Niners he was 66. Fred Allen *(see Chapter 23)*, captain of the side, said this was the first tragic mistake by the organisers of the tour.

There have been claims through the decades since that at the first training run in South Africa McDonald was ignored, and that Allen called the backs to go with him and the forwards to be coached by vice-captain Ray Dalton. Later in the tour, as he watched a liner steam out of Cape Town harbour, McDonald is alleged to have said he wished he could have been on it.

But Allen denies any suggestion that McDonald was isolated and ignored by the team at any stage. 'He was a lovely old man,' he said when interviewed by the author in 1997. 'The team and I liked him and he was never shut out. But he was sick a lot and was 66 years old. Eventually, I did end up doing a lot of coaching.'

Dr Ron Elvidge, who captained the team in the third and fourth tests when Allen became unavailable, confirmed to the author in 1997 that any claims that McDonald had been ostracised were completely false.

The great All Black fullback Bob Scott, who was on the tour, reckoned the worst misfortune of the Forty-Niners was that they were sent to South Africa with so much at stake.

'We were [meant] to wipe out the memories of 1937 and re-establish New Zealand rugby at the peak of 1924,' said Scott. 'So much were these aspects discussed and so deeply did New Zealand feel . . . that a sense of the religious importance of our mission inevitably gripped us . . . I am quite certain that the tension was the greatest problem we encountered.'

Like the previous All Blacks who toured South Africa in 1928, this team was unable, early in the tour, to match the Springboks' scrummaging. 'Bo' Wintle, the side's South African liaison officer and formerly a fine player, took the All Blacks behind closed doors to explain his countrymen's scrum formation. Later the Springbok coach himself, Danie Craven, did the same. This caused a furore back in New Zealand, where it was claimed the All Blacks had been humiliated.

Compare the aged McDonald, not withstanding his record, with the Springboks' Craven, and the difference in the two sides is obvious.

Craven was one of the brains behind the great Springbok touring team which whipped the All Blacks in 1937. Though primarily a halfback with a superb dive pass, he had played for South Africa from 1931 to 1938 in no fewer than five positions. He was now in his forties. He was a player and coach of enormous depth and breadth of vision.

He deliberately narrowed that vision to get what he sought from his players. The Craven doctrine was simply never to play beyond your limitations. Later a great rugby politician, Craven knew he had to provide victories for the South African public. He did not delude himself about expansive or 'entertaining' rugby.

'Hence,' wrote Bob Scott, 'the No. 8 forward, whose sole purpose was to wreck rugby as a conventional game of man against man; hence the South African method of hooking; hence the South African lineout, in which the element of fair

CHAMPION CHARLIE: Charlie Saxton, the All Black halfback, has scored as Wallaby and All Black forwards tower over him during the first 1938 test in Sydney. Saxton got two tries in this game and another in the third test. Coached by Alex McDonald, the side won all three tests.

competition between man and man had been cut down to the irreducible minimum; hence the kicking for touch by the flyhalf, to reduce the game to a mauling struggle between forwards until a penalty goal could decide the issue.'[7]

The 1949 All Blacks were considered a potentially great side when selected, but they did not produce the results expected of them so cannot be rated a successful team. But were they as bad as the 4-0 whitewash suggests? With an ounce of luck they could have tied the series, or won it 3-1.

None of their losses was by a substantial margin and, remarkably, only eight tries were scored against them in an arduous tour of 24 matches. In fact, 18 opposition teams failed to score a try against them. That demonstrated outstanding defensive resilience.

However, the team kicked only 15 penalty goals, as against 35 kicked by opponents. Even allowing for Scott's woefully out-of-form goal-kicking, there remains more than a hint that the refereeing was sometimes more parochial than was fair and reasonable, especially considering that this All

THREE WISE MEN: Alex McDonald, Harold Strang and Norm McKenzie finalise their 1949 team to tour South Africa. This would be the last time these long-time servants of All Black rugby would convene. A new panel, led by Tom Morrison, would replace them in 1950 and begin to rebuild from the ashes of the 1949 situation.

Black team had the experience to keep within the laws and not deliberately offend.

After initial problems with the revolutionary new tactics adopted by all South African teams in scrums and lineouts (see Chapter 39 for further details), the All Blacks often outscrummed and outjumped their opposition later in the tour. The selecting of the team in 1948, after a campaign that simplistically favoured size over skill in the forwards, had contributed to some players being overweight upon arrival, and hindered the side early in the tour.

Of the individual performances, Scott caused the South African pressmen to run out of superlatives in their praise for him. Fellow backs Elvidge, Morrie Goddard and Peter Henderson also had outstanding tours, and Kevin Skinner, only 20, emerged as a prop of exceptional ability. A future All Black captain, Skinner had begun to build the record that would make him the most capped All Black by the mid-1950s. He, Johnny Simpson and Has Catley formed a front row that dominated the opposition by the end of the tour. Lachie Grant was an outstanding lineout jumper, while Jack McNab, Pat Crowley and Peter Johnstone all developed well.

But other careers, especially among the inside backs, were destroyed during the tour. There is no doubt a schemer of the calibre of Cavanagh could have altered the way the All Blacks dealt with the problems presented by Hennie Muller.

Cavanagh did leave behind some ideas of how he would have handled Muller if he'd had the chance. He wrote a series of coaching articles, remarkable for their simplicity and the way they explain the game's supposed mysteries in easily understood passages, in the *Dunedin Evening Star* in the early 1950s.

In one he said he'd have had his winger throwing directly to Muller at the end of the lineout. With one or two All Black forwards close-marking him, Muller would have risked being scragged each time and might have given up hounding the inside backs so often. The only problem would have been the accuracy of the throw right out into the midfield, where Muller used to stand.[8]

A few months before Cavanagh died in July 1980 he was interviewed about why he'd quit.

'Maybe I've been a bit stuffy about it all,' he said. He reiterated why he'd retired from coaching, and added: 'I must say I found it a reasonably easy decision to make in view of the fact that I did not think much of the way the NZRFU went about making their appointments.'[9]

In one of his last articles for the *Evening Star*, in 1950, he touched on the problems that had followed the disastrous 1949 tour. 'One of the great weaknesses of rugby in New Zealand is that there is no organisation set up to provide for an exchange of views between selectors and coaches of provincial teams. It is difficult to avoid the conclusion that there is an alarming lack of appreciation by the administration of the playing problems at present.

'I cannot understand why the tour . . . was not examined thoroughly when the team returned. So many contentious issues arose in South Africa . . . that it is incomprehensible why the manager's report to the NZRFU was received "without comment".

'Such lethargy is fantastic. Is it too much to suggest that it is one of the biggest handicaps to the game in New Zealand at the moment?'[10]

Those were to be the last words by Cavanagh, in public, on the subject. Meanwhile, McDonald, who had served New Zealand rugby for nearly 50 years, took the brunt of criticism for the Forty-Niners' failures. He did not serve on another national selection panel after 1948, but remained on the NZRFU council until 1950.

. . . .

VIC CAVANAGH

The greatest coach never to coach the All Blacks

Vic Cavanagh has been called the finest rugby coach never to have coached the All Blacks — and a prophet without honour in his own land.

Known as Young Vic so as not to be confused with his father, Old Vic, he was undoubtedly the greatest New Zealand coach of his day. His triumphs with Otago are legendary, but in 1949 his outstanding claim to the All Black coaching job was passed over for Alex McDonald, one of the New Zealand selectors and a member of the NZRFU executive. While he was idolised in the south, in the north his success seems to have made him actively disliked. The originator of the great rucking game, it was claimed, lacked enterprise and adventure and was too negative. Yet his backs scored hundreds of tries.

Cavanagh started at Otago as assistant coach to his father in 1936, a year after the shield had been won by the province for the first time. There was a Cavanagh in charge of the team from then until 1949. Otago lost the shield in 1950, with Charlie Saxton as coach. Otago and Southland shared the shield from 1935 until 1950, a remarkable span, even allowing for World War II. Young Vic was in charge between 1946 and

1949, when the shield was successfully defended 19 times, a tenure reminiscent of the Hawke's Bay era of the 1920s.

The All Blacks on the 1949 tour to South Africa were plagued by Hennie Muller, the ferocious, swift and magnificent Springbok No. 8 who stood off the back of lineouts, opposite the five-eighths, as the rules of the day allowed, and destroyed all hopes New Zealand had of expansive rugby. The All Blacks stood deeper to try to combat Muller, sometimes 10-20 metres behind the advantage line. They would often end up a long way back from the previous phase, rather than going forward, after a Muller raid. They never solved the problem.

Interviewed by the author in August 1997, Vic Cavanagh's son, Dick, said a number of myths had developed about his father and the 1949 series.

'In discussing the 1949 series and the possible tactics that could have been used, VC made it clear nobody was interested in listening to him pretending he could have won, when he was far from sure himself,' he said.

However, his father did say he would have 'buried' Muller. The All Blacks would have been forbidden to run with the ball while Muller was on his feet. The forwards would have run at Muller, rather than away from him, and Muller's resolve 'would have been tested'. Vic also said the combination of McDonald and Fred Allen was ineffective. Allen, the captain and first five-eighth, was not then the Allen who would coach the All Blacks so masterfully 17 years later.

Dick Cavanagh agreed his father had retired for business reasons. His employers, the Smith family, had actually encouraged him to continue coaching. But he had a strong desire to retire while on top. This was probably caused, back in 1937, when his father's — Vic Snr's — Otago team was heavily beaten by the Springboks. The family felt Vic sen had been unfairly judged on that game and perhaps should have retired earlier.

The men who played under Cavanagh still worship his memory and it would be hard to find one from the Forty-Niners who still didn't think Cavanagh's absence cost them the series.

'He had that immediate rapport with players, and that analytical mind would undoubtedly have helped us get very quickly to the heart of our problems,' Dr Ron Elvidge, Otago and All Black captain and 1949 tourist, told the author. 'Vic was the Graham Henry of the 1940s. At an Otago team meeting he could go through a game played several days before and recall all the moves, incidents, and what each of us had been doing. You could hear a pin drop at those meetings.'

Cavanagh and his methods are still talked about with

LIKE FATHER, LIKE SON: Vic Cavanagh Snr and Junior, otherwise known as 'Old Vic' and 'Young Vic'. 'Old Vic', a former New Zealand selector, developed second-phase play in the 1920s. His son took the rucking game to new levels. From 1935 to 1949 either Cavanagh, or both, ensured that Otago, with Southland, maintained a stranglehold on the Ranfurly Shield.

awe by older rugby men. All Black coaches have openly admitted they adopted his methods. Dick Everest, the outstanding Waikato and All Black coach, Bob Stuart, Neil McPhail, Fred Allen, Eric Watson and Laurie Mains have all paid tribute to the man. Allen once had Cavanagh run his record-breaking Auckland Ranfurly Shield team while the Otago man was on a business visit.

A knee injury had ended Cavanagh's rugby-playing career, after he had built a reputation as a promising young loose forward for Otago in 1931 (he played seven matches in a team coached by Alex McDonald). He played cricket for Otago from 1928 to 1936, became an outstanding captain and was 12th man for New Zealand v. Douglas Jardine's MCC in 1933.

It was in the period from 1922 to 1934 that Vic Cavanagh sen developed the idea of second-phase play, which up until then had only been tried in its crudest form. Because his forwards were lighter than their opponents and outplayed for first-phase possession, he had them follow their backs, recovering ball at the breakdown and heeling it back.

Vic jun used second-phase far more deliberately. It was the pedestal of his game. A designated runner in the backs, such as Ron Elvidge, would deliberately create the ruck, just

ALEX McDONALD

as a player like Ian McRae would do with the All Blacks nearly 20 years later. Continuity of possession was a key factor.

Vic jun said he had learned from his father. 'I had the benefit of watching his teams play. I was impressed with the way they created tries.'

His loss to the game was immeasurable. We can still see how his brilliant rugby brain operated by reading the clear, concise coaching articles he wrote in 1949-50. An example is his answer to the problem that would plague New Zealand rugby for more than 40 years — the loss of the 2-3-2 scrum and its attacking potential for back play. His own final year as a player was 1931, the year the 2-3-2 scrum was outlawed. The new 3-4-1 scrum put chains on back attack. Yet he could show how his development of the 'loose scrum', or rucking game, could bring back the attacking chances of old.

The beauty of the 2-3-2 scrum had been the uncertainty of who would win possession, so both back lines stood deep, ready to attack. But with the new scrum (and the loose head) the teams could almost always predict who was going to win possession. This meant the defending back line stood up flat, negating any chance of attack by its opponent.

But with the rucking game, according to Cavanagh, 'because of the various uncertainties, the opposing backs are generally in reasonable depth. Consequently, all the methods that were successful behind the 2-3-2 scrum can be put into operation from the loose scrum. The essential here is that your own forwards are able to get to the loose scrum more readily than the opponents'.

In 1971, during the great tour by the British Lions, the doyen of New Zealand rugby writers, Terry McLean, arranged a meeting in Dunedin between Lions' coach Carwyn James and Cavanagh. The older man got to talking about patterns, players and possibilities. 'A long time later, James and I sat in a taxi returning to our hotel,' said McLean. 'Carwyn uttered only one word. "Fascinating", he said. It was the perfect tribute.'

REFERENCES
1. Terry McLean, *New Zealand Rugby Legends*.
2. *New Zealand Rugby Legends*.
3. *New Zealand Sporting & Dramatic Review*, 1 September 1921.
4. *New Zealand Herald*, 14 September 1921.
5. Terry McLean, *The Best of McLean*.
6. *Evening Star*.
7. *The Bob Scott Story*.
8. *Evening Star*, 1950.
9. 'The Vic Cavanagh Story: Why I quit rugby', *New Zealand Truth*.
10. *Evening Star*, 1950.

BIOGRAPHICAL DETAILS

Alex McDonald

Born: Dunedin, 23 April 1883

Died: Wellington, 4 May 1967

Position: Loose forward

Represented NZ: 1905–08, 1913
41 matches (8 internationals)

Points for NZ: 50 (16 tries, 1 conversion)

Provincial record: Otago 1904, 1906–09, 1911-14, 1919 (Kaikorai); Otago-Southland 1904; South Island 1904-07, 1913

NZ selector: 1929-32, 1944-48

NZ coach: 1921 (shared), 1938, 1949

Other service: Otago RFU management committee 1914-16, 1920-28; Otago RFU vice-president 1928-32; coached Wellington College Old Boys to championship 1933; NZRFU management committee 1935-36, NZRFU council 1937-50; elected life member of NZRFU 1951

Occupation: Brewery worker.

NEW ZEALAND COACHING RECORD

1921: beat South Africa 13-5; lost to South Africa 5-9; drew with South Africa 0-0

1938: beat Australia 24-9, 20-14, 14-6

1949: lost to South Africa 11-15, 6-12, 3-9, 8-11

CHAPTER 15

NEW ZEALAND COACH 1950, 1952, 1955-56

TOM MORRISON

Never lost a series in seven years

TOM MORRISON NEVER LOST A SERIES AS ALL Black coach. But his long career as an All Black, convenor of the national selectors, All Black coach and chairman of the NZRFU is also remarkable for the times he decided to allow 'outsiders' to coach, or help coach, the team.

More than 40 years after the event, it seems difficult to imagine why an incumbent All Black coach would do this. But when one considers the enormous challenge which confronted Morrison, the expectations of the nation, and the worrying form of the All Blacks the previous year, it becomes more understandable why he decided to bring Bob Stuart into the frame in 1956.

Perhaps forgotten is that Morrison had already stepped aside twice while he was convenor of selectors to pass the coaching job, temporarily, to other men. Len Clode, an 'outsider', coached the All Blacks in Australia in 1951, while one of Morrison's fellow selectors, Arthur Marslin, coached the team on the epic tour of Britain and France in 1953–54.

Morrison's actions in this regard beg the question why some other national selection chairmen did not similarly see fit to put the team before personal ambition or reputation.

Another forgotten, but no less unusual, feature of Morrison's career was that he became an NZRFU executive member while still a player, and that he was just 36 when he began his All Black coaching stint, four years after quitting first-class rugby.

Morrison thus delivered a powerful message that was ignored for many a long day — that a national selector-coach who is young and closely in touch with the players and the game's strategies may have a stronger chance of success than sometimes much older men, even though they have faithfully moved through the tried and trusted NZRFU selectorial/coaching system.

Morrison, together with fellow selectors Marslin and Jack Sullivan, co-opted the 1953–54 All Black tour captain, Stuart, to help coach the All Blacks in the 1956 series against the touring Springboks. Stuart was designated the forward coach, but it is clear from the large amount of original source material available that Morrison had long planned the campaign and retained a strong hand in proceedings to ensure his team became the first All Black side to win a series against the Springboks. The NZRFU had also done its part by appointing its selectors for a two-year stint late in 1954 and providing Morrison with unprecedented powers concerning playing policy and preparation.

Stuart was probably the most influential coach of the 1950s in terms of playing style. A surprise choice to some as captain of the 1953–54 team — he turned 33 on tour — he had played in all five tests and proved to be an inspirational leader. There is little doubt that Marslin, with

TOM MORRISON

HIGH STANDARDS: Tom Morrison's days as an All Black three-quarter were ended by World War II, but he became a young and very successful All Black coach and long-serving NZRFU chairman after that.

the benefit of having observed Stuart's tactical and man-management skills at first hand in 1953–54, also had a major influence in the decision to co-opt him. Stuart exerted a lot of influence in New Zealand rugby circles from that time on. He was already one of the country's 'most passionate theorists' and became a coach of Canterbury in 1958.

Included among the documents accessed for researching this chapter were Morrison's personal letters, handwritten team plans and schedules, including the tactics to be used against the Boks, notebooks and newspaper clippings.

The gem of the Morrison 'memoirs' is a 16-page handwritten letter to Bob Stuart on his appointment, dated 11 March 1956. It sets out Morrison's vision of how they were going to beat the Boks.

'I only hope that when this season is completed you will have the satisfaction of being associated with a New Zealand side that has for the first time beaten the Springboks in a test series,' wrote Morrison.

'The playing of three games, namely against The Rest, North Island and South Island teams, will give an opportunity to develop teamwork . . .

'The players this year, I am sure, are going to be fitter by far than they have been for a long while. This will enable us to spend much more time practising than would be the case should they only be half fit.'

The team would be brought together for 10 days for the three games in late May, and then would disperse for a month until the first test. Because of this lapse of time, Morrison believed 'the spadework of developing team spirit must be accomplished' during their short time together. He was mindful that All Black teams had rarely, especially in the postwar era, been given the opportunity by the NZRFU to spend such time together before a home series.

'It is imperative that the players are "living football" . . . [The development of] morale will be the most important aspect . . . and also the absolute determination — I don't think we'll have any trouble with this — that they must be prepared and keen to give their all for New Zealand.

'As I told you, Bob, it would not be fair to ask you to assist without your being consulted re the policy, and as I said then, I don't think that there is anything that we can't iron out where there is a difference of opinion. The main thing is to be working for the same end!'

With great honesty, Morrison added that in 1955 'we were taken apart for our performances and for that I take full responsibility. Arthur and Jack are two fine types to be associated with and are particularly loyal. I know that there were features last year that both did not fully agree with, and Arthur in particular was worried about our lack of drive in the forwards . . .'

Morrison explained he had deliberately attempted to play to Australia's strengths in 1955, and, thinking ahead to the Boks, had tried to make the All Blacks more mobile. 'I also know, Bob, that we can't beat the Springboks without hard, honest forward play first. You have to win the ball to play with it.'

The All Black weaknesses of 1955, pinpointed in the letter, were lack of fitness, lack of quickness in the loose forwards, and backs being caught behind the advantage line.

While he had previously refused to employ the spoiling tactics of 'Hennie Mullerism' in his All Black teams, Morrison told Stuart that 'it appears that this activity is the accepted practice and that teams not indulging in it are giving their opponents an advantage'.

'I have no desire to come out of the encounter other than with New Zealanders on top . . . we will have to play active flankers who will force their opponents into playing the ball behind their forwards . . .'

Morrison mentions only one player in his letter, Bill Clark. He would become one of the stars in the 1956 series win as a constructive/destructive flanker who wreaked havoc among the Springbok backs, but Morrison's comments are not flattering. 'I would be happy to play a blind and open-side flanker, but of all the flankers I saw last year none reached the standard of ability to warrant his selection for that role. Bill Clark was the nearest, but was not fit enough and missed far too many tackles.'

In a handwritten plan of the three-game build-up, Morrison referred to the necessity for punctuality, a team curfew of '11 p.m. at the latest', 'liquor to be off the menu, excepting after the games and then very few', and that 'dances' were 'right out'. It was thinking that was not too different from that of the All Black World Cup campaigns or camps of 1987 and 1995 — just 30 to 40 years earlier.

Morrison also had special meetings in May with the coaches of all the provincial teams of the North and the South Islands, explaining objectives and laying out policy. He did not direct provincial teams how to play the tourists, however, stating instead that their own strengths and weaknesses should dictate their tactics.

He had already spent four days between Christmas and New Year's Eve 1955 personally addressing and mailing out a standard letter to 820 players — all those who had taken part in first-class rugby in 1955 — urging them to get fit for the Springboks. Auckland had set up a training school over summer, while Canterbury could state, early in December, what every member of its team was doing fitness-wise, or planned to do, over the summer. After the series, Morrison would thank everyone in New Zealand rugby, down to club players and officials and coaches, for the way they had tackled the fitness campaign so that the Boks had been harried relentlessly, from first to last, in virtually every match they had played.

The loss of the second test, which meant the series was squared, caused consternation in higher New Zealand rugby circles. Some thought it was a sign the Springboks would repeat the success of the previous series in New Zealand, in 1937.

The All Blacks' leaders realised changes had to be made. Key players introduced were Kevin Skinner, Don Clarke, Ponty Reid, Peter Jones and Tiny Hill. Jones and Clarke had not been considered fit enough to play until that point. The All Blacks then completed their first series win over South Africa, with outstanding victories in the third and fourth tests *(see also Chapters 22 and 29)*.

Morrison's All Blacks of 1955 had really struggled against the touring Wallabies. It was not an impressive rehearsal for the long-awaited visit by the Springboks the following winter. There was a lot of chopping and changing and experimenting.

TOM MORRISON

Afterwards there was a fair amount of foreboding among the panel, the public and the critics.

The side had a relatively new look about it. A number of players had retired from international rugby after the mammoth 1953–54 tour of Britain and France — including Bob Scott, Bob Stuart, Nelson Dalzell, and Bill McCaw — while young players such as Colin Loader, Brian Fitzpatrick, Des Oliver and Guy Bowers were never to represent New Zealand again.

Newcomers for the first test included Pat Walsh (just turned 19), Ivan Vodanovich, Mark Irwin, Lindsay Townsend, Robin Archer, Ross Smith and Kevin Stuart, a younger brother of Bob Stuart. Others would be tried during the series.

The experience in the team came from Ian Clarke, Ron Jarden, Alan Elsom, Peter Jones, Tiny White, Peter Burke, Bill Clark and Ron Hemi. Ian Clarke, the captain, played at No. 8 throughout the series rather than prop.

A feature of Morrison's long era as the national selection/convenor, and sometimes coach, was that he never took the All Blacks away on tour. A menswear retailer, and on the NZRFU executive throughout those years, he was never able to take extended time off.

Morrison had been convenor of selectors since he was first voted onto the national panel in 1950. Merv Corner and Arthur Marslin were his fellow selectors for four years, then Corner dropped off the panel, to be replaced by Jack Sullivan. Marslin, Sullivan and Morrison did the job through to 1956.

Morrison was thrown in at the deep end in 1950. The panel was completely new. The year before had been the most disastrous in New Zealand rugby history. The All Blacks had lost four tests in South Africa and another two to Australia, whose team toured New Zealand while the South African tour was on. That was six out of six — a psychological disaster that has never been repeated, and a programme that has never again been attempted.

The touring British Lions were to present Morrison with many problems. They were a more mature team than usual, a result of World War II, after which players 'made up for lost time' by continuing their careers into later years. They delighted New Zealand spectators with their open game. Jackie Kyle, at first five-eighths, was their star. He was a genius, especially running with the ball, in an era when loose forwards usually ruled the roost.

The Lions drew the first test at Carisbrook 9-all, but winger Peter Henderson, a finalist in the Empire Games 100 yards that year, and first five-eighths Laurie Haig, playing his first test, were brought into the All Black side for Lancaster Park. The All Blacks won 8-0, although the press was to condemn New Zealand's consistently obstructionist lineout play.

In the third test, at Athletic Park, the All Blacks lost a player when the great prop Johnny Simpson had to leave the field with a knee injury which finished his career. No replacements were allowed. Then the All Black captain, Ron Elvidge, was badly injured just before halftime. He returned to the field with one arm hanging loose and obviously in great pain. Elvidge took up a position as rover or stood behind the back line and gave what help he could on defence. Down 0-3, the All Blacks drew level when Elvidge joined an attack and dived through Billy Cleaver's tackle to score. New Zealand won 6-3.

The All Blacks eventually took the fourth test, at Eden Park, 11-8, but not without a tremendous battle. The highlight was the try by Lions winger Ken Jones, after fullback Lewis Jones had run from his own line to halfway before unloading to the sprinter, who outpaced the All Black cover to score under the bar.

DEADLY FOEMEN: The fictitious world crown of rugby was at stake when Danie Craven (left), the Springboks' manager and coach, and Tom Morrison, the All Blacks' head coach, discussed matters during the 1956 tour of New Zealand. Craven had helped the Boks beat the All Blacks in 1937 (as a player) and 1949 (as coach), but Morrison was to prove his nemesis this time.

THE POWER BEHIND THE ALL BLACKS

That 1950 season was the last for a lot of established All Blacks. Henderson, Meates, Roper, Beatty, Elvidge, Bevan, Crowley, Harvey, Hughes, McNab, Simpson, Cherrington and Mexted would not play another test. Bob Scott retired, although he would be tempted back for the 1953–54 tour.

Morrison and his panel would from this point begin to focus on the big 1953 tour, with a tour to Australia in 1951, reciprocated by the Wallabies in 1952, as their yardstick. The 1952 series, shared one test each, would be the only series Morrison would not win outright in his time as All Black coach.

By the end of his seven-year era, Morrison and his colleagues had lifted All Black rugby from the ruins of 1949 to take the mythical world crown from New Zealand's arch-rivals, the South Africans, and created an excellent record throughout. In a total of 21 tests, 15 had been won, five lost and one drawn.

'Mr Morrison was unique in becoming top New Zealand selector while young and active, with the modern game at his fingertips,' wrote Fred Boshier when Morrison retired. 'A longtime admirer of his predecessor, Alex McDonald, he shared Mr McDonald's conviction that players are not employees. He has done a tremendous amount to make players see the New Zealand union as a benevolent rather than an unfeeling organisation.'[2]

Boshier added that 'for all his sunny nature Mr Morrison did not hesitate to show as a selector a tough streak'. He had pitted dour forward strength against the 1950 Lions, even in the face of fierce opposition from his closest friends, because he believed New Zealand, above anything else, needed victories. Conversely, he had employed the 1955 Wallabies as guinea pigs, using every expedient to find the right material for the Springboks, even at the risk of defeats.

There was some irony that Morrison himself, at the end of 1956, would worry publicly that New Zealand rugby was getting too stereotyped and that 15-man rugby and running back play needed to become a greater part of the game.

'Now that we have reached the top it is our responsibility to try to stay there. But more than that, we should use our strength and the position we have gained to develop and round out our play,' he said.

'We should have the confidence to bring our backs, all our players, into the game. Certainly, we cannot sit

CAPTAIN COURAGEOUS: Ron Elvidge scores the famous try which helped save the All Blacks in the third test at Athletic Park, Wellington, in 1950. Billy Cleaver cannot prevent the try. Elvidge had earlier left the field with collarbone and head injuries and could not play the next test. New Zealand won 6-3.

MEAN BUSINESS: The Springboks mean business as All Black captain Pat Vincent is harried by Dan Retief in the second 1956 test at Athletic Park, Wellington. Retief scored a try in South Africa's 8-3 victory to tie the series. Anxious All Blacks, from left, are Ron Jarden, Dennis Young, Bob Duff and Don McIntosh.

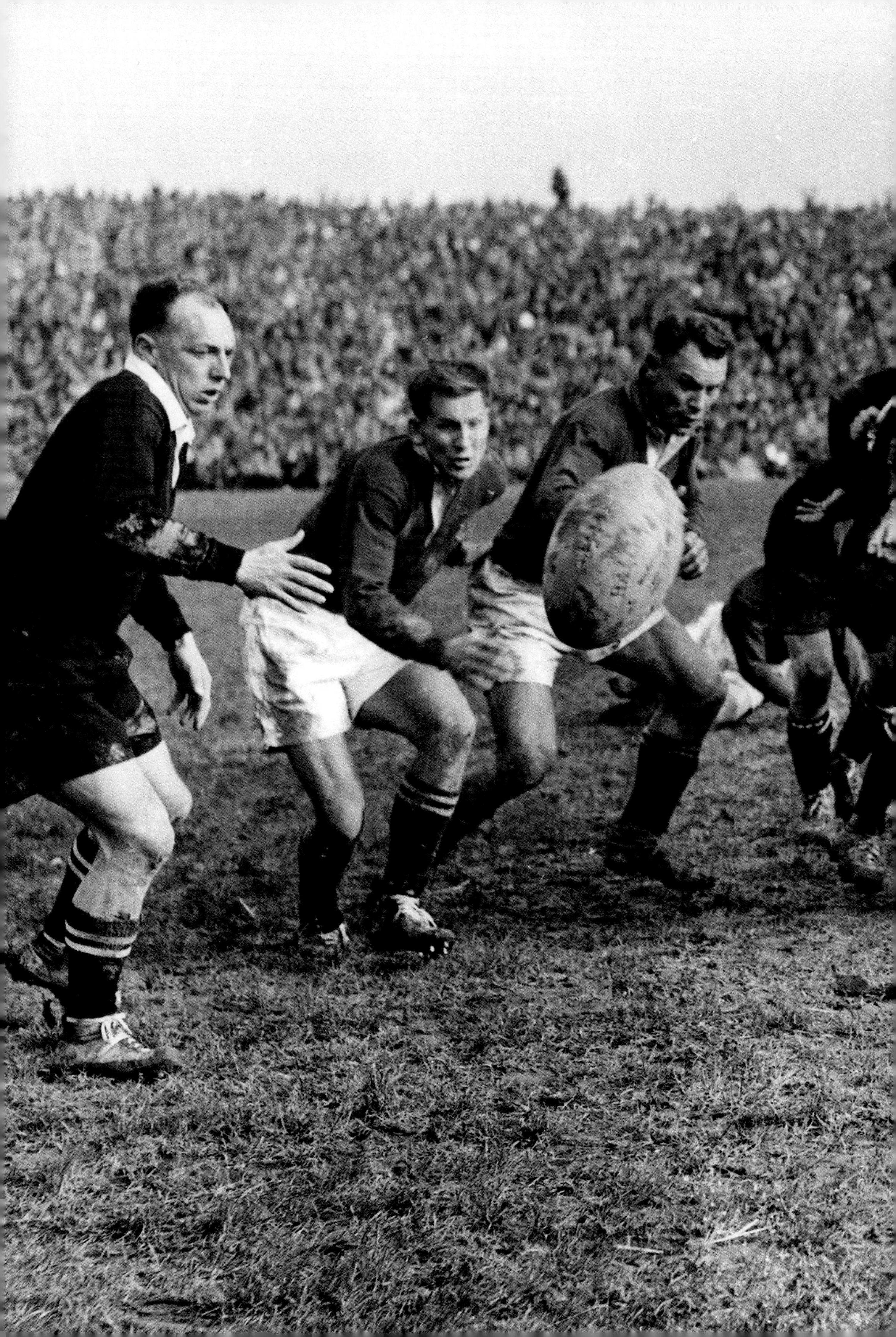

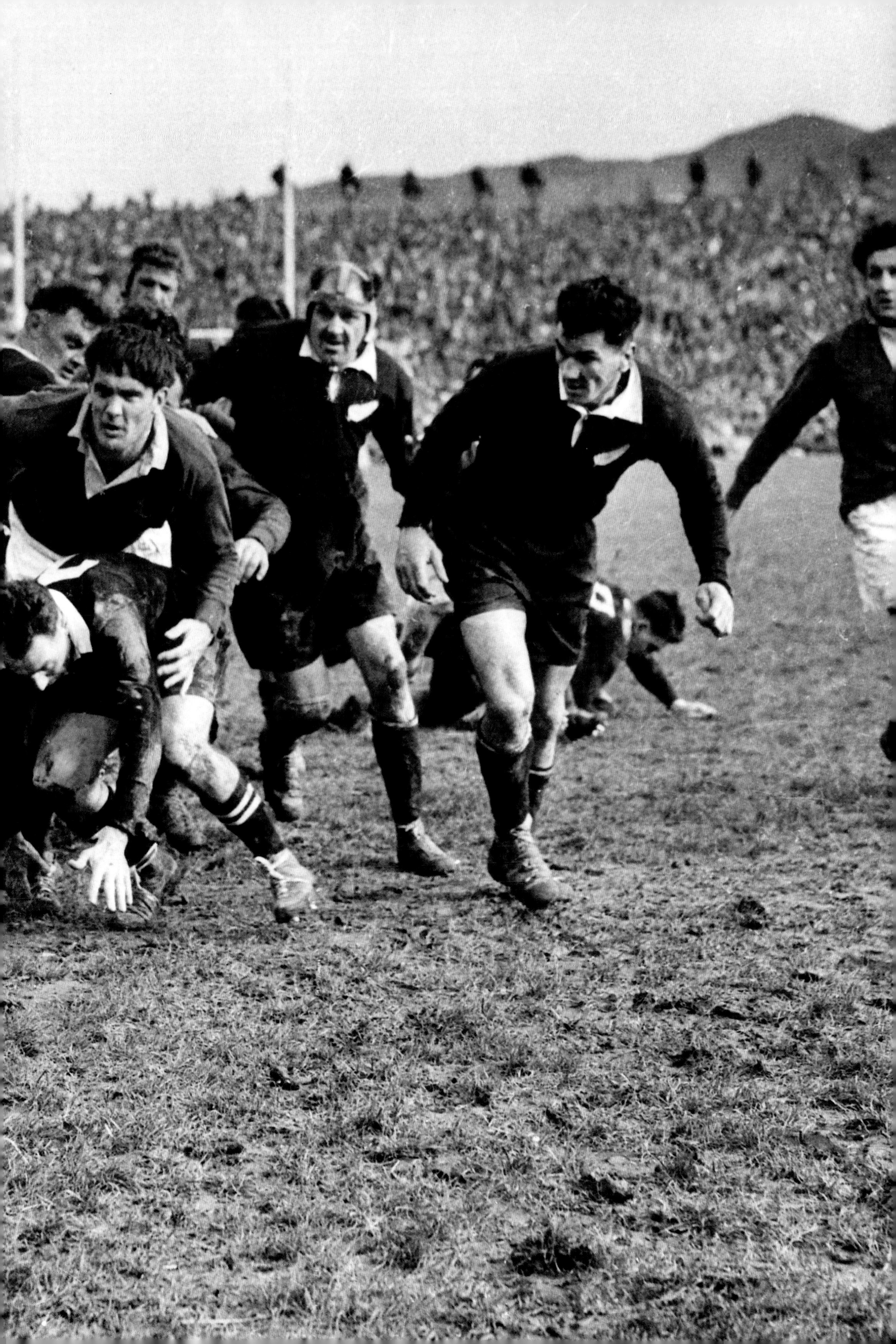

still. There is all the necessary inducement.' He spoke of the upcoming tour to Australia in 1957, the Lions touring in 1959 and the tour to South Africa in 1960. 'No young player should need to think twice as to whether a special effort will be worthwhile.'[3]

Morrison had had an unusually long playing career for a three-quarter, refusing to let the intervention of World War II cut him short.

He first played for South Canterbury, aged 18. In 1935 he scored 10 tries in seven games for the province, played in the first of his six interisland matches, and appeared in three All Black trials but did not win selection for the tour of Britain.

Morrison was among the 20 players selected to train at Otaki before the first test against the Springboks in 1937, but fractured his sternum playing for South Canterbury against Mid-Canterbury the Saturday before and had to withdraw.

Morrison finally won All Black selection for the 1938 Australian tour, playing in all three tests in an outstanding back line which included Charlie Saxton, Trevor Berghan, Jack Sullivan and Brushy Mitchell. He also played four times for the South Island before the war. Renowned as a hard, determined runner and fierce tackler, as well as a capable goal-kicker, he stood 6ft tall and weighed 12st 7lb at this stage of his career.

While serving in the war Morrison played for the Middle East Army team and New Zealand Services before returning home to represent Wellington and play in two more interisland fixtures in 1944 and 1945, this time for the North Island. He played some of his best rugby in this 'second half' of his career, exploiting the role of an attacking fullback in a way which delighted crowds. By this time he weighed 14st 6lb and combined the physique of a forward with the pace of a three-quarter. He could exploit an opening with a speedy burst and then use the fend or side step, while his kicking (place, drop or punt) was exceptional. Playing for the North Island in 1944, he kicked six goals out of six.

He joined the Onslow club, then a 2nd-division team, at the urging of his good friend and later inspirational NZRFU chairman Cuth Hogg, and led the team on its meteoric rise to all but take the 1st-division championship. He continued playing club football, intermittently, until 1948, and his last game was for the Centurions in 1950, aged 36.

Morrison gained a place on the NZRFU executive in 1946, the year he retired from representative rugby, aged 32. Within four years he would be convenor of national selectors, probably the youngest in history. Morrison went on to devote many years of service to the game. He served on the NZRFU executive from 1946 to 1968, and as chairman from 1962 to 1968.

. . . .

RUGBY FANS KNEW HOW TO SUFFER IN SILENT ECSTASY

All Black rugby fans are just as fanatical about supporting their team nowadays as they have been in the past. The thousands who fly off on excursions to overseas destinations, or maintain their bleary-eyed vigil in front of pay-TV screens in the middle of the night, bear strong witness to that fact.

But younger followers may have difficulty relating to the level of stoicism in the face of hardship displayed by their predecessors. Occurrences such as are described here were repeated, to a greater or lesser extent, throughout the nation in the winter of 1956, including outside Tom Morrison's central Wellington shop, which sold the tickets for the second test.

Christchurch hosted the third test against the Springboks, with the series all square. It was early August and the city's climate at that time is cold, especially at night, and often wet. The first person to queue for tickets at the Canterbury union booking office in the central city came at 6 a.m. on the Saturday a week before the game, and about 51 hours before the tickets would go on sale on the Monday morning.

By Sunday night the queue stretched a block and a half. The police had been busy trying to prevent traffic jams in the surrounding streets as sightseers drove in to see the queues — on Sunday afternoon. They had tried to move some of the people in the queue because they thought they might endanger themselves or others. Two potential patrons had then sought legal advice — and resumed their original positions on the street after being advised they were not breaking the law.

The queuers favoured shop verandahs for shelter, but also used tents, packing cases and the entrances to doorways as they maintained their vigil. There was impromptu musical entertainment, although card games and reading were the preferred occupations. Those who had kerosene heaters, or Primus stoves for a nosh-up, were enviously noted. One group of students brought their own iron bedstead and mattress. When told to move it off the footpath, they promptly pushed it onto a parking space, inserted three pence in the meter, and cheerily continued their wait.

The Canterbury union surveyed the throng and helpfully issued numbered tickets to their customers to prevent queue jumping.

Many hundreds of people who joined the queues on the Monday were informed by officials that they did not stand a chance of actually getting a ticket. Most philosophically preferred to remain in line — just in case. Most did miss out. The blackmarket and 'scalpers' were very active during the week, inserting classified advertisements in the daily newspapers with offers for tickets at greatly inflated prices. There were plenty of takers.

One cad is reputed to have advertised with an offer of marriage that week. He requested a photo — not of the lady, but of the tickets she had to have for the big game.

In those days the official capacity of Lancaster Park's huge embankment was 34,500 standing spectators. The official attendance on Saturday 18 August was 51,000.

BIOGRAPHICAL DETAILS

Thomas Clarence Morrison

Born: Gisborne, 28 July 1913

Died: Wellington, 31 August 1985

Position: Three-quarter

Represented NZ: 1938
5 matches (3 internationals)

Points for NZ: 14
(2 tries, 2 dropped goals)

Provincial record: South Canterbury 1931–39 (Star club); Wellington 1944 (Trentham Army); 1945–46 (Onslow Club); South Island 1935, 1937–39; NZ Services 1944; North Island 1944–45

NZ selector: Convenor 1950–56

NZ coach: 1950, 1952, 1955–56

Other service: NZRFU executive 1946–68, chairman 1962–68, life member NZRFU 1969; Referees' Appointment Board 1957–59; Appeal Council from 1971

Other: Won Canterbury triple jump title; represented Canterbury at national athletics championships; represented South Canterbury as senior freestyle swimmer and at tennis; played in NZ tennis championships 1936; CBE

Occupation: Managed a menswear shop in Wellington in partnership with fellow All Black and All Black coach Ivan Vodanovich

NEW ZEALAND COACHING RECORD

1950: drew with Lions 9-9; beat Lions 8-0, 6-3, 11-8

1952: lost to Australia 9-14; beat Australia 15-8

1955: beat Australia 16-8, 8-0; lost to Australia 3-8

1956: beat South Africa 10-6; lost to South Africa 3-8; beat South Africa 17-10, 11-5

REFERENCES

1. *Evening Post*.
2. Spiro Zavos, *Winters of Revenge*, Penguin Books, 1997.
3. [page 103]

CHAPTER 16

NEW ZEALAND COACH 1951

LEN CLODE

The right man in the right place at the right time

LEN CLODE WAS CERTAINLY A MAN IN THE RIGHT spot at the right time when he decided to apply for the coach's job of the All Blacks in 1951.

Whereas many outstanding provincial coaches over the decades have sought the job, and not been able to obtain it, Clode was lucky. Though he had captained his club team, Invercargill (Blues), to a championship win, coached the senior team and been a Southland selector when it won the Ranfurly Shield against Otago in the mid-1940s, he had never coached a provincial team. But he was living in Wellington at the time and had been on the NZRFU executive committee since 1949, representing his old province of Southland.

Interviewed in 1997, Clode, almost 89 and the oldest former NZRFU executive member, recalled how he had got the job.

'Of the three New Zealand selectors that year — Merv Corner, Arthur Marslin and Tom Morrison, the convenor — none were available to take the team to Australia,' he said. 'I was coaching at the Khandallah club with Tom Morrison and he said, "Why don't you apply for the job?" So I did and I was appointed.'

Although he knew a number of the Otago players in the team, such as Ray Bell, captain Peter Johnstone, Norm Wilson, Laurie Haig and Kevin Skinner, and the Southlanders Bill McCaw and Eddie Robinson, Clode was only introduced to some of them on assembly. But that didn't make much difference. The 1951 team rates with the best. It maintained an unbeaten record, scored a record number of points for a New Zealand team in Australia, and regained the Bledisloe Cup.

The winning of the series against the British Lions in 1950 had done much to raise the prestige of the All Blacks from the ashes of the previous year. In 1949 New Zealand had lost all its six tests — four in South Africa and two when Australia toured New Zealand at the same time and uplifted the Bledisloe Cup.

It was also a time for rebuilding, with the 1953-54 tour to Britain and France coming into the focus of the national selectors. Many of the older players from the postwar era retired at this point. More than half the test players of 1950 were unavailable to tour in 1951. The loss of Bob Scott (retired, but to make a comeback for the British tour) and the injured Vince Bevan was badly felt. Most of the 15 new All Blacks were backs.

The veteran of the team was Lachie Grant, who had toured Australia with the 1947 All Blacks. Three other forwards, Johnstone, Skinner and Norm Wilson, had, like Grant, toured South Africa.

Those wearing the All Black jersey for the first time were Cockerill, Bell, Ercerg, Jarden, Lynch, Wightman,

THE POWER BEHIND THE ALL BLACKS

FILLING THE BREACH: When the three All Black selectors were all unavailable to coach the 1951 All Blacks on their unbeaten tour of Australia, Len Clode stepped in. These photos of the tourists show the way All Black teams were often depicted pictorially.

Fitzpatrick, Len Wilson, Reid, Steele, Burke, Duff, Hammond, McCaw and Robinson.

The star of the 1951 team was Ron Jarden. He 'was a sensation in every match he played' and ended the tour with 88 points, 45 of which came from tries (three points a try). Already in Australia when the All Blacks arrived, playing for New Zealand Universities and 'wearing a beaten track to Australian goal-lines,' he was regarded by the Australians as the finest winger to have toured that country since World War II.[1]

Clode confirmed this opinion. 'Without doubt. Ron was in outstanding form throughout our tour. I later had him in the Wellington team I helped coach with Clarrie Gibbons.

'After the first two tour matches, I had made up my mind on the choice of players for the first test,' said Clode. 'After the team aquitted itself well in the first test, and being a believer in never changing a winning team if all played to their ability, I then stuck to the same players, where possible, for the remaining two tests.'

Snow Cockerill, Bell, Haig, Tom Lynch and John Tanner, the vice captain, all had fine tours. Of the forwards, McCaw, Grant, Robinson, Tiny White, Skinner and Hec Wilson were the most impressive. The team beat Australia comfortably in all three tests.

'They were a marvellous team all right,' recalled Clode. 'There was absolutely no trouble with any of them on the tour.'

The All Blacks had to play Auckland just six hours after returning to Auckland on their Sunderland flying boat. They had had a busy time shopping and celebrating in Sydney for two days after the third test in Brisbane and had flown into the Waitemata Harbour just before 8.00 a.m. on the day of the match.

'I remember I put the team that was playing to bed

LEN CLODE

as soon as we arrived at our hotel, so that they could catch a few hours of sleep,' recalled Clode. 'My desire was to end a successful tour without a loss, so again the same team which had played the third test played against Auckland.'

Twenty-five thousand people turned up at Eden Park for the game, one that the All Blacks would have preferred not to play. It was a dull occasion, won 9-3 by the national side.

Johnstone, who, as captain, had played a leading part in the tactics and preparation of the touring All Blacks, and Hec Wilson both retired at the end of the 1951 season, while Lynch accepted a league offer in England.

A number of young players from the tour were never called on again to wear the All Black jersey. Of that team only seven players — Jarden, Fitzpatrick, Haig, Tanner, McCaw, Skinner and White — would go on to tour in 1953-54.

Clode became a Wellington selector the year after the tour, serving for three years, and was assistant coach to Gibbons when the team beat Waikato on 1 August 1953, ending the Mooloos' long tenure. Wellington held the log for five matches and then lost it to Canterbury that same season.

Wellington had just changed its selection system from a sole selector to a three-man panel. Clode shared selecting duties with Norm Millard, Gibbons and, later, Jack Taylor, at a time when the capital had a wealth of outstanding talent to choose from.

Clode, who was a company manager in the motor industry, then returned to Southland and bought a farm. He became a Southland selector for another 11 seasons (1957-67). In 1959 Southland thrashed Taranaki 23-6 to uplift the shield and end a long Taranaki tenure, but Southland did not survive its first defence, losing to Auckland 13-9. In 1965 Southland almost took the shield from Taranaki again, drawing 6 all.

Now retired, Len Clode lives in Tauranga.

Len Clode.

BIOGRAPHICAL DETAILS

Leonard Alfred Henry Clode

Born: Colac Bay, Southland, 14 August 1908

Position: Side row or lock

Provincial record: St George Old Boys; Invercargill RFC; Pirates (Dunedin)

Selector/coach: Southland selector 1944-47, 1957-67; Wellington selector 1952-55

NZ coach: 1951

Other service: Invercargill RFC and Southland RFU administrator over many years; NZRFU executive 1949-55

Occupation: Retired; was director of several companies and farmer in Southland

NEW ZEALAND COACHING RECORD

1951: beat Australia 8-0, 17-11, 16-6

REFERENCES
1. Rod Chester and Neville McMillan, *Centenary: 100 Years of All Black Rugby*, Moa, 1984.

CHAPTER 17

NEW ZEALAND COACH 1953-54

ARTHUR MARSLIN

Cavanagh's treatment opened the door

FEW MODERN-DAY RUGBY FANS WOULD remember the name of Arthur Marslin. But the Otago man, who never coached at provincial level, came close to being the first All Black coach to win the grand slam.

One reason Marslin didn't coach a provincial team was because the great Vic Cavanagh jun. always stood in his way. Marslin, a stud-sheep farmer from near Alexandra, could probably not have taken on the Dunedin city-based job anyway, and was content to assist Cavanagh as the country selector in identifying the many magnificent rural players who would make Otago the dominant province of the 1940s.

What is remarkable is that at the exact moment Cavanagh realised he had no future as a coach on the national scene, the quiet, mild-mannered Marslin stepped in to fill the master's shoes — and steadily ascended to the top.

After being dropped from the South Island panel in 1950, the year after the disastrous 4-0 whitewash of the All Blacks in South Africa, Cavanagh quit rugby coaching and submerged his talents, energy and disappointment in business. Marslin took his place on the South Island selection panel and joined the New Zealand selectors that same year. The national selectors retained their places for the next four years. Who is to say that Cavanagh, given his chance even after the NZRFU botch-up of 1949, could not have done the same? It is interesting to surmise how the 1953–54 team would then have fared.

Marslin's team, captained by Bob Stuart, beat three of the home unions, but lost to Wales, 8–13, after giving the Welsh pack one of the worst beatings critics could recall. Its record compared favourably with that of its immediate predecessor, the 1935–36 team. The All Blacks were on tour for five months, playing 36 games, of which they won 30, drew two and lost four. Two of the defeats were in France, at the end of the mammoth tour (the 1935 team did not play there). Critics were to claim that, but for some injudicious selection for key matches, the team could even have matched the 1924 Invincibles, who did not play Scotland.

The coaching of the team was the delegated NZRFU responsibility of Marslin. But he operated in full co-operation with the captain, Stuart. There was a team selection committee of Norman Millard (manager), Marslin, Stuart and Bob Scott, the players' representative.

'Marslin is a very sound judge of players and of the play,' wrote John Hayhurst in his tour book. 'With Bob Stuart appraising individual forward merit on the field, and Arthur watching the whole side from the touchline, they were able to spot defects, however small, and correct them, whenever that was possible, from match to match. These two worked admirably together.'[1]

Stuart was a surprise choice to some as captain — he turned 33 on tour — but he played in all five tests and proved to be an inspirational leader. Terry McLean wrote

ARTHUR MARSLIN

COUNTRY MAN: Arthur Marslin is second from left in this 1926 photo of the Otago Country Districts team. As an Otago selector Marslin would introduce many Country players to the great Vic Cavanagh-coached Otago Ranfurly Shield teams of the 1940s.

that Stuart 'personally revived great captaincy in New Zealand rugby . . . no finer leader of forwards could have been imagined, and if his captaincy tended to emphasise caution at the expense of adventure, the general effect was such that tribute to his ability as a field-captain of the old-fashioned kind could be made with utter sincerity.'[2]

But the long tour was arduous, and no All Black team has attempted to repeat such an itinerary since. It is doubtful today if any coach would accept a tour of that nature. There were matches against the four home unions, plus France, Canada and the United States.

Marslin and his team, the first to embark on a 'grand tour' since World War II, were faced with many problems and challenges that could not be foreseen. France, for instance, had become strong, and would become the first side this century to win a series in South Africa four years later. The games against France were 'tacked on' to the end of the tour, after the exhausting time in Britain. It is to the credit of Marslin that, with a minimum of back-up support, he kept the players fresh and relatively free of injuries.

The All Blacks were also surprised at the consistent strength of British sides. 'The backs, individually, were extremely accomplished,' said Stuart. 'They had speed, they could definitely teach New Zealand a lesson in accuracy of passing, they had a venturesome spirit which was probably superior to the like spirit in the New Zealand game.'

However, the All Blacks invariably dominated possession and thus severely restricted the opportunities of their opponents.

At the conclusion of the tour the *Daily Express* said: 'Let us remember R. C. Stuart's fourth All Blacks as they were in their terrific, awe-inspiring grand finale at Cardiff, handing a terrible thrashing to what on paper looked like the mightiest-ever Barbarians side. Let us remember the noblest of all fullbacks, Scott, giving his last and perhaps finest performance on the playing fields of Britain. Let us remember Stuart leading the All Blacks to their greatest moment. They crushed and brought to an impotent standstill just about the hardest, toughest pack Britain could field. Yes, let us remember the All Blacks as they finished in top gear, tearing the stuffing out of the Barbarians to the last second.'[3]

Marslin, a breeder of Southdown sheep and 53 years old at the time of the tour, had, as a farmer, spent much of his life in his own company. He cultivated a bluff manner to cover up a shyness.

Terry McLean said Marslin 'in the best sense, had simplicity of character, accepting men as he found them and walking his own straight path'.

'Had he appreciated the warmth of feeling towards him among all in the party, he might have conquered the lack of confidence which occasionally beset him. He was as straight as a die.'

But McLean was critical of the training methods used by Marslin and Stuart on the tour.

'The team of the day would take a ball and under the eye of Stuart or Mr Marslin gallop up and down the field, the forwards going over the top of a man trapping the ball to make a heel and the backs spinning away in passing rushes until a whistle or shout or a combination of both compelled them to stop and let the forwards take over,' he wrote.

'The only trouble was that it had a certain unreality, for there was no opponent and all situations were contrived.

'It did not seem to me that the cause of back play was substantially advanced by the training sessions. It also seemed unfortunate that little if any time was devoted to discussions of a technical nature at team-talks.'[4]

However, Ron Jarden, the great All Black winger of the early 1950s and a member of the 1953–54 team, recalled how the senior players had been asked to contribute suggestions as to how to beat the stifling British loose-forward play.

'Each of the players in [manager] Mr Millard's room that day had the opportunity to come forward with his ideas on combating the spoiling rugby which we were meeting in every game,' he wrote. 'Not one of us had any solution to offer other than what was already being tried by the team committee.'[5]

Though critics like McLean thought Marslin a quiet, shy man, that is not how some of the players remember him. Bob Duff, who captained the 1956 All Blacks when they beat the Springboks in a series for the first time and himself became an All Black coach, recalled that Marslin had a caustic wit.

'I had "words" with Arthur once or twice during my playing career,' laughed Duff, who got to know Marslin much better years later, especially through their love of horse racing.

He recalled an incident in 1955, when the All Blacks were struggling with the touring Wallabies. Ian Clarke was the All Black captain that year and asked

LAST GREAT TOUR: Arthur Marslin's 1953-54 All Blacks at London Airport to begin their tour of the British Isles and France. Marslin is in the second row, third from left, with captain Bob Stuart (fourth from left).

ARTHUR MARSLIN

ADVENTURE TOUR: Captain Bob Stuart expected the British opponents of this 1953-54 All Black team to play their rugby like the adventurous 1950 Lions who toured New Zealand. How wrong he was. The team is: Back Row: C. J. Loader, A. E. G. Elsom, J. W. Kelly, W. A. McCaw, K. L. Skinner, R. C. Hemi, J. M. Tanner, I. J. Clarke; Second Row: C. A. Woods, H. L. White, P. F. H. Jones, K. P. Bagley, R. J. O'Dea, D. O. Oliver, G. N. Dalzell, W. H. Clark: Sitting: R. A. Jarden, J. T. Fitzgerald, D. D. Wilson, R. C. Stuart (captain), J. N. Millard (manager), A. E. Marslin (assistant manager), L. S. Haig (vice captain), R. W. H. Scott, B. P. Eastgate, V. D. Bevan; Front Row: B. B. J. Fitzpatrick, R. G. Bowers, K. Davis, M. J. Dixon, W. S. S. Freebairn.

Duff for his opinion on tactics at halftime in the second test in Dunedin. The match then descended into a dull kicking game, and Marslin ticked Duff off afterwards by asking, 'And who asked you to be captain?' Duff's rejoinder was that he'd 'gone out on the field to play rugby, not be a harrier'.

Marslin's playing career with Otago had been short, from 1927 to 1929. However, he was an All Black trialist in 1927 and 1929, and came close to touring with the 1928 All Blacks to South Africa, being named as one of the eight official forward emergencies. He was an All Black reserve on other occasions.

He later turned to refereeing, selecting and coaching, and gave great service to country rugby in Otago. After World War II, as Otago sub-unions selector, he was co-opted to assist the Otago selection committee headed by Vic Cavanagh jun. This was the period of Otago's greatest ascendancy in provincial rugby. Otago and Southland shared the Ranfurly Shield from 1935 to 1950, including during Otago's prime period of 1946–50.

Otago's team had always been based on its great old city clubs, such as Alhambra, Kaikorai, Zingari-Richmond, Pirates, Southern and University. Country players had virtually needed to play city rugby to have any chance of recognition. Now, for the first time, the best players of Otago's vast rural areas were identified, initially by Marslin, and their raw but rugged potential was knocked into shape by Cavanagh. Tough players like Charlie Willocks and Lester Harvey, who farmed the hill country, and miners like the Haig brothers, Jimmy and Laurie, were introduced. In fact, country players formed the core of Otago's teams of the 1940s. Others included Doug Hamilton and Jack McNab in the pack, and Jim Kearney partnering the Haigs in the five-eighths.

Great sacrifices and feats of organisation had to be made to achieve this marriage of town and country. The country players had to be cheaply but comfortably accommodated for their frequent stays in the city, which might take up most of the week. It meant time away from farming duties, which had to be organised through friends or family.

Cavanagh, who should have got the job of coaching the All Blacks in South Africa in 1949, was a South Island selector in 1948–49 but was dropped from the panel in 1950. Marslin replaced him, and also began his term as a New Zealand selector. The entire New Zealand panel were dropped and he was appointed with two other new selectors, Merv Corner and Tom Morrison. The trio were to carry through until 1954.

It was also a time of great change among the players. After the close-run series victory over the 1950 British Lions, many of the test team retired, and in 1951 the selectors began to look towards the next big tour, in 1953–54. Fifteen new All Blacks toured Australia that year, and the team were unbeaten and scored a record number of points under captain Peter Johnstone. Ron Jarden was the sensation of the tour. Then Australia toured New Zealand in 1952 and the series was shared with a test apiece.

Thus was the stage set for the first tour of Britain and France in 18 years. There was tremendous public interest. The selectors worked hard, touring the country for five months before the extensive trials, which lasted three weeks. The whole exercise was completed at tremendous cost, and it was to be the last time the NZRFU would undertake such a system of selection. But the effort made gave an indication of the level of importance placed on the tour.

Marslin retained his place on the national selection panel in 1955 and 1956, with Morrison (as convenor) and Jack Sullivan (who had replaced Corner in 1954). In 1956, facing the Springboks and following a difficult 1955 season against Australia, the selectors decided to co-opt Bob Stuart as forward coach. It is believed Marslin's excellent relationship with Stuart and his high opinion of Stuart's tactical nous formed during their 1953–54 tour partnership was highly influential in this decision.

So Marslin completed seven invaluable years as a New Zealand selector and sometime coach. Over that momentous period, during which a series had never been lost and the All Blacks had emerged as 'world champions', Marslin had assisted convenor Morrison to give the team a sense of confidence and continuity.

There was a recognition among good rugby judges that Marslin had some unique qualities. Some selectors are also competent coaches, but not all coaches are necessarily astute selectors. Unlike Arthur Marslin, they do not always develop that special ability to spot new talent, choose the right player for the right position and match players to a particular game plan.

REFERENCES

1. John Hayhurst, *The Fourth All Blacks 1953–54*, Longmans, 1954.
2. Terry McLean, *Bob Stuart's All Blacks*.
3. *Daily Express*.
4. Terry McLean, *Bob Stuart's All Blacks*.
5. Ron Jarden, *Rugby on Attack*, Whitcombe and Tombs, 1961.

BIOGRAPHICAL DETAILS

Arthur Edward Marslin

Born: Alexandra, 6 March 1901

Died: Alexandra, 1 December 1977

Position: Forward

Provincial record: Otago 1927–29 (Alexandra club); All Black trialist 1927, 1929

Selector/coach: Otago co-opted selector 1949; South Island selector 1950–56

NZ selector: 1950–56

NZ coach: 1953–54

Other services: Otago RFU president, life member

Occupation: Southdown sheep breeder, Springvale Farm, Alexandra; chairman of Otago Central Electricity Board 1963–74

NEW ZEALAND COACHING RECORD

1953–54: lost to Wales 8-13; beat Ireland 14-3; beat England 5-0; beat Scotland 3-0; lost to France 0-3

CHAPTER 18

NEW ZEALAND COACH 1956

BOB STUART

A mastermind of the 'greatest series win in history'

BOB STUART, WORKING CLOSELY WITH TOM Morrison, is credited with masterminding the downfall of the 1956 Springboks, as co-opted forward coach of an All Black team which became the first to win a series over the South Africans.

His appointment, though highly successful, was the last time a coach was co-opted to guide the All Blacks. In the last 40 years the coach has always come from the selection panel, whereas, previously, there had been a number of co-opted coaches, both in partnership and in a sole capacity.

Stuart was All Black captain just two years before the momentous 1956 series and was probably the most influential coach of the 1950s. A surprise choice to some as captain of the 1953-54 team to Britain and France — he turned 33 on tour — Stuart played in all five tests and proved to be an inspirational leader.

Terry McLean wrote that Stuart 'personally revived great captaincy in New Zealand rugby . . . no finer leader of forwards could have been imagined, and if his captaincy tended to emphasise caution at the expense of adventure, the general effect was such that tribute to his ability as a field-captain of the old-fashioned kind could be made with utter sincerity'.[1]

Stuart exerted considerable influence in New Zealand rugby circles from that time on. He was already one of the country's 'most passionate theorists' and quickly became a coach. He assisted the national panel, led by Morrison, to defeat the Springboks and selected and coached Canterbury in 1958-59, a highlight being the defeat of the British Lions, 20-14, in 1959.

Casting his mind back to the 1956 Springbok tour, Stuart said the entire prestige of New Zealand rugby seemed at stake to anyone closely involved in planning the defeat of the tourists.

'I worked closely with Tom Morrison, Jack Sullivan and Arthur Marslin [assistant manager on the 1953-54 All Black tour]. I think they had changed the tactics after the '53-'54 tour, and the forward play had become loose. They thought perhaps I could restore cohesion and drive again, a component of our forward skills that no team in the world could match.

'I knew Tom, Arthur and Jack very well. The only reason I accepted was that I trusted their honour and integrity absolutely and we had always enjoyed a good relationship,' Stuart said. 'I'd have my say in the selections, but the final decisions were made in the other room, or another city. Maybe I didn't agree with every decision, but that was natural and part of the deal. Players' form was erratic early in the season, but by the time of the third test I couldn't fault the chosen teams.

'I used to say to Arthur, who was quite humorous, that

TURNING POINT: Bob Stuart and Tom Morrison coached this All Black team which won the third test against the Springboks at Christchurch, 17-10, after the series had been 1-all. The team went on to take the series 3-1, the first time New Zealand had beaten South Africa in a series. Back Row: Bill Clark, Don McIntosh, 'Tiny' White, Nev MacEwan, Peter Jones, 'Tiny' Hill, John Buxton; Middle Row: Robin Archer, Ross Brown, Kevin Skinner, Don Clarke, Ron Hemi, Bill Gray, Ian Clarke, Pat Walsh; Seated: Ron Jarden, Bob Stuart (coach), Tom Morrison (selector-coach), Bob Duff (captain), Lou Carmine (manager), 'Ponty' Reid, Arthur Marslin (selector), Jack Sullivan (selector), Morrie Dixon. In Front: Dennis Young, Keith Davis.

when we won I couldn't get into the photo, but when we lost I seemed to be the only one around for the interviews.'

Though designated specifically as the forward coach, Stuart's plans depended very much on the entire 15 ensuring the tactics were successful. The decision to have him running the forwards, who were very much the dominant component of a test team in the 1950s, had been discreetly handled. Amazingly, the critics, and therefore the public, were not aware of Stuart's larger role in the great victory. It was only later, as players began to talk of the coach's influence on the series, that the fascinating full story emerged.

It had not all been plain sailing for Stuart in the series, though. In a 1997 interview for this book, he revealed there had been a move to oust him after the loss of the second test.

'Unbeknown to me at the time, there was a special meeting called. My understanding is that Tom Pearce [the Auckland administrator] wanted Johnny Simpson [the former All Black, also of Auckland] in my place. To his credit, Tom Morrison held out for the status quo.'

Independent research by the author has confirmed this revelation.

The selection of Kevin Skinner for the last two tests, and the way he subdued the Springbok props, Jaap Bekker and Chris Koch, by switching positions in the scrum at halftime in the third test at Christchurch, has become part of All Black folklore. But Stuart recalled new details about Skinner's involvement.

'At the start of 1956 Kevin phoned me and wanted to know if I was interested in coaching. He said, "I'm not coming back if they are going to play like the 1955 team."' (Skinner had not been available in 1955.) Once his coaching role had been clarified, Stuart contacted Skinner and said, 'I'll take it on if you come back.'

'Some of the players' form was erratic right through the many trials. Don Clarke did not play well. Peter Jones was overweight and out of condition. So there were players who should have had form, but didn't have at the start. The selectors got the blame for not picking them, but you couldn't,' Stuart said. Skinner was nowhere to be seen.

With a win and then the loss at Wellington in the second test, the All Blacks' leaders realised changes had to be made.

'To be fair to the selectors, they realised that changes were necessary on the form in the first test. Had the series comprised only three tests, such changes would have been made immediately,' said Stuart. 'However, with a four-test series, and the first test won, the selectors were in an invidious position. If they had made changes and lost the second test, they would have been in a no-win situation. In a sense, then, the second test became expendable. It was a gamble, yes, but one which had splendid outcomes.'

All the strands came together for the third and fourth tests, both tactically and individually, in terms of selections and form.

'But, in essence, it was the explosive All Black forward drive, especially at the breakdowns, that gave us that critical edge,' recalled Stuart. 'Tom Morrison agreed with my suggestion to play Bill Clark as our only covering forward and release Peter Jones as a straight-up forward with no cover worries, nothing, just up on that ball. It was the style of play Peter understood and could put into devastating effect with that tremendous strength and explosive speed.

'We gambled that the Springboks would not drive from the lineouts. We took that risk. Bill Clark was a magnificent thinker who had a double cover job to do, which he did brilliantly.'

The All Black tactics worked, and Stuart said much the same was planned for and successfully implemented in the final test.

He did say, though, he hoped New Zealand would never approach another series in the same sort of atmosphere as in 1956.

'I don't think nationalism should come into sport like that. I didn't see that we were going to be any worse off as far as the country was concerned politically, economically, morally or in any other way, if we lost. But we hadn't won a series at home, let alone over there, and opportunities to do so were years apart. Thus, "to win at all costs", if not conducive to the soul of rugby, was understandable. Today, with international matches played so regularly, to a degree there is an erosion of the status of test rugby, with an importance that is more immediate than long term.'

Stuart was only 35 in 1956. A question to be asked of him, therefore, is why did he not seek to continue his career as an All Black selector and coach? Stuart said he was offered a nomination on the South Island panel the year after the Springboks. 'I then asked Neil McPhail [the Canterbury coach] if he was interested. He said he was, so I didn't stand,' he recalled.

McPhail would go on to be a national selector and coach the All Blacks most successfully in the 1960s. Stuart meanwhile took on the Canterbury coaching job, his major achievement being the win over the 1959 Lions. Other priorities then prevented him climbing further. His work as an agricultural economist and the responsibility of a young family were two. Then, late in 1959, he went to Rome to represent New Zealand at the United Nations Food and Cultural Organisation and other trade talks and was away for many months.

He returned to the game over a decade later to serve as an administrator at the highest levels for more than 20 years. He sat on the NZRFU executive from 1974 to 1989, and was the NZRFU delegate on the IRB from 1977 to 1989. Later he was the IRB honorary development officer, from 1990 to 1996. He had an especially close association with the development and organisation of the Rugby World Cup.

Stuart's only matches as an All Black before the 1953-54 tour were when he played No. 8 and flanker in two tests against the 1949 Wallabies. He was vice-captain, and the legendary Johnny Smith captain, of that team, which lost both matches at home to a strong Australian team.

The national selectors were not to call on Stuart again for four years, but it was during that time he got his grounding in captaincy and tactics. Otago had drubbed Canterbury 31-0 in its 1948 Ranfurly Shield challenge, but with its next opportunity, in 1950, Canterbury was to win 8-0. However, it was not without a lot of behind-the-scenes drama.

Stuart wanted to employ tactics that would counter Otago's famous second-phase game. 'In Canterbury at that time the general tactic was to "open her up and let's run it". It was a bit of an airy-fairy style to play Otago, although reasonably successful up to that time.

THE POWER BEHIND THE ALL BLACKS

'The Cavanaghs had developed Otago's game to perfection over many years and the reason was simple — you couldn't do a lot from set play under the rules of the time, except against weak teams. However, control of the secondary phases of a match provided an ideal platform for launching a range of attacks against a more disorganised defence.

'I'd examined Otago's game fairly closely and felt it was vulnerable only by its predictability. But how to capitalise on that identification, against a superbly drilled team, was another matter.'

Stuart contended that the way to counter Otago was not to get sucked into their rucks. If you arrived at the breakdown second, the sensible tactic was to commit the minimum number of forwards and keep the remainder back 'to counter and capitalise on the coming attack via the backs'. If you were first, to the breakdown, it was often possible to continue the drive onwards.

However, Stuart's theories were not accepted by the Canterbury management. 'I was led to believe I would be captain that year, but I forfeited the leadership to Doug Herman because of my opposition to Canterbury's tactics.

'So we staged a revolution. I guess it was one of the first players' revolutions in New Zealand. I had Garth

BOXING DAY: All Black halfback Keith Davis is in danger of getting his ears boxed as a British Combined Services forward, A. Valentine, wraps him up. It is Boxing Day, 1953, during Bob Stuart's All Blacks' long tour. The other All Blacks are Arthur Woods, Peter Eastgate, 'Tiny' White and Peter Jones.

BOB STUART

NOW IS THE HOUR: The long 1953-54 tour is over and opponents link arms after the All Blacks' defeat of the Barbarians, 19-5. From left, Guy Bowers, Bob Stuart, Ivor David (referee), Clem Thomas and Kevin Skinner. Clem has the ball.

Bond, one of the 1946 Kiwis, and Larry Savage, one of the youngest team members, on my side.

'We were placed before the rugby union and explained our position. We said, "If you're going to go with those tactics, we're not keen on going to Dunedin. If we try these other tactics, we've got a chance and we'll support them to the hilt."'

'Anyway, we received a very fair hearing and won our case. To the credit of our coaches, Jack Rankin and George Mortlock, there was agreement to disagree. The outcome was agreement to adopt the fundamentals of the approach I was advocating.

'Jack and George, and Doug, in the ensuing weeks, added the polish and enthusiasm. The shield was won and, in retrospect, this was the catalyst for a great red-and-black resurgence.'

The shield went onto a merry-go-round from this point, until a Stuart-led Canterbury team whipped Wellington in 1953, 24-3, to begin one of the great shield eras, lasting until 1956 (although Stuart retired after the 1953-54 All Black tour).

Regarding Stuart's return to the All Blacks in 1953-54, and his elevation to the leadership after so long away and at the end of a long career, we need to look to others. Kevin Skinner had led the All Blacks in a split series with Australia in 1952. Only 24 and already with a wealth of experience behind him, Skinner was being groomed for a longer-term tenure, but he was never at ease with the captaincy. He admitted as much to Lindsay Knight, adding he felt the front row was not the ideal position to lead from, and found speech-making nerve-racking.[2]

With the emphasis the British placed on formality and black-tie dinners, Skinner began to dread the thought of captaining the All Blacks as the tour loomed, so he was a relieved man when Stuart got the job.

According to Stuart, other factors apart from personal ambition kept him playing when he could easily have retired to concentrate on his career. One was that his younger brother, Kevin, the Canterbury fullback, was well in the running for a tour place, although he eventually missed out to Bob Scott and Jack Kelly as a utility back.

Stuart says he was 'brought down to earth very quickly' at the start of the 1953-54 All Black tour by the opposition's tendency to kill the ball at breakdowns and the toleration by referees of offside play.

'I thought we would encounter teams that would play a style not unlike the 1950 Lions in New Zealand, a brilliant team. In fact it was the opposite. We had difficulty creating clean platforms to get quality ball and it was very difficult to develop back play. We had some excellent backs and two sets of forwards that consistently won 60 or 70 per cent of possession. But you couldn't open it up when you had opposition offside in your back line.'

Stuart said the 36-match grand tour was arduous and that no All Black team had attempted to repeat an itinerary containing five internationals over a five-month period since.

BIOGRAPHICAL DETAILS

Robert Charles Stuart

Born: Dunedin, 28 October 1920

Position: Loose forward

Represented NZ: 1949, 1953-54
27 matches (7 internationals)

Provincial record: Manawatu 1941 (St Patrick's Old Boys); Canterbury 1946-53 (University club) — captain from 1951; South Island 1948-49

Selector/coach: Canterbury 1958-59

NZ coach: 1956 (v. South Africa)

Other service: NZRFU executive 1974-89; NZRFU delegate IRB 1977-89; IRB honorary development officer 1990-1996; close association with development and organisation of the Rugby World Cup

Other: Younger brother Kevin was an All Black fullback in 1955 and represented Canterbury 1949-56, another brother, John, played for Canterbury in 1957. Served with the Royal Navy during World War II in England, the Atlantic and Burma; OBE for services to agriculture and rugby 1974

Occupation: Retired; was an agricultural economist with the Department of Agriculture and the NZ Dairy Board, and first director of the Vocational Training Council

NEW ZEALAND COACHING RECORD

1956: beat South Africa 10-6; lost to South Africa 3-8; beat South Africa 17-10, 11-5

REFERENCES

1. Terry McLean, *Bob Stuart's All Blacks*.
2. Lindsay Knight, *They Led the All Blacks*.

CHAPTER 19

NEW ZEALAND COACH 1957

DICK EVEREST

*Could have bestrode the
All Blacks' 'Everest'*

122

THE POWER BEHIND THE ALL BLACKS

IT WAS DICK EVEREST WHO PROVIDED THE inspiration and the method for the All Blacks and New Zealand provincial sides when the 1956 Springboks, the 'world champions', trotted out for their first tour match.

Perhaps the pity of this outstanding coach's career was that he was not provided the opportunity to cross swords with the Springboks four years later, when they proceeded to win back their crown.

Everest had proven his worth by leading a record-breaking All Black team in Australia in 1957. Before that he had unified a ragtag Waikato union for the first time, introduced the fabulous Cavanagh style to the North Island, taken his province to unimagined riches, and unearthed many future All Blacks. But these qualifications were never to be weighed up against those of possible rivals for the 1960 tour job and put to a vote by the NZRFU.

Before Waikato's triumph over the 1956 Springboks, Everest had been working for some years on this country team and had pulled off some great victories. It was said his players had developed such a level of trust in him 'they would gladly set out to grapple with all the demons in hell itself if he directed them to'.

According to veteran rugby journalist and author Morrie Mackenzie, Everest's and fellow coach Has Catley's battle plan, with the restricted resources of country selectors, 'was of the basic simplicity with which great conflicts are won'.

'Borrowing partly from the terrific, non-stop rucking that Cavanagh brought to a pitch of perfection in the far south, and partly from the Otago maestro's dictum about keeping the ball in play just ahead of the advantage line, Everest had evolved a system of play which, while not pretty to watch, gave him maximum use of his own strength, and covered his weak points... right from the opening whistle, the Waikato pack tore in like a pack of fiends, hitting the first man who took the ball with such an ungodly wallop that they cleaved the Springbok defences asunder like a hard-hit wedge in splitting a log.

'Before the bemused world champions could gather their startled wits, Ponty Reid had worked the blindside as no other half in New Zealand could do since Jimmy Mill,

COACH'S DREAM: Don Clarke played under five All Black coaches in an international career from 1956-64. He made life easier for each of them by winning countless tests with his extraordinary goal-kicking.

and Malcolm McDonald, the Waikato wing, was over for the first try of the tour.'[1]

Waikato continued their barrage, with Don Clarke driving the Boks back with his range of kicks and coolly landing goals when opportunities arose. Hard, low-trajectory throw-ins to the lineout with the greasy ball largely nullified the Springboks' size and leaping skills, while high kicks kept them floundering in the loose. The home side extended its lead to 14–0 by half-time, after a Rex Pickering try and a dropped goal, conversion and penalty from Clarke.

As the Waikato effort flagged, the Springboks fought

TOUR TRIUMPHANT: Dick Everest (front row, third from left) coached this outstanding team on its unbeaten tour of Australia in 1957. The side, which set many records was: Back Row: B. P. J. Molloy, R. H. Brown, W. R. Archer, P. T. Walsh, R. F. McMullen, H. J. Levien; Third Row: D. Young, I. J. Clarke, R. C. Hemi, W. N. Gray. W. J. Whineray, A. J. Soper, T. R. Lineen; Second Row: J. R. Watt, D. N. McIntosh, P. S. Burke, I. N. MacEwan, E. A. R. Pickering, W. D. Gillespie; Front Row: F. S. McAtamney, D. B. Clarke, R. A. Everest (manager), A. R. Reid (captain), W. A. Craddock (manager), S. F. Hill (vice-captain), C. E. Meads; In Front: M. J. Dixon.

DICK EVEREST

back to 14–10 with two converted tries. Continued Mackenzie: 'And then when the Waikato forwards looked completely done, little Ponty Reid rallied them in the most emotional incident of a memorable game.

'Astonished observers gasped as a 9st halfback, a pigmy among Springbok giants, came charging through a gap at the head of a dribbling rush, flanked by Ian Clarke and the equally lion-hearted Jim Graham. There was no holding men who could call on such reserves of will, when their physical powers were almost exhausted. Waikato with their 14 men saw it out. They not only won, but they struck a moral blow for New Zealand, which was both the beginning and the end of the 1956 Springbok tour.'

A quietly spoken, thoughtful man, Everest had played as a five-eighth in the celebrated Waikato–King Country–Thames Valley team which had almost toppled the great 1937 Springboks in their second match. The Boks had won 6–3. It was at that time that Everest gained his keen sense of the disunity of rugby in the area. His team did not even have a coach.

He also played during World War II, representing New Zealand Combined Services at home, until a shoulder injury ended his rugby — and also curtailed a promising cricket career.

After the war Everest joined Dr Jim Mackereth, a Matamata doctor with a highly developed sense for winning rugby, in the selecting and coaching of Waikato teams. When Waikato challenged Otago for the Ranfurly Shield in 1949, losing 5–27, during the southern province's great 1947–50 tenure, Everest witnessed the superb forward techniques and incessant pressure tactics that had been evolved by Vic Cavanagh jun. He became an instant convert to Cavanaghism, and learnt a hard lesson from the defeat. 'You always learn a lot more from your losses than your wins,' he said. 'That loss in the long term was a real help to us.'

He sought Cavanagh out after the challenge. He sought a much longer meeting with the master when Otago toured north the following year and was heartened by Cavanagh's comment after watching Waikato train: 'Yes, I think you can make something of this lot.'

Meanwhile, he had begun team-building. He dropped Bill Conrad, the 1949 All Black halfback. To add to the experience of the legendary Has Catley were newcomers such as Hugh McLaren, George Nola, Jim Graham and 'Ponty' Reid. Then came the Clarke brothers, Ian and Don.

Everest's team took the Ranfurly Shield from North Auckland in 1951, Don Clarke, then just 17, kicking Waikato's points. Everest would recall that on the morning of the match in Whangarei it began to rain, which suited Waikato. McLaren, the captain and a humorist, went round the team's hotel singing 'Oh What a Beautiful Morning'.

Thus began a tenure through to 1953 — interrupted when Auckland won the shield in the third challenge of 1952 and lost it back to Waikato a fortnight later — when Wellington took the log. Many critics were surprised, because Waikato had previously been looked upon as a loosely organised province of players from isolated country subunions.

Waikato's climb under Everest continued, despite the loss of the shield. Later in 1953 it beat the South Island's big three of Southland, Otago and Canterbury. In 1954, it drew with Canterbury in a shield challenge. But its greatest triumph, the ambush of the hapless South Africans, was still to come.

It is amazing that Everest, with Waikato's meagre resources and unsophisticated, semi-rural approach to the game, could muster a team and an approach that would in some ways anticipate today's All Black and Waikato methods. He always laid down a seasonal and match-by-match plan. Every player knew the job expected of him. Player participation was strongly encouraged in pre- and postgame meetings, even from the reserves. The team had a doctor and a physiotherapist on call and did calisthenics (stretching exercises) before all training and games.

He also believed in utilising his limited resources as best as possible. 'If you've got a plough horse, you don't take it to the Ellerslie races. Similarly, if you had a crack racehorse you wouldn't make it pull a plough,' he said.

Everest was a combination of affable personality and acute rugby brain. A planner supreme and a master psychologist, he may have been ahead of his time. Some credited him with genius, even clairvoyant powers. An illustration fondly recalled was his moving the young Rex Pickering, later to become an All Black flanker, out to the wing during a Waikato trial before the Springbok game. Disgruntled observers thought it a waste of time and talent. But during the big match, with replacements for injured not allowed under international rules, Pickering indeed had to go to the wing, where he scored one of Waikato's two tries. But, Everest would suggest the more likely role of luck.

Everest's short but outstanding career as All Black coach took place when he guided the team on its 1957 tour of Australia. The team rated as one of the best international sides ever to visit Australia. It set all sorts of records, including a total of 463 points in 13 official games.

THE POWER BEHIND THE ALL BLACKS

Don Clarke, with 163 points, eclipsed Ron Jarden's record for a New Zealand player in Australia. Russell Watt, with 17 tries, equalled Opai Asher's record from the 1903 tour. Other records set were: most points in a match (86); most tries on tour (92); most conversions on tour (50); most tries by an individual in one match (seven, by Watt); and most conversions by an individual in one match (13, by Clarke).

The All Blacks won the first test 25–11 and the second 22–9. In the opening test in Sydney, two forwards who were to play hugely influential roles during the next decade of All Black rugby, Wilson Whineray and Colin Meads, made their test-match debuts. So did the Auckland midfield backs Terry Lineen and Frank McMullen.

Pat Walsh, who had played at second five-eighth, fullback and centre for the All Blacks since 1955, had a fine game on the wing. He joined the back line from the blind-side on two occasions that led to tries being scored, and scored another himself.

Critics were unanimous in their praise of the New Zealand win, Whineray earning special praise.

Everest decided on an unchanged team for the second and last test, in Brisbane, while the Wallabies made five changes. As in the first test, the All Blacks scored four tries to one.

An especially memorable highlight of the match was a try by Colin Meads, deputising on the wing, who received the ball on the end of a passing rush and dived over for the first of the seven tries he would score in a long international career.

Then, midway through the second half, Don Clarke took a fair catch near the Australian 25-yard line. He moved the mark back to about 45 yards from the posts to improve the angle, and with his brother Ian holding the ball, kicked the first goal from a mark for New Zealand since Mark Nicholls had landed one against the 1930 British Lions at Lancaster Park.

Whineray, who would become captain the following year, remembers Everest's style being consultative. 'We would go back to the team's hotel after the game, and before attending the official function that evening. There Dick Everest would go over the game with us. He did it in a very constructive way, which was very helpful to the young players in the side like myself. I thought he was a very good coach.'

Everest was keen to coach the 1960 team in South Africa. Jack Sullivan and he were both nominated for the position, and the pair discussed the issue. Everest decided Sullivan, because he was chairman of the selection panel, had prior right, so withdrew his nomination. That was the way All Black appointments were usually decided in those days.

We can only wonder how Everest would have fared in South Africa. As a hands-on coach with a long, proud and very recent provincial coaching record who had also shown he could handle the international level on tour with aplomb, Everest may have done a better job than Sullivan.

People hark back to the Alex McDonald-Vic Cavanagh coaching controversy of 1949. But perhaps the Everest-or-Sullivan debate provides an equally tantalising question. The challenge of a South African series, where success had already eluded New Zealand for more than 30 years by 1960, would continue to elude its teams for yet another 36 years. During Dick's time, it was indeed to remain New Zealand rugby's Everest.

REFERENCES
1. Morrie Mackenzie, *All Blacks in Chains*.

BIOGRAPHICAL DETAILS

Richard Alan Everest

Born: Hamilton, 12 May 1915

Died: Hamilton, 28 February 1994

Position: Midfield back

Provincial record: Waikato 1937–38, 1940–41, 1944: Waikato–King Country–Thames Valley v. South Africa 1937; North Island Combined Services 1944

Selector/coach: Frankton club coach 1947; Waikato selector/coach 1950–56; North Island selector 1957–60

NZ selector: 1957–60

NZ coach: 1957

Other: His brothers also represented Waikato: E.W. Everest 1929. J.K. Everest 1939–40

Occupation: Company representative

NEW ZEALAND COACHING RECORD

1957: beat Australia 25–11, 22–9

CHAPTER 20

NEW ZEALAND COACH 1958-60

JACK SULLIVAN

Craven's revenge awaited Sullivan and Whineray

JACK SULLIVAN WAS LINKED WITH SOUTH Africa over six decades — as a player, selector, coach and administrator.

Highlights of his long rugby career were his superb tries in the All Blacks' test efforts against the great 1937 Springboks, being one of the victorious All Black selection panel which plotted the downfall of the 1956 Springboks, coaching the All Blacks in South Africa in 1960, and leading an administrative resurgence of the game.

Sullivan had served on the New Zealand selection panel for seven years by 1960. When Tom Morrison, the convenor until 1956, retired, Dick Everest coached the All Blacks in Australia in 1957. Then Sullivan took over.

His record during 1958–60 was 11 tests played, for six wins, four losses and a draw. His greatest success was the hard-fought series win over the 1959 British Lions, while the series loss in South Africa, as we shall see, came down to one poor refereeing decision in the fourth test, when the series was tied up one win each and one draw.

The record of the 1960 All Blacks was subjected to the usual post mortems suffered by touring teams. They were compared with their predecessors of 1928 and 1949.

In the four-test series, South Africa won the rubber with an 8-3 victory in the final test at Port Elizabeth. The first had been won 13-0 in the altitude of Johannesburg by the host side; the second, down at sea level in Cape Town, by the All Blacks, 11-3; the third, on the low veldt at Bloemfontein, had been drawn, 11-all.

That is the bare-bones summary of a hard-fought series which had its exhilarating moments in spite of the dour nature of the battles. Though they had dominated the second half of the second test, for instance, the All Blacks only managed to score a try (by Colin Meads) and a conversion and a dropped goal (by Don Clarke), all in sensational circumstances in the dying minutes.

In the third test, the Boks were up 11-3 with six minutes remaining. Clarke then placed a 60-yard penalty kick.

Needing five points to save the match, the All Blacks threw everything into attack. Whineray opted for a tap kick from a penalty. With 90 seconds remaining, the All Blacks won a ruck 15 yards inside the South African half and Briscoe threw a desperate, hurried pass along the ground past Nesbit, where it was picked up by Lineen, who quickly fed Laidlaw. The centre ran through a gap before putting a kick towards the left-hand corner, where Frank McMullen, sprinting past Antelme, gathered a favourable bounce and scored five yards in from the corner.

Clarke, faced with an acute angle and a slight head wind, showed incredible poise to steer the conversion between the posts to draw the game.

The series might have been squared if an

THE POWER BEHIND THE ALL BLACKS

undoubtedly fair try had been allowed in the fourth test. All Black centre McMullen broke into the clear, only to be ankle-tapped just short of the Springboks' line. He was not held in the tackle and, regaining his feet, made the try line. But referee Burmeister ruled no try and penalised McMullen for tackled ball.

Nevertheless, the Springboks probably deserved the series. They scored five tries to two, and 35 points to 25 overall. Though the rugby was seldom memorable, the 300,000 spectators were thrilled by the intensity and emotionalism of the struggles.

The 'predator' of 1949, Hennie Muller, returned to haunt the 1960 All Blacks. Not only was he the Springbok coach, but his playing methods influenced the selections and tactics the All Blacks adopted. The backs stood up flat and, therefore, were seldom willing or able to launch a full-blooded passing movement.

The fear of being penalised out of the game, as in 1949, produced a team policy of promptly kicking their way out of their own half — an almost invariable tactic, which meant Briscoe passed back to Clarke to kick for touch in game after game.

The 1960 All Blacks' manager, Tom Pearce, said after the tour that the team had been chosen with the 1949 disasters well in mind. 'We had devoted the intervening 11 years to building up our forward strength to what was

TALENT TO BURN: Jack Sullivan had much fabulous talent to work with – as this second test All Black team of the 1959 series shows. The team is: Back Row: Adrian Clarke, Dick Conway, Des Webb, 'Tuppy' Diack, Ron Hemi, Ralph Caulton, Frank McMullen; Second Row: Dick Everest (selector), Kel Tremain, Stan ('Tiny') Hill, Nev MacEwan, Colin Meads, Don Clarke, Terry Lineen, Bill Gillespie; Sitting: Ron King (selector), John McCullough, Wilson Whineray (captain), Tom Pearce (manager), Kevin Briscoe, Ian Clarke, Jack Sullivan (selector). In front: Roger Urbahn.

HAPPY HOOKERS: All Black captain Wilson Whineray relieves the pressure as opposition hookers Ron Hemi and Ronnie Dawson 'discuss' tactics during the first test of the 1959 British Lions tour. Nev MacEwan (headgear) watches progress. Don Clarke's six penalties gave New Zealand a 18-17 win.

probably the most powerful array of forwards to represent New Zealand over the decade.

'We left for South Africa with the firm intention of developing back play if the conditions made this possible.

'In no circumstances were we prepared to sacrifice forward strength, because a team without strong forward play is like a house with termites in the foundations. It looks good until one day it falls down.'[1]

So the tourists played a winning, no-risk style that disappointed the critics. It was known as 10-man rugby.

Sullivan was not the sole architect of this general game plan. The tour committee consisted of Pearce, Sullivan, captain Wilson Whineray and vice-captain Mick Bremner, and they were responsible for broad policy. But it was Sullivan who adhered strongly to the philosophy of forward domination — in spite of strong dissension among some of the All Blacks after the first-test whitewashing.

The playing style caused adverse comment among the South African hosts. This was ironical considering the Springboks' one-dimensional winning tactics on the two previous All Black tours. But that did not prevent Louis Babrow, an opponent of Sullivan from the great 1937 Springbok team in New Zealand and in the Western Desert, from consenting to having an open letter published under his name in the *Cape Times*. It began, 'Please Jack, do something about this pathetic, unattractive All Blacks' rugby . . . which is completely without precedent,' and continued in like vein, lambasting the All Blacks.

A little-known fact about the series is that Sullivan's task was not helped when Pearce suffered a breakdown during the tour, meaning Sullivan, officially the assistant manager, had to take on temporary extra duties.

The tour's outstanding player was Don Clarke, at the peak of his powers. He contributed a third of the team's points, scoring a massive 175. Besides his match-winning kicking, his general play was consistently outstanding.

'Never so great a fullback, as such, as Bob Scott and

George Nepia, he was superior to both as a matchwinner; it may be that he is the greatest matchwinner in the history of the game,' wrote McLean at the time.[2]

Colin Meads had a fine tour and was the best of the forwards. He was well supported by Kel Tremain, who developed well on tour, and Dennis Young, Peter Jones, John Graham and Red Conway. In the backs, Kevin Briscoe, Kevin Laidlaw, Russell Watt and Frank McMullen were the most consistent.

The Springboks had many mighty players also. Martin Pelser, the one-eyed flanker, was the best loose forward in the series, in either team. Hugo van Zyl, another flanker, was not far behind. Johan Claassen, the lock, was superb. Piet du Toit was the scrum scourge of the All Blacks and improved his tight and line-out support as the series developed. The Boks' halfback pairing, Dick Lockyear and Keith Oxlee, was superior to New Zealand's combinations, while further out Hennie van Zyl was a menace on the wing.

The 1960 All Blacks were the first New Zealand team to use air travel to move from game to game throughout South Africa, South-West Africa and the Rhodesias.

'The most boring journey on the whole tour was a 220-mile rail journey taking 22 hours,' said Pearce. 'Consequently, we felt keenly for previous New Zealand teams that had traversed this vast continent by train and bus.'[4]

The tour also served to remove the bitterness that had developed following the 1949 series (won by South Africa 4–nil) and the 1956 series (won by New Zealand 3-1) especially over refereeing. Pearce, a strong but 'magnanimous, humorous and genuine' character, to quote McLean, was to play a pivotal role in the vastly improved relations.

Sullivan had become chairman of selectors in 1957, and took over almost complete control of coaching the All Blacks.

'It was strange to see his fellow selectors [Dick Everest and Ron King], both with ample experience in provincial coaching, plodding the touchline at training runs while Mr Sullivan or a deputy named from among the players took charge of activities,' recalled Terry McLean.[3]

Sullivan's era with the All Blacks had begun with a fanfare when his team demolished the touring Wallabies 25-3 at Athletic Park in 1958. Whineray, captaining New Zealand for the first time, scored two of the seven tries. But the Australians shocked an overconfident All Black team at Christchurch, winning 6-3. With the injured Clarke brothers, Ian and Don, restored to the team, the third test in Auckland was won 17-8, though the tries were one apiece.

The 1959 British Lions proved a popular team. They had a host of fast and adventurous backs prepared to attack from anywhere, and a forward pack which was to prove it could hold its own. But they did have defensive weaknesses and showed a penchant for foolish infringements, which All Black fullback Don Clarke often punished heavily.

Sullivan's team took the evenly contested series 3-1. A remarkable feature of the first test, won 18-17 at Carisbrook, was Clarke's six penalties, against the Lions' four tries. Clarke saved the second test at Athletic Park with a famous try in the last minute of play, but the All Blacks had outscored the Lions three tries to one. New Zealand pummelled the Lions 22-8 at Lancaster Park, scoring four tries to one. But the Lions finally got home in the fourth test at Auckland, deservedly winning 9-6, three tries to two penalties.

'Sullivan's strong point was an ability to select the right players', Whineray notes. 'On tour, I was involved, with some input in the selections. But it was Jack who had to wear these decisions in the end and he was not afraid to make hard decisions. I can remember conversations with him when I thought a particular player might be more suited and he would eventually select another. There were times when I could come off the field and think, "Well, Jack was right about that one."'

Sullivan is remembered as a dour character in public, but Whineray said this was probably a front to hide a basic shyness in the man. As for his lukewarm relationship with the media this was partially caused by the pressures of touring, Whineray contends today. 'He often didn't have the time to devote to those jobs. Apart from him and the manager, Tom Pearce, we had no support team. Injuries meant days filled with getting players into taxis to doctors and physios, on top of all the travel and the 32 matches of that tour.'

Sullivan had played nine games for the All Blacks, including six tests, from 1936 to 1938, and would undoubtedly have built a more impressive record had not World War II ended his serious sporting career. He was a certainty for the projected 1940 All Black tour of South Africa.

Sullivan was a fast and very powerful three-quarter, with the ability to make play for his wings. He was renowned as an intensely competitive player, with a deadly tackle. He first played senior rugby at 16 and was an All Black by 21. Winston McCarthy, commentator and author, would later state Sullivan was the 'player of his decade'.

With Taranaki he made a sensational debut against

JACK SULLIVAN

Wanganui as a teenager, scoring four tries. The next year he scored nine tries in 10 games.

In 1936, he made the first of four appearances for the North Island, was a test reserve against Australia and gained his All Black jersey in a match against South Canterbury.

Against the 1937 Springboks, Sullivan played two matches at centre and the third on the wing. After the All Blacks won the opening test, it was Sullivan who kept New Zealand in the second test in Christchurch, scoring two superb tries, New Zealand's only points in the 6-13 loss.

His second try was sensational. The Springboks were attacking the All Blacks' line when a pass from Babrow to Harris was intercepted by Sullivan, who took the ball almost out of Babrow's hands.

'In a flash Sullivan was in the clear but Williams turned to chase him. As the flying Springbok wing drew level with him, Sullivan kicked over the head of Brand, the fullback . . . Running shoulder to shoulder, Sullivan and Williams chased the ball with the All Black always getting to it just a little in front and kicking it on as the crowd went wild. With inches to spare Sullivan dived on the ball to score one of the most thrilling tries in test match history.'[5]

Sullivan's All Black career ended with the unbeaten 1938 tour of Australia, where he played in all three tests, at second five-eighths in two and centre in the other, scoring one try in the series. In a first-class career of 60 matches, his strike rate was exceptional for he managed a total of 50 tries, six for the All Blacks.

During the war Sullivan led a Second New Zealand Division team to victory over a South African Army team in Baggush, Egypt. It was the greatest battle, sans firearms, of the war. The win was celebrated by Sullivan and General Freyberg with a bottle of beer, said to be the only one in the entire desert. There were no glasses. First it was Tiny Freyberg's turn, then Jack's, then the general's again, then the corporal's . . . until, with the final swig, the beer was gone.[6]

A serious shrapnel wound in 1942 ended Sullivan's rugby career.

Sullivan was Taranaki's selector-coach from 1947 to 1952 and then served on the North Island and national selection panels from 1952 to 1960. He coached the 1958 New Zealand under-23 team on their undefeated tour of Japan and Hong Kong. He was a member of the NZRFU executive committee from 1962 to 1965 and 1967 to 1977.

Between 1969 and 1977, as chairman of the union, Sullivan was the target of anti-apartheid demonstrators during a period when the All Blacks toured South Africa twice and a tour of New Zealand by South Africa was cancelled. He became famous as the 'no comment' leader because of his refusal to become involved in public debate on the issue.

As the anti-apartheid movement became more aggressive. Sullivan and his family were subjected to abusive, threatening and indecent telephone calls, but he refused to take an unlisted number. Instead, he carried on in the face of threats of assassination, eight in all, sent by post by a person who called himself the Black Knight and who said he would spill Sullivan's 'guts all over his front doorstep'.

People who knew Sullivan well said he would have preferred to speak out on the issue but the executive he served wished to remain silent. He never wavered from his view that sport and politics should remain separate, while the bridge-building argument of rugby administrators concerning apartheid was strongly and sincerely felt.

'My conscience is clear,' said Sullivan. 'I am sure history will prove that the decisions of the union to keep up associations in sports with other countries, notably South Africa, were 100 per cent right.'

Referring to the selective morality of tour opponents, Sullivan added that the union had not sent the All Blacks to Romania because it believed in communism, or to Argentina because it believed in a fascist, military dictatorship. It had not sent the All Blacks twice into Northern Ireland because it believed in the holocaust that was going on there.[7]

Sullivan made a major contribution to New Zealand rugby when the NZRFU, under his leadership, became a truly democratic organisation. He was noted by all for his knowledge and fairness. Those close to the top of New Zealand rugby spoke of him with reverence.

Sullivan's era as NZRFU chairman saw tremendous progress. This included the introduction of Junior All Black and Colt tours; age-group tournaments and interisland matches; the national and regional coaching schemes and promotions of schools for promising players; the first contact with New Zealand rugby and coaching by developing rugby nations such as Argentina, Uruguay and Romania; club rugby's peak membership of 600,000 (the majority nonplaying); and the start of the National Provincial Championship. Internal All Black tours were less enduring, though they served their purpose, while the All Blacks toured South Africa with players of non-European descent for the first time.

Sullivan would say, upon retirement, that he had found all aspects of his association with the game appealing. 'The

CLOSE-RUN THING: Jack Sullivan's All Blacks struggled against the classy Lions of 1959. (Above) All Black second five-eighth John McCullough punts ahead in the second test at Athletic Park, Wellington. Ralph Caulton scored twice in his debut match in this test, but it took Don Clarke's try (below) and conversion with one minute to play to rescue the match, 11-8.

fellowship of players and administrators endeavouring to do something for the game' had pleased him.

Sullivan's sense of humour is not legendary, and was known only to family, friends and those he trusted. Terry McLean told a story illustrating his sense of both occasion and humour.

On the night before the All Blacks left for their tour of South Africa in 1970, NZRFU officials Sullivan, Ces Blazey and Bert Rippin were bidden to attend the office of Acting Prime Minister John Marshall. Marshall carefully explained that in the political climate of the time, his Government believed it would be imprudent for the All Blacks to fulfil their engagements against Rhodesia and South-West Africa.

'If you are prepared, sir,' said Sullivan, 'to announce to the New Zealand public that you as a Government wish us not to play the All Blacks in those games, naturally we will cancel them immediately.'

Marshall demurred. He did not, he conveyed, wish to put the matter so bluntly. It would be more suitable if the Rugby Union, of its own initiative, announced that, as a gesture to world opinion, it had decided to so act. Discussion ranged here and there. Rippin, the union treasurer, would tell McLean how he had been fascinated by the dexterous swordplay of the principals, Marshall and Sullivan.

Sullivan put his point again. Marshall hesitated. He knew, as did Robert Muldoon a decade later, that direct political interference would not be tolerated by the New Zealand voting public. He said he was not prepared to speak to the public. Sullivan smartly took his cue to 'exit at left'.

Outside the prime ministerial office he told his two compatriots: 'The first lesson you learn as a salesman is this — when you have made the sale, get out!'[8]

Sullivan's fistic ability is even less well known, but in researching this book the author was made aware of at least two pugilistic incidents involving the NZRFU chairman. 'He was a tough bastard,' said one informant about the scuffle Sullivan had with longtime NZRFU executive committee member Morrie Ingpen, when Ingpen, a former member of the 1946 Kiwi team, was knocked down. On another occasion, an incumbent All Black declined to accept an invitation by Sullivan, by then in his sixties, to 'come outside' after a particularly heated argument.

Sullivan's business career, after his playing days were over but running parallel with his enormous workload in national rugby coaching and administration, is probably worthy of a book on its own — not of the 'think and grow rich' type, but the 'how to succeed by perseverance' variety. Several publishers did enquire of Sullivan, then approaching retirement, if they could handle his autobiography. But it would not have suited his modest character to have complied.

Sullivan's formal education was limited. Born in Tahora in 1915, the fourth of six children, he received his only schooling at remote Tangarakau School. His father was a tunneller working on the building of the new Ohura–Stratford railway line. The family were of very modest means, and, being the height of the Depression, young Jack never wore shoes until in his teens. He started working life, after standard VI, in a grocer's shop, then laboured in a New Plymouth timber merchant's yard, and then drove a petrol tanker for Caltex (it was called Texaco then) before and after the war.

It was about the time of his marriage to Mary in 1947 that he switched from tanker driving to selling the product. After a few years, in the early 1950s, he first encountered Caltex's managing director Horace Hansen, himself a great sports lover, who took a shine to the shy and serious young man from the Taranaki hills. Hansen would later initiate the move which would start Sullivan on the path to the peak of the company, and national rugby administration, by appointing him assistant branch manager in Wellington.

In 1961 Sullivan was appointed national sales manager of Caltex. In the same year the company began its promotion of Boron, an improved petrol brand. The promotion was sensationally successful. It was talked about all over the world as one of the great selling campaigns.

'We had a great product,' said Sullivan years later. 'But timing and promotion assisted. I don't know whether it was because of this that I started to move upwards.'[9]

In 1966 he spent a year at head office in New York. When he succeeded Hansen as Caltex's managing director the next year, it is said that directors of competing companies were incredulous. Many unkind remarks were made of him. Sullivan heard these things and, characteristically, was silent. But his 13 years as head of the company would prove immensely successful.

'If my competitors want to think that that has been a failure, I suggest they count their own share of the market,' he commented when he retired from the firm. 'I don't mind critics. I can't wear fools. Just let it be said the company has had its greatest success over those years.'[10]

Sullivan seldom spoke publicly of his charity work, which he continued after his retirement. He was president of the Paraplegics and Disabled Persons' Association and chairman of the trust set up by the Society for the Intellectually Handicapped.

He would leave us all something to think about when he said: 'Paraplegics get more fun out of life than the physically able. It's an education, to see them dance in their wheelchairs and see how much more full of life they are than we who are apparently physically fit.'[11]

Terry McLean, who had been, at times, critical of his methods as All Black coach, interviewed Sullivan on his retirement in 1980. He travelled to Wellington to do so. With the interview completed, Sullivan apologised for not personally being able to take McLean to the airport. He explained it was his carless day, it being a time of petrol shortages. The irony was not lost on McLean, who wrote, 'He did not believe that he, despite his senior place in an oil company, was entitled to an exemption sticker.'

Buffeted by tackles, buffeted by war wounds which ended his rugby career, so violently buffeted by controversy as to have cause to fear, so it seemed, for his life, Jack Sullivan had the qualities of fortitude, dedication, determination and, not least, of humour, concluded McLean.[12]

BIOGRAPHICAL DETAILS

John Lorraine Sullivan

Born: Tahora, 30 March 1915

Died: 9 July 1990

Position: Centre three-quarter

Represented NZ: 1936–38
9 matches (6 internationals)

Points for NZ:

Provincial record: Taranaki 1934–40 (Tukapa club); North Island 1936–39

Selector/coach: Taranaki selector-coach 1947–52; North Island selector 1952–59; NZ Juniors coach, Japan, 1958

NZ selector: 1954–60

NZ coach: 1958–60

Other service: NZRFU executive 1962–65, 1967–68, chairman 1969–77, life member 1977; represented NZ on IRB

Other: Brothers Colin and George also played for Taranaki (also three-quarters), and George refereed NZ v. Lions fourth test 1950; Taranaki 100-yards champion 1934–35; president, then patron, NZ Paraplegic and Physically Handicapped Federation; chairman, IHC trusteeship; Queen's Jubilee Medal 1977; CBE 1978

Occupation: Labourer; driver, Caltex Oil Co.; managing director, Caltex Oil Co.

NEW ZEALAND COACHING RECORD

1958: beat Australia 25-3; lost to Australia 3-6; beat Australia 17-8

1959: beat Lions 18-17, 11-8, 22-8; lost to Lions 6-9

1960: lost to South Africa 0-13; beat South Africa 11-3; drew with South Africa 11-11; lost to South Africa 3-8

REFERENCES

1. Terry McLean, *Beaten by the Boks*, Reed, 1960.
2. *Beaten by the Boks*.
3. *Beaten by the Boks*.
4. *Beaten by the Boks*.
5. R.H. Chester and N.A.C. McMillan, *Men in Black*, Moa, 1978.
6. Paul Donoghue, *Rugby Versus Rommel*.
7. Terry McLean, *New Zealand Herald*.
8. Terry McLean, *New Zealand Herald*.
9. Terry McLean, *New Zealand Herald*.
10. Terry McLean, *New Zealand Herald*.
11. Terry McLean, *New Zealand Herald*.
12. Terry McLean, *New Zealand Herald*.

CHAPTER 21

NEW ZEALAND COACH 1962

RON BUSH

Helped throw off chains of 1950s

RON BUSH'S 1962 ALL BLACK TEAM WAS ONE OF the most experienced and successful New Zealand teams to tour overseas.

Bush, a New Zealand selector from 1961 to 1964, served on a three-man panel with Neil McPhail and Jack Finlay until 1963, when the panel was expanded. McPhail, the selection convenor, coached the All Blacks through this period with great success. But in the early part of 1962 he was unavailable to take the All Blacks to Australia, and Bush did the job. McPhail was back in the hot seat after the tour though, when he coached the All Blacks to two victories over the Wallabies in New Zealand.

Although Bush's side lost its second match of the tour 11-12 to New South Wales, the early reversal galvanised the tourists. It won its other nine matches, scoring 426 points with only 49 against and breaking numerous records.

When the opposition allowed, the All Blacks played an attractive game of rugby, scoring 91 tries in 10 games. Wilson Whineray and Des Connor, captain and vice-captain, provided outstanding leadership. Every player in the party, except Whineray, scored points.

There were seven new All Blacks — Kevin Barry, John Creighton, Jules Le Lievre, Waka Nathan, Bruce Watt, Ray Moreton and the New Zealand sprint champion, Rod Heeps. Of the others, eight had toured Australia in 1957 and 11 had been to South Africa in 1960. The old hands in the forwards were Ian Clarke, the Meads brothers, Graham, MacEwan, Tremain, Whineray and Young, while Don Clarke, Ross Brown, Briscoe and Connor were in the backs.

The All Blacks won the first test in Brisbane 20-6, with an efficient rather than inspiring performance, but the second test in Sydney, won 14-5, was a harder-fought encounter. After the Wallabies led early with a Dick Thornett try, Don Clarke swung the game New Zealand's way with a massive 72-yard penalty kick to make the score 6-5 at the interval. Nathan and Russell Watt scored tries in the second half.

The match was a triumph for Connor, who had been an Australian test halfback before moving to New Zealand. He outplayed Ken Catchpole, a player most Australian observers regarded as his superior.

A match against Northern New South Wales yielded a score of 103-0. It was a world record by a touring team, while the eight tries scored by Heeps set a record for an All Black in one game. It was the first time a century had been scored in a first-class rugby match and the first time the All Blacks had scored 20 tries in a game (they actually scored 22). The only All Blacks not to score in the game were Stan Meads and Neil Wolfe.

'They were a very good team and I thoroughly enjoyed the tour,' recalled Bush years later. 'I remember Don Clarke missing a few goals in the first game and getting behind him at practice and helping him straighten out his run. With

THE POWER BEHIND THE ALL BLACKS

EARLY SHOCKER: Ron Bush's 1962 All Blacks swept through a triumphant Australian tour after an early shock 11-12 loss to New South Wales. Here Dennis Young and Colin Meads forage for loose ball in the first test, as Wallaby captain John Thornett (headgear) turns to cover.

the round-the-corner kicking of the more modern game, you wouldn't do it like that. Anyhow, he didn't fail for long.'

Bush spoke fondly of some of the players he had in the team. Wilson Whineray, as captain, 'was the ideal leader. He never pushed his authority, it was just natural — he just said what he wanted to be done and it would be done'.

'We tried to get the loose forwards to meld in more between the forwards and backs — to be the linkage on both attack and defence,' said Bush.

Bush became a casualty of the New Zealand rugby shake-up of 1964. Five national selectors were appointed that year — McPhail, Les George, Fred Allen, Les Christian and Bush. But after the home-series win against Australia, when the third and final test was decisively lost 5-20, the panel was reduced to three again. Bush and Christian lost their places. It was said a five-man panel was too unwieldy.

'He was a happy man, always ready with a joke,' said Whineray, remembering the meetings he had attended in Bush's small Auckland office. 'But for all his gregariousness, he also knew how to lift a team and devise tactics to stretch the strongest opponents. For all his smiles, who's to say his message wasn't equally as valuable as that of the stern-faced coach?'

Whineray's first experience of Bush's methods had come in his first year of big rugby. Only 20, he'd been put into the 1956 Canterbury team by its then coach, Neil McPhail. He'd already had a win over the touring Springboks, with Canterbury, when chosen for the New Zealand Universities team.

'We weren't given a bolter's show that day,' said Whineray. 'We were just a bunch of boys really, though we did have lots of talented young players, especially in the back line. Ron had a big hand in that team and the victory that day.' The students won 22-15.

Standing more than 6ft tall and weighing 14st 6lb, Bush had been a versatile player who appeared at fullback, in the three-quarter line, occasionally at five-eighths, and, for Auckland and the North Island in 1934, as a loose forward.

His only match for New Zealand came in 1931, when he played fullback at Eden Park in the single test against Australia, kicking four penalty goals and a conversion in the 20-13 victory. Only 15,000 spectators watched the game, probably because the Wallabies had had such a poor record in the lead-up matches. But, as has been so common with Australian touring teams, the Wallabies turned on a superb performance. They outscored the All Blacks by three tries to two and it was only the goal-kicking of Bush which saved the day.

'I kicked a few goals. They went over for a change,' recalled Bush years later. 'I don't think I did much wrong.'

It was the dawn of a new era for New Zealand. After the brilliant teams of the 1920s, and the series win over the 1930 British team, household names such as Nepia, Lucas, Cooke, Nicholls, Mill, Irvine, Stewart, Porter and Finlayson would play no more international rugby.

Bush, an Auckland representative since 1928, was attending Otago University on a one-year course. Rusty Page, who was to go on to become a brigadier and win decorations for bravery and leadership in World War II, had his first game for the All Blacks. Normally a first five-eighth, he played at centre after Charlie Oliver withdrew the day before the match.

Wing Kelly Ball also made his debut, as did Frank Solomon at wing forward, the last player to fill that position. It was the last occasion the traditional seven-man scrum was used. The other new forwards, Metcalfe, Purdue, Max and Jessep, were all All Blacks the next year.

Archie Strang, the All Black first five-eighth and captain, who had been outstanding in 1928 and 1930, retired after the game at the age of only 24.

'The following year the All Blacks went to Australia,' Bush said. 'But I had mucked up my knee in a club game so I wasn't in the trials and wasn't considered.'

Bush said that Vincent Meredith, the long-time Auckland selector-coach who managed and coached the 1935–36 All Blacks in Britain, was largely responsible for his versatility as a first-class footballer.

'I always recall going down to Hamilton for the June 3rd game against Waikato. At the railway station Vinny came up to me, asked if I was all right and said, because of an injury to another player, I might be playing at first five-eighths.

'That was the start of it. From then on anywhere he didn't have anyone to put, he seemed to put me there.'

Bush said it was Meredith who influenced him to have a year in the forwards with Auckland in 1934. Meredith, who had been Auckland's sole selector-coach in 1923–24, 1927–29 and 1934, was also a New Zealand selector in 1934.

'He said to me, in chatting at an Auckland practice one day, "I would like to have you on this tour [the 1935–36 tour of Britain]. I don't say that you won't get in as fullback, but you'd be a great help as a utility man."'

BIOGRAPHICAL DETAILS

Ronald George Bush

Born: Nelson, 3 May 1909

Died: 10 May 1996

Position: Fullback

Represented NZ: 1931
1 match (1 international)

Points for NZ: 14
1 conversion, four penalties

Provincial record: Auckland 1928–30, 1932–37 (University club); Otago 1931 (University club); South Island 1931; North Island 1934; NZ Universities 1929–1931, 1933, 1936

Selector/coach: NZ Universities selector 1947–57; North Island selector 1959–64

NZ selector: 1961–64

NZ coach: 1962

Other service: Co-founder, with Hugh McLean, of New Zealand Barbarians club 1937; Auckland RFU president 1966–68

Other: Represented Auckland at cricket 1933; father, George, played rugby for Canterbury 1898–99, 1901

Occupation: Partner with indent agents Thompson Bush; before that a schoolteacher

NEW ZEALAND COACHING RECORD

1962: beat Australia 20-6, 14-5

'Seeing he was chairman of the national selectors and the manager, what do you do? You go where you're put, so I had a year in the forwards. That was the main reason,' said Bush.

Bush was a member of the New Zealand Universities team which was the first New Zealand side, in 1936, to tour Japan. The team travelled on a Japanese boat, stopping at Hong Kong for a match on the way. Bush recalled how they had taught the Japanese crew the haka on the way over.

'The Hong Kong team was full of retired colonels and so forth, from the British that were there. The crew came to the game, and every time there was a pause they would do the haka.'

CHAPTER 22

NEW ZEALAND COACH 1961-62

NEIL McPHAIL

Outstanding record in combination with great captain

NEIL McPHAIL SHOULD BE HAILED AS ONE OF the finest All Black coaches.

He reclaimed the 'world crown' from the Springboks and guided his team to arguably the best touring performance of the modern era. He suffered only two test losses, both in series which he comfortably won, in the five years he coached the All Blacks.

But his legacy didn't stop there. When he handed over the reins to Fred Allen after 1965, he had created such an air of stability and invincibility about the team, and built up such a store of brilliant young players, that Allen was able to continue undefeated for another three years. Eleven of McPhail's 1963 team would return to Britain with Allen in 1967.

At the same time, and while restricted by the rules of the day, McPhail had bestrode two eras — that of the ultraconservative, loose-forward-dominated game of the 1950s, and that of the freer running game. Rule changes in 1963 changed the offside law, restricted loose forwards and gave inside backs more room and time. This opened up McPhail's All Black style, and the potential would be further exploited when Allen took the team back to Britain in 1967. McPhail's All Blacks scored 118 tries in 36 games in 1963–64, whereas Allen's strike rate, 71 tries in 17 games, would be even higher.

When McPhail died late in 1994, aged 81, the seasoned Christchurch rugby journalist John Brooks wrote that, as All Black coaches go, 'none would match the mix of sound judgement and strength of purpose which distinguished Neil McPhail from the rest.'[1]

Brooks recalled the time, against Australia in 1962, when McPhail had dropped four 'icons' of All Black rugby — Colin Meads, Kel Tremain, Dennis Young and Ian Clarke — in one fell swoop. Such a move took a lot of courage and vision, but it helped him win the series and set the stage for his triumphant tour of Britain and France the next year.

That 1963–64 tour produced perhaps the finest performance of all New Zealand teams, with just a 0-3 loss to Newport in its third game and a 0-0 draw with Scotland as blemishes on its record.

Subsequent All Black teams have had more success, including perfect records, but on much shorter tours. Among earlier teams, the 1905 Originals and 1924 Invincibles had many easy matches and many close scores, while the 1935 and 1953 All Black tourists had inferior records. The 1963–64 team was remarkable for its consistency over the five-month period.

Apart from the tour leadership and quality and depth of the players, a primary reason for such success was the rules of the day. With unlimited lineouts and control of the loose ball, the All Blacks were able to plan and control their matches.

The All Blacks' lineout was awesome. The Meads

NEIL McPHAIL

brothers, Alan Stewart, Ron Horsley, Brian Lochore, Keith Nelson, Ken Gray and Tremain were, to quote one of the halfbacks of that tour, Chris Laidlaw, 'So good in the lineouts that a scrumhalf could plan his game around an unending supply of the ball.

'If all went well the game could be played at precisely the pace the halfback wanted. When it was fast it was exhilarating. When it was slow it was frighteningly efficient, and immensely satisfying to participate in; however boring it may have been to the uneducated spectator.' Laidlaw, more forthright than possibly any other player who had written a book on rugby, described his coach as 'exactly the right man at the right time'. Neil 'Grumpy' McPhail was 'a blunt, definite man whose insight into the motivations of players rivalled that of his successor, Fred Allen'.

But he had many other assets. 'Essentially a man who identified with the players, he understood very clearly the basic differences between New Zealand and British players and temperaments, and exploited it ceaselessly.

'His team talks before important matches were a blending of the best of Montgomery and Churchill — so eloquent at times that discussion of tactics was completely forgotten in euphoric and highly effective flashbacks to wartime analogies and visions of the future in which grey-haired old men round the fireside would be proudly telling their grandsons that their team, the 1963–64 All Blacks, never lost a test match.'[2]

While the leadership was top quality on that tour, wrote Laidlaw, it was not perfect. He claimed there was a distinct division between the older, experienced players and younger players. He said the younger group, including himself, sometimes felt estranged, and pointed to the treatment of

OLD HEADS: All Black coach Neil McPhail had some of the shrewdest tactical heads in this 1963 team which beat England 21-11 and 9-6 on the first Home Unions tour to New Zealand. Captain Wilson Whineray was backed up by vice-captain Des Connor, an outstanding halfback who had played for Australia in 1957-59 before moving to Auckland in 1960. The team is: Top Row: Don Clarke, Brian Lochore, Alan Stewart, Colin Meads, Kel Tremain, Barry Thomas; Second Row: Bruce Watt, Pat Walsh, Don McKay, Ralph Caulton, Waka Nathan, Ian Clarke, John Graham; Front Row: R. G. Bush (selector), Dennis Young, D. Ross (manager), Wilson Whineray (captain), Des Connor (vice-captain), N. J. McPhail (coach), Mac Herewini, J. L. Findlay (selector); In Front: Neil Wolfe, Ian Uttley.

PARTNERSHIP: Possibly New Zealand's greatest captain Wilson Whineray is cheered from the field after the All Blacks' first 1963-64 tour match against Oxford. Whineray and coach Neil McPhail forged a profitable partnership.

Earle Kirton, who had taken much of the blame for the Newport defeat, as the worst case of neglect.

Wilson Whineray, captain of the team, rebuts such criticism. 'What Chris and Earle forgot was that we took three first five-eighths on that tour — Mac Herewini, Bruce Watt and Earle Kirton,' he told the author. 'There were 32 tour games and if you take out the five tests and the Barbarians match, if you played 12 or 13 games, as Earle did, then you were getting more than your share. And it needs to be remembered that Herewini and Watt were experienced test players, whereas Earle was not.'

Whineray pointed to the benefits of such an 'apprenticeship' for many of the young players in the side. The likes of Laidlaw, Brian Lochore, Ian MacRae, Bill Davis and Kirton (though it took him longer) would soon become test mainstays.

For his part, McPhail said he had enjoyed watching and influencing the development of the youngsters in the team, and specifically mentioned Laidlaw, Lochore, Ken Gray and MacRae. He thought the tour too long though, and considered 10 weeks and about 15 matches to be the optimum.

The 1963–64 team was to become the nucleus of All Black sides for the next five years or so. But it was not as smooth a ride for McPhail and his fellow selectors as for some of the players in those times. In 1964 the NZRFU appointed five national selectors. At the end of the season, after the series against Australia, only McPhail, Allen and Les George were to emerge as incumbents.

McPhail was the master, and Allen the assistant, for the series against the touring Springboks of 1965, which was again to attempt to wrest the mythical world crown from the South Africans. McPhail made an excellent job of securing the rubber in the series by retaining the same team virtually intact (the forwards were the same in all four tests) and keeping spirits high, in spite of the embarrassing loss in the third test in Christchurch after the All Blacks had held a commanding 16-5 lead at half-time.

'You simply felt that winning was inevitable so long as you did not lose your head,' recalled Laidlaw. 'McPhail was no lover of instinctive rugby. Every contingency was prepared for . . . The Springboks arrived and performed with an enigmatic inconsistency. Personnel, experience and power were all there, but the spirit wasn't.

'One could sense internal strife at several receptions thrown for them in Wellington beforehand. At Government

NEIL McPHAIL

House I happened to notice a violent argument, one day before the test match, between several senior players and the management. A remarkable sight in public, and naturally enough something of a boost for a supremely integrated All Black team.'[3]

The Springboks came into the first test with eight wins and a loss on tour. Five of their latest test team — Lionel Wilson, John Gainsford, Keith Oxlee, Lofty Nel and Abe Malan — had helped win the series over the All Blacks in South Africa in 1960. Just four of the All Blacks — Colin Meads, Whineray, Red Conway and Kel Tremain — were veterans of that series.

A 50-mile-an-hour Wellington wind influenced the game. New Zealand took it, with tries scored by Bill Birtwistle and Tremain by the interval. The South Africans could manage only a dropped goal, by Oxlee, in the second half, giving the All Blacks a 6–3 win. The second test, on a heavy Carisbrook, was won by New Zealand 13-0. It was the biggest margin the All Blacks had achieved over their illustrious rivals. Tremain, Ron Rangi and Bruce McLeod scored tries.

Gainsford and Gert Brynard scored two tries each for the visitors in the third test on a holding Lancaster Park ground. All were superbly executed. Down 5-16, the Boks began their comeback straight after the interval and were to snatch victory with a Tiny Naude penalty with two minutes remaining. The score was 19-16.

With morale high and the chance of tying the series realistic, the Springboks looked forward to a firm Eden Park. But the predatory All Black forwards exerted pressure that eventually told. Up only 3-0 at the interval, the All Blacks scored three tries in the space of 11 minutes afterwards, all the result of breakdowns by the Springboks in running out of their own half. Five tries were scored in the 20-3 victory.

The victory was again the largest scored by New Zealand over South Africa, and the worst loss a Springbok team had suffered in a test.

'The plan simply was to put South Africa under pressure quickly from their errors or our play, and get some quick points,' McPhail said afterwards.

'This would cause South Africa to do one of two things

COACH'S DREAM: The task of coach Neil McPhail – and four other All Black coaches who had Colin Meads in their teams – was made easier by the abilities of Meads (with ball) and other exceptional players in the 1960s. From left, Alan Stewart, Wilson Whineray, Meads, Waka Nathan and Kel Tremain attack the Welsh in the 1963 test at Cardiff, won 6-0 by New Zealand.

THE POWER BEHIND THE ALL BLACKS

— try to slog it out with our forwards, or the South African backs would try to run the ball from insecure positions. With our cover defence forcing them into errors, we would be in a position to quickly turn defence into offence from a good position, as the Boks would be rather wide open. This is actually what happened on the day.'[4]

The series win was a private victory for McPhail over his opposite, the famed Hennie Muller. Tactically speaking, McPhail had won almost all of his battles in his time as All Black coach. Muller, the brilliant destroyer of All Black hopes as a player in 1949 and coach in 1960, had lost his final challenge. McPhail would now retire.

An important reason for the All Blacks' success during McPhail's tenure as coach was the rapport enjoyed between him and Whineray, his captain. Whineray had captained the All Blacks since 1958, but did not enjoy complete success at the beginning. Though he won the two series, his teams struggled against the Australians (1958) and Lions (1959), and then suffered the narrow series loss in South Africa in 1960 under Jack Sullivan. McPhail's accession seemed to coincide with a new confidence and self-belief in Whineray as both captain and prop.

Between the pair there was an excellent chemistry which can be traced back to Whineray's two years' studying at Lincoln College, in 1956-57, when McPhail was the Canterbury coach. Whineray was 20 when he came to Canterbury, but had already played for Wairarapa, Mid-Canterbury and Manawatu.

'Neil gave me my first big break, because he needn't have gone with a student like me, who would not be there for as long as others,' Whineray told the author.

McPhail's intuition quickly proved correct. Whineray's advancement was rapid, and during that season he was to gain his first taste of international victory, with wins by Canterbury and New Zealand Universities over the touring Springboks.

Whineray, perhaps the greatest of All Black captains, retired after the Springbok series of 1965 (he had taken the 1964 season off from international rugby). He had played 77 times for the All Blacks, 68 of those games as captain. He had led the All Blacks in 30 of the 32 tests in which he had taken part. The previous highest tally of games as captain had been Cliff Porter's seven.

Fundamental to McPhail's coaching philosophy, Whineray told the author, was that 'good teams do the simple things well'.

'He insisted that we had to win good possession and build up a cushion of points before we did anything flashy. We liked to play it in our opposition's half. Once we got well ahead he didn't mind how we handled our attack.'

McPhail's gruffness and occasionally abrupt manner earned him the nickname Grumpy from his players, but it was undoubtedly a term of affection. The players recognised his deep knowledge of rugby and appreciated his understanding of the strains they were sometimes under on tour or in the test arena.

McPhail had been a Canterbury prop before World War II and an All Black trialist in 1939 for the scheduled tour to South Africa the following year. That tour never took place because of the war, and the team selected by sole national selector Norm McKenzie was never announced. McPhail perhaps thus saw his long All Black coaching/selection career as compensation for the loss of opportunity to become an All Black.

Nevertheless, he enjoyed a fine autumn to his playing career. In the early days of the war he played for the Second New Zealand Division against South Africa in Egypt. Later he was captured by the Germans at Bel Hamed, in the Western Desert. He spent more than three years in a prisoner-of-war camp, so it was a tribute to his stamina that he could resume his rugby career at the conclusion of hostilities. It is said that he and Pat Rhind, a fellow Canterbury front-row forward and later Canterbury coach, ran the risk of court martial when they deliberately missed troopships home from England so they could play in the Kiwi trials. If so, it was worth it. Both won places in the famous Kiwis team captained by Charlie Saxton which toured Britain and Germany in 1945–46. They were also both in the team which beat Wales at Cardiff, the first New Zealand side ever to achieve the feat.

In 1955 McPhail took over as Canterbury coach from Jack Rankin. Canterbury had held the Ranfurly Shield since 1953 and would become even stronger under McPhail. In 1956 his Canterbury team beat the Springboks 9-6 in a famous victory, while many Canterbury All Blacks played key roles in the defeat of the Boks for the first time in a series. Those players included Pat Vincent, captain of the All Blacks in the first two tests, and Bob Duff, captain in the decisive third and fourth tests.

Later that season Canterbury lost the shield to Wellington. McPhail took the Canterbury team for one more year and became the All Black selection convenor in 1961.

'Rugby is a wonderful game, and what you put into it you will get back tenfold,' he said more than 40 years ago. 'You are enemies for 80 minutes and friends for life.'[5]

He seldom if ever had cause to regret that statement throughout a long and fruitful career serving the game.

THE SELECTOR MUST GET THROUGH

'Snowbound, fogbound, wet to the skin, and in mud over their ankles, New Zealand's rugby selectors are travelling thousands of miles and suffering a hundred discomforts in their search for playing talent,' wrote a reporter for the Christchurch *Press* in the lead-up to what would be the last grand tour of Britain and France by an All Black team in 1963–64.

The writer suggested the vast amount of travel on the tour would mean nothing to Neil McPhail, the All Blacks' coach and chairman of the national selectors. He was well into 'travel training'. McPhail's total mileage for the 1963 New Zealand season had already exceeded 10,000 miles, with more than 30 days away from home.

New Zealand's rugby talents were far more geographically widespread in the 1960s than today, with the majority of the All Black forwards coming from rural backgrounds, particularly farming.

While the All Black selectors of today cover 2nd- and 3rd-division teams, almost all recent All Blacks have been playing for 1st-division sides when chosen. But that was not the case in McPhail's day. There was no national championship then, so players were able to remain in their home provinces and still gain national recognition.

An example of the lengths to which McPhail and his co-selectors were prepared to go to search out talent was provided in the article in the *Press*.

'The road to the West Coast was blocked [by a big landslip] as an impatient motorist left his car to speak to the weary workmen who had been clearing the snow and rubble all night. They assured him he simply could not get through, but were shaken when he insisted he must.

'Who are you?" asked the foreman.

'"McPhail, rugby selector," came the reply. "I could not get through to see West Coast play Canterbury. Now West Coast is playing Buller, and I must see these boys."

'"And by heavens, you will," promised the foreman.'

'Like a rugby team, these weary men rallied. Additional bulldozers were brought in; men sprang from all sides to the attack anew. The hours slipped by, but a path was cleared, and Mr McPhail saw the match,' wrote the *Press* reporter.

REFERENCES

1. *Press*, 1994.
2. Chris Laidlaw, *Mud in Your Eye*, Reed, 1973.
3. *Mud In Your Eye*.

BIOGRAPHICAL DETAILS

Neil James McPhail

Born: Christchurch, 24 September 1913

Died: Christchurch, 7 November 1994

Position: Prop forward

Provincial record: Canterbury (High School Old Boys) — 32 games; All Black trialist 1939; Kiwis Army team, Britain, 1946

Selector/coach: Canterbury selector/coach 1955–57

NZ selector: 1961–65

NZ coach: 1961–65

Other: Father Alex McPhail was NZRFU president 1933 and long-serving Canterbury official (from 1913); brother Clem was Canterbury representative centre 1933–36, played for South Island 1935–36 and was Canterbury RFU president 1968–70; son Bruce represented Canterbury 1973–75; other sons Alex and Hamish played for Old Boys seniors; uncle 'Nuts' Hasell was All Black hooker before and after World War I and toured South Africa with NZ Army team

Occupation: Retailer

NEW ZEALAND COACHING RECORD

1961: beat France 13-6, 5-3, 32-3

1962: drew with Australia 9-9; beat Australia 3-0, 16-8 (NZ had toured Australia earlier in the season, winning all three tests, coached by Ron Bush)

1963: beat England 21-11, 9-6; beat Ireland 6-5; beat Wales 6-0; beat England 14-0; drew with Scotland 0-0; beat France 12-3

1964: beat Australia 14-9, 18-3; lost to Australia 5-20

1965: beat South Africa 6-3, 13-0; lost to South Africa 16-19; beat South Africa 20-3

CHAPTER 23

NEW ZEALAND COACH 1966-68

Fred Allen

*'The Needle' had what others strive for
— the perfect record*

MUCH-LOVED TEAM: Fred Allen was a member of this Second New Zealand Expeditionary Force team – known universally as the 'Kiwis' – which toured Britain, France and Germany in 1945-46. Captained by Charlie Saxton, the team played marvellous open rugby for a war-torn, sports-starved Europe. The side contained 16 past and future All Blacks and players who would surely have been All Blacks but for World War II. The Kiwis, pictured outside the Versailles Palace in France, won 32 of their 38 games, including wins over England, Wales and France (twice).

THE POWER BEHIND THE ALL BLACKS

FRED ALLEN IS PERHAPS THE MOST successful All Black coach of all time.

It is impossible to objectively compare the All Black coaches of the different eras, just as it is impossible to compare the All Blacks themselves. However, Fred the Needle's unbeaten run through the late 1960s established a record which has never been matched by any other All Black coach, before or since.

Allen coached the All Blacks through 1966, 1967 and 1968, his teams cutting a swathe through the best the rugby world had to offer — with the notable exception of South Africa (although he assisted Neil McPhail in beating the 1965 Springboks in New Zealand). Then he quit.

His run of 14 straight test victories has only been approached by the magnificent efforts of Alex Wyllie, who was unbeaten until his thirteenth test as coach and established a record of just two losses in 23 tests (one of which was when he was co-coach with John Hart — the 1991 World Cup semifinal).

Had Allen continued through 1969 — when the All Blacks, coached by Ivan Vodanovich, destroyed the Five Nations champions, Wales — and taken the team to South Africa in 1970, could he have achieved the elusive series win?

Like Wyllie, whose era of dominance came when South Africa had not quite emerged from the political wilderness, Allen never locked horns with that great rival — to his eternal regret.

'I do regret it very much, because that was my intention in 1967,' he said. 'We were supposed to tour South Africa, but went instead to the UK and France when the tour was cancelled.

'I would love to have done the South African tour and I would love to have stayed on as All Black coach. But I sensed behind the scenes that people weren't fully supportive of me. Perhaps there was a bit of jealousy about the unbeaten record? I wasn't going to give them the opportunity to dump me, so I packed it in.'

Allen made his sixth trip to the republic in 1996. The first one was in 1949, when he captained the All Blacks on the tour that produced a 4-0 whitewash by the Springboks. It left an indelible mark on Allen, who was never to play big rugby again. It was a pain the whole of New Zealand rugby was to feel, but it was also one of the formative influences which made Allen such a formidable coach in later years.

A number of factors contributed to the losses in South Africa: choosing the team after trials in 1948; not having any international matches in 1948; the choice of

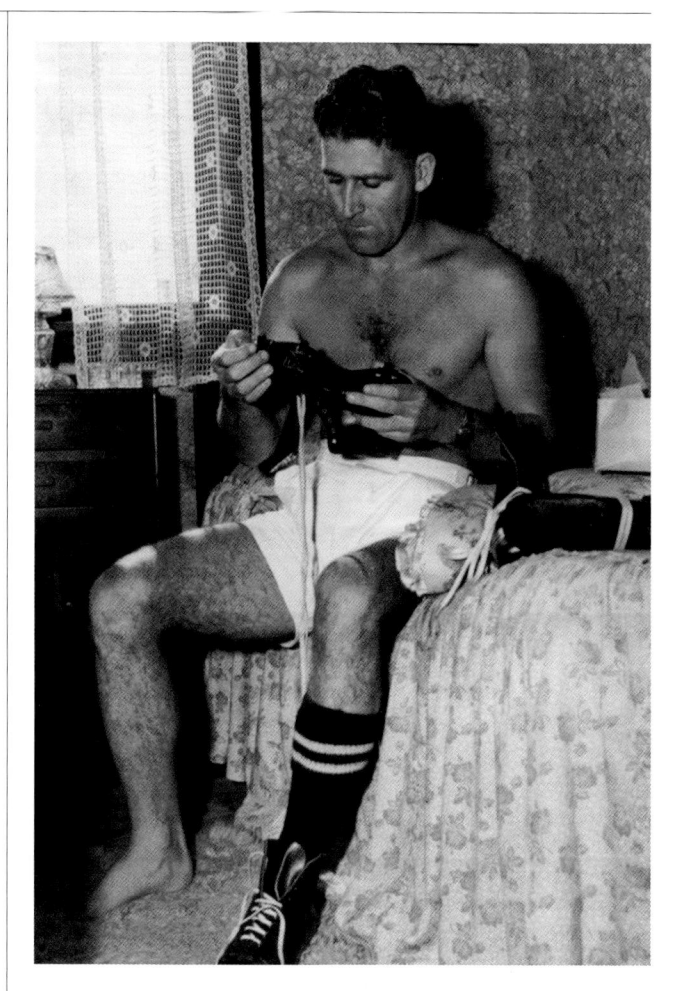

TESTING TIME: Fred Allen prepares for a test during the 1947 All Black tour of Australia. Allen captained New Zealand in two tests against the touring Wallabies in 1946, two in the 1947 series and the first two tests of the 1949 series in South Africa. Commentator Winston McCarthy said Allen was 'one of the finest first five-eighths of all times'.

the All Black coach; the 27-day journey by boat; the immense distances travelled by train between games; the 'No Maoris' policy of the time, which prevented fine players such as Johnny Smith, Ben Couch and Vince Bevan from possible selection; the refereeing; the poor goal-kicking form of Bob Scott, who converted only two penalties in the series; All Black shortcomings at halfback; the devastating influence of Springbok No. 8 Hennie Muller; the unerring boot of Springbok Oakey Geffin; the brilliant scheming of Danie Craven . . .

The All Blacks were clearly up against it before they began, and it would have taken a miracle for any captain to have beaten the odds. That the All Blacks would take almost another half-century to win a full-blown series in

FRED ALLEN

South Africa would come as no surprise to Allen.

Allen strongly rejected any suggestion that Alex McDonald, the 66-year-old coach of the team, who had been a 1905 All Black Original, captained the All Blacks on their 1913 tour of North America, and first coached or co-coached the All Blacks against the Springboks in 1921, was cynically rejected by the team as being too old.

'Alex was a lovely old man. But it was hard enough for young people to be up on the high veldt and he was sick a lot of the time,' said Allen.

'I'm not making excuses for it. I'm quite proud of that side. But we had 27 days on the boat on the way over. What could you do on the boat? It wasn't the Queen Mary. We jogged around the deck with the Indian Ocean rolling a bit and people twisting ankles. And then you retire to the bars and everything's going on.

'Once we got there, about four of the fellas were three stone overweight. They'd eaten too much. At Hermanus, for a week before our first game, we were fêted and wined and dined by high society. Danie Craven really sewed us up.

'We travelled by train and at one stage spent 10 out of 13 days travelling and playing two games. It got so that at night we used to get off the train while it was filling up with water and coal and work out in the dark.

'Just for good measure we had a train smash in Rhodesia — head-on, about one o'clock in the morning. Our big lock, Charlie Willocks, buggered his shoulder and several of us were thrown out of our bunks. One rail employee was killed.'

The All Blacks had their line crossed only eight times in 24 games on tour. There was little in it. Allen still firmly believes if the team had had Vic Cavanagh as coach, it would have at least squared the rubber.

'He was the greatest coach never to coach the All Blacks, no doubt about it,' he said.

'I only played the first two tests. I started to take over the training because old Alex was crook. Something had to be done. Some of the other players didn't like the fact I wasn't playing. But I felt I couldn't do any more by playing, so when it came to picking the third test, I said, "Start with me — I'm out." Then I basically took over the test-team training, with Alex taking the dirt trackers when he could. It was a hard tour.'

Why, then, was Allen, the captain, so proud of that team?

'When we boarded the boat for home, I asked our manager, Jim Parker, and Alex to let me talk to the team in private, because I'd like to straighten out a few things. The team was a bit hot with Alex and Jim, who were pretty good guys really. I'd already retired. I'd kicked my boots into the Indian Ocean.

'I just said, "It's all over and in a thousand years' time the score is still going to be 4-0." I said, "All the complaining and bleating and blaming of management and referees, which I believe you're thinking of doing, just let's cut it." For about 15 years it never came out. Although the tour's results almost broke my heart, the attitude of the team afterwards made me very proud.'

Among those who felt Allen should have remained the on-field commander was team-mate Johnny Simpson, who would later forge a fabulous coaching partnership with Allen at provincial level.

'Fred, unfortunately, blamed himself for our problems, but none of them were of his making,' said Simpson. 'That was the nature of the man — he was so conscientious. But our players couldn't vary the tactics, which was needed to counter the menace of Hennie Muller in the loose.'[1]

As a player, Allen made his reputation as a beautifully balanced five-eighth with the Kiwis, the New Zealand Army team which toured Europe at war's end in 1946. Allen had been wounded twice in the war. The great commentator Winston McCarthy wrote:

'Allen was one of the finest five-eighths of all times . . . one of the greatest of side-steppers off either foot. He could make them, big or small, but always at pace. He was an immaculate player, neat in all he did. There can be no doubt that in blind-side play there was never his equal.'[2]

Allen captained the All Blacks in the two-test series in 1946 and led them to Australia in 1947, playing in two tests. Weighing 12st 6lb and standing 5ft 10in tall, he was one of the best postwar players, equally at home at first or second five-eighth.

Allen's early coaching triumphs were with Auckland between 1957 and 1963, in partnership with Simpson. This included a then-record tenure of the Ranfurly Shield for 25 matches (1960-63).

In 1964 he became an All Black selector, under the convenorship coach Neil McPhail. Allen helped McPhail plan the defeat of the 1965 Springboks in New Zealand.

The following year Allen became All Black coach and thus began the most successful era of any All Black coach. The 1966 British Lions became Allen's first victims, whitewashed 4-0, the All Blacks scoring 79 points to 32 against. Only the second test at Wellington produced a reasonably close score, 16-12.

That year, too, Allen made the first of many

THE POWER BEHIND THE ALL BLACKS

CHANGED FOREVER: Fred Allen dives over for one of the six tries he scored as captain of the ill-fated 1949 All Blacks in South Africa. The Boks had brilliantly rewritten the scrummaging and line-out tactical manuals and rugby the world over would immediately adapt to the changes after 1949.

outstanding decisions which were to lift him from the 'pack' as an international coach. He chose Brian Lochore to replace the long-serving Wilson Whineray as captain. Others would have ranked Kel Tremain, Ken Gray, Colin Meads or Chris Laidlaw ahead of Lochore. This was not exactly a gamble by Allen. He told the author in 1996 he had been thinking about the need to find a replacement for about 12 months and had been observing Lochore's demeanour of quiet dignity.

'A successful captain has to have patience, good observation and be a student of human nature. Brian had all those qualities. I chewed it around with some coaches and players, but in the end it was my decision. He had broad shoulders and the common touch. He developed tremendously. He came up trumps all right.'

Lochore led one of the strongest and most consistent packs in All Black history. Stalwarts of this time included Waka Nathan, Stan Meads, Bruce McLeod, Colin Meads, Alister Hopkinson, Ian Kirkpatrick, Sam Strahan, 'Jazz' Muller, Ken Gray, Kel Tremain and Jack Hazlett, but others were to follow, and the 16 forwards who made Allen's triumphant 1967 trip to Britain and France must rank as probably the finest grouping of any All Black touring side.

Among all the marvellous rugby played by the

FEARLESS FERGIE: The All Blacks under Fred Allen reached new attacking heights. In this photo of the 1967 test against France at Colombes Stadium, Paris, Fergie McCormick counter-attacks from fullback with captain Brian Lochore in support. A McCormick run produced a try for Malcolm Dick, while Sid Going, Ian Kirkpatrick and Tony Steel also scored tries in the 21-15 victory.

HIGH TIMES: All Black captain Brian Lochore introduces the Queen to Jack Hazlett at Twickenham in 1967.

tourists, two incidents stand out for the historian. One was the ordering off of Colin Meads during the victory over Scotland at Murrayfield. Meads thus joined 1924 All Black Cyril Brownlie as one of only two players to have been ordered off in an international at that time.

The other, less obvious development was Allen's changing of the guard against France. He dropped the great Kel Tremain for the untried 21-year-old Ian Kirkpatrick, and replaced Chris Laidlaw with the fast-improving Sid Going. It was another example of how Allen would not hesitate to make the hard decisions to maintain his team's quality of performance.

The 1968 season, which was to become Allen's last with the All Blacks, provided series wins over Australia (away) and France (at home). But the All Blacks did not put away their opposition with the same precision as of old. There was the famous penalty-try test at Brisbane, won 19-18, when Australian referee Kevin Crowe 'saved' the All Blacks (and Allen's unbeaten record) by awarding a penalty try in the dying moments of the game. However, injuries to key players, such as Lochore, Gray and Tremain, had affected the team's performances.

It was after this that Allen decided to retire. He was at the height of his coaching powers, but it seems his position — even after 38 matches without a defeat — was in jeopardy.

Allen will not speak ill of the dead. But the author has learned from other parties that Allen's coaching job may well have been in jeopardy. Chairman of the NZRFU then was the late Tom Morrison, himself a former All Black coach. The man who replaced Allen as coach was the late Ivan Vodanovich, who was to become an NZRFU councillor. Morrison and Vodanovich were business partners. There was criticism made by councillors of Allen's handling of certain All Blacks, and their tactics, during the 1968 Australian tour. A coup was a possibility, though the dumping of an unbeaten All Black coach would have caused a furore.

Allen has led a busy life since he wound down his women's clothing company and retired to Whangaparaoa. In 1995 he travelled to the World Cup, to the 100th test between New Zealand and Australia, and to Europe with the Kiwis' reunion party. In 1996 he followed the All Blacks in South Africa.

At 76 he looks fit and strong. 'I've had my whack and had my fun out of [rugby] and I've got no regrets,' he concluded before adding a special word of thanks for his wife, Norma, for her support during his years in the game.

REFERENCES
1. Lindsay Knight, *They Led the All Blacks*.
2. Winston McCarthy, *Haka! The All Black Story*.

. . . .

A COACH FOR ALL REASONS

Fred Allen was often called upon to coach and advise teams at various levels after his All Black days. In 1970 he wrote with Terry McLean a coaching book which became a worldwide bestseller.

Some of his lesser-known coaching exploits follow:

In 1950, when the British Lions toured with many talented players, but no coach, Allen, upon request, took them for a training session. For his troubles, after the team improved to draw the first test and run the All Blacks close in the other three, he was called a traitor by one weekly newspaper.

In 1973, at the request of Marlborough chairman Pat Dwyer, Allen spent several days in Blenheim helping to prepare the Marlborough team which lifted the Ranfurly Shield from a shocked Canterbury and held it for six challenges into 1974.

BIOGRAPHICAL DETAILS

Frederick Richard Allen

Born: Oamaru, 9 February 1920

Position: Five-eighth

Represented NZ: 1946, 1947, 1949
21 matches (6 internationals)

Points for NZ: 21 (7 tries)

Provincial record: Canterbury 1939–41 (Linwood club); Marlborough 1944 (RNZAF); Waikato 1944 (Army); Auckland 1946–48 (Grammar School)

Other matches: 2nd NZEF 1945–46 (Kiwis) in Britain; Barbarians (UK) 1946

Selector/coach: Auckland 1957–63, including 25-match tenure of Ranfurly Shield

NZ selector: 1964–68

NZ coach: 1966–68 (won all 14 tests played)

Other: Co-author, with Terry McLean, of a rugby coaching book, *Fred Allen on Rugby* (Cassell, 1970)

Occupation: Retired; was women's clothing manufacturer

NEW ZEALAND COACHING RECORD

1966: beat Lions 20-3, 16-12, 19-6, 24-11

1967: beat Australia 29-9; beat England 23-11; beat Wales 13-6; beat France 21-5; beat Scotland 14-3

1968: beat Australia 27-11, 19-18; beat France 12-9, 9-3, 19-12

Before the advent of the North Harbour union Allen was asked to coach lowly Silverdale, the club which serves the Whangaparaoa area. Allen helped them out of the Auckland third division into the second.

CHAPTER 24

NEW ZEALAND COACH 1969-71

IVAN VODANOVICH

Fine servant of game but coaching record unenviable

THERE IS LITTLE DOUBT THAT IVAN VODANOVICH spent his time as All Black coach in the shadow of the great Fred Allen.

Faced with international rugby's toughest assignments: the Springboks and the Lions, in successive years, Vodanovich took the blame for failing both challenges. It was one of the darkest periods in All Black rugby history, perhaps worse even than 1949, when the All Blacks lost all six tests that year. While the All Blacks had never beaten the Springboks in South Africa, the loss to the Lions was the first time New Zealand had been beaten in a series by that team. It was also the first time a full-strength All Black team had been beaten in a series at home in 33 years.

But good was to emerge from disaster. Wise heads among New Zealand rugby, with Vodanovich working as hard as anyone, would move swiftly to perform an 'autopsy on the corpse' and come up with answers. Support groups, such as national coaching schools and the feeder New Zealand Colts and Junior teams, were vastly improved from 1972 onwards. Between 1964 and 1972 there had not been a Colts team, while the Juniors, who had played just one match a season (and none in 1971) graduated to eight- and nine-match tours overseas and at home. The game never looked back.

A member of the NZRFU executive while All Black coach, Vodanovich later became the strong right arm of successive council chairmen Tom Morrison, Jack Sullivan (both former All Black coaches) and Ces Blazey. He served from 1969 to 1991 and was made a life member that year. The chairmen cherished Vodanovich because he gave them respect, total integrity and inexhaustible physical energy.

'His whole bearing, his rugged stance, the straight look from piercing eyes immediately gave the impression Vodanovich was a straight-shooter, that rare person who is the completely honest and earnest man,' recalled the *New Zealand Herald's* veteran rugby journalist Don Cameron on Vodanovich's death. 'He mixed with the lords of the game but was more comfortable among the commoners.'[1]

Vodanovich and Morrison owned a menswear shop in downtown Wellington, and it was 'out the back' of the shop that the elect were invited. 'The talk was that there were more serious matters decided at the back of the shop than in the NZRFU offices, or even the back bar of the Midland Hotel,' added Cameron.

Vodanovich was the last of the 'sweat-and-strain, hellfire-belching' All Black coaches who seemed to believe that all playing problems could be corrected by even harder work on the training field. He won only four tests. From 10 played he suffered five losses and a draw.

SILKY SKILLS: Barry John, aided by the superb service of Gareth Edwards, almost always managed to evade the defensive traps set by Vodanovich's 1971 All Blacks.

He began strongly, with resounding victories over the touring Welsh, the reigning Five Nations champions, in 1969. All Black fullback Fergie McCormick claimed a world record of 24 points during the 33-12 second test win. The Welsh contingent included such players as J.P.R. Williams, Gerald Davies, Mervyn Davies, Barry John and Gareth Edwards, all of whom would return to haunt Vodanovich two years later under the guidance of the great coach Carwyn James.

It was the tour of South Africa the following winter which would reveal the limitations of Vodanovich as a top-level coach and begin the unravelling of a fabulous All Black era. The All Blacks had gone undefeated in a test match since 1965 when they began the 1970 tour of South Africa. They had not lost a test series in 10 years – since their previous visit to South Africa in 1960, when they had lost two tests, won one and drawn one for the tightest of series defeats. They began the 1970 tour with unprecedented ease and were undefeated outside the tests. But the three test losses, which were the only international defeats suffered by Brian Lochore as captain, marked the beginning of a downward spiral that could not be immediately arrested.

Among the reasons for the fall was that the nucleus of the All Blacks had been together for a decade. Age had caught up on many. It was a situation akin to Alex Wyllie's long, unbeaten run and seemingly abrupt stall in 1991. With the home series against the Lions, Vodanovich and his team tried to plug the gaps, but the once-well-oiled machine had well and truly coughed its last.

The incomparable Fred Allen had guided his All Blacks to an incredible unbeaten record. He undoubtedly gained the maximum capacity from his charges, but his unblemished copybook was in jeopardy in 1968 when he won a test against Australia 19-18 only with the aid of a sensational penalty try in the eightieth minute, a try which took away a deserved win from the Wallabies.

Some have suggested the tide was already turning, and that Allen, had he chosen to remain as coach, would have suffered a similar humiliation to Vodanovich in 1970. We shall never know for sure, but we can be certain Allen would not have stood for the loss of discipline in playing methods that marked the 1970 tour. Poor tactical judgement and errors in handling and tackling contributed to the series loss. Most basic of all, the All

Black greats did not give Vodanovich the commitment Allen would have commanded.

The 1970 All Blacks lost only three tour matches. They accomplished many huge scores, totalling 687 points in 24 matches, easily a record, and scoring 135 tries – 41 more than any other team of modern times had scored in South Africa. But the three losses were in the test series, and the defeats in the first and third tests were demolitions. The All Blacks might have returned unscathed by criticism if they had played at their best in those three losing games, but they made too many mistakes.

Veteran rugby writer Bob Howitt recalled visiting the seaside resort of East London in South Africa and eyeing the sandhills at the eastern end of the beach.

'These were the sandhills for marvelling at, for photographing, perhaps even for tumbling down. They were never designed for running up. But Ivan Vodanovich, who obviously had a masochistic side to his personality, determined that the 1970 All Blacks would be better prepared to tackle anything the South Africans might throw at them if they conquered these sandhills.'

Howitt believed Vodanovich, who 'inherited a sensationally good All Black team from Fred Allen, fell into the old trap in South Africa of revealing his hand too easily'.

'Shrewd old campaigners like Danie Craven lavished praise on Vodanovich's All Blacks as they swept aside their provincial opponents.

'They flattered the tourists, lauding them as the finest running team to visit South Africa. It was an invitation to produce more of the same. And Ivan's All Blacks obliged.'[3]

The Boks hit their guests like a whirlwind in the first test, and the All Blacks never truly recovered.

Even in the second test, which the All Blacks won, and in which they were dominant for much of the game, the score was only 9-8.

While manager Ron Burk would say that winning all the provincial matches and being in contention to tie the series right up to the final whistle of the fourth test made the tour a success, Vodanovich did not agree. He said he was decidedly uncomfortable with such an appraisal and could not live with it.

'We failed in what was the most fiercely burning ambition of my time: to beat South Africa in a series in South Africa. Were I to believe the tour was a success, how could I explain the deep depression I felt at the end of it?

'We made selection errors and were too much influenced by Hawke's Bay holding the Ranfurly Shield. I was never very confident about my understanding of fitness and I don't like coaching the team on my own,' he added in an honest, frank retrospective of the tour.

If Vodanovich did not obtain 100 per cent from his players either on or off the field in South Africa, there was reason to fear the same when his All Blacks met the Lions the following winter. There is little doubt that among the experienced players still available there were some who had become even more disillusioned by his methods.

Future New Zealand coach Laurie Mains made his All Black debut under Vodanovich, replacing Fergie McCormick for the second test against the Lions in 1971, after Barry John had outmanoeuvred McCormick to help the Lions win the opening test. Mains contributed to a stunning 22-12 victory at Lancaster Park in a game made famous by the extraordinary 55-metre solo try by Ian Kirkpatrick. It was to be the Lions' only loss of the tour, for they came back to Wellington to win the third test and then drew the fourth in Auckland 14-all.

Mains remembered the fitness work required by Vodanovich two or three days before the tests with disquiet.

"It staggered me that that would happen at that level. The amount of fitness work relevant to team work was unbelievable. There were heaps of meetings, but the coach did all the talking."[3]

If Mains, flushed with the excitement of his first series, was to make such observations imagine the disenchantment of the more experienced players in the side. Not for no reason had many an All Black called their coach Ivan the Terrible!

The mild-mannered Vodanovich had hit world headlines just as the series kicked off. After the Lions' particularly fiery match against Canterbury, Bob Howitt had asked Vodanovich what he'd thought of the day's brawling spectacle, expecting little more than a shrug of the shoulders. As Howitt was to recall:

"'I'll give you a statement," he said, his nostrils flared. "The first test will be another Passchendaele. The Lions' crude attempts to nullify our second phase play by lying on the ball are ruining a delightful part of rugby," Vodanovich said.'

'Once I worked out how to spell Passchendaele, I realised I was on to a major scoop. Ivan's comments were headlines throughout the world, with the lead-up to the first international dominated by reaction to Ivan's inflammatory comment.

'In the event, there was no Passchendaele at

Carisbrook, scarcely a fist raised in anger. The Lions didn't so much nullify second-phase play as the All Blacks overall. They tackled themselves to a standstill to register a famous victory, going on to clinch the series.

"Ivan stepped down after that . . . He deserved better, for no more conscientious individual ever filled the role."[4]

The fourth test of 1971 also marked the end of the career of Colin Meads, who had been captain for the series. He had played in 55 tests since 1957 – a period of 15 years. He was 35 in 1971, past his best but still worthy of the jersey.

Eleven new test players were introduced during the series. Seven came into the first test team, including Tane Norton and Peter Whiting, who would develop into key All Blacks over the years. Two newcomers, Mains and Howard Joseph, came into the second test team, while Phil Gard and Mick Duncan were introduced for the fourth test.

Meads was to state that Vodanovich had 'unfairly taken the blame for everything' that went wrong in the two series. He said it had been easier for an All Black coach and captain in the 1960s. 'Then we had at least six of the pack who were provincial captains and who were always thinking positively.'

Meads' greatest disappointment during his 15 All Black years was that he had failed to lead his team to victory over the Lions. 'They were a great side, but we had the beatings of them, specially in the first test in Dunedin. It was hard for so many inexperienced players to go straight into their first tests.'

Vodanovich had had a long first-class career, beginning with King Country in 1949. He played 112 matches for Wellington from 1950 to 1960, proving a strong, durable and consistent prop. As an All Black he played in the three tests of the home series against the Wallabies in 1955, scoring a try on his debut. He weighed 15st 12lb and stood just over 6ft tall.

After his retirement as a player, he was a keen and tireless organiser, coach and administrator who was involved with rugby for most of his life. He coached at club level in various grades, taking the Marist Old Boys to the Wellington Jubilee Cup championship in 1963.

He was a member of the NZRFU executive committee for more than 20 years, being on the coaching committee. This body produced a large number of coaching films under the direction of Peter Coates. Vodanovich was also the technical editor of a fine coaching book, *New Zealand Rugby Skills and Tactics*, published in 1982.

BIOGRAPHICAL DETAILS

Ivan Matthew Henry Vodanovich

Born: Wanganui, 8 April 1930

Died: Wellington, 2 September 1995

Position: Prop forward

Represented NZ: 1955 (3 matches)

Points for NZ: 3 (1 try)

Provincial record: King Country 1949 (Taumarunui club); Wellington 1950-60 (Marist); North Island 1955, 1960; NZ trials 1955-60

Selector/coach: Club coach in various grades, including Wellington senior championship with Marist 1963; North Island selection 1966-72

NZ selector: 1967-72

NZ coach: 1969-71

Other service: NZRFU executive committee 1969-91, elected life member 1991; NZRFU coaching committee; involved with production of many coaching films; technical editor of *NZ Rugby Skills and Tactics*, published 1982

Occupation: Menswear retailer in Wellington, in partnership with fellow former All Black, All Black coach and NZRFU chairman Tom Morrison

NEW ZEALAND COACHING RECORD

1969: beat Wales 19-0, 33-12

1970: lost to South Africa 6-17, beat South Africa 9-8, lost to South Africa 3-14, 17ñ20

1971: lost to Lions 3-9, beat Lions 22-12, lost to Lions 3-13, drew with Lions 14-all

REFERENCES
1. Don Cameron, *New Zealand Herald*, September 1995.
2. Bob Howitt, Vodanovich obituary, *Rugby News*, 1995.
3. Robin McConnell, *Inside the All Blacks*, HarperCollins Publishers, 1998.
4. Bob Howitt, *Rugby News*, 1995.

CHAPTER 25

NEW ZEALAND COACH 1972-73

BOB DUFF

History should not judge 'Duffer' unfairly

BOB DUFF MAY LONG BE REMEMBERED FOR TWO chapters in All Black rugby folklore.

One tells of an achievement as famous as any in the archives of New Zealand rugby history — his leading the All Blacks to their first series win, after 35 years of trying, over the Springboks, in 1956.

The other tells a tale as infamous as the first is famous, and most unfairly so for the gentlemanly Bob — to do with his coaching of the touring 1972–73 All Blacks from which Keith Murdoch was banished.

But Duff's contribution to rugby in general, and to the evolution of the professional All Black coach of today in particular, is much greater than the events of those few fleeting months in 1956 and 1972 might suggest.

Although he has received little credit for the achievement, Duff's brief era as coach of the All Blacks was to lay the foundations for a brilliant decade through the 1970s. How else can one explain the fact that so many of the promising youngsters he took to Britain and France in 1972 became the backbone of the All Blacks, season after season?

For some, the 1972 tour — and Bob Duff himself — are remembered only for the Keith Murdoch incident, the actions of the so-called Mafia within the All Black ranks, and the loss to the Barbarians in a splendid running match which the British have dined out on and employed as a textbook lesson ever since.

But that's not how Duff and the team remember it. Grant Batty described it as 'the happiest tour I ever went on'.[1] 'Bryan Williams recalled the preparation for the great victory over Wales as 'the best build-up to any test in which I played'. He found Duffer, as the players affectionately called him, to be a 'quiet man, a serious thinker, but able to relax and exhibit humour. But I was disappointed he was a forward-oriented coach, who never encouraged the backs greatly. He essentially left us to our own resources.'[2]

Alex Wyllie, who would return to Britain as coach of the All Blacks nearly 20 years later, said that the 1972–73 team bore an unjust reputation. The team could have faltered with the expulsion of Keith Murdoch after the first of its five tests. Instead, in adversity and under pressure, it grew stronger.

'Bob Duff was vital to us. He got on well with all the players, and he was well respected. He had such a young team, probably one of the youngest the All Blacks ever had on tour,' said Wyllie.[3]

Sid Going was another who felt Duff unfairly took the blame for problems on the tour. He related how Duff had cleverly played to the young team's strengths. 'He wanted the forwards to dominate and the backs to keep play close and eliminate mistakes. He restored tightness to the forwards that had been lost in South Africa and against the Lions [of 1971].' He strove to return New Zealand scrummaging to its former glory, ensuring the flankers did their share.[4]

The 1972 All Blacks should have been the first to win the grand slam. They beat Wales, Scotland and England and then suffered the ignominy, after dominating throughout, of a 10-all draw when Ireland scored in the final moments.

'The team did not carry out the plan I had asked of them,' said Duff of the Irish test, when interviewed in 1997. 'We were superior and should have won it. They knew I was annoyed too. I didn't speak to them for quite some time, which wasn't usually my style if we lost.'

Duff will never forget the Murdoch incident. It came after Murdoch had been one of the All Black heroes, scoring New Zealand's only try in the 19-16 win over Wales. He punched a Welsh security guard in the team's Cardiff hotel, the Angel, during the celebrations on the night of the test.

It was Duff who finally persuaded Murdoch to go to his room, which he shared with Lin Colling, an old friend from his days with the Ponsonby club. The next day Duff and captain Ian Kirkpatrick, and later Sid Going, spent a lot of time with team manager Ernie Todd trying to ensure Murdoch got a fair hearing.

'I went to bed believing Keith was not going home and he was actually chosen for our next game,' recalled Duff.

He also remembered taking a call from NZRFU chairman Jack Sullivan in New Zealand. Todd was not at the hotel at the time.

SON OF ANAK: Bob Duff, a huge man for the times, dribbles the ball through despairing Springbok defenders during Canterbury's triumph on the 1956 tour. Duff, with 'Tiny' White, locked the All Black scrum in a grip of iron throughout the series and took over the captaincy for the decisive third and fourth tests.

BOB DUFF

'"I understand you're having some problems. Get Ernie to ring me,"' Duff recalled Sullivan saying. 'I believe the NZRFU told Ernie, "You're in charge — you do what's best." I think they were passive, not active observers.'

But that is not what rugby author Ron Palenski believes took place. He wrote that Jack Sullivan made the final decision and ordered Todd to send Murdoch home.[4]

Asked by the author in 1997 how he came to this conclusion, Palenski said he could not break a confidentiality, but had 'no doubts whatsoever that the information is true'. He also said he could understand Bob Duff and the players would not have been privy to the inside story.[4]

He confirmed Duff's understanding that on the Sunday morning Todd had decided Murdoch would be severely reprimanded, that no police charges would be laid, and that he would continue on the tour. But the home unions were not placated, and after a series of phone calls between Sullivan and the unions, it became clear the rest of the tour was in jeopardy. Sullivan then phoned Todd and gave the order.

Duff believed Todd, who had become increasingly unwell on the tour and was to die of cancer in November 1974, was put under enormous pressure by the home unions.

Duff kept a tour diary, and he noted, when interviewed for this book, that Todd had taken ill during the first tour match at Gloucester. Duff had given the team speech in his place and, according to many of the players, was to take on more and more of the management duties as the tour proceeded.

It is notable that Duff's team's achievements came between the two great Lions tours of 1971 (when they beat the All Blacks in New Zealand) and 1974 (when they beat the Springboks in South Africa). British rugby was at its strongest ever. Duff's tyros faced defensive-minded teams with shallow back lines and they often played in bleak, cold and wet conditions. They still scored 103 tries in 34 matches, averaging more than three tries per game.

The grand slam was left for Jack Gleeson's 1978 All Blacks, with many of the same players. But it was that feature of the 1972 team — that they contained at least eight youngsters who were to go on to cement places in the All Blacks for, in some cases, as long as the next decade — which is part of the Bob Duff legacy.

'As a proving ground for many of the stars of the next decade, the tour had to be branded an enormous success,' concluded Bryan Williams.[5] Kenny Stewart was 19, Kent Lambert, Joe Karam and Bruce Robertson 20, Grant Batty and Ian Hurst 21, and Andy Haden and Bryan Williams 22.

Duff lost the coaching berth to J. J. Stewart for the England test in 1973 and was dropped from the panel at the end of that season. He said it would be less than honest of him to say it didn't disappoint him.

'I'd have thought it would have been a natural progression, having had me coach the team on the long 1972–73 tour, to possibly have me continue.'

The All Blacks returned to Britain in 1974 under Stewart and new captain Andy Leslie. The team did well and it seemed a bold new era. But the team which beat Wales in 1974 contained 11 players from Duff's side: Karam, Batty, Williams, Robertson, Hurst, Going, Kirkpatrick, Macdonald, Whiting, Lambert and Norton. It was a new-look team with old-look players.

Like other former All Black coaches, Duff eyes the resources behind John Hart's All Blacks with wonderment and not a little envy. He firmly believes the modern All Black coach is the result of 'evolutionary progress' to which he and others contributed.

He learned a good part of his coaching skills from Jack Rankin, Bob Stuart and Neil McPhail, who had preceded him as coaches of Canterbury and, in the cases of Stuart and McPhail, the All Blacks. The 1972–73 All Blacks practised squad drills, and the team was issued with a specialist fitness programme, upon selection, before the tour. The players' weights were regularly monitored and action taken when required.

Duff said his written tour report was 'never required by the NZRFU'. That amazed him, because he felt the knowledge to be gained for future touring teams was invaluable. He understood Ernie Todd made only a verbal report to the union. He feels strongly that the NZRFU should have had an 'archive of tours' to assist planning.

When the 1978 grand slam All Blacks toured under Jack Gleeson and Russ Thomas, Duff took it upon himself to make recommendations. A doctor and a physio with the team was one which became reality.

'To me it's natural evolution. In my playing days, if you wanted two balls the union would look long at you. As a coach, I always demanded six balls out on the training field. Laurie Mains was still fighting for things. Now John Hart has 36 players on a short but intense tour.'

Duff's All Black playing career spanned from 1951 to 1956, all of it spent in the mighty engine room, locking the scrum with the legendary Tiny White. Duff played in all of the three tests when the All Blacks toured Australia in 1951, clean-sweeping the series. Two tests followed when the Wallabies toured New Zealand in 1952.

He was unavailable for the decade's most important tour, the 1953–54 trip to Britain and France, on which the team was captained by Bob Stuart, his Canterbury captain and the man who would assist the national selectors in plotting the downfall of the Springboks with Duff at the helm *(see Chapters 19, 21 and 22)*.

He made a comeback in 1955 against the touring Australians, after being unavailable for the opening test through injury. He replaced Peter Burke for the second and third tests in a 2-1 winning series that did not augur too well for the coming of the Springboks the following winter.

Yet another of the many ironies of Duff's long rugby career came when he replaced Pat Vincent as All Black captain for the third and fourth tests against the Springboks. He had been vice-captain when Vincent had led the All Blacks to a first-test win and second-test loss, after which Vincent and others were axed for a new-look side which now included Don Clarke, Kevin Skinner, Tiny Hill, Ponty Reid and Peter Jones.

Duff had played under Vincent's leadership for many years. They had first played together in the Christchurch Boys' High School first XV in 1943. They made their debut for Canterbury in the same game, against Ashburton, in 1945. The pair later helped spearhead the successful Canterbury team which held the Ranfurly Shield from 1953 to 1956.

Another irony was that Vincent would be dumped after leading two teams, the All Blacks in the first test and Canterbury a week later, to victory over the mighty Springboks. He was believed to be the first person to have accomplished this feat, within that time frame, and possibly remains so.

Two of Duff's strongest personal qualities as a champion player, captain, selector and coach were patience and imperturbability. He has needed both in great quantities over the years since that fateful afternoon on 18 August 1956 when he led the All Blacks out from under a Lancaster Park stand to face the mighty Boks with the series locked at 1-1, with a certain Kevin Lawrence Skinner jogging behind him.

The veteran Springbok props, Jaap Bekker and Chris Koch, had proved powerful opponents earlier in the series. Koch had dominated All Black loose-head props

COMETH THE HOUR: Bob Duff (right) had almost always played under the captaincy of Pat Vincent (left) through school, representative and international rugby. But in 1956, after leading the All Blacks to a win and a loss against the Springboks, Vincent was dropped and Duff elevated to the captaincy to lead New Zealand to its first series win over South Africa.

Mark Irwin (who retired with damaged ribs after the first test) and his replacement, Frank McAtamney (dropped to the reserves after the second test).

Skinner was brought in to partner Ian Clarke. He swapped sides with Clarke at half-time, causing years of speculation and debate that he had been chosen primarily to deal to the Bok giants one after the other. There were certainly some fisticuffs, first as Skinner marked Koch and later with Bekker. The outbreaks led

BOB DUFF

to referee Bill Fright calling aside the captains, Duff and Basie Viviers.

The legend goes that Skinner had a vendetta to settle with the Boks, especially Koch, whom he had marked in two tests way back in the humiliating 4-nil whitewash of the 1949 All Blacks. But Duff rubbishes that theory, as well as any other sinister motive for the swap that had been proposed.

'The exchange of Kevin and Ian Clarke was simply because Ian had a very sore cauliflower ear,' he explained. 'He asked me at the interval whether they could change positions and I said I was happy for them to swap.

'Kevin was not going to take a backward step from either Koch or Bekker and he settled their differences in the quickest way possible. But there were only two incidents that I can recall — the whole episode has been blown out of all proportion in the years since.'

It is also true Skinner was a former New Zealand heavyweight boxing champion. But that had been in 1947, a decade before the 1956 series. He had also been the New Zealand captain in 1952 and played in 61 matches for the All Blacks — equalling Maurice Brownlie's then record — before retiring after the 1953–54 tour. All that time and service without being noted as anything other than a hard but fair footballer . . .

South African journalist Max Price probably contributed to the legend when he wrote that at the third test dinner 'there were several bruised and patched faces to be seen, and very jocularly Jaap Bekker remarked to Skinner that he hoped to see him in action at the Olympic Games in Melbourne later in the year'. Bekker's brother, Daan, represented South Africa in boxing at those Olympics, winning a bronze medal. He went one better four years later in Rome, taking silver.

BACKBONE: Pocket battleship Grant Batty rounds in for another All Black try. He was one of many youngsters nurtured by coach Bob Duff on the 1972-73 tour. Duff was sacked but these players became the backbone of the All Blacks for many years.

Price summed up the Springbok response to the manner in which the All Blacks beat them for the first time.

'We had been aware long before of the great forward strength of New Zealand teams, but when it hit the Springboks full blast at Waikato with fierce rucks flattening out roads to the Springbok defence line, we sat back almost stunned.

'This was something entirely new. However tough it was thought the forward play of New Zealand would be, none, not the Springboks nor the selectors, press and public of South Africa, were prepared for forward play of this hard-hitting, commando-like character.'

Morrie McKenzie, in his 1960 book, *All Blacks in Chains*, discussed that 1956 All Black side, so swiftly elevated from years of mediocrity to the slippery heights of world supremacy.

'The two best previous sides of our modern era were the 1924 All Blacks and Philip Nel's 1937 Springboks. I do not think that either could have beaten Bob Duff's All Blacks, certainly not in the third and fourth tests.

'Such tremendous physical strength and controlled power as the 1956 All Blacks possessed up front, plus the goal-kicking fullback of the majestic range, under pressure, of Don Clarke, will swamp and crush to death the most brilliant footballers who ever lived.

'What a collection of human tanks were these. Skinner, Hemi and Ian Clarke in the front row; two sons of Anak, Duff and White, locking the pack in a grip of iron; with Hill behind them driving it relentlessly forward; while the superheavyweight sprinter Jones and the ghostlike [Bill] Clark alternately angled their pushing power or sped like guided missiles to their targets in mid-field.

'Here (alas, for one test series only) was gathered together the finest set of forwards I have ever seen.'[6]

It was high praise indeed from a journalist who had observed generations of international rugby players.

Duff, who later became Deputy-Mayor of Lyttelton, where he ran his accountancy practice for about 40 years, can take some credit for the publication of *The Power behind the All Blacks*. It was while interviewing Duff soon after he had been sacked from his All Black coaching position that the author first had the germ of an idea for a book on all the All Black coaches, and began to work on the huge subject.

Duff now lives in retirement in Christchurch with his wife, Neroli. They both play bridge and golf. He said he 'threw out my principles and got Sky in 1995' to watch the big rugby occasions.

BIOGRAPHICAL DETAILS

Robert Hamilton Duff

Born: Lyttelton, 5 August 1925

Position: Lock forward

Represented NZ: 1951–52, 1955–56
18 matches (11 internationals)

Provincial record: Canterbury 1945–53, 1955–57; South Island 1952–53, 1955–57

Selector/coach: Canterbury 1963–66
South Island 1967–72

NZ selector: 1971–73

NZ coach: 1972–73

Other: Life member Canterbury Park Trotting Club; former chairman Addington Raceway; former board member NZ Racing Industry Board (formerly NZ Racing Authority)

Occupation: Accountant

NEW ZEALAND COACHING RECORD

1972–73: beat Australia 29-6, 30-17, 38-3; beat Wales 19-6; beat Scotland 14-9; beat England 9-0; drew with Ireland 10-10; lost to France 6-13

REFERENCES
1. Bob Howitt, *Grant Batty*, Rugby Press, 1977.
2. Bob Howitt, *Beegee: The Bryan Williams Story*, Rugby Press, 1981.
3. Bob Howitt, *Super Sid*, Rugby Press, 1978.
4. Ron Palenski, *Our National Game*.
5. *Beegee: The Bryan Williams Story*.

CHAPTER 26

NEW ZEALAND COACH 1973-76

JOHN ('J.J.') STEWART

'J.J.' was rugby's gentleman revolutionary

THE POWER BEHIND THE ALL BLACKS

ONE OF THE GREAT ACCOMPLISHMENTS OF J. J. Stewart as All Black coach was that he took a large group of provincial also-rans and quickly converted them into a team that climbed back to the top of the international ladder.

But more lasting was his influence on New Zealand rugby coaching at all levels over at least the next decade. His pragmatic but sympathetic coaching ethos, especially the value he placed on a balanced game plan and player input into tactics, rubbed off on all who came in contact with him.

With his background as a teacher, coach, original thinker and man manager, his success is not surprising. What is surprising is the way he returned from 'Mission Impossible' — another All Black tour of South Africa frustrated by biased and incompetent refereeing — to be dumped by the union, only to rise again inside that same organisation as an NZRFU councillor bent on reform.

Stewart was a man ahead of his time. He was an enlightened rugby coach who involved his players in decision-making and responsibility. A visionary, he never shrank from expressing honest views and criticisms, even at the expense of earning the ire of rugby's establishment. Nor has any other All Black coach written with such simplicity, skill and understanding about rugby coaching and rugby's heritage as a constantly developing game.

Stewart's background, if not unique among All Black coaches, was different from most. Injury ended an unremarkable senior playing career during the war years, but meant Stewart, as a teacher, started coaching at a young age.

He began with junior teams at New Plymouth Boys' High, but in 1950 was asked to coach the first XV. He was to do the job for 15 years.

From 1957 to 1962, he had unprecedented success, his teams being unbeaten in traditional interschool fixtures. During that time he was also appointed coach/co-manager of the New Zealand Colts team which toured Australia and Ceylon (now Sri Lanka) in 1955. Then came a seven-year stint as coach of Taranaki, including the famous 1963-65 Ranfurly Shield tenure. Two years as Wanganui's coach followed.

According to K. J. Gledhill, Stewart's knowledge of the rules, especially the potential of rule changes in a team's tactical approach, helped his school teams.

'His innovative methods did not escape criticism however, most notably from beaten teams and commentators, who didn't appreciate or realise the impact the laws were having on constructive backplay. A noted commentator of the time was to label New Plymouth Boys' High's style as "ruinous of secondary school rugby", yet had overlooked the positive backplay his teams were producing.'[1]

Stewart realised early what a 'winning habit' required, specially developing a style of play around a team's strengths and weaknesses. He became skilled at analysing the opposition and communicating his philosophy — an intellectual approach to the game plan by all involved.

The rules of the day, up until 1963, meant back lines were 'eyeball to eyeball'. Stewart's answer to this included a shallow-standing back line (deeper-standing back lines were in danger of being caught behind the gain line) skilled at passing the ball quickly to their outsides; the kick in behind as an alternative; loose forwards to recover possession; and second-phase attacks. In 1959 alone, his wingers scored 100 points each (at three points a try).

Stewart's move to coach Taranaki coincided with the momentous 1963 rule changes. Their impact was not immediately apparent to some, and he was able to exploit his knowledge. The 'What would a bloody schoolteacher know about dealing with men or rep rugby?' sceptics in the squad were quickly won over.

As the team developed, he became a sort of 'chairman of the board', encouraging player participation and responsibility in pre- and after-match analysis — 'player ownership of tactics', as he called it. He could 'fade into the background' and 'allow his captain and team to get on with it'. Team spirit was high, and not only because this was the province's finest hour. However, again, he was to experience criticism for the way his teams played.

From 1970, when he ran the first of many annual national coaching schools, Stewart was to place his mark on New Zealand's coaching methods at a more influential level.

From 1973 to 1976 Stewart was the All Black coach. He came after the intense disappointments of the 1970

FIRST AND LAST: The 1973 test against England at Auckland, lost 10-16, was J.J. Stewart's first test as All Black coach and the last as All Black test captain for Ian Kirkpatrick. It was also the last international appearance for a number of players as Stewart and his selectors made wholesale changes in 1974. Back Row: John Dougan, Ian Hurst, Bob Lendrum, Bryan Williams, Duncan Robertson, Dave Pescini; Third Row: Kent Lambert, Mike Parkinson, Tane Norton, Alex Wyllie, Terry Morrison; Second Row: Bill Bush, Ken Stewart, Alan Sutherland, Sam Strahan, Hamish Macdonald, Murray Jones; Front Row: Bob Duff (selector), Lin Colling, Ian Kirkpatrick (captain), J.J. Stewart (convenor), Sid Going, Grant Batty, Jack Gleeson (selector).

tour to South Africa and the unprecedented series loss to the 1971 Lions. Although his legacy was to leave a remarkable number of young All Blacks as the cornerstone of New Zealand teams for years to come, Bob Duff's short reign as coach in 1972-73 had caused some disquiet because of the emphasis on forward domination and a halfback who linked with loose forwards. Stewart seemed the right man for the time. Reflecting the freer society of the day, players were increasingly unprepared to slog it out unquestioningly. They wished to know the reasons behind a strategy and that their own ideas might be listened to. Stewart's background was perfect for encouraging participation, thereby stimulating players and boosting their self-confidence.

With far greater talent than he had ever had access to before, Stewart knew he had only to choose the right players for any particular job or game and he could once again be 'chairman of the board'. His philosophy of method in all phases of team management was to reach new levels.

It has long been presumed the NZRFU wanted Stewart and his fellow selectors to alter the direction of the game. But Stewart is adamant he was 'never given any instructions or guidelines by the NZRFU or any individual member'. He nevertheless switched the axis of the All Blacks' game from a halfback/loose forward to a wing/loose forward orientation. Meanwhile, backs were encouraged to run, pass, initiate moves and 'take whatever opportunities presented themselves' to reach the try line. Forwards were not neglected — the All Blacks' scrummaging of 1974 and 1976 was among the best of the decade.

In harness with his captain, Andy Leslie, Stewart steered his All Black teams such that they gained a reputation for harmony, sociability and attractive rugby and helped restore the All Black image at home and abroad. His impact as New Zealand coach set the standards and the modus operandi for his immediate successors and therefore went far beyond his simple win-loss record.

Stewart himself claimed that, in retrospect, he 'should never have been appointed in 1973'. His fellow selectors were Duff, who had coached the big 1972-73 tour, and Jack Gleeson, coach of the 1972 internal tour. 'I recall we drove from Hamilton to Whakatane to watch a game. I sat in the back seat and offered one or two suggestions from this unfavourable position, which were considered to have little merit — and rightly so, I guess,' said Stewart. 'They were more au fait with the top player merit order than I.

'The team finally selected did not contain one player I had previously had anything to do with. It was hard work. I was expected to yell and rant in the coaching tradition of the times, and that wasn't what I did.'

Stewart ruefully recalled his first test match as All Black coach, beaten in 1973 by the touring England team 10-16, after it had lost their three provincial games.

The All Blacks stayed at the Station Hotel in Auckland, on a floor of bedrooms 'that were no longer used because they did not meet the statutory standards,' according to Stewart. 'Two All Blacks to each little room, no individual room facilities, a bathroom-toilet at the end of the passage. It was prewar facilities,' he told the author in 1997.

'Although Auckland officials were very helpful, and since the NZRFU had not appointed one, I was supposed to be the manager, the organiser of homeward transport, organising pick-ups for players when they arrived in Auckland. In retrospect, there was just no way that any team could have won that game. I was disappointed and I thought, well, if this is rugby at the top level, that'll do me.'

But Stewart was persuaded to stick with it. With fellow selectors Gleeson and Eric Watson (who had replaced Duff), they began one of New Zealand rugby's most daring revolutions. Two-thirds of the All Black team that toured Australia in 1974 were new, including the captain, Andy Leslie.

The NZFRU gave Stewart a manager this time, the genial King Country undertaker Les Byars. The team prospered, which was not actually surprising since many of the newcomers had been hardened by years of experience in provincial football.

The end-of-year trip to Ireland was to be capped by an extraordinary conclusion — three 'tests' in eight days. The Ireland international, won 15-6, was followed by the midweek Wales XV game, won 12-3, and then by the Barbarians fixture, drawn 13-all. The Barbarians had stacked their team with players from the Lions team which had been unbeaten in South Africa earlier in the year, including the entire forward pack.

'We had to play through the "hate" thing between New Zealand and Wales, a bit media-fanned I must say, that had developed since the Angel Hotel incident involving Keith Murdoch a year earlier,' said Stewart.

'Then the Barbarians decided our team weren't going to get out of the British Isles undefeated. So we were into it at the deep end.'

Stewart's All Blacks were to keep improving. One of the most famous games was their masterful display in the 24-0 win over Scotland at the waterlogged Eden Park in

THE POWER BEHIND THE ALL BLACKS

NO QUARTER: All Black halfback Sid Going is in trouble during the 1973 Eden Park test against England. It was the first test in charge for All Black coach J.J. Stewart and one he does not fondly remember. England won 16-10.

1975. Andy Leslie recalled that, unbeknown to the All Blacks, the Scots had wanted to call the game off and play the next day.

The 1976 tour of South Africa, begun so optimistically, was almost inevitably to follow a pattern similar to that of some of its predecessors. The series was lost 1-3, the chance of tying the rubber hanging in the balance until the final whistle of the fourth test, lost 14-15.

It is probably of little succour to Stewart and his players that the series was the last to be played with referees from the host country. It was widely reported, and is probably regarded as fact today, that the NZRFU had declined the offer of neutral referees, a decision that proved crucial in the final outcome of the series. But that was not correct, according to Stewart.

'I don't think an offer of neutral referees was ever made to the NZRFU. It may have been made in conversation in a rather non-serious way, and rejected in the same manner,' said Stewart. 'I have never been able to find any written record of such an offer.'

One instance of questionable refereeing occurred late in the fourth test, with the score 12-11 to the home team. South African referee Gert Bezuidenhout was called upon to make a decision that clearly called for a penalty try. All Black Bruce Robertson chipped into the in-goal area, a try for the taking, only to be taken out of the play by Springbok fullback Ian Robertson. Instead of six points, and the likely winning of the game, the referee awarded a penalty, which yielded three points.

So the tour ended on a sour note. There had been some selection blunders, and the goal-kickers, as on previous tours, had been unable to match the Springboks. But this team had played themselves to a standstill and failed to share the series by the tiniest margin possible.

A myth that arose from the Stewart era was that he handpicked Andy Leslie to lead the reformation of All Black rugby. Not so, according to the coach.

'It happened underneath the stand at Athletic Park. Jack Sullivan, the NZRFU chairman, had come in to give the selectors a hurry-along and then reminded us that we'd have to pick a captain. The others said, "Well, it's got to be Kirky." But I had got the impression from my

163

JOHN STEWART

association with him in 1973 that the captaincy wasn't sitting very easily with Kirky at that time.

'Don't misunderstand me. He's one of the greatest persons I've ever met, certainly one of the greatest footballers you'd ever meet. But I didn't feel that being captain was pleasing him and I said that. They said, "Well, who else have we got?" Then we started to look at the list. People have said that Leslie was selected to be captain, but that isn't true. He was selected in the team and then we started to look for the captain.'

Leslie's elevation came as a surprise to him. He was 29 and had long given up any serious hope of becoming an All Black. His place in recent trials had been 'just to make up the numbers'. Remarkable proof of this belief was in a letter he had written to his wife, Leslie, during a pre-season trip to South Africa by his club side, Petone. Andy wrote that he would not go on any more trips without her. Fortunately, for his All Black future, delivery of the letter was inexplicably delayed. Leslie received it as Andy was in the middle of leading the 1974 Australian tour. Had it arrived on time, he might have been forced to uphold his promise and try to break with the then tradition of excluding wives and partners on a tour.

The hardest part for Andy Leslie was taking over from Ian Kirkpatrick, although if we accept Stewart's version of events, Kirkpatrick was probably relieved to have the burden of captaincy lifted from his shoulders. He certainly played like it in Australia, tackling his new-found freedom with enthusiasm and taking his game to a new level. He was also one of the first to congratulate Leslie after the announcement and became probably Leslie's most able and faithful supporter over the next several seasons.

But others didn't see it that way. Leslie's appointment was not well received at first, and he recalls players giving him a hard time on the night of the selection, whether celebrating or drowning their sorrows.

STRETCHING OUT: Andy Ripley is about to haul in Grant Batty during the shock 1973 win by England, 16-10, over the All Blacks in J. J. Stewart's first test as coach.

'That was the hard part in becoming captain,' Leslie said. 'I was taking the place of the most popular player in the team and it was a case of overcoming a sort of wall. There was a certain amount of animosity — towards me.'[2]

Leslie found Stewart a marvellous All Black coach. 'It was amazing how much we were on the same wavelength in our attitude to the game. He could have been the All Black coach 10 years beforehand. I think our group were lucky to have him when we did.

'We weren't a great side. We were labelled Dad's Army at first. But he certainly turned us into a very competitive one. I think probably the greatest moment was on our tour of Ireland, when we actually pushed the Irish pack [then a far greater international force than it is today] back in the scrum. I think he fulfilled a little dream that we were going to turn New Zealand rugby around. I think it was at that moment when it all happened.'

Stewart can take credit for the transformation of All Black scrummaging from a weak, seldom-practised phase to a dynamic art form, equipped so that the All Blacks have seldom had to struggle since.

'Throughout the 1974 Australian tour we spent hours and hours at scrum practice. We virtually had to reinvent the wheel in this respect — the setting: grips, feet position, body position; and the dynamics: joining, foot movement, the push, sustaining the push, and so forth.

'By the end of that tour I thought we had a pretty good scrum. Later in the year, when we got to Ireland and after the first game, I found we didn't. So it was back to the drawing board — hours of discussion and hours of practice. By the end I knew we had a good scrum. The Barbarians, who chose a pack which had done so well in this phase in South Africa earlier that year, could not move us.'

Good humour was an essential ingredient on any tour led by Stewart. He saved some of the best for when prying opposition eyes were watching the All Blacks practise. He would have the team completing weird and inventive moves out of no textbook. One was the 'up the jumper' move, performed when prying Australian selectors were watching a practice at Dubbo before the game against NSW Country. Later, NSW Country made the move famous when it actually scored a try using it. The move was then banned.

'We had a move where we threw Grant Batty over the scrum to score tries,' Leslie said. 'Another was where our back line ran backwards, towards its own goal line, with Joe Karam throwing gridiron-style across the field to Beegee Williams, who would be steaming through.'

A feature of Stewart's time with the All Blacks was that he took into account the views of senior players in choosing his teams. Whether this was a strength or weakness depends on your point of view. More than one former All Black under Stewart complained about the habit.

Andy Haden was to write of his belief, from conversations with selectors, that he had done enough in the trials for the 1976 team to South Africa to be selected. But Stewart, he claimed, had allowed himself to be influenced by certain players into taking Gary Seear, a specialist No. 8, as the fourth lock.

'This probably pinpoints J. J. Stewart's weakness as a selector and coach, his allowing players to influence his selections. This trend certainly changed after J. J. Stewart dropped from the scene,' wrote Haden. However, he said he had enjoyed his brief association with Stewart in 1973 as a replacement on the All Blacks' internal tour, after the team had been beaten by the New Zealand Juniors. 'It was an awkward time for a coach, but J. J. handled the situation with considerable dignity. He was certainly one of the best thinkers New Zealand rugby had had at top level in modern times.'

Haden revealed Stewart had written to him after that tour to encourage him. Showing remarkable foresight, considering Haden was subsequently to remain in All Black limbo for several years, Stewart predicted Haden would go on to play many games for New Zealand.

'He said that what All Black rugby required was a continually changing unit with a stable central core which could be coached by anyone, it didn't matter who. How right he was.

'Tragically, the same brilliant thinker and coach was held responsible for the failings of the 1976 All Blacks in South Africa and dumped by the New Zealand union upon his return.'[3]

While Stewart's fate after the 1976 tour was harsh, particularly in light of the refereeing decisions, Bryan Williams was to assert the coach had made some blunders in selections on tour.

J. J. appointed himself sole selector for the tour but confided in two or three of the senior players before announcing his choices. Pole Whiting and Grant Batty were two of his confidants and I personally believed they had too great an influence in team selection.'

In Williams' opinion it had been a major mistake to drop Doug Bruce and Kevin Eveleigh for the third test, and Bill Bush, despite an injured ankle, should have played instead of newcomer Perry Harris. The sending home of

JOHN STEWART

injured Brad Johnstone instead of the ill Kerry Tanner had been another mistake, he said.

Former All Black and later All Black coach Laurie Mains has also criticised Stewart for some of his test selections on the tour. Mains never got a test, Stewart instead playing his Otago team-mates Duncan Robertson, a first five-eighth, and Kit Fawcett in two tests each. With goal-kicking so crucial, Mains found the use of part-timers Sid Going and Bryan Williams hard to understand and was supported in this contention by the results. He felt he warranted at least third- and fourth-test selection on that basis alone.

'I found it incredible that he could put Duncan at fullback. Duncan and I both knew he could not do the job as well as me. He simply didn't understand the strategy of fullback play. He'd never played there before and he didn't appear there subsequently.' Fawcett, who had been a fringe player for Otago, was 'a player with tons of talent but no application'.

Mains claimed cliques developed on that tour and that these 'dictated the selection'. He believed several players retained their places in the test team on reputation and through the 'old boy network'.[4]

Stewart won a place on the NZRFU council in 1985, a decade after his last tour. He would lose his seat in 1989 to Kel Tremain.

He was primarily involved with the NZRFU coaching committee, which was attempting to make the game safer. The advent of power scrummaging had been the major cause of deaths and paralysing injuries among young players. The committee would make domestic rule changes that improved the safety aspect.

Asked to comment on the future direction of rugby, Stewart said: 'The council as I knew it has all gone now. It won't be long before someone like Brierley buys the New Zealand union.

'We are right on the track of professional soccer and the major American professional sports. That's the shaky road we've put our foot on . . . '

Stewart, now 76 and retired, completed a philosophy degree from Massey University, a degree he started 48 years earlier. He was honoured with the MBE in 1983. 'The Govenor-General, in presenting the award at the investiture, did mention rugby and my coaching at schoolboy, provincial and national levels, which was very considerate of him. But the award was really made for my contribution to agricultural and horticultural education and training,' said Stewart in typical droll humour.

BIOGRAPHICAL DETAILS

John Joseph Stewart

Born: Northcote, Auckland, 18 July 1923

Provincial record: Massey University 1941, 1943; Manawatu 1944; Auckland Teachers' College 1946-47; New Plymouth High School Old Boys 1948

Selector/coach: New Plymouth Boys' High School first XV 1950-64; Taranaki 1963-69; Wanganui 1970-71; North Island 1972, 1977; coach NZ Colts, Australia and Ceylon, 1955

NZ selector: 1973-77

NZ coach: 1973-76

Other service: NZRFU council 1985-89

Occupation: Retired; was principal Flock House Farm Training Institute, Bulls; before that master at New Plymouth Boys' High School 1948-69

Other: Historian, rules of rugby; published works — Creative Rugby, Rugby Law: A Player's Guide, Gumboots & Goalposts (rural short stories), Rugby: A Tactical Appreciation, Rugby: Developments in the Field of Play (history of rule changes and influence on the game); MBE for services to agricultural and horticulcural education 1983.

NEW ZEALAND COACHING RECORD

1973: lost to England 10-16

1974: beat Australia 11-6; drew with Australia 16 all; beat Australia 16-6; beat Ireland 15-6

1975: beat Scotland 24-0

1976: beat Ireland 11-3; lost to South Africa 7-16; beat South Africa 15-9; lost to South Africa 10-15, lost to South Africa 14-15

REFERENCES

1 K. J. Gledhill, *Rugby Coaching: The JJ Stewart Way*.

2 Andy Haden, *Boots 'n' All*, Rugby Press, 1984.

3 Bob Howitt, *Beegee: The Bryan Williams Story*, Rugby Press, 1981.

4 Bob Howitt and Robin McConnell, *Laurie Mains*, Rugby Press, 1966.

CHAPTER 27

NEW ZEALAND COACH 1972, 1976-82

JACK GLEESON

All Blacks' first Grand Slam didn't tell the whole story

JACK GLEESON'S GREATEST FEAT AS ALL BLACK coach was that he led New Zealand to their first grand slam.

Without denigrating the accomplishment of that outstanding Graham Mourie-captained team of 1978, it should be pointed out that four of Gleeson's predecessors had been unbeaten in their tests in Britain. The 1924 Invincibles were not invited to play Scotland, the 1963–64 All Blacks drew with Scotland, the 1967 side did not play Ireland and the 1972 All Blacks drew with Ireland.

From a historical perspective, therefore, the Grand Slam, while a marvellous achievement, was only slightly better than the accomplishments of those other All Black tourists, especially the 1924 and 1967 sides. It should be mentioned, too, that Laurie Mains' All Blacks achieved the grand slam in a different way — by beating all four home unions in the space of a couple of weeks at the 1995 World Cup. But on hard, fast grounds away from their old sod, that, of course, was a different proposition from Gleeson's efforts.

Gleeson's All Black coaching career was inextricably linked with the brilliant All Black captain of that era, Graham Mourie. Although Eric Watson, who would succeed Gleeson as All Black coach in 1979, had played a major role in the development of Mourie's leadership and loose-forward skills, it was Gleeson who would take the Taranaki man the final few steps to All Black captaincy and success.

The rise and rise of Mourie and Gleeson went hand in glove. Gleeson had his first real contact with Mourie on the Argentine tour of 1976. Mourie was almost certainly headed for All Black captaincy even before the circumstances of that tour evolved. Yet it was the meeting of the two men, their style of dealing with players and their tactical approach to the game, which were to form a bond that would see All Black rugby rise immediately from the disappointments of South Africa only a month or two earlier in the year.

'Gleeson, a man of shrewd intellect, with the gift of being a good listener and a talent for man management, shaped more the way Mourie teams played, rather than the way Mourie himself was required to play,' wrote Ron Palenski.

'Gleeson was not of the shout-at-them, die-for-your-country school of coaches, a breed which thankfully seems not to have survived into the 1980s. Standing on the sideline during Gleeson training sessions, you could rarely hear him. What you could hear wasn't a command: "Do this." Rather, it was a suggestion which brought all his players into the decision-making process: "What do you think about this?"'

Gleeson's strategy was not to play into the hands of

JACK GLEESON

DOUBTFUL HONOURS: Jack Gleeson's All Black coaching era began in 1972 with the internal tour of New Zealand. The All Blacks, in their first tour match, were beaten by the New Zealand Juniors, who had had eight matches in preparation. The team is: Back Row: Tane Norton, Richie Guy, Bruce Robertson, Ron Urlich, Keith Murdoch; Second Row: Alan McNaughton, Graham Whiting, Alan Sutherland, Hamish Macdonald, Ian Eliason, Bevan Holmes; Sitting: Bryan Williams, Phil Gard, Ian Kirkpatrick (captain), J. Gleeson (manager), Sid Going (vice captain), Trevor Morris, Lin Colling; In Front: Duncan Hales, John Dougan, Ken Carrington, Bob Burgess.

the power-obsessed Argentinians. He sacrificed some lineout height for loose-forward mobility, running their big forwards around and controlling secondary possession. These tactics were to bubble up again and again, when required, during the Gleeson–Mourie and Watson–Mourie eras, against the Lions in 1977, in France later that year, and on the British tours of 1978, 1979 and 1980.

Shortly before his death from cancer in 1979, in a television interview with rugby commentator Keith Quinn, Gleeson explained his belief in the importance of getting players to think. 'The whole game is thought; gone is the day of brute strength and ignorance. Rugby is a game of thought. Play the game at pace and be a thinker.'

The third test against the Lions in 1977 had exemplified rugby as he had wanted it played, he continued: '. . . we were winning very little ball, but we went out there with the plan to run whatever ball we got from anywhere and everywhere. That we did, and to see an All Black side running the ball from their own goal line, putting it right through to the wing three-quarters — and winning — possibly gave me the greatest pleasure.'

In an understandable show of unanimity, the All Blacks who played under Jack Gleeson have recorded a mass of favourable comments that approach levels of beatification of the man:

THE POWER BEHIND THE ALL BLACKS

'Jack never waved the big stick. He approached, he encouraged, he coaxed — and above all, he made us believe in ourselves,' said Stu Wilson, the 1976–83 All Black winger.[1]

'Jack was a thorough gentleman — and an optimist. He appreciated that rugby was a game in which attacking brought its own rewards. He believed in making the play, rather than concentrating on stopping the opposition,' said Bryan Williams.[2]

Dave Loveridge described how his coach slipped into the bus seat next to him on the way to Cardiff Arms Park for his first international: 'He could probably see that I was getting nervous and he just sat down and didn't say much — just encouraging me by being there.'[3]

Bryan Williams recalled how Gleeson had shown signs of illness during the grand slam tour.

'Three times while I was in his company he doubled over and winced in pain. Each time he passed it off as indigestion. At training he became less mobile. He had always been an active coach but by the end of the tour he was just standing in the middle of the field, getting the players to come to him.'[4]

When Gleeson realised he was not going to recover, he gave up the coaching job but remained on the New Zealand selection panel during 1979 with his successor, Watson, and Peter Burke.

Gleeson died on 2 November 1979, while the All Blacks, under Mourie and Watson, were on their tour of England, Scotland and Italy. It was the day before the All Blacks were to play the tough Midland Division side at Leicester, and the All Blacks, especially those who had come to know Gleeson well, like Mourie and Watson, were subdued, but steadfastly determined to pay tribute to their old coach and comrade the next day.

The Midlands had no chance. The All Blacks put together a stunning 33–7 victory as both a salute to Gleeson and as a living example of what his methods had left behind for New Zealand rugby.

FINEST HOURS: This 1977 first test team began Jack Gleeson's fine era with the All Blacks, culminating in the first All Black Grand Slam tour of Britain in 1978. Gleeson would die of cancer the following year. The team is: Back Row: Colin Farrell, Duncan Robertson, Kent Lambert, Peter Sloane, Bruce Robertson, Kevin Eveleigh, Mark Taylor, Doug Bruce; Second Row: Bill Osborne, Ian Kirkpatrick, Laurie Knight, Andy Haden, Gary Seear, Frank Oliver, Brad Johnstone, Bill Bush, Bryan Williams; Front Row: J. J. Stewart (selector), Lyn Davis, Tane Norton (captain), R. M. Don (manager), J. Gleeson (selector), Sid Going, Grant Batty, E. A. Watson (selector).

JACK GLEESON

The same trio who had succeeded in Argentina — Gleeson, Mourie and manager Ron Don — had taken the All Blacks to France at the end of 1977. There were seven new players in the party, including Andy Dalton, John Ashworth and Gary Knight, the trio who would eventually form the most durable front-row combination in All Black history and become known affectionately as the Geriatrics.

But it was a baptism of fire for many of the youngsters. On the field the French softened their visitors up with powerful and 'overcommitted' French selection XVs. Off the field the sometimes poor accommodation and endless substandard meals were among the many problems faced by feisty manager Don.

Knight recalled how the team had been quartered in a castle in Angouleme. 'I roomed with Mark Donaldson in one of its vast wings, and all we had was a sheet and one blanket. We were so cold that we took the curtains down from the windows and wrapped them around ourselves to try and get warm.'[5]

France is famous for its cuisine. But on that tour, confined to set menus (because of budgetary reasons of the host union), the All Blacks chomped their way through record quantities of bread rolls and croissants, occasionally bacon and eggs, and, almost always as the main daily fare, steak and chips.

Brad Johnstone became so frustrated with the food he eventually took direct action. He stood up in a hotel dining room and deposited his plate, upside down, on the table, informing one and all he was not going to stand for it any more.

The All Blacks lost the first test, in Toulouse, 13–18. The French fielded a huge pack which included Gerard Cholley, one of France's leading amateur boxers who also had a reputation as a dirty player. With the tiny but clever Jacques Fouroux dictating the pattern behind his mammoths, the French used intimidatory tactics throughout the game. Playing in his first international, Gary Knight had an early exit when Cholley gouged him. Bleeding from a slit eyelid, Knight had to be led off and thought that he might have suffered very serious damage, possibly blindness.

'Cholley came out of a lineout and stuck his fingers right in my eyes,' Knight said. 'I was completely blinded. I couldn't see anything out of my left eye for at least 15 minutes and had no hope of continuing playing. I had done nothing to provoke it. His only reason for doing it was obviously to get rid of me.'[6]

After the first test, Gleeson was to show the genius which was the mark of his successful tenure as All Black coach. Realising his players must not meet the French head-on in the second test in Paris, he began formulating a plan that was to astonish everyone, friend and foe alike. They would call short lineouts and play the game at tremendous pace, so as to tire the opposition and thereby impose their will on the French.

The plan worked a treat. With Dalton, in his first test, throwing immaculately, Laurie Knight, who had a spectacular game, and Andy Haden gained short lineout possession as the All Blacks swept to a 15–3 victory.

The highlight of the day was the try just after halftime, when the All Blacks caught the French napping with a quick throw-in by Mourie. Donaldson sent his backs away and Robertson sliced through before sending a pass, cutting out Osborne, direct to Stu Wilson. The winger thrust back infield to elude the cover and dot down for a fabulously engineered try.

Brian McKechnie, who had been nervous in the first test after being deputed to replace the injured and only fullback on tour, Bevan Wilson, had kicked well, including a fine drop goal from the touchline to start things off. Gary Seear's 45-metre penalty goal was another memorable contribution.

Future NZRFU chairman Russ Thomas replaced Ron Don in the successful management triumvirate which took the All Blacks to their first grand slam of Britain in 1978. There were eight newcomers in the side, and followers were generally not too hopeful. But the All Blacks won all but one of their 18 tour matches and all four internationals. Three tests were comfortably won, but the Welsh match was saved only in the dying moments.

Mourie would later state of the grand slam team: 'There was a pretty limited physique and in some ways a limited skill level in that team, but they really put everything on the line every time they took the field and the attitude was tremendous on and off the field.'

The most controversial feature of the tour, apart from the furore caused when John Ashworth accidentally scraped J. P. R. Williams' head in a ruck in the Bridgend match, was the dive by Andy Haden in the Welsh international.

Replacement fullback McKechnie kicked a penalty a minute from full time after a lineout infringement, taking the score to 13–12. Haden had thrown himself out of the lineout in a desperate and highly questionable attempt to save the game for New Zealand.

All hell was to break loose immediately the Welsh

THE POWER BEHIND THE ALL BLACKS

NATIVE CUNNING: Tane Norton leads the All Blacks into battle. He capped off a fine career as captain of the 1977 All Blacks who eventually triumphed over the touring British Lions. Norton called for a three-man scrum in the fourth test before his team pipped the visitors 10-9 to take the series 3-1. Three-man scrums are now outlawed. Phil Bennet leads the Lions.

BIOGRAPHICAL DETAILS

John 'Jack' Gleeson

Born: Manakau (near Levin), 24 May 1927

Died: Feilding, 2 November 1979

Position: Wing three-quarter

Provincial record: Manawatu 1947, 1949–50, 1953, 1955 — 30 matches, 12 tries

Selector/coach: Manawatu 1962–69; North Island 1970–76; NZ Colts coach 1974–76

NZ selector: 1972–79

NZ coach: 1972 (NZ internal tour), 1976, 1977, 1978

Other service: Feilding club coach 1958–61; president 1978–79; life member 1979

Other: Deteriorating health forced him to give up coaching 1979; remained on national selection panel; died of cancer later that year

NEW ZEALAND COACHING RECORD

1976: beat Argentina 21–9, 26–6

1977: beat Lions 16–12, lost to Lions 9–13, beat Lions 19–7, 10–9; lost to France 13–18, beat France 15–3

1978: beat Australia 13–12, 22–6, lost to Australia 16–30; beat Ireland 10–6; beat Wales 13–12; beat England 16–6; beat Scotland 18–9

---

realised they had lost the match. A quarter-century of disappointments and humiliation at the hands of successive New Zealand teams surfaced in the Welsh psyche, fanned by the media, who said Wales had been robbed by a devious, disgusting act.

Ron Palenski recalled being in the press box at that moment. 'Barry John, that king of first-fives who was normally unflappable on the field, was sitting behind me . . . he jumped up, shouting "You bloody cheats, you bloody cheats", all the while thumping me on the shoulder in rhythm with his ranting [because, I hope, it was the nearest shoulder and not because it was a New Zealand shoulder].'[7]

The trouble was, it had not been Haden's act which had won the game. Referee Roger Quittenton, as TV replays clearly showed, had actually penalised the Welsh lock, Geoff Wheel, for jumping off New Zealand lock Frank Oliver's shoulder.

REFERENCES

1. Alex Veysey, *Ebony and Ivory*.
2. Bob Howitt, *Beegee: The Bryan Williams Story*.
3. Ron Palenski, *Loveridge: Master Halfback*.
4. *Beegee: The Bryan Williams Story*.
5. Lindsay Knight, *The Geriatrics*.
6. *The Geriatrics*.
7. Ron Palenski, *Our National Game*.

CHAPTER 28

NEW ZEALAND COACH 1979-80

ERIC WATSON

*Eric plotted the ruin of the
Welsh centenary party*

THE POWER BEHIND THE ALL BLACKS

ERIC WATSON TOOK OVER THE ALL BLACKS after Jack Gleeson had taken them safely through the first grand-slam tour of Britain in New Zealand rugby history. It was a hard act to follow.

A year later, Watson undertook a similar, though less arduous tour. The 1979 All Blacks were without 19 of the grand-slam party of 1978. The death of the much-loved Gleeson while the team were on tour also had its effect. Yet Watson's team won their two tour internationals.

After another year of mixed results, partly caused by the unavailability of key players, Watson returned to Britain with a team which rated as the finest in more than a decade. The result was the trouncing of the Welsh in that union's centenary match — a game many of the All Blacks present remember as their 'finest hour'.

New Zealand rugby fans privileged to view the Scotland test of the 1979 tour will not forget the try scored by Murray Mexted. Short lineouts were organised to neutralise the expected Scottish obstruction and gain better-quality possession. It was from one such lineout that Mexted weaved through despairing Scottish tacklers to score what remains one of the finest individual tries an All Black forward has ever scored.

Nor will enthusiasts of the same vintage forget the game 12 months later, when Watson was at last able to put onto the field players of the calibre he'd wanted for two years: Rollerson, Wilson, Robertson, Fraser, Osborne, Nicky Allen, Loveridge, Mexted, Mourie, Shaw, Haden, Higginson, Ketels, Knight and Reid. In a game described by those All Black veterans as the fastest-paced test they ever played and the high point of their careers, the Welsh were tamed 23-3 and were probably lucky to get away with that.

These were the highlights of the short but eventful All Black coaching career of Eric Alexander Watson, affectionately known to his many teams as Bugle.

Sports journalist Ron Palenski relates how Graham Mourie pointed to a meeting with Eric Watson, when the Junior All Blacks assembled at Timaru for their 1973 tour, as the turning point in his career. Watson's 25-man team did not have an obvious open-side flanker and he decided to try Mourie there.

'Yes, Mr Watson, I'll give it a go, but don't expect too much of me,' said Mourie.

Watson thanked him and said: 'OK then. But by the way, I'm Eric. Only managers have to call me Mr Watson.'

The team beat South Canterbury and then prepared to play Southland, which would have Ken Stewart off the back of the lineout. Watson, who liked to call the team 'my wee Juniors', worked his players hard at Carisbrook on the way to Invercargill. Attired in an Otago jersey and All Black tracksuit pants tucked into Zingari-Richmond socks, Watson stood on the 22 as the players went through simulated moves.

'The adrenalin seemed to course through him when he was back out on his beloved Carisbrook turf, the scene for him of earlier rugby and cricket triumphs,' wrote Palenski. 'The player that commanded a lot of his attention was Mourie.'[1]

The Juniors beat Southland and, after eight tour matches, upset the All Blacks, having the first of a four-match internal tour, at Carisbrook. They won 14-10, and Mourie scored a try.

'Graham's a young lad,' Watson was heard to comment during the tour. 'He'll be all right.' Thus, in his inimitable, laconic way, the future All Black coach predicted the fortunes of a player who would develop into one of the All Blacks' greatest leaders.

Watson first considered Mourie perhaps too shy a man to lead the All Blacks. By the time he took over from Gleeson, however, Mourie had been captain for two years and struck Watson as possibly too assertive and influential for him to carry through the transition from the Gleeson era.

Mourie, for his part, recognised Watson was in a difficult position, taking over from a successful coach after a grand slam and needing to continue the All Blacks' winning streak. He was sympathetic and keen to help his new coach as best he could, but the financial strain being placed on All Blacks at the time by the amount of big rugby would force him and other key players to miss parts of Watson's programme. But come the emphatic victory at Cardiff Arms Park on 1 November 1980, it was clear Watson and Mourie were compatibility itself.

'As a captain and player, Graham has been first class,'

TALL ORDER: Eric Watson's task with this 1979 All Black team that toured England, Scotland and Italy was to attempt to emulate the Grand Slam the year before by Jack Gleeson's side. The team beat England and Scotland but played inspired rugby after hearing of Gleeson's death while on tour. The team is: Back Row: Gary Cunningham, Brad Johnstone, Murray Mexted, Vance Stewart, Andy Haden, John Fleming, Mike Burgoyne, Brian Ford; Third Row: Eddie Dunn, Barry Thompson, Ken Stewart, Richard Wilson, Rod Ketels, Alan Hewson; Second Row: Brian McKenzie (physiotherapist), Tim Twigden, John Spiers, Bernie Fraser, Murray Taylor, Peter Sloane, Kieran Keane; Front Row: Stuart Wilson, Dave Loveridge, Russ Thomas (manager), Graham Mourie (captain), Eric Watson (coach), Andy Dalton, Mark Donaldson.

ERIC WATSON

Watson wrote. 'He was my type of captain because he believed in what we were doing, he was intelligent and certainly right behind myself. He led and talked with plain common-sense and he, like myself, couldn't take too many theorists.

'There was always complete and honest teamwork, no little groups, and that is the secret of All Black successes under him. I was fortunate to have him from novice to an All Black captain. There are some who sound honest, but he was completely honest, to himself and others.'[2]

Mourie's summation of Watson's influence on the New Zealand game in the 1970s is interesting. While 'other coaches' (presumably J. J. Stewart and Jack Gleeson) were more successful, Watson was 'the dominant influence on the rugby played, particularly in the forwards'. Mourie justified this claim by pointing to Watson's involvement with New Zealand's junior national teams from 1972 to 1978. He was to leave his stamp on literally dozens of future All Blacks.

'As an All Black captain, I was always pleased when a player selected had been, as I had been, through the Watson training school. If they had graduated with Watson's approval, it meant they were halfway to adapting to the harsher demands of international rugby, and it meant that, having survived, they had the right mental toughness to carry on.'

Mourie described Watson's coaching style 'as honest and simple as the man himself. Rather than take players and develop them into a team, allowing the game to evolve from the individual styles of the group to suit their disparate abilities, Watson moulded the players to his game'.

His game was based on the age-old style of low-packing, hard-driving forwards who delivered ball from the ground in rucks. The major difference from the game a decade and a half earlier was that 'the backs got the best ball, the forwards the rest'. Watson's only demand of the backs was that they must never kick away good ruck ball.

'Given the right players, Watson's rugby was unbeatable,' said Mourie. 'But with a team unable to carry out his basics, it faltered. If Watson had a fault, it was that when his sides did fail, he tended to exhort greater efforts rather than try something new.

'My last experience with Watson was in Wales, when he gained the success he deserved. He was a good coach but, like so many, he had served too long as the master's apprentice before he became the master.'[3]

In his book, *Boots 'n' All*, Andy Haden, whose long All Black career began under Bob Duff in 1972 and ended under Brian Lochore in 1985, devoted a critical chapter to coaches he had played under. He wrote far more about Eric Watson than any other.

Watson's reputation as an ultratough training coach had been so exaggerated that certain All Blacks mentioned to New Zealand councillors that if he ever became All Black coach, they would be unavailable. But Haden, who first played under Watson on the New Zealand Juniors' Australian tour in 1972, found the training sessions 'hard, but even I concede they were enjoyable, and they always contained that essential ingredient of humour, so neglected by most coaches'.

'Although his concepts were sometimes basic, even to the extent of being unashamedly old-fashioned, they were workable . . . He insisted on the simple things being done well, an obvious basis for any good team.

'Wales was the climax of Watson's career and a just reward for his services. He was not a self-seeker — losing his chance of knighthood years before! — but thoroughly merited acclaim for the Welsh tour successes.'[4]

Murray Mexted, the All Black No. 8 who began his international career under Watson, took a similar view to Mourie.

'He had a special influence on my career. But it was when he was in harness with Graham Mourie that he most confidently approached team coaching. He was rather stereotyped otherwise, too constricted in style and pattern. And it was here that Mourie's perception was of great help to him.

'When we went to Australia [in 1980] without Mourie, playing on fields foreign to much of Eric's coaching experience, the need for a freer rein became obvious . . . Eric insisted with setting up rucks . . . a compulsion to slow down the game to control . . . when in these conditions we should have been spreading our wings.'[5]

Watson, now 73, but only retired from his signwriting business 'for a couple of years', still watches his Zingari-Richmond club team each weekend and attends all the Otago and Otago Highlanders' home matches. He says today's forward play could still sometimes do with 'some old-fashioned driving and rucking, sweeping over the ball, with the clean possession fed back quickly from the ground. I believe the ball we produced for the backs in my

WINNING WILSON: Stu Wilson always had the ability to make the most of any try-scoring opportunity. Between 1976 and 1983 Wilson scored 50 tries for 200 points for the All Blacks. Four All Black coaches were delighted to have Wilson available, including Eric Watson when he gate-crashed the 1980 Welsh Centenary celebrations.

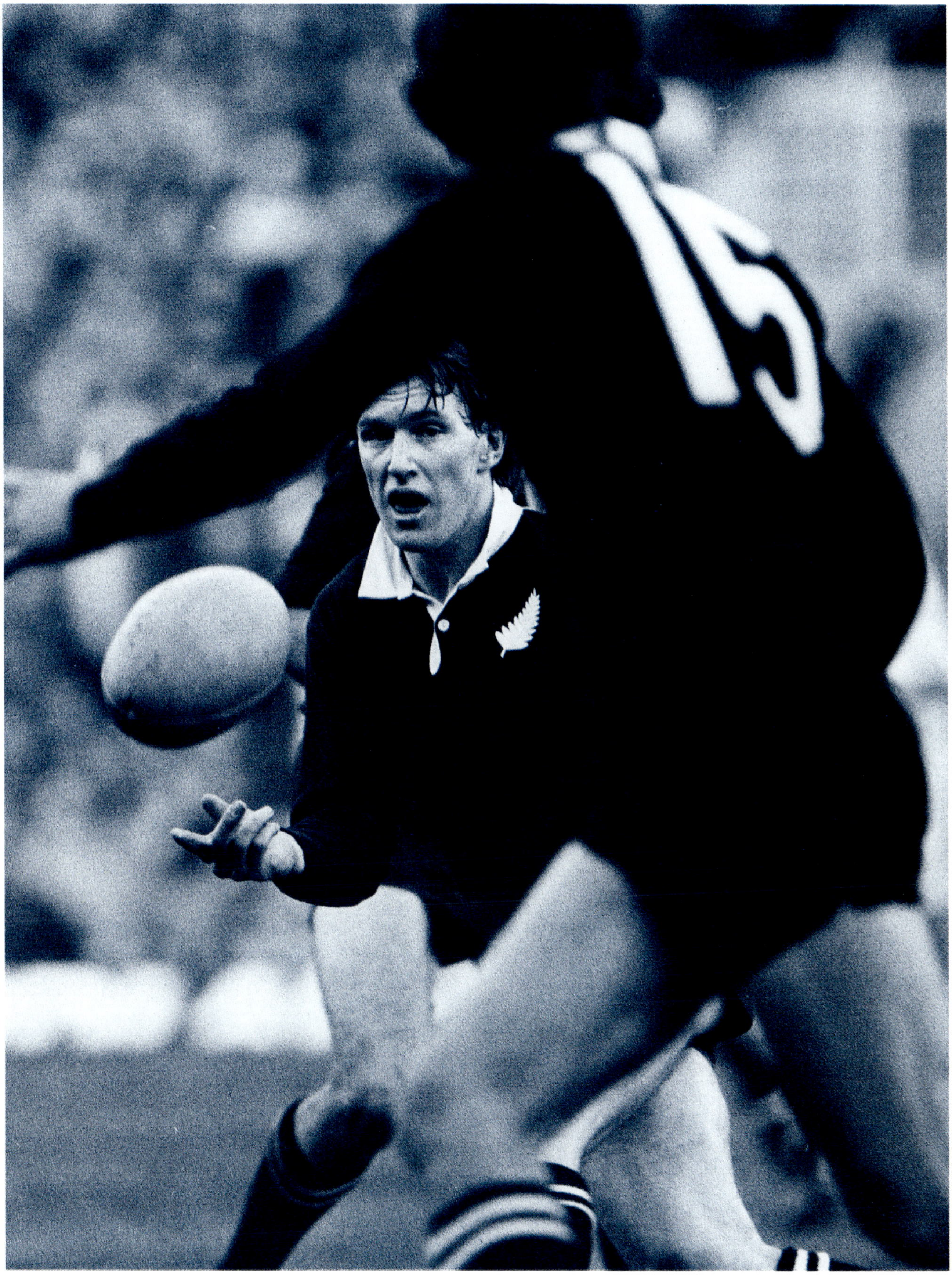

day was often 10 times better than the way they do it, under different rules of course, today.

'I also never had a top goal-kicker in my All Black test teams. They were all toe-kickers, and I recall Mike Gibson, the former great Lion, telling me we needed to develop round-the-corner kickers. How right he was. Look at them all today.'

Watson fondly recalls the first All Black panel he worked with. It also included Jack Gleeson and J. J. Stewart. Watson had replaced Bob Duff as a selector in 1974, and this trio stayed together for four years, until Peter Burke replaced Stewart in 1978.

'At first I was a bit tentative, but we began to work really well as a panel. It should be remembered that I became All Black coach only because Jack got sick.

'There was never any bias or arguments. I read about the personality clashes in more recent years and wonder if jealousy has become a factor.'

Regarding his own coaching philosophy, Watson said it was all those winters standing at second five-eighth or centre with the Zingari-Richmond seniors that formed his views.

'We played 10-man rugby and I hardly ever got the ball, and I hardly knew what to do with it when I did get it. I was a good little tackler, but we played dour rugby. When I began as coach I was determined that the backs in my teams should run with the ball and score tries.'

Watson's humour was, and still is, legendary. Some called it 'graveyard humour'. It was sometimes self-deprecating, usually affectionate, and used both as a motivating tool and a method to lighten moments when training could be looked on by some players as drudgery. It was a form of psychology and it did make players sit up and listen.

The forwards were more often than not the butt of Watson fun, especially the front row. Of an Otago front row of the early 1970s, which included Keith Murdoch, Watson said 'they wouldn't get School Cert between them'. Front rowers were told not to worry about tactics or 'intellectual things' like signals and calls. 'I'll come out at halftime and point you in the right direction,' he would say.

But some undiscerning players, especially North Islanders, couldn't understand Watson's wit when they first came into contact with him. They thought he was being harsh and insensitive and unfunny.

'The thing about the biting lines he could sometimes deliver, he always had a good reason and most of the players accepted that,' said Dave Loveridge. 'Sure, he used to goad players, but most of them enjoyed it, especially the props, who felt they had a particularly affectionate relationship with Eric.'

Watson's All Blacks sometimes took revenge on their coach. Laurie Mains recalled two classic Watson stories in his book. One was when Keith Murdoch came up with the nickname Skellerup for the Otago coach. When Watson asked the reason for the name, Murdoch told him he had a face like a twisted gumboot. Even Eric laughed. The other, later that season, was when the team were having a day out at a team member's farm at Gimmerburn. A prankster, Roger House, embedded a pair of gumboots in a coal heap, then summoned Watson in an apparent state of panic. 'There's been a fall of coal, one of the players is trapped, come quickly,' he shouted. 'Eric was completely sucked in and started digging frantically until he realised the gumboots were empty,' said Mains.[6]

If Watson ever had doubts about continuing as coach after the 1980 Australian tour, they were dispelled by a 'delegation' of senior All Blacks. He knew he had been completely accepted when he was thrown, fully clothed, into a swimming pool in Fiji, quickly to be rescued by Murray Mexted. Watson cannot swim.

Andy Haden recalled one incident which much amused the 1980 All Blacks at Watson's expense. The team were in Wales, and the Manawatu contingent was holding one of their 'shed meetings', which had become a regular occurrence after training. The players had a few beers and occasionally invited a guest. This time it was Watson, who was summoned to answer a few 'charges' against him.

'Eric got so involved in the discussion he forgot about the bath he had been running back in his own room, until the hotel management arrived at speed, seeking to stem the flow of water that was drenching the wedding cake and disrupting the function on the floor below. Accidental as it was, Eric was brought to justice at the team's next court session.'[7]

Watson has been a fine all-round sportsman. He played in the Zingari-Richmond senior team's rugby back line with two of his three brothers, Albie and Len, and represented Otago, briefly, in 1945 and 1946.

The three brothers all played senior cricket for Albion, but Eric was the best. An all-rounder, and an outstanding slips fieldsman, he played senior grade for 25 years, until the age of 42. He also represented Otago from 1949 to 1960, scoring 1746 runs and taking 40 wickets. The Otago side of those days included Bert Sutcliffe and John Reid, and Watson described himself as 'just a grafter'. He got one first-class century, 103 against Central Districts, in the 1951-52 season.

'The game was played at Napier and I opened in

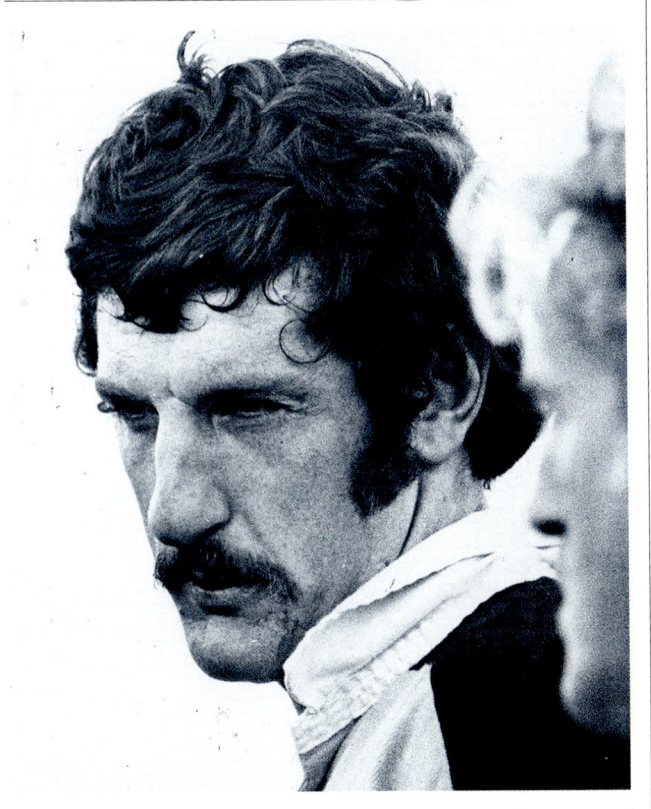

CAPTAIN SUPREME: Graham Mourie assisted the fortunes of All Black coach Eric Watson in 1979-80. Mourie recognised Watson was in a difficult situation taking over from Jack Gleeson, after New Zealand's first-ever Grand Slam.

BIOGRAPHICAL DETAILS

Eric Alexander Watson

Born: Dunedin 20 July 1925

Position: Five-eighth

Provincial record: Otago 1945-46 (Zingari-Richmond club 1945-55)

Selector/coach: Otago 1962-71; South Island 1973-79

NZ selector: 1974-80

NZ coach: 1979-80

Other service: Zingari-Richmond club coach and president 1972; Otago RFU management committee 1973-80

Other: Represented Otago at cricket 1949-60

Occupation: Retired; was signwriter

NEW ZEALAND COACHING RECORD

1979: beat France 23-9; lost to France 19-24; lost to Australia 6-12; beat Argentina 18-9, 15-6; beat Scotland 20-6; beat England 10-9; beat Italy 18-12

1980: lost to Australia 9-13; beat Australia 12-9; lost to Australia 10-26; beat Fiji 30-6, 33-0; beat United States 53-6; beat Canada 43-10; beat Wales 23-3 (Welsh centenary test)

Bert Sutcliffe's place,' recalled Watson. 'For the first 20 runs I scored, Sutcliffe's name was on the scoreboard and the crowd was applauding all my shots. Then they realised it wasn't Bert and stopped clapping.'

Watson was a 16-handicap golfer, and took up bowls in 1971. In 1978, he was a member of a St Clair four which came third in the nationals in Christchurch. He was on his honeymoon at the time with his second wife Daphne.

Life has not always been easy for Watson. His father, Ernie, who had played 48 games for Otago as fullback from 1910 to 1923, separated from his mother, Isabella, when Eric was only 12. He later had to turn down a university art scholarship because of hard times. Instead, he became a signwriter. At 25 he went into business on his own and remained self-employed for the rest of his working life. Watson has been happily married – twice. He lost his first wife, Billie, after 25 years of marriage and a four-year battle with cancer, in 1976. They had two daughters. He then met Daphne, a widow whose husband, Harold, had been president of the Southern RFC, and they were married 18 months later.

When Watson retired as All Black coach at the end of 1980, the *Otago Daily Times* sports editor, Brent Edwards, wrote that 'probably the greatest tribute to Eric Watson is that he has emerged from the maelstrom of international rugby with his humour and his appreciation undiminished of the simple pleasures of life'.[8]

REFERENCES

1. Ron Palenski, *Graham Mourie: Captain*, Moa Publications.
2. Eric Watson.
3. *Graham Mourie: Captain*.
4. Andy Haden, *Boots 'n' All*.
5. Alex Veysey, *Mexted: Pieces of Eight*.
6. Bob Howitt, *Laurie Mains*.
7. *Boots 'n' All*.
8. Brent Edwards, *Otago Daily Times*, 1980.

CHAPTER 29

NEW ZEALAND COACH 1981-82

PETER BURKE

Regained 'world crown' from besieged Boks

PETER BURKE SECURED A PLACE OF HONOUR IN All Black coaching history when his team regained the mythical world crown from South Africa.

The 1956 Springbok series is remembered by New Zealanders as perhaps the greatest of all in the days before the World Cup made international supremacy a clear-cut matter. But the 1981 series, with its outcome undecided until the Alan Hewson penalty in the dying seconds of the third test, was as great a challenge for players and coaches of both teams. The distractions of the unprecedented political situation and civil unrest which grew as the tour proceeded, ensured the on-field combatants had to focus on the job at hand as never before.

Burke's place in history is therefore secure. He became only the fourth coach, after Tom Morrison and Bob Stuart in 1956 and Neil McPhail in 1965, to beat the Boks. Since then, Laurie Mains (in 1992 and 1994) and John Hart (in 1996 and 1997) achieved the feat.

The question that has been raised by critics, possibly unfairly, and encouraged by some players of the time, is what role did the All Black coach actually play in preparing the team?

Burke was blessed with two fine captains in Graham Mourie and Andy Dalton. It has been correctly surmised that each played a greater role in the preparation and tactical approach of the All Blacks under Burke than was usual. But what is forgotten is Burke's clever assessment of the situation he faced. Rather than let ego damage the delicate balance needed to ensure the team's potential was realised, Burke happily let first Mourie, then Dalton, and then Mourie once again, play their leader's role to the full.

Burke's successful man management and shrewd judgement averted one potential crisis when he had to find a new captain to help plan the Springboks' defeat. Mourie had stood down on conscience grounds, and Dalton was chosen to step into the breach. A number of former test captains and provincial coaches were canvassed by the selectors on the subject, and the majority clearly saw in Dalton qualities that made him the wiser choice.

With the South African series won, Burke faced the dilemma of whether to stay with the faithful Dalton or return to the still keen Mourie. It was a decision few coaches would have wanted to make.

In 1981 the All Blacks played eight tests, more than any New Zealand side had been asked to play before. Mourie led them to a 2-nil series win over the touring Scots in June, then Dalton assumed the captaincy against the Springboks in August and September, leading them to a 2-1 series win.

Dalton was not firmly entrenched as the test hooker at the time. After he had been unavailable for the tour of Australia in 1980, Hika Reid had been preferred for the

UNITED WE STAND: Peter Burke (left), with Bob Duff at his shoulder, support their tackling captain, Peter Johnstone, in the match against Australian United Services on the unbeaten 1951 All Black tour of Australia. Burke was an All Black in 1955 and 1957 also.

Welsh centenary test. There may also have been feelings among some senior players when the All Blacks lined up for the first test against the Springboks at Lancaster Park that he might struggle in the captain's role. Dalton recalled how two players, Andy Haden and Murray Mexted, had approached him before the team meeting the night before the test and asked if he realised how important his team talk would be.

'I said quite sharply I was aware of that. They said nothing more and left the room. I am still not quite sure what point they were making. Anyway, I much appreciated Mark Shaw coming up to me, about the same time, and saying, "We're right behind you, pal."'[1]

The series, largely because of off-field activities that even invaded the Eden Park pitch from above in the third test, would have provided the ultimate test of the most experienced leader's character. Dalton came through with flying colours.

With honours shared after the first two tests, the third was played in the most bizarre circumstances. While flour bombs regularly splashed the ground, one scoring a direct hit on Gary Knight, the combatants somehow focused on the rugby and some superb play and spectacular tries resulted.

Among the many memories, Dalton recalls two incidents in particular. One came five minutes from the end, when referee Clive Norling called Dalton and the Springbok captain, Wynand Claassen, together and asked if they wished to call the game off. The score was then 22-18 to the All Blacks. 'What a good idea,' thought Dalton, but readily agreed with Claassen that the game must go on.

Dalton's other abiding memory is of Alan Hewson winking in confidence at him as he was handed the ball to take the final winning penalty. Hewson's goal gave the All Blacks a 25-22 victory.

Mourie had to sit back and watch with some trepidation as the Springbok tour unfolded. He desperately wanted to go to France and Romania and recalled being comfortable with the idea that he might have to tour under the captaincy of Dalton, a popular and accomplished player. What concerned him was the form of the other flankers during the series. Would the All Black selectors still want him afterwards?

As it turned out, Peter Burke and the selectors did want him. For the sixth year in a row he led the All Blacks

PETER BURKE

overseas after the New Zealand domestic season — on the tour of France and Romania at the end of the year and the series against Australia in New Zealand in 1982.

In Mourie's absence Dalton had done such a grand job a number of his team-mates thought he should have continued as captain, but it was Dalton's action that eventually saved a decision having to be made. He was to state later he had clearly seen the cause of All Black unity might be further damaged if Mourie was penalised for following his personal convictions. He advised Burke he would be more than happy to tour under Mourie's leadership.

'I had great respect for Graham's ability,' Dalton said. 'He was a great captain. I was aware of the speculation that I should be kept on as captain, so I thought I would make it easier for Peter Burke and the selectors. It didn't worry me touring under Graham.'[2]

The Scotland team of 1981 was led by Andy Irvine and won four of its five matches leading up to the first of its two internationals. Features of the New Zealand first-test selections included the absence of Andy Haden, who had been suspended after an ordering-off in a club match, and the selection of former Canterbury second five-eighth Andy Jefford, now playing for East Coast. Hud Rickitt, 6ft 8in tall, replaced Haden.

The All Blacks won 11-4, and Burke, after his first game as coach, said he wanted to eliminate mistakes from the team's performance in the second test. The All Blacks did their best for him in Auckland, scoring three tries in the last 10 minutes to win 40-16. In the seven-try bag Stu Wilson collected three and Alan Hewson two. Their efforts represented some of the finest running, timing, positioning and finishing to be seen in New

ALL TIED UP: Lachie Cameron props inside a Springbok, with Stu Wilson in support, during the second test of 1981 at Wellington's Athletic Park. The Boks won the game 24-12 to tie the series up.

Zealand. Bruce Robertson, who retired after that match, scored the last of his 42 tries for New Zealand.

Andy Haden said both Eric Watson, Burke's predecessor, and Burke were 'a decade too late in occupying the driving seat in the All Black van. Both had ideas better suited to the time when they were involved at provincial level.

'To Burke's credit, he recognised that in Mourie he possessed the best general in the rugby world and was content to use his outstanding example and experience in the preparation of his teams.'

Haden claimed that, at least in the late 1970s and early 1980s, few fresh ideas came from the national coach or selectors, innovations coming from players who had a wealth of experience at home and overseas.'

'This isn't the fault of the appointed selectors, who have waited patiently in the wings for their turn, all victims of the system.'

A selector's role is thankless, he argued. 'His worthiness is gauged solely on scoreboard statistics. Such matters as the calibre of the opposition, or the quality of the talent available for selection are considered irrelevant. Defeats are more often attributed to coaches and selectors than players — unfairly, I know, but a fact of life.'[3]

Burke pointed out he had completed a thorough grounding when he took over the All Blacks from Eric Watson. Beside his long All Black career and his time selecting in Taranaki and serving as a national selector, he'd built up strongly to the top position in the seasons immediately before 1981. He'd coached the North Island in 1978–79, the New Zealand Colts in 1978, and the New Zealand Juniors in 1979 and 1980.

'I was extremely fortunate to have Mourie and Dalton as my captains. They both had vast experience. They were outstanding leaders. I never had a cross word with either of them,' said Burke in 1997.

'Naturally, it is the coach's job to confide in his captain. During our time together we discussed tactics and the type of game we wished to develop, our training methods, the playing personnel and so forth.'

He added that, with fellow selectors Bryce Rope and Tiny Hill, the policy had always been to select only the best players but never to play them outside their permanent position. 'We were never tempted to play men out of position. It is difficult to experiment at this level in a home series and there was a lot at stake.

'We can all dream and carry out all these inspiring objectives at training. However, in the field of play, on match day, it doesn't often happen, because the opposition have a say in how you are going to perform.'

Every All Black coach is under enormous public and media pressure to win, so every selection of a player is vital, he said.

'But it was always my objective for our team to play attractive rugby, and at times we achieved that goal. We required players who could take part in all phases, not just their specialist role. We always chose players who could carry out that plan if things worked out.'

While the Springbok series is the part of his era best remembered by the public, there were two other tests which Burke recalled as being more illustrative of what he attempted to achieve. These were the 40-15 win over Scotland in 1981, already described, and the 33-18 victory over Australia in 1982, both games at Eden Park. He singled out the sometimes maligned fullback Alan Hewson for special mention.

'He was the outstanding individual when it came to modern fullback skills and a sense of adventure. People will always criticise his defence, but with us, using the three-fullback game on defence, with Stu Wilson and Bernie Fraser covering back when Hewson was up in the line, and Murray Mexted as the third cover, we had that aspect well sewn up,' said Burke.

'These four players came from the Wellington team. I could not find a better combination. Ian Upston, the Wellington coach, had adopted the same pattern. I had extensive discussions with Ian and as All Black coach had no hesitation in carrying this pattern on to the higher level of rugby.'

Burke relished the huge Bok challenge in a different sense. He fondly recalls his manager, Pat Gill, who was with him throughout his time as a selector and coach, and their planning and execution of goals.

'I don't think we would ever want to go through those pressures again. We had 50 of the police's Red Squad escorting us wherever we went — surrounding the field when we trained and having the bomb dogs check out our rooms at each hotel.

'When I think back, it was pressure from daylight to dark and our boys had to be focused on winning a test series against the mightiest opposition in the world!'

While today's All Black coach is a highly paid professional, Burke believed the general public had little conception of the huge amount of time, work and travel that went into All Black coaching and selection in his day, when the position was gratis. While some of the players were involved in shamateurism, often earning a good

PETER BURKE

FIRST BLOOD: This Peter Burke-coached All Black team won the first test of the 1981 series at Lancaster Park, Christchurch. The team is: Top Row: Brian McKechnie, Stu Wilson, Lachie Cameron, John Ashworth, Ken Stewart, Rod Ketels, Andy Jefferd, Alan Hewson; Middle Row: Mark Shaw, Stan ('Tiny) Hill (selector), Murray Mexted, Andy Haden, Peter Burke (coach), Graeme Higginson, Geoff Old, Malcolm Hood (physiotherapist), Gary Knight; Bottom Row: Dave Loveridge, Bryce Rope (selector), Bernie Fraser, Andy Dalton (captain), Fred Woodman, Doug Rollerson, Peter Gill (manager), Mark Donaldson.

living by playing in both hemispheres each year, the coaches certainly neither sought nor gained any monetary award.

'You were required to travel the length and breadth of New Zealand, watching players perform, discussing performances with provincial coaches, selecting trial teams, colts, juniors, island and All Black teams,' he said.

'Then there was the assembly of the All Black squad, the training and the build-up for the home series, or going overseas on tour to a foreign country where you soon found out the rest of the world is against you. It was an enormous commitment.

'On top of that one had one's own private commitments such as family and job responsibilities. It was all part of the day's work.'

Burke played in six matches on the 1951 All Black tour of Australia. But he did not make his test debut until 1955, when he was called into the side against the touring Wallabies when Bob Duff was unavailable. He played two more tests in Australia in 1957, as No. 8. He was a surprise omission from the 1953–54 All Black team which toured Britain and France.

Burke played 121 matches for Taranaki, many of them as captain and lineout jumping expert. He led the side in their successful Ranfurly Shield challenge against Otago in 1957 — the beginning of a shield tenure that was to last into the 1959 season.

Otago might have underestimated Taranaki, which won 11-9. But the young Taranaki team had given fair warning of its potential the year before when it had drawn 3-all with the Springboks in a game which it could, with an ounce of luck, have won. That match had given Taranaki the confidence boost it needed.

'We knew then we could hold our own in any company,' said Burke. 'Before we played the Springboks everyone had written us off and the best we were hoping for was, if they were to beat us, that it would not be by much.'

Taranaki had won the shield just once before, in 1913. In 1934 it had drawn with Canterbury and in 1953 had drawn with Waikato. The welcome home for Burke's team was memorable. Burke reckoned there were at least 20,000 people waiting for them when their DC3 touched down.

'As we came into New Plymouth airport our pilot did a circuit. "There are a few people here to see you," he said. A few people! From our plane we could see one line of cars stretching back, bumper to bumper, from the airport way into the city. It was a beautiful spring day and what a sight it presented . . .'

The shield brought a boom period to the province. The 1958 season became known as the Fabulous Winter. Taranaki, incredibly, used the same set of forwards in all nine defences. In the backs, it had the choice of two inside-back combinations, Urbahn and Bill Cameron or Kevin Briscoe and Ross Brown. It stuck mostly to the first pairing that year, with Brown further out. But the Urbahn–Briscoe rivalry was to bubble healthily for years, culminating in their sharing the test series against the Lions in 1959 and touring South Africa in 1960. John McCullough would become the test first five-eighths the following year and Roger Boon and Terry O'Sullivan would win their All Black jerseys in South Africa.

Burke felt that Taranaki started the 1959 season stronger than ever and seemed set to withstand the winter's challengers. After magnificent wins over Otago and Wellington in the space of four days, it had defended the shield 14 times. But unexpectedly, in a match that could offer up no excuses for the holder, Southland, superbly drilled by coach Ron Ward, a 1937 All Black, thrashed Taranaki 23-6. Taranaki players still speak of that Southland performance with awe.

'They beat us at our own game,' said Burke. 'They put the eight-man shove on us and thus prevented our loose forwards from detaching. Then they broke our scrum. Later, we tried to run it in the backs, but just made mistakes.'

Ross Brown recalled the game as a nightmare for the backs. Southland's midfield pairing of Kevin Laidlaw and Watson Archer, brother of the first five-eighths and captain Robin Archer, were crash tacklers. 'That Watson Archer nearly cut me in half,' recalled Brown.

Burke, now retired, has been involved with rugby all his life and in 1997 was made an Officer of the New Zealand Order of Merit. He says he has been helped by many wonderful people. 'I am sure I had the respect of the players and I will always respect each and every one of them for their dedication. I wouldn't have missed it all for quids.

'I remember when I was first appointed All Black coach. I was at the Taranaki Gentlemen's Club in New Plymouth that evening. A prominent person, a Dutchman, who was at the time involved with the energy development in our area, asked about my new position and whether I received a salary. When I told him not, he said if it had been an appointment to the Dutch national soccer team I would have immediately been on a salary of $100,000, at least, and a new Mercedes Benz. "Nothing like that here," I said. How things have changed.'

BIOGRAPHICAL DETAILS

Peter Standish Burke

Born: Tauranga, 22 September 1927

Position: Lock

Represented NZ: 1951, 1955, 1957

Points for NZ: 6 (2 tries)

Provincial record: Bay of Plenty 1946 (Edgecumbe club); Auckland 1947 (Marist club); Taranaki 1948–51 (Stratford club), 1952–54 (Tukapa club), 1955–59 (Hawera club); North Island 1951–54, 1957

Selector: Taranaki selector 1960–68; North Island selector 1970–75

NZ selector: 1978–82

NZ coach: 1981–82

Other: President NZRFU 1994, ONZM 1997

Occupation: Retired; was an oil company executive

NEW ZEALAND COACHING RECORD

1981: beat Scotland 11-4, 40-15; beat South Africa 14-9; lost to South Africa 12-24; beat South Africa 25-22; beat Romania 14-6; beat France 13-9, 18-6

1982: beat Australia 23-16; lost to Australia 16-19; beat Australia 33-18

REFERENCES

1 Lindsay Knight, *The Geriatrics*, Moa, 1986.
2 Lindsay Knight, *They Led the All Blacks*, Rugby Press, 1991.
3. Andy Haden, *Boots'n'All*.

CHAPTER 30

NEW ZEALAND COACH 1983-84

BRYCE ROPE

The full range of highs and lows

BRYCE ROPE'S TWO-YEAR PERIOD IN CHARGE OF the All Blacks produced an impressive record. In 12 tests he recorded nine wins, two losses and a draw. Then he was dumped.

Rope's tenure began with the 4–0 whitewashing of the 1983 Lions, a feat to equal that of Fred Allen's 1966 All Blacks. The only major blemish on his record was a draw with Scotland and a loss to England on the short tour at the end of 1983 — for which, as we shall see, there were extenuating circumstances. Nevertheless, after recovering strongly in 1984 by winning a home and an away series, Rope was dropped to make way for Brian Lochore. The NZRFU thinking was that Lochore was the right man to lead the All Blacks on another trek to South Africa in 1985. Rope had no strong argument with that decision. His only regret was that, because the tour was stymied by legal procedures and never took place, he lost the chance to have a third year with the team.

'Ces Blazey, the NZRFU chairman, had much earlier told me there was a move to bring Brian Lochore in. I said I'd be disappointed to lose the position, but if it was to the benefit of the All Blacks, I'd gladly step aside. Ces asked me if I'd be prepared to assist Brian and even if I would go to South Africa as his coaching assistant. That was why the NZRFU retained me on the selection panel in 1985,' recalled Rope.

Rope inherited an extremely experienced and successful All Black team in 1983. By then he was in his late sixties, and observers noted he did not take a particularly active role in the team training sessions. Instead, the direction seemed to come mostly from Andy Dalton, the captain, or, if it concerned back play, from senior players like Stu Wilson or Dave Loveridge.

Dalton was the usual captain, but in his absence Wilson led the All Blacks on the tour of Scotland and England, while Loveridge captained the All Blacks on their 1980 Australian tour.

But Rope sees his role entirely differently. While he did not initially have to coach the All Blacks in the technical aspects of their game, he certainly laid down the pattern they played in beating the Lions. Then, when the young, inexperienced team toured Scotland and England in late-1983, he had to work hard on their technical deficiencies.

Rope had certainly served his 'apprenticeship' to become an All Black coach. He had been a North Island selector from 1972-79 and was unbeaten in all the national trial teams he coached in those same years. His run with the New Zealand Colts (1979-81) and New Zealand Juniors (1982) was very successful, including a double over the Australian Colts. In the eras of his immediate predecessors, Eric Watson and Peter Burke, as a national selector Rope had also helped with the back coaching.

'I was fortunate to have a great captain and such an experienced side, especially that front row, in our first season,' he said in 1997. 'But it moved from the sublime to the ridiculous by the end of the year, when we took that young team away.

'However, then the challenge to bring them up to standard became the thing. We worked extremely hard on our game, sometimes having 100 scrums at a session and achieving a very presentable scrum by the tour's end.

'I always enjoyed the pressure of tests, when the adrenalin flowed. I was a pattern coach, who tried to pick the right players and then adapt them to the pattern we wanted to play.'

'I used to say to the Geriatrics: "You know the front-row requirements better than me or anyone. Play this test like you did the last one, only better!" That was my team talk to those three. They used to laugh, but it was right.

Rope is still adamant today that 'you can't buy experience. To have changed that forward pack would have been suicide for New Zealand and for me. One great thing that came out of the 1981 Springbok tour was a very special bonding of these forwards, who had survived tremendous pressure and adversity both on and off the field.'

In fact, when Rope announced the first test team of 1983, to play the Lions, the only forward change was Jock Hobbs for the retired Graham Mourie.

'It was at this point the press labelled our front row the "Geriatrics". Well, there was no motivation needed for them after that. Perhaps they were in their twilight years as All Blacks, but the results of 1983-84 spoke for themselves and silenced the critics. That pack was never mastered,' Rope said.

The case of the backs was different. Only Dave Loveridge, Bernie Fraser, Stu Wilson, Alan Hewson, Wayne Smith and Stephen Pokere were available from the previous test team. Over the next two years Rope would promote players from his Colts and Junior sides, including Ian Dunn, Warwick Taylor, Arthur Stone, Bruce Smith, Craig Green, John Kirwan, Andrew Donald, David Kirk and Grant Fox.

'The nucleus of the 1987 World Cup team would be made up of these players, who were by then match-hardened,' Rope said. 'Having received from my predecessor, Peter Burke, a great All Black pack, I was in turn able to pass on to Brian Lochore this group of brilliant backs.'

'That pack had been through so much together. They were like a machine. You don't try to tamper with something as good as that. The critics had said, after Peter Burke retired, that I would bring through all my players from the Colts and Juniors sides.

'But I didn't, at least not until I had to later in the year. And then, with so many unavailable to tour in 1983, and lacking a core of experience, I couldn't take some young players. John Kirwan was in that category.'

Dalton was later to state his preference for specialist forward and back coaches, an approach that was yet to be adopted.

In all the years in which he had been in the All Blacks there had not been one coaching overlord who had contrived a master plan and moved his players about as if they were pawns in a gigantic chess game. The coaching had to be tended to by committee. He said that this was not necessarily the best system for all circumstances and there were times 'when player power might need to be curbed'. Specialist All Black forward coaches were his preferred options.

'Compatibility, however, is the key here and human nature and individual ambitions being what they are, the best possible systems might not always be realistic,' Dalton said with remarkable prescience, considering the coaching events which were to rock New Zealand rugby in the early 1990s.

The arrival of Brian Lochore as coach in 1985, who moved to have assistant coaches Alex Wyllie and John Hart for the World Cup, was to herald a system along the lines Dalton thought best. But given the All Blacks were operating under a well-tried system in 1983-84, Dalton felt there could be no more admirable person in charge than Bryce Rope.

'He really was a great guy,' he said. 'Bryce Rope wouldn't have an enemy among any of the players and they all respected him as a person. I'd say, to use one of his own expressions, he gave you a warm glow.'

Common sense, loyalty to his players, a gentle humour and unfailing optimism were the qualities which endeared Rope to his players, Dalton added.[1]

If Eric Watson's graveyard humour had taken some of the All Blacks a little time to get used to, the vocabulary of Bryce Rope was to puzzle others a few years later.

'At Bryce's first team talk I thought I needed an atlas and that we were getting a geography lesson,' said John Ashworth, former All Black prop. 'He kept on talking about Mt Everest, Katmandu and the South Col.'

It turned out these Himalayan places related to the way Rope expected the forwards to win and distribute their line-out ball. He didn't want it tossed down from a great height, like Mt Everest or even the South Col, but from a more comfortable level, like Katmandu. He also had players like Ashworth entranced by terms like 'top hinges', 'middle hinges', 'bottom hinges' and 'pressure gaps'.[2]

BRYCE ROPE

DEMOLITION JOB: Bryce Rope's 1983 All Blacks were a vastly experienced team and made short work of dismembering the unfortunate touring British Lions. They whitewashed the visitors, 16-12, 9-0, 15-8 and 38-6. The second test team is: Back Row: Kevin Boroevich, Geoff Old, Gary Whetton, Andy Haden, Murray Mexted, John Ashworth, Mark Shaw, Gary Knight; Middle Row: Alan Hewson, Wayne Smith, Stu Wilson, P.G. Stokes (physiotherapist), Jock Hobbs, Robbie Deans, Warwick Taylor, Andy Donald; Front Row: Steve Pokere, P. W. Mitchell (manager), Bernie Fraser, Andy Dalton (captain), Dave Loveridge, Hika Reid, D. B. Rope (coach), Arthur Stone.

ANOTHER BLINDER: David Loveridge clears the ball against the 1983 British Lions. 'Trapper' Loveridge eventually became one of New Zealand's finest halfbacks, with a long, swift, accurate pass and elusive blindside running.

Rope's tenure as All Black coach was assisted by the elevation of Dalton to the captaincy. Dalton had captained the team to a series win over the Springboks in 1981 under coach Peter Burke, but that had been in Graham Mourie's absence when Mourie had declined to play on conscience grounds. Dalton had been happy for Mourie to take up the captaincy again on the late 1981 tour to Romania and France, and again in Australia in 1982. Then, when Mourie retired, Dalton led the team against the Lions and to Australia for one test. The Rope-Dalton partnership of that year produced a 5-0 winning run.

Dalton was not available for the tour of Scotland and England in late 1983, a side captained by Stu Wilson. He came back 1984 to lead New Zealand to a 2-0 series win at home against France and 2-1 series win in Australia.

Dalton's leadership record under Rope was therefore a mighty nine wins from 10 tests. In all, Dalton would captain the All Blacks in 17 tests between 1981 and 1985, losing only two of them. Many of these victoies were by the closest margins.

But if Rope's successful introduction to test rugby was also a tribute to a very experienced and effective team, he was to pay the price a few months later. The 1983 tour of Scotland and England was to bring him down to earth with a thump. The tourists drew with Scotland and lost to England and Midland Counties on the eight-match tour.

Yet there were many extenuating circumstances behind the team's problems. A large group of senior All Blacks had come to, or were approaching, the end of their careers, and the tour highlighted the gap that had opened between the experienced and the newcomers. A positive consequence was to be the large number of players blooded to international football.

A number of older players were unavailable, including all six who had played in the lock and front-row positions earlier in the year. Loveridge, halfback in 22 successive tests since 1979, was also unavailable. There were 12 new players in the side selected, and then 13 when Alan Hewson had to withdraw through injury. Of the nine tight forwards, only hooker Hika Reid had previously represented New Zealand. A further restriction was that Rope was allowed only 25 players for the eight-match tour.

Stu Wilson was a reluctant captain. He had been an outstanding performer for New Zealand on the wing over seven years, but his temperament was probably not suited to the captaincy, especially of a team such as this. Being out on the wing also meant he was a long way from most of the action. He was to state later that had he been asked beforehand if he would do the job, he would have declined.

'But I suppose I was one of the few who had been around a while,' he said. 'Unfortunately, we didn't have much firepower. It wasn't an enjoyable way to bow out of the All Blacks.'[3]

Rope is positive Wilson was approached before being appointed captain. However, the panel did not have him, Loveridge or Haden down as candidates, but did seriously consider Murray Mexted, who had been the All Blacks' test No. 8 since 1979.

'Stu did find it difficult to captain from the wing, especially such a young side. Perhaps it put pressure on his own game. He did a good job, but given the nature of the tour, and the formalities encountered off the field in England and Scotland, Murray Mexted probably should have been given the chance to lead New Zealand.'

The Scottish test was drawn 25-all, the All Blacks being considered unlucky not to win after scoring three tries to one. Inexperience and lack of discipline did not aid their cause, and two kickable penalties awarded the All Blacks were reversed by a touch judge, including one in the dying moments of the game.

The England selectors recognised the achievement of the Midlands team in beating the All Blacks by including seven of its number in the test side. England deservedly won the game 15-9. The home forwards maintained pressure on the All Blacks, and the tactic of kicking high for the All Black three-quarters to sometimes mishandle paid off. The penalty count, 3-12 against New Zealand, again reflected the inexperience of the side. It scored 19 tries on tour and conceded only six, but the penalties goaled were 20 for and 23 against.

Rope was on the national selection panel from 1980 to 1985. At first he worked with Eric Watson (coach in 1980) and Peter Burke (coach in 1981-82). Tiny Hill replaced Watson in 1981 and would remain a selector for six years, but never became coach. Lochore came on in 1983, and Meads replaced Rope in 1986. Rope rates Hill, a former All Black strongman of the 1950s who became an army sergeant major, as one of the unsung heroes.

'Tiny was a man of few words. But he was an excellent selector and judge of men and players. It must have been the army background. You could ask him to do a particular task and it would be done impeccably.'

In Rope's time the All Black selectors always worked well together. When the occasional difference in opinion over a player's merits arose, the convenor got the final choice. Rope can remember only one time, before Peter

BRYCE ROPE

Burke took the All Blacks to Romania and France in 1981, when they had strong differences.

Rope was involved at a time of major upheaval in the game at the international level. There was the 1981 Springbok tour, with its attendant civil unrest, and the banning by the courts of the projected tour to South Africa in 1985.

There were other controversies. On tour in Australia in 1984 Rope crossed swords on the field with the inimitable and previously highly successful Alan Jones. The Wallaby coach caused a furore two days before the All Blacks' game with New South Wales when he withdrew all the Wallaby players. It is a common enough occurrence today, but was unusual at the time, especially at such short notice.

'Simon Poidevin came to our hotel and apologised to the whole team for what had happened. I felt sorry for the New South Wales coach, because it devastated his team and planning. I actually sent a message out to the team at halftime, suggesting they ease up. It was the only time I ever did that. But it gave me lots of motivational ammunition for the next game, the test.'

Rope never coached a provincial team. Of the other postwar All Black coaches only Len Clode and Arthur Marslin had not done so before they coached the All Blacks. But Rope had a wealth of playing and coaching experience all the same. He played as a loose forward for Auckland and New Zealand Universities between 1947 and 1953.

He recalled playing for NZU when Australian Universities toured New Zealand in 1950. NZU won the first test comfortably, but for the second, in Dunedin, the visitors were prepared by the great Vic Cavanagh, who had just lost his place as a South Island selector and had a long association as coach of the Otago University team. 'Vic transformed them. They won that test and drew the third,' said Rope.

Rope became the NZU coach for a long period, involving overseas tours and matches against international sides. In the 1965 Springboks v. NZU game, because replacements weren't allowed under international rules, his team was reduced to 12 players after three backs, Ian Uttley, Mick Williment and Chris Laidlaw, went off injured in the first 10 minutes or so.

Rope coached New Zealand in sevens from 1983 to 1987. New Zealand won the Hong Kong Sevens in 1986 and 1987 and other major tournaments. Players such as Wayne Shelford, Mark Brooke-Cowden, Zinzan Brooke, David Kirk, Frano Botica, Wayne Smith, John Kirwan, Terry Wright, Craig Green and Mike Clamp excelled at the game.

BIOGRAPHICAL DETAILS

Douglas Bryce Rope

Born: 11 February 1923

Position: Loose forward

Provincial record: Auckland 1947–52 (University club); NZ Universities 1948–49, 1951–53

Selector/coach: University senior coach 1958–64; NZ Universities selector 1965–73; NZ Universities coach, North America, 1962; North Island selector 1973–79; NZ Colts coach 1979–81, NZ Juniors coach 1982

NZ selector: 1980–85

NZ coach: 1983, 1984

Occupation: Shipping company and construction company owner, and farmer; now retired

NEW ZEALAND COACHING RECORD

1983: beat Lions 16-12, 9-0, 15-8, 38-6; beat Australia 18-8; drew with Scotland 25-25; lost to England 9-15

1984: beat France 10-9, 31-18; lost to Australia 9-16, beat Australia 19-15, 25-24

Rope, who piloted Mosquito aircraft in Britain and Canada during World War II, became managing director of the Rope Construction Company, a business started by his father. It built more than 200 bridges and wharves in New Zealand, including projects on the Auckland Harbour Bridge, in Haast Pass and Opua (in the Bay of Islands) and at Chelsea and Ferguson Wharfs (in Auckland). It was sold to Wilkins and Davies, and Rope Shipping Ltd, specialising in tow boats and barges, was started.

Rope, now 74, is retired and living in Auckland with his wife, Adrienne, but still owns a farm, with a manager, on Rakitu (Arid) Island, off Great Barrier Island.

REFERENCES

1. Lindsay Knight, *The Geriatrics*.
2. Lindsay Knight, *They Led the All Blacks*.

CHAPTER 31

NEW ZEALAND COACH 1985-87

BRIAN LOCHORE

All Blacks' guide to victory in first World Cup

BRIAN LOCHORE WOULD HAVE BEEN guaranteed a place in rugby's hall of fame if his sole achievement had been to coach the All Blacks to victory in the first World Cup.

But he has had many other successes — as a player, as captain of possibly the strongest All Black team ever to tour overseas, as coach of a small union which he guided into the first division, as a New Zealand selector, as coach of international XVs, and, much later, as campaign manager of an All Black team which raised rugby tactics and skills to dizzying heights at the 1995 World Cup. Then he was called upon to lead the NZRU's player negotiations with the advent of professionalism. Later he led the NZRFU committee charged with improving the National Provincial Championship. He became Sir Brian Lochore when he was knighted in 1999.

If there is a single, dominant theme to Lochore's rugby career, it is that he always responded to requests for help — to lead, coach, select or manage a team. He seldom, if ever, went looking for a job. Such was the case in 1982, after he had coached Wairarapa-Bush into the first division. Ivan Vodanovich, his 1969-71 All Black coach and now a member of the NZRFU council, was Lochore's staunchest advocate for his standing as an All Black selector.

South Africa beckoned again, too. Lochore was to recall that in 1982 people in high rugby positions were already thinking about the tour scheduled for 1985. They saw him as an ideal coach with the experience to win a series there for the first time, after he had served his "apprenticeship" on the panel. So he joined, with coach and convenor Bryce Rope, and Tiny Hill, in what was a happy relationship.

New Zealand rugby was still struggling to recover from the woes of the 1981 Springbok tour of New Zealand. Though a tour to the republic would be looked at with alarm or even revulsion by some, for most of the players it was an exciting prospect — a reason to hang in there and extend their playing careers. But according to Lochore, the ambivalent feeling about a tour did affect the players, and it was not until five years later, at the 1987 World Cup, that they were to become unequivocally proud to don the black jersey again.

Lochore played no part in the coaching of the All Blacks while he was a selector. He did not even attend the training sessions. An indication of his role is given by the fact that he and Hill were only insets in the 1983 team photo.

When Lochore became the All Black coach in 1985 and began planning for the South African tour, 70 or so top players were looking to crown their careers with a victorious series. While the vicious among the anti-tour fraternity pointed to the krugerrand as the motivation, they couldn't have been further from the truth.

The All Blacks had previously made five unsuccessful treks to South Africa. The proposed tour was something they wanted to do because victory had so far been elusive — it was the All Blacks' Everest! Failing victory, at least they would experience the simple joy of trying again. Like the players, Lochore did not ever think the tour might not go ahead.

In the end, though, it was scuppered by legal action. It was claimed it would not be in accordance with the NZRFU's constitution, which undertook to promote and foster rugby. This contention was initially thrown out but went to the Appeal Court. Five days after Lochore and his panel had chosen the team, the case was back in the High Court. Lochore was asked to take the stand by the NZRFU lawyers. 'The intention was for me to talk about how I thought the tour would break down attitudes in South Africa and would help rugby among the blacks and the coloureds. I was to talk about my experiences there in 1970 and 1979 and how the situation in South Africa was not exactly how it was painted in New Zealand.'[1]

Lochore added that the plaintiff's lawyers then asked that his evidence be given as an affidavit, instead of from the witness stand, because time was short, and the union's lawyers agreed. He claimed it was 'a cunning ploy', because it weakened the union's case considerably.

An Argentinian tour was organised for end-of-season, with Jock Hobbs taking over as captain from the unavailable Andy Dalton. But Argentina, though a fun and interesting place to tour and with a team strong enough to draw the second test, wasn't South Africa.

The drive to beat South Africa was to prove as disruptive to Lochore's plans in 1986 as it had the previous year. It was to be the year of the Cavaliers and the Baby Blacks!

Lochore was asked to coach the Cavaliers, but turned down the opportunity because of the conflict of interest with his NZRFU duties. Instead, early in 1986, he coached an international XV at the IRB centenary celebrations. Meanwhile, Colin Meads, a national selector, accepted the job.

Beaten in the 'test series' by the Boks, the Cavaliers had returned to New Zealand by the time the French had arrived. But the NZRFU, angry at the tour and the duplicity of the South Africa union, declared the Cavalier players ineligible, citing residential reasons, and then banned them from the first test against the Wallabies as well.

Meads, who had been reprimanded by his national union, joined Lochore and Hill to select an almost entirely new All Black team to meet the French. Apart from David Kirk and John Kirwan, who had declined to join the Cavaliers, the side was absolutely raw, and its preparations underlined that fact.

'I think the French in their hotel must have been laughing like hell and thinking what a cakewalk they would have,' Lochore recalled in 1997.

It is part of the New Zealand game's great folklore that Lochore was able to calm his young charges down in their build-up to the test at Lancaster Park to prepare a game plan that would beat the French. It was a David and Goliath story.

The fairy-tale came to an end a week later when the Wallabies, under Alan Jones, scraped to a one-point win, 13-12, in Wellington. Lochore felt some of the Baby Blacks, as they'd been dubbed, were already anticipating the threat to their positions from the Cavalier players. Media speculation about who might replace whom was rife, and a little of the magic they'd discovered against France had disappeared.

Never a crowd to miss the opportunity to be contrary, the media then barrelled Lochore, Hill and Meads for 'overreacting' in their second-test choices. They made 10 changes. Greg Cooper, John Kirwan, David Kirk, Joe Stanley and Frano Botica survived the sweep, as did Mike Brewer when Buck Shelford had to cry off with an injury.

Lochore still maintains there was no great split among the selectors over the choice of Baby Black or Cavalier, though there were some long discussions. He also did not detect any rancour among the players over the new team, even after the All Blacks made it home 13-12 — an exact reversal of the first-test score.

Though it was not made public for some years, by the time of the third test in Auckland, Lochore had become aware of a degree of resentment between the two factions over who had the greater right to wear the black jersey. David Kirk, who had declined to play for the Cavaliers to protect his Rhodes scholarship, was one target of some in that party. The third test was lost 9-22.

Lochore took the team to France later that year for what seemed set to be a very successful tour — until it struck an incredibly fired-up French team in the second test in Nantes. The side had set a variety of point-scoring records earlier in the tour, including a dominant 19-7

THE POWER BEHIND THE ALL BLACKS

BEATING THE WORLD: The inaugural World Cup was hosted by Australia and New Zealand in 1987. This All Black side, captained by Andy Dalton (who did not take the field because of a hamstring injury) would go on to trounce France in the final at Eden Park, Auckland, under the coaching of Brian Lochore. The team is: Back Row: Andy Earl, John Kirwan, Albert Anderson, Gary Whetton, Murray Pierce, Alan Whetton, Zinzan Brooke, Wayne Shelford; Third Row: Joe Stanley, John Drake, John Gallagher, Michael Jones, Richard Loe, Bernie McCahill, Kieran Crowley; Second Row: N. D. Familton (physiotherapist), David Kirk, Grant Fox, Warwick Taylor, Mark Brooke-Cowden, Bruce Deans, Craig Green, Dr D. R. Laing (doctor); Front Row: B. J. Lochore (coach), Sean Fitzpatrick, Steve McDowell, Andy Dalton (captain), Frano Botica, Terry Wright, R. A. Guy (manager).

BREAKING AWAY: A youthful Sean Fitzpatrick deals to a Frenchman in the 1987 World Cup final. He had got his break when captain Andy Dalton was injured in the days leading up to the opening game and would go on to many triumphs with later coaches, Alex Wyllie, Laurie Mains and John Hart.

victory in the first test in Toulouse, and had completely healed any wounds that remained from the Cavaliers-Baby Blacks saga. Hence the 3-16 thumping in the second test was unexpected, especially the ruthlessly efficient manner in which the French pack went about its work.

'The All Blacks were shattered by that loss,' Lochore said. But it was the best thing to happen in terms of the World Cup in 1987. 'Remember Nantes' became the rallying cry which enabled Lochore to get his players focused on the task ahead and remind them they could take no opposition for granted.

Alex Wyllie and John Hart, the dominant provincial coaches for several years, joined convenor Lochore on the national selection panel soon after the French tour. The trio gelled immediately, all three instantly recognising how they wanted to play to win the World Cup in 1987. They were always harmonious. There was never any hint of rivalry, difference in philosophy, or rancour between Wyllie and Hart while Lochore ran the cutter. Such sourness developed only after Lochore had retired as coach.

ABSENT FRIENDS: They would become four of the strongest candidates for any 'Greatest All Blacks' team. Colin Meads, Ken Gray, Kel Tremain and Brian Lochore are about to begin the last 'great tour', the 1963-64 tour of Britain and France under All Black coach Neil McPhail. Meads and Lochore have gone on to administrative and coaching roles, as did Tremain. Gray and Tremain both died suddenly in 1992.

The trio wanted to play an expansive style in the tournament, with accuracy and pace, to negate the bigger packs of France, Australia and England. To get the players fitter than they had ever been and to peak for the May event, fitness guru Jim Blair, who had fine-tuned Canterbury and Auckland to success, was called in. Individually tailored fitness programmes were organised, probably the first in international rugby.

The first World Cup provided unknown challenges. The best teams would play a maximum of six matches, two of them peaking for the final, so it was not like a test series. Twenty-six players were allowed, and, sensibly, the best team needed to be chosen for each game. Lochore and co. chose cleverly — a test XV, six reserves and five other versatile players. It was obvious not all opposition countries looked at the team componentry like New Zealand — or understood the planning and preparation necessary.

Andy Dalton, who had missed the latter part of 1986 because of a broken jaw suffered with the Cavaliers, and had not captained the All Blacks since the test against Australia in June 1985, was appointed captain. David Kirk had captained the All Blacks in four tests in 1986, and Jock Hobbs had been captain in Argentina in 1985 and France in 1986. But Hobbs, on medical advice, had retired during the summer, and the panel decided Dalton's vast experience was essential to lead the cup campaign.

But it was not to be. Dalton pulled a hamstring on the day the team assembled, when he was running the training in the absence of Lochore, whose flight to Auckland had been delayed by fog. Kirk, appointed captain for the first game against Italy, kept the job on-field throughout the tournament as Dalton's injury failed to heal. But Dalton still played a very worthwhile part as captain off-field. Both players held the World Cup aloft after the final against France.

The All Blacks seemed to peak anew at each stage of the arduous World Cup series. That was no accident. The Grand Plan worked at every step. Home advantage also helped the All Blacks, although it brought an entirely different set of challenges, such as overcoming staleness, familiarity and domestic distractions.

It was to be New Zealand's year. No team came near to seriously challenging the All Blacks — not even France, which couldn't counter early New Zealand control and was well beaten. The achievement of 1987 becomes richer with each passing year, particularly as the feat had not been repeated.

Lochore retired after the 1987 Bledisloe Cup win and his rugby involvement decreased. But in 1995 he was back in the fray once again, joining Laurie Mains' World Cup efforts as campaign manager. He covered the food-poisoning episode that ended the All Blacks' hopes in his autobiography. Meads was so ill that Lochore, who was not poisoned, had to take over the management of the team the day before the final.

'We decided to keep the situation quiet, to keep it within the team,' he said. 'We didn't want word of it leaking out. We didn't want the South Africans to think they had any physical or psychological advantage over us. When it did get out later, it sounded like sour grapes.'

The All Blacks were probably able to keep their terrible secret because the media were deeply distracted by the announcement that day that professional rugby had arrived with plans for the News Limited-sponsored Super 12 tournament. Though many were suffering, and Jeff Wilson couldn't even get out of bed, the team went to Ellis Park that Friday morning. The players were told that all 26 would need to think about playing, because management did not know who would emerge fit enough to compete.

'In the afternoon, instead of sitting around the hotel worrying and wondering, we took them to a nearby park, just for a wander around in the fresh air,' said Lochore. 'Some didn't wander at all, but just slumped down and leaned against the nearest tree.'[2]

It was a tragedy. The final was already lost — Lochore knew it in his heart of hearts. Mehrtens and Wilson were still ailing on the day of the match. Others were too, though they didn't say much. Lochore and the rest of the non-playing team were so proud of the All Blacks as they stretched the Boks into extra time in a match of attrition that 'insiders' knew could only have one outcome.

Lochore had ended his playing career with a brilliant record as captain of the All Blacks. In 18 tests he led New Zealand to 15 wins and three losses — a success rate of 83.33 per cent.

He had made his debut for Wairarapa as an 18-year-old flanker in 1959. By 1963 he was an All Black reserve playing against the touring England team, and later that year was chosen in Wilson Whineray's 1963-64 side, which toured Britain and France with resounding success under coach Neil McPhail. He

UNHAPPY TOUR: All Black captain Brian Lochore's 1968 Australian tour is over. He leaves the field in the first test in Sydney for the second time in the game. He broke a thumb after eight minutes, went back onto the field and retired with a hamstring pull late in the first half.

played in two internationals on that tour — the English and Scottish tests.

After John Graham had led the All Blacks against Australia in 1964, Whineray returned from a season off to complete his career with a 3-1 series win over the 1965 Springboks. Lochore had missed the three Australian tests, but played in all four against South Africa.

From 1966 to 1970, Lochore captained the All Blacks to many triumphs. His ascendancy to the captaincy, which

BRIAN LOCHORE

coincided with the change of All Black coach from McPhail to Fred Allen, caused controversy. More senior players like Colin Meads, Ken Gray, Kel Tremain and even Chris Laidlaw were seen as the more likely contenders. Allen told the author in 1997 he was never in doubt about raising Lochore to the captaincy.

'It was my decision to make and it was the one least expected by my fellow selectors, Des Christian and Les George. I could not go past Lochore.

'It was the integrity and the quiet dignity of the man. Whineray had it. The Army had taught me about the qualities of leadership and Brian had what I always looked for — strength of character, the capacity to provide discipline by example. He had a resilience. He would have been a leader of men in any field.'

Allen's faith in Lochore was soon rewarded. A 4-0 whitewash of the Lions in 1966 was followed by a resounding win over the Wallabies in the test to celebrate the New Zealand union's 75th jubilee in 1967.

The unbeaten tour of Britain and France at the end of 1967 was probably the peak of Lochore's time as captain. The tour had been arranged as an alternative to the scheduled tour of South Africa, cancelled by the NZRFU when the South Africans would not agree to host non-white players. The All Blacks cut a swathe through their opposition. England were defeated 23-11, Wales 13-6, France 21-15 and Scotland, in the game made infamous by the dismissal of Colin Meads, 14-3.

The two sets of forwards made up what must rate as perhaps the best-equipped and most efficient packs an All Black touring team has ever assembled.

A broken thumb in the first test in Australia in 1968 ruled Lochore out of rugby until the second and third tests against the touring Frenchmen. Although the All Blacks were to win the series 3-0, it was evenly contested but, apart from Sid Going's superb tries in the third test, often lacklustre. Lochore's return from injury for the second test coincided with one of rugby's legendary acts. This was the penalty goal kicked by Pierre Villepreux in the 28th minute. Laughter around Athletic Park soon turned to cheering when the Frenchman sent his attempt soaring over the bar. The kick is rated one of the longest achieved in international rugby, variously estimated at between 65 and 70 yards.

The team that undertook Wales' first tour to New Zealand, in 1969, was the Five Nations' champion, so big things were expected of it. But it was outclassed by Lochore's men, losing 0-19 at Lancaster Park and 12-33 at

ECSTACY AND AGONY: David Kirk has the world at his feet. He has just led the All Blacks to Victory over France in the first World Cup final. Andy Dalton, the non-playing captain after injuring a hamstring before the opening game, watches on. To his great credit, Kirk pulled Dalton 'into the frame'.

Eden Park. The series was a triumph for the All Black forwards, who dominated the Welsh. Fergie McCormick set a world record in the second test scoring 24 points, including a 55-yard dropped goal.

The Welsh series also represented a changing of the guard, in that Allen had quit as All Black coach and selection convenor, citing unnecessary interference from the NZRFU. He had been replaced by Ivan Vodanovich, and while the "mean machine" that was the All Black team ticked along against the Welsh just as before, it was to stutter and splutter in South Africa a year later. In spite of being undefeated outside the tests and racking up many huge scores, the All Blacks lost the series 1-3. The two losses were to be the only international defeats suffered by Lochore as captain of the All Blacks.

Coach Vodanovich was to take much of the blame for the failure from a disappointed New Zealand rugby public. His methods were seen as old-fashioned, and it appears he overtrained the side in the hot, hard and harsh South African conditions. A famous quip of the day came from 'Jazz' Muller, who said he needed more games to get fit for Ivan's training sessions. Most of his teammates heartily concurred.

Other factors lay behind the reversals, including a degree of overconfidence prior to the first test, for which the All Blacks were tipped as strong favourites. They had played 10 matches in the republic by the time of the first test, and the South Africans had analysed their game and worked out how to counter it.

'In the first test I think we took them too lightly,' said Lochore. 'By then we had played most of the Springboks in provincial games and we didn't see them individually as great players. But we found they were very different when they put on that green and gold.'[3]

Even in the second test, which the All Blacks won, and in which they were dominant for much of the game, the score was only 9-8.

In 1971, in semi-retirement, Lochore was surprisingly recalled by the All Black selectors to lock the scrum with Colin Meads in the third test against the Lions, after an injury to Peter Whiting. Both Lochore and the selectors were criticised for the decision after the game, but for Lochore there was no choice other than to oblige when selector Bob Duff called him.

'How could I possibly have lived with myself knowing I had been approached to help New Zealand in an emergency and turned my back?

'Of all the challenges I took up in my life as a player this was probably the greatest. I do not regret confronting it. I regret bitterly only that I was not better prepared for it.'

BIOGRAPHICAL DETAILS

Brian James Lochore

Born: Masterton, 3 September 1940

Position: Back row and lock forward

Represented NZ: 1963-67
68 matches (24 internationals)
Captain in 18 tests, for 15 wins and three losses

Points for NZ: 21 (7 tries)

Provincial record: Wairarapa 1959-70 (Masterton club); Wairarapa-Bush 1959, 1965-66, 1971; North Island 1964-69

Selector/coach: Masterton club 1966-67, 1975-78; Wairarapa-Bush 1980-82

NZ selector: 1983-86

NZ coach: 1985-87

Other: Coached overseas teams in IRB centenary 1986; OBE; Appointed to Halberg Trust, The Hillary Commission, chairman of the Sports Foundation 1999. Knighted 1999.

Occupation: Farmer in Hastwell, near Eketahuna

NEW ZEALAND COACHING RECORD

1985: beat England 18-15, 42-15; beat Australia 10-9; beat Argentina 33-20; drew with Argentina 21 all

1986: beat France 18-9; lost to Australia 12-13; beat Australia 13-12; lost to Australia 9-22; beat France 19-7; lost to France 3-16

1987: World Cup Pool matches: beat Italy 70-6; beat Fiji 74-13; beat Argentina 46-15. Quarterfinal: beat Scotland 30-3. Semifinal: beat Wales 49-6; Final: beat France 29-9 (who beat Australia 30-16)

REFERENCES

1. Alex Veysey et al., *Lochore: An Autobiography*, Hodder Moa Beckett.
2. *Lochore: An Autobiography*.
3. Lindsay Knight, *They Led the All Blacks*.

CHAPTER 32

NEW ZEALAND COACH 1988-91

ALEX WYLLIE

More wins than any other All Black coach

ALTHOUGH ALEX 'GRIZZ' WYLLIE'S TERM AS ALL Black coach ended with the disappointment of watching the World Cup slip from New Zealand's grasp into Australia's, he fashioned a win-loss record that was rivalled only by that of the great Fred Allen. And no other All Black coach in history, including Allen, had achieved Grizz's record of 24 test victories, three losses and a draw.

Wyllie's All Black coaching record for all matches was 64 games for 58 wins, five losses and a draw. This gave him an overall success rate of 90.6 per cent, bettered among his predecessors only by Allen (97.3 per cent), Jack Gleeson (92.3 per cent) and Neil McPhail (90.7 per cent). And he had coached for many more matches.

Beginning with the 1987 World Cup victory (Wyllie did not become coach until after that year's 1987 Japan tour), the All Blacks went undefeated in 50 matches and 21 tests, a world record. The team brought a level of fitness, commitment and sophistication to the game unmatched by any opponent. It contained the greatest try-scorer the All Blacks had produced, John Kirwan, and the greatest points-scorer, Grant Fox, as well as a host of champion players.

Such was the sophistry of this team that its lineout calls sometimes contained a reference to where the referee was standing, so the players knew whether they should risk 'stretching the rules'. There had never been a test team as dominant as Wyllie's All Blacks. A winning margin of 15 points was regarded as a close-run result. Closer scores were a rarity.

After playing some fabulous rugby and going three years without defeat, New Zealand was installed as odds-on favourite to retain the World Cup. But that was before the rot set in in 1990-91. Wyllie would have problems motivating his 'invincible' team as its standards, imperceptibly, began to drift. However, it was pressure from above which initially placed a straitjacket on the great coach and eventually led to the lessening of his side's cup prospects.

Interviewed in 1997 for this book, Wyllie revealed he had made up his mind to resign as coach just before the World Cup. It was 'the last straw' as far as he was concerned, after a series of interfering and undermining actions by the NZRFU and its chairman, Eddie Tonks. Tonks' efforts to promote John Hart had resulted in his appointment as co-coach of Wyllie's World Cup team. Given the well-publicised history of tension and rivalry between the pair, it was an incredible move. As the 1987 All Black World Cup-winning coach, Brian Lochore, would state, it was a decision which took both men out with one shot.

Wyllie believes Tonks was also behind the action which drove another stake into the All Blacks' hearts and

THE POWER BEHIND THE ALL BLACKS

TOIL AND SWEAT: Bill Bush and Alex Wyllie, surrounded by other tired but triumphant Canterbury players when they lifted the Ranfurly Shield from Auckland, 12-6 in 1972. Wyllie had helped lift the shield from Hawke's Bay in 1969 too. As Canterbury coach in 1982 he made it a 'hat-trick' by depriving Wellington of the 'log'.

World Cup hopes — the NZRFU decision not to allow loose forward Mike Brewer to go with the team. Brewer was given an 'impossible' fitness test for a heel injury on the eve of the team's departure. It involved a jumping/landing exercise, but he was not allowed to wear the support he would have worn if he'd been playing. The test made no sense to Wyllie and the team.

'That was it for me,' said Wyllie. 'I went to John Sturgeon, our manager, and told him I was going to quit. I had had enough of all the bullshit. I had been talking to Tonks on the phone and got nowhere. The whole thing wasn't gelling at all. But Sturge cooled me down and we talked it through. There were the players and all the hard work we had put into the campaign by that stage to consider.'

Former NZRFU councillor Sturgeon, a cheerful West Coaster who was Wyllie's manager throughout his time with the All Blacks, told the author in August 1997 that he believed the team would have retained the World Cup if Wyllie had remained in full control of coaching and preparation. Although past its peak, he said, the All Black team was still capable of asserting enough control to beat Australia in the semifinal, and had already proven, in the tournament opener, it could handle England, the eventual beaten finalist. But the differing styles and actions of Wyllie and Hart eventually took away some of the All Blacks' traditional ability to focus on their objective.

'There was no major split between the players at the tournament that I was aware of. But the differences between the two coaches became quite a task for me,' said Sturgeon. 'When I came home, I was quite a nervous wreck after having to "adjudicate" at up to four meetings a day between the pair. They hated one another. It was shocking at times.'

The loss of the World Cup in 1991, especially after the 1987 triumph and the invincibility of the All Blacks for so long afterwards, seemed a tragedy at the time. But with the failure to regain the cup in 1995, even under the most unfortunate of circumstances, and the passing of time,

ALEX WYLLIE

Wyllie's end needs to be kept in perspective. His team failed in only one match, after all — the semifinal against Australia. That is the way Wyllie likes to look back on his era.

'We had started off the World Cup quite well with the victory over England,' he said. 'Though we struggled a little to maintain form in later matches, I was still reasonably confident we could do the job. With the amount of ball we won against Australia, we should have beaten them easily.'

Though Wyllie was never a coach to bag his players publicly, it isn't hard to see he thinks the All Black backs that day did not do themselves justice.

In answer to criticism that he should have dropped more players than just his skipper, Buck Shelford, when the All Blacks began to struggle, Wyllie said it was all very well being wise after the event, but the test team had been performing consistently.

'I didn't have the option of taking 36 players away on tour like they do now. In 1988, when we had a 14-match tour of Australia, I wanted to take 30 players, so we could develop some young blood. But we were allowed only 26.'

Wyllie was also badly hit by rugby league ambushes. Frano Botica was the first to go, and then the All Blacks lost two fullbacks, John Gallagher and Matthew Ridge — in the same week!

'Looking back, we never properly recovered from that week,' said Wyllie. 'Gallagher had been in fabulous form for several years, perhaps the best in the world. Matthew was his understudy. Shane Philpott got injured. We used Terry Wright in the first three cup games at fullback, then John Timu. Kieran Crowley had to be flown over during the tournament. He played in the semifinal.'

When Wyllie had won the All Black coaching job he had been 'warned' by one of John Hart's ardent disciples to 'Remember — rust never sleeps.' These people were

WORLD BEATERS: Alex Wyllie's All Blacks had just begun their (almost) three-year unbeaten run when this photo of the 1988 side that toured Australia was taken. The team is: Back Row: Andy Earl, Mike Brewer, Alan Whetton, Murray Pierce, Gary Whetton, Albert Anderson, John Kirwan, Kevin Boroevich; Third Row: Jasin Goldsmith, John Schuster, Michael Jones, John Gallagher, Zinzan Brooke, Richard Loe, Ron Williams, Warren Gatland; Second Row: P. L. Penn (assistant coach), Sean Fitzpatrick, Joe Stanley, David Abercrombie (physiotherapist), Terry Wright, Warwick Taylor, Graeme Bachop, Dr R. J. Mayhew (doctor); Front Row: J. A. Sturgeon (manager), Grant Fox, Bruce Deans, Wayne Shelford (captain), Steve McDowell, Frano Botica, Alex Wyllie (coach).

THE POWER BEHIND THE ALL BLACKS

known as Harty's Army and, 'led' by Andy Haden, became an increasing embarrassment to Hart as the seasons of the late 1980s wore on.

Wyllie's All Blacks played some fabulous rugby. They went unbeaten for almost three years. But the moment Wyllie's momentum faltered — in 1990, in the third test against Australia, after the series had already been secured — Haden and the army resurfaced.

Hart had perhaps been too eager to take up and wear the laurels in 1987. After the inaugural World Cup success earlier that year, the All Blacks trampled their way through Japan with him at the helm and Wyllie as assistant. But the New Zealand councillors became alarmed at stories about that tour. It was said the 'Auckland connection' had been too strong among 'management'. Players from outside Auckland, including Gallagher in his autobiography, would say Hart's treatment of Wyllie was so condescending he must already have believed the coach's job was in the bag.

Hart also became involved in the voting process. After Wyllie defeated him at the ballot box for the coach's job, Hart announced he would not be available for the selection panel. There was too much time involved, he said, in hopping on and off aircraft all over the country without the final say in the team. It was an arrogant stance, some councillors reckoned. Hart changed his position two years later when he accepted a place on the panel.

Haden, who had served New Zealand well over many seasons on the field and was a leading protagonist for players' rights, was at full throttle on Hart's behalf, using TV and radio as a platform to undermine Wyllie. One publication summed it up: 'Publicity is to Haden what a jolt of electricity was to Dr Frankenstein's monster. Let him off the slab and in front of the cameras, and he's out of your control.'

There were some incredibly ugly and untrue whispering campaigns against Wyllie. At an NZRFU council meeting in 1991, team manager Sturgeon had to get team doctor John Mayhew to confirm to those present, in a telephone conference call, that a particular story was untrue.

It was during the winter of 1991 that Wyllie strongly suspected Hart was trying to undermine him. He thought Hart was feeding anti-Wyllie stories to the media, especially in Auckland. According to Phil Gifford, Wyllie's biographer, the All Black coach was right.

'I am not the only journalist to have a tape of off-the-record statements by Hart in which he suggests that the All Blacks had lost faith in Wyllie,' Gifford wrote, 'and that the situation demanded that he be allowed to take over the team for the World Cup, or at least have equal weight with Wyllie in the coaching of the team.'[1] Hart would rebut these claims.[2]

AS STRAIGHT AS A DIE: Alex Wyllie's All Blacks were at their most punishing best in 1989, midway through his (almost) three-year unbeaten run.

As a leading player, Wyllie was always tremendously fit, toughened by heavy farmwork and running. His technical knowledge, later to make him one of the world's great coaches, was good as a player and captain. He could play all the loose-forward positions, fill in as a lock, and even deputised in a test match against Scotland as a prop.

His dedication to the game, especially as a player in Canterbury, became legendary. He made the long, boring drive from his farm at Omihi, North Canterbury, into Christchurch and back two or three times a week for Canterbury training and matches, year in, year out, in good weather and bad, without complaint, for 16 seasons.

These characteristics, combined with his size (1.85m, 101.6kg), gave him awesome forward endurance until he retired, aged 35.

Wyllie's hard, unremitting style of play became equally legendary. He led by example and expected much of his Glenmark club, Canterbury Country and provincial team-mates. He picked up the nickname Grizz from Lyn Davis, longtime Canterbury halfback and team-mate, back in the mid-1960s, when the pair faced each

ALEX WYLLIE

other in the annual Town-Country match. Davis reckoned Wyllie grizzled all the way through the game.

Wyllie credited his first provincial captain in 1964, John Graham, who was also All Black captain that year, with teaching him many of the finer points of the game, and a later coach, Dr Jim Stewart, with inspiring him to lead from the front. Playing with other exceptionally durable players, such as Davis and Fergie McCormick, also assisted Wyllie.

From a fiery, brash youngster in the 1960s, Wyllie matured into a fine All Black forward in the early 1970s. In between times, he built the legend of one of the truly hard men of New Zealand rugby. There was the 1971 Lions-Canterbury fracas, labelled a disgrace by some, in which he was a participant. On the 1972-73 All Black tour of Britain and France, he was one of the so-called Mafia figures, a sinister, anti-authoritarian bunch in the eyes of the media.

Wyllie did not take the step up to All Black rugby easily. After years of outstanding provincial and interisland performances, he finally made the All Blacks for the 1970 tour of South Africa. He lacked the height of team-mates like Ian Kirkpatrick, Brian Lochore and Alan Sutherland, but was quicker and could play off the back of the lineout.

His ruggedness, energy and dedication quickly brought him the recognition he deserved and made him one of the successes of the tour. He played in the second and third tests, but was surprisingly dropped for the fourth. He regained a test spot in 1971, against the Lions, when Sutherland broke a leg.

It was on coach Bob Duff's 1972-73 tour of Britain and France, however, that Wyllie came into his own. The team was young and largely inexperienced. Its strength was the loose-forward trio of Wyllie, Sutherland and Kirkpatrick, who, with halfback Sid Going, were able to dominate many opponents, in a side which was unbeaten in the home union tests. Wyllie played in all the tests, though his gruff exterior on and off the field caused one British journalist to label him 'a man of ill-repute'.

Wyllie was one of the 'old guard' dumped in 1974 after the unimpressive loss to England the year before. He had played 40 matches for the All Blacks, including 11 tests.

He was to go on for another five seasons with Canterbury, rewriting the record books as a provincial player and captain. A provincial captain whose team lost 28 times might ordinarily be considered unsuccessful, but Wyllie became a centurion as a captain and a double centurion as a player!

He captained Canterbury in 108 games over eight seasons, winning 78, losing 28 and drawing two. It was quite a record in its time, especially with its Ranfurly Shield highs and lows. He played for Canterbury for 16 years, an unusually long career by any standards, especially considering the competition within a major union. In that time he was almost always a first-choice player, and finished with a tally of 210 games played for the province.

Wyllie said in 1997 his greatest thrill as a player had been in 1972, when he captained Canterbury to a 12-6 Ranfurly Shield challenge victory over Auckland.

'We'd played well in 1969 when we lifted the shield from Hawkes Bay,' he said. 'There were some mighty footballers in that Canterbury side — Fergie McCormick, Lyn Davis, Alistair Hopkinson, Wayne Cottrell and Ian Kirkpatrick among them. The 1972 game was actually a dour affair, not the best of games, but it was satisfying to lift the log again.'

None of those triumphs as a player, however, could match the feeling of coaching Canterbury to its shield win in 1982, said Wyllie. 'A team that weren't very well placed the season before went right to the top of New Zealand rugby — which is where I think the shield should be. It was a marvellous feeling all right.'

A year after retiring from playing, Wyllie had put his hand up again — this time for coach of the province. He said later he hadn't really expected to get the job immediately, especially as his aggressive reputation would be seen negatively by some administrators. But the union gave him his chance, and Wyllie repaid their faith tenfold, transforming a poorly performing team into one which prised the Ranfurly Shield from Wellington in his opening season.

By the time he retired from the job to head for higher honours, Wyllie's well-disciplined but adventurous team had equalled the shield record of 25 defences, and his provincial coaching record (for 1982-86) was 76 wins, 12 losses and four draws from 92 matches.

The players knew Wyllie as a tough but fair coach and quickly grew to respect his enormous fund of knowledge and his winning methods and psychology. Once more the legend was extended. His team talks could be inspiring — and brief! At halftime in one challenge he walked on to the field, said the team was bloody hopeless and stomped off. In the challenge of 14 September 1985, when Auckland lifted the log, Canterbury trailed 0-24 at the break. Wyllie kept it simple and calm. Pointing to the ball he told his players they couldn't win without it. 'If Auckland can score 24 points in one half,' he said, 'so can you.' The faithful believed him, scoring 23 points to lose 28-23 in a remarkable game.

Before Canterbury had travelled to Wellington for the 1982 challenge, Wyllie asked Jim Stewart, who had guided Canterbury to two earlier Ranfurly Shield victories, in 1969 and 1972, to address his players. Stewart told them they might be facing the one chance of greatness in their entire careers. 'Miss it and you may never get another one. For the rest of your lives you will wonder if there was any more you could have done.' Those words obviously had the desired effect, and Wyllie would himself use such language later in his career. Both men had learned an appeal to pride, rather than fist-banging and shouting, was the more effective way to motivate a side.

In 1987 Wyllie and Hart joined Lochore on the national panel to choose and prepare the All Blacks who comfortably won the first World Cup. Then, with Lochore retired, Wyllie beat Hart in the ballot for All Black coach. He was to beat off further challenges from Hart later.

Wyllie stuck faithfully to his trusted squad and test XV, who repaid him with excellent results. But he dropped his aging captain, Buck Shelford, who became the first long-term All Black captain to lose the job while unbeaten. In the aftermath of the 1991 World Cup campaign, it seems he should perhaps have dropped other players also, at least to give them a shake-up.

Shortly after he was dropped as captain in mid-1990, Shelford published his book. In it he said that though both Wyllie and Hart were outstanding coaches, he related better to Wyllie 'because Alex is so straight and to the point'.

'There is no nonsense and you are left in no doubt about what he wants and expects. You always know his intentions, his plans, and where you fit in the All Black scheme of things. I find his up-front manner refreshing.

'Grizz Wyllie is not your smooth, sharp, city-slicker coach, but is as talented as any I've had. His tactical appreciation is enormous and he has earned the All Blacks' undeniable admiration.

'There are a lot of Aucklanders in the All Blacks and at times they have made it clear they don't want to alter their provincial tactics. However, they can't argue because the All Blacks, under Grizz, are unconquered.'[3]

But the All Blacks, by 1991, had been in a gradual

SO NEAR, SO FAR: All Black Alex Wyllie makes a 50-yard burst for the 1972-73 All Blacks against Hawick. The All Blacks won 26-6.

decline. This was not necessarily noticeable to the casual observer, or the diehard fan who hoped against hope as the All Blacks began their World Cup campaign by beating England that the team would lift its performance. But the rot was well set in by then.

Auckland had been New Zealand's outstanding team for eight years, through the Hart and Maurice Trapp-Bryan Williams coaching eras. Other provinces were lucky to come second. There were now 14 Auckland players in the All Black squad, a record number. Not surprisingly, the Aucklanders carried much weight in team tactics and

WORLD RECORD: Alex Wyllie's All Blacks were an unrivalled team when this action, from the 1989 home series against France, took place. Beginning with the 1987 World Cup (when Brian Lochore was coach) the team went 50 matches and 21 tests undefeated, a world record. A pack containing, from left, Alan Whetton, Steve McDowell, Gary Whetton, Murray Pierce and Richard Loe allows Frenchman Laurent Rodriguez little chance to contest the ball.

culture, particularly the captain, Gary Whetton, who had replaced Shelford, and Grant Fox.

But Auckland's standards had also been imperceptibly slipping. Motivation, morale and fitness were three key areas which, with habitual success, almost inevitably suffered a decline, leading to a loss of performance, even though the team kept winning. The senior players' influence kept getting stronger and stronger, and everyone seemed quite happy about it all, but Auckland's problems became the All Blacks' problems.

Shelford also said the power of the Auckland team rubbed off on the All Blacks. 'It was inevitable. Gary Whetton, Grant Fox, Alan Whetton called the shots . . . everyone was used to getting what they wanted.

'None of this would have mattered, but by 1990 the politics had taken over from the rugby . . . it was most noticeable in the fitness. Players were not putting in the hard graft. The basic attitude at training was "a short time's a good time."'[6]

Confirmation that Auckland had reached this sorry state came when Graham Henry took over as its coach after the 1991 World Cup. Facing an unenviable task, Henry knew he had to ring the changes if he was to survive and a new era be born. He said he confronted apathy, disrespect and hostility as he did so, but out went Gary and Alan Whetton, Steve McDowell, Terry Wright, Bernie McCahill, Ant Strachan, John Kirwan, Pat Lam and Daniel Manu (who became a Wallaby), while Grant Fox retired.

The author believes some influential factors were beyond Wyllie's understanding at the time, and certainly beyond his control. The 'Auckland factor', evident in the selectorial actions of Graham Henry and Laurie Mains after 1991, supports this theory. The co-coach move by the NZRFU only helped to cement in place the near-inevitability of the All Blacks' 1991 disappointments.

Team manager Sturgeon said, in 1997, that but for his ministrations on Wyllie's behalf at NZRFU council level, Wyllie would have been dropped by the NZRFU altogether, such was the politicking during 1990-91.

Wyllie was a precursor of rugby's professional era. After retiring as an amateur All Black coach in 1991 he became one of the first former national coaches to take his experience overseas and coach for a living. He coached Eastern Province in South Africa in 1993-94, and Transvaal in 1995, and was on the Argentina national team's coaching staff from 1995 to 1999.

Wyllie returned to his farm at Omihi in 1998. It had been leased while he had been overseas. It is his base, and he travelled for specific Argentine coaching tasks, including the 1999 Rugby World Cup.

REFERENCES
1 Phil Gifford, *Rugby News*, 1992.
2 Paul Thomas, *Straight from the Hart*.
3 Wayne Shelford with Wynne Gray, *Buck: The Wayne Shelford Story*.

. . . .

BUCK SHELFORD

THE CAPTAIN'S 'PERFECT' RECORD WAS NOT GOOD ENOUGH

When Alex Wyllie dropped his famous All Black captain, Wayne Shelford, midway through 1990, he unwittingly abandoned the one person who stood between World Cup success and the disunited, cynical and eventually ignominious mess the campaign became.

'At the end of the day, I was probably Grizz's biggest ally — if only he had talked to me,' Shelford told the author in 1997.

Instead, Shelford became the only long-term unbeaten All Black captain ever to have been dropped, permanently, from the team.

Seven years after his demise and the heralding of the unprecedented 'Bring Back Buck' campaign, Shelford was adamant he held no grudges against his former coach. He recalled the partnership with Wyllie with fondness. 'But to this day, Alex has never spoken to me about the matter,' he said. 'One day we shall have to sit down and talk it all through.'

His relationship with Wyllie aside, the intervening years, and frank conversations with a number of his former All Black team-mates, have unravelled a thread of

POWER PLAY VICTIM: Wayne 'Buck' Shelford became the only long-term and undefeated All Black captain to be permanently dropped from the team. Shelford says he now knows how and why it happened.

All Black intrigue increasingly disturbing to Shelford. He believes both Wyllie and himself became victims of the 'Auckland mafia' in the rugby game.

'Grizz became the victim of player power from the Auckland faction of the team, coupled with the ambitions of John Hart at that time,' said Shelford. 'To some extent, looking back, so did I.'

The tragic consequence of player power for New Zealand rugby, according to Shelford, was that the dominant Auckland players 'could run the All Black show while the going was good, but didn't know how to put things right when it got tough'.

'They thought they knew it all, but they had never coached. That's why teams like the All Blacks have coaches with years of experience in playing, selecting and coaching.'

Serious undermining of Shelford began on the 1989 tour, when he led the All Blacks to big victories over Wales and Ireland.

'Some of the team began to complain to me about Grizz's hard training methods,' he said. 'I should stress they were only ever Aucklanders — the players from all the other provinces didn't gripe. They just got stuck in.

ALEX WYLLIE

'There was a brigade of them trying to run the show. I can see it now, years down the line . . . But I just told them to stop being soft and get on with it. I actually enjoyed Grizz's methods and felt we were going well. Grizz was hard, but also a lot of fun. 'I knew nothing about what else was happening on that tour, but have subsequently learned a great deal.'

Shelford said a group of Auckland players had been 'having secret meetings, behind closed doors', in a move which 'basically amounted to trying to get rid of me'. Pressed for the source of these allegations, Shelford said Mike Brewer had told him a lot. 'Mike was invited to those meetings, but refused to attend.'

Brewer, when coach of the West Hartlepool club in England, told the author Shelford's recall of events was accurate. 'It was at Swansea when I was asked my opinion about the test no. 8,' he said. 'I was meant to say Zinny should get the job, but my response was that it should go to whoever was playing the best. It was all part of a move to install Gary [Whetton] as the captain.'

Brewer summed up the move as 'probably one of the worst decisions in All Black rugby. Zinny took several years to round out his game and become one of the best, while the All Blacks missed Buck's quiet, inspiring leadership. He was like a mountain. If I was asked who I wanted in the All Black pack for a particularly tough test match, I'd have to say Buck Shelford would be the first I'd pick.'

Shelford said he had also discussed the issues with a number of other players from the team and gradually learned about the 'power play' that had taken place.

'In 1991 I attended the two dinners, at the beginning and the end of the World Cup. The All Black camp was disunited. There were two completely split camps. I don't know what the numbers were, but many of the players say it was the worst team they had ever played for in that respect. It was the major reason for the side not performing as it could have.'

It was hard for Shelford to come to grips with the fact All Black team-mates for whom he was constantly laying his body on the line had secretly been plotting to overthrow him.

'It was disappointing to go through such a great era of three or four years and then have it all dissolved by arrogant men with giant egos,' he said. 'I have made an awful lot of friendships from rugby — hundreds of good friends at all levels of the game. But with regard to some of my old All Black team-mates..... well, I couldn't call them friends really, just acquaintances.'

BIOGRAPHICAL DETAILS

Alexander John Wyllie

Born: Christchurch, 31 August 1944

Position: Loose forward

Represented NZ 1970-73
40 matches (11 internationals)

Points for NZ: 42 (12 tries)

Provincial record: Canterbury 1964-79 (Glenmark club) played 210 games for Canterbury, more than 100 as captain; South Island 1966-69, 1971-73, 1976. Played 278 first-class matches.

Selector/coach: Canterbury 1982-86 (played 92, won 76, lost 12, drew 4); NZ Colts 1987

NZ selector: 1987-91

NZ coach: 1988-91 (played 28 tests, won 24, lost 3, drew 1)

Co-coach with John Hart, 1991 World Cup team

Other: MBE for services to rugby 1986

Occupation: Professional rugby coach in South Africa and Argentina since soon after retiring as All Black coach; was farmer at Omihi

NEW ZEALAND COACHING RECORD

1988: beat Wales 52-3, 54-9; beat Australia 32-7; drew with Australia 19-all; beat Australia 30-9

1989: beat France 25-17, 34-20; beat Argentina 60-9, 49-12; beat Australia 24-12; beat Wales 34-9; beat Ireland 23-6

1990: beat Scotland 31-16, 21-18; beat Australia 21-6, 27-17; lost to Australia 9-21; beat France 24-3, 30-12

1991: beat Argentina 28-14, 36-6; lost to Australia 12-21

World Cup Pool matches: beat England 18-12; beat USA 46-6; beat Italy 31-21. Quarterfinal: beat Canada 29-13. Semifinal: lost to Australia 6-16. Play-off for third place: beat Scotland 13-6

CHAPTER 33

NEW ZEALAND COACH 1992-95

LAURIE MAINS

Poisoned chalice robbed Mains of glory he earned

WHEN LAURIE MAINS RETIRED AS ALL BLACK coach at the end of 1995, there were some critics, particularly north of the Bombay Hills, who claimed his reign had produced only moderate success. The advent of fully professional rugby, with its high-powered resources, fuller itineraries and smooth-as-silk marketing, had, within a few short months, seemingly overshadowed the achievements of Mains and his team.

But to categorise the Mains era — from 1992 to 1995 (virtually from the 1991 World Cup to a little beyond the 1995 World Cup) — as moderate is to do a disservice to the achievements of a coach in a highly transitional period.

The record books show Mains' 34 tests yielded 23 wins, 10 losses and a draw. But the level of success early in his term was never going to be good enough for his detractors, and he was forced to fight off challenges from John Hart, who had also challenged Alex Wyllie and brought about the unfortunate co-coach experiment at the 1991 World Cup.

Mains was able to see off the most serious of Hart's attempts in September 1994 and continue to lay the foundations for what should have been a glorious World Cup victory over South Africa in 1995. Yet critics remained thick on the ground, even after the World Cup. However, the requirements of the four-yearly cup cycle put new pressures on international coaches.

Analysis of Mains' era reveals a number of heady achievements:
- The 1995 All Blacks perfected the most sensational attacking style (with unprecedented match-try totals) world rugby had witnessed, the superb 1996 All Black victories notwithstanding. This without the aid of rule changes which opened up the game further in 1996.
- The 1995 All Blacks completed a 12-test programme — the longest any international side had undertaken — with 10 victories. This was comparable to the 1996 All Black 10-test, one-loss record although 1996 opposition was tougher.
- The 1995 All Blacks scored 574 points in those tests, averaging a phenomenal 48 points a game, and including 71 tries, an average of six tries a game.
- Mains' legacy included a large group of test-hardened All Blacks for his successor, in vivid contrast to the aged, jaded and disillusioned players he had inherited in 1992. Those players he developed into world-class players — and who were seen as courageous selections at the time — included Josh Kronfeld, Craig Dowd, Robin Brooke, Andrew Mehrtens, Jeff Wilson, Jonah Lomu, Taine Randell and Justin Marshall. In the 1996 test-starting line-ups only Christian Cullen was new.

LAURIE MAINS

CRITIC OUTRAGE: It is 1994 and Laurie Mains is in the midst of the toughest of schedules – against France, South Africa and Australia, including five tests in five weeks – ever undertaken. Critics said his most outrageous moment was trying to sell his theory that the All Blacks were holding back some ammunition until 1995. How wrong the critics turned out to be.

- Mains' All Blacks beat every major rugby-playing nation away from home (something to which even the great Fred Allen could not lay claim), and achieved the grand slam in the World Cup.
- The World Cup match against Japan produced a stack of records: most points, most tries, most individual tries and points, the near-perfect game.
- The World Cup semifinal against England, with Jonah Lomu scoring four tries, will go down in international coaching manuals into the next century as the textbook way to start and consolidate a test-match victory.
- Mains' team was the first to play five tests in five weeks (in 1994).
- Mains' was the first All Black team to be unbeaten in a series against South Africa, when it won the 1994 series.
- Mains was the first All Black coach to win a one-off or series in South Africa — after 64 years of endeavour.
- On that tour of South Africa, in 1992, Mains became the first coach of an international touring side to win all its matches in the republic.
- He was the first international coach to beat the Springboks in series at home and abroad.
- Mains had won more tests than any other All Black coach except Alex Wyllie.

Mains told the author that, of all those achievements, the depth of talent he left for his successor is probably the one he was most proud of.

Mains' detractors — it is common knowledge he did not enjoy a happy relationship with some media personnel — accused him of getting many things wrong.

Part of Mains' problem was he had to swiftly weed out all the past-their-best players who had gone on a year or two too long under Alex Wyllie. The Wyllie era had produced an incredible run of success — 20 wins and a draw in 23 tests to 1991, with not one loss in the first three years. But apart from Buck Shelford — the only unbeaten All Black captain to be dropped after a long tenure — Wyllie was especially loyal to incumbent test players. With the experience of only one World Cup, the significance of experimentation and the blooding of new players with the four-yearly peak in mind seemed largely lost on Wyllie. But Mains did not want to make the same mistake — and could not have done so even if he had wished to, because the cupboard was so bare.

Another major factor in Mains' turnover of test players was the losses to rugby league. John Schuster, Craig Innes, Inga Tuigamala and John Timu were the All Blacks to go. All were backs, and left holes in terms of talent and experience that could not easily be filled. The worry of league and the vast sums it offered were factors Mains, unlike any All Black coach since the Depression, had to deal with as best he could. The meagre allowances allowed by the last of the amateur-minded NZRFU officials must have made him feel impotent. The shadow of Japan and its vast resources also disrupted his planning when players like Herb Schuler were attracted by the yen.

The great tragedy for Mains came with the 12–15 loss, in extra time, of the World Cup final. The All Blacks had shown a tactical and skill level several grades above any other team at the tournament — until then. If the team had won Mains would have silenced most of his critics for good.

But the cruel hand of fate — or something more sinister — when 18 members of the All Black team came down with food poisoning two days before the final shortened the odds to nigh on impossible before the starting whistle blew.

Although the All Blacks remained competitive throughout the game and lost only with the Joel Stransky drop goal near the end of extra time, the form which set them apart from the other contenders had deserted them. They lacked all spark in the final.

Critics have said the Springboks did not allow the All Blacks to play their usual game. It is true that Jonah Lomu, following his four-try annihilation of England in the semifinal, was marked out of the game after Shell South Africa disgracefully offered $2000 a tackle — and Freek Burger, the director of SARFU referees, had been designated to judge who qualified to gain the 'tackle bounty'. But it was Springbok conservatism that actually allowed the All Blacks to stay in the game. The All Blacks' energy levels, courage and timing, and the instant decision-making of key players, had all been affected — and it was gastroenteritis that was to blame.

The experts are unanimous that a minimum 48 hours is required to recover from gastroenteritis — time the All Blacks unhappily did not have at their disposal after their hotel tea and coffee (medical analysis points to this source) had been contaminated.

Mains would quote a detective he hired as saying a kitchenmaid with a name like Susie was paid to spike the drinks. He was also told by a leading New Zealand financier that British bookmakers, facing big pay-outs if the All Blacks won the final against odds made before the tournament when the All Blacks were far from favourites, might be behind the poisoning. Installed as strong favourites by the time of the final, the All Blacks' loss instead created a bookmakers' bonanza.

'I don't have an opinion. I have no evidence to point the finger, though I'm still working on it,' said Mains. 'But I'm a lot more relieved to know what did occur.[1]

All Black campaign manager Brian Lochore said he knew the day before the game that it was already lost. 'In the afternoon, we took the team to a nearby park, for a wander around in the fresh air. Some didn't wander at all, just slumped down against the nearest tree. It was a tragedy.' The campaign had gone exactly as it had in 1987, when Lochore had coached the All Blacks to win the

MOST CAPPED: Sean Fitzpatrick – with the Bledisloe Cup after the All Blacks' 28-16 and 34-23 victories over Australia in 1995 – was captain throughout Laurie Mains' era. He would go on to play 128 matches, including a record 92 tests, between 1986 and 1997. The durable 'Fitzy' made his debut in the same game as Joe Stanley and would have Stanley's son, Jeremy, as an All Black team-mate by 1997.

first World Cup tournament. Until then he had had no doubts whatsoever that the All Blacks would win.[3]

Manager Colin Meads was one of the team hit hardest by the poisoning, and spent the only day sick in bed in his life! Lochore became de facto manager in his absence. Meads said that, in retrospect, the All Blacks should have pulled out of the final and asked that it be played later.

According to author Spiro Zavos, the team doctor's room was turned into 'an emergency ward along the lines of *MASH*' on the Thursday night before the final. 'Players stumbled, almost crawled to it for injections and pills.'[2]

Ian Jones thought he wasn't going to make it through the night. Andrew Mehrtens, who would play some of the final with double vision, and Jeff Wilson, who left the match at halftime to go to the toilet and then departed for good later in the game, only to be seen vomiting on the sideline by TV viewers, were the worst affected. Craig Dowd had to be replaced by Richard Loe in extra time, while most of the players reported later they had found it hard to breathe, their legs had been much wearier than usual and their concentration had wavered.

The All Black medical staff confirmed at the time of the incident that the poisoning had not affected several team members, including Sean Fitzpatrick and the Brooke brothers. But it was found that this group had arrived late for a team meal, so had not eaten it and had drunk freshly made tea or coffee.

According to Mike Bowen, the All Black team doctor, 'Susie', who was subsequently sacked by the hotel management, probably used Indian Trick, a herb known in South Africa to produce a particularly virulent stomach upset. 'The herb is odourless and flavourless, and was probably added to the team's tea and coffee,' wrote Zavos.[3]

For Mains and his players the incident was a tragedy. It is also disgraceful there was no official IRB enquiry. It is an interesting proposition, but if the All Blacks had requested a postponement, the IRB would have had to act, one way or another. It is an eventuality the IRB needs to be prepared for at future World Cups.

Hardly had the realisation hit Mains that the major goal of his coaching career had escaped when he was faced with another huge dilemma — the arrival of fully professional rugby, intertwined with the battles between WRC (backed by Kerry Packer) and the NZRFU (newly contracted to Rupert Murdoch's News Corporation).

Mains had played a key part in getting the NZRFU to negotiate with Murdoch. He had long been a vocal opponent of the way British and Australian rugby league was 'raping' the New Zealand rugby game. He had been the closest observer of all as he watched helplessly as key members of his back line were picked off during his term. The All Blacks Club had been partially effective in fighting off the predators from league and Japan, but its resources were only enough to put up a 'rearguard action'.

Back in April 1995, Mains had taken it upon himself to ask Kevin Roberts, then the chief operating officer of Lion Nathan, the All Blacks' major sponsor, and by then a personal friend, to approach Murdoch's people.

'My reasoning was that rugby was more entertaining than league and a more global sport and that if Murdoch was prepared to invest so much money in Super League, why would he not be prepared to pick up rugby too, particularly on a southern hemisphere basis?' he explained.[4]

A series of meetings ensued from which came the historic agreement for Murdoch to fund rugby's entry into fully fledged professionalism, to the tune of $US555 million.

The first Mains had heard of WRC was at Jan Smuts Airport, Johannesburg, as the All Blacks were preparing to return to New Zealand after the World Cup. Colin Meads said he'd been told the Australian team was holding a meeting with the organisation that day. Mains dismissed the idea as impossible, given Murdoch's entry into the game. But by the time the All Blacks spectacularly beat Australia in the second Bledisloe Cup match of 1995, in Sydney, he had already become inextricably entangled in the battle that emerged between WRC and the establishment of the game.

That test was historic. It was the 100th between the two countries. Large numbers of former All Blacks and Wallabies were present as guests of honour. It might, because of WRC developments, have been the last time an All Black team would play. It was the last such game between so-called amateurs.

Afterwards, before the official dinner, the All Blacks attended a meeting at the home of Brian Powers, Kerry Packer's lieutenant, to look at the WRC proposals. Meads, Mains and Earle Kirton, the assistant coach, sat outside in the team bus. Mains was initially dead set against WRC, but listened to his senior players, who clearly liked the proposed set-up and the money offered.[5]

WRC and the NZRFU waged a behind-the-scenes battle for the minds and bodies of the All Blacks through June, July and August of 1995. Eventually, Mains became convinced rugby would benefit, regardless of which party won the war, with better conditions for players in a professional environment.

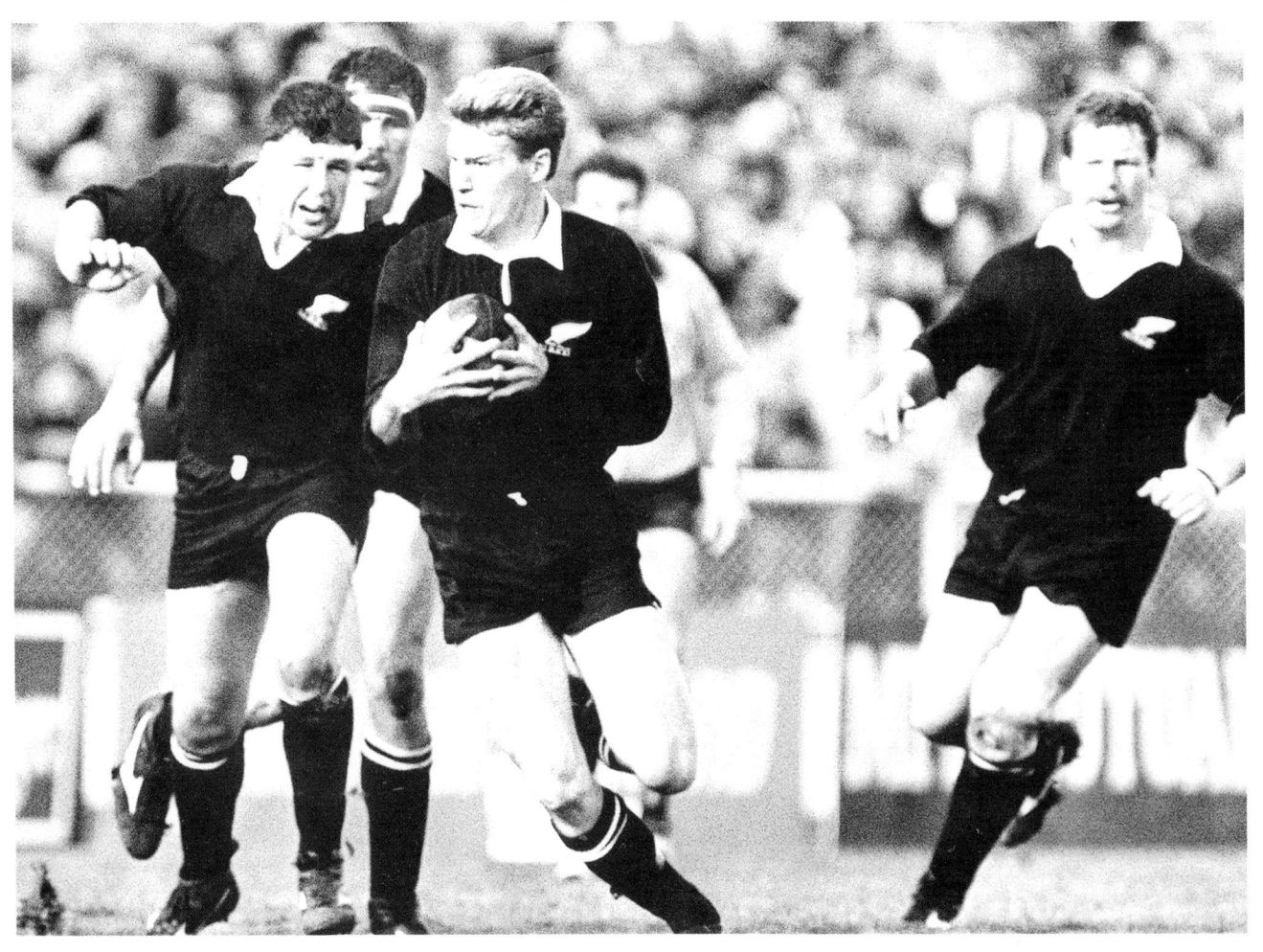

SCORING MACHINE: John Kirwan scored 35 tries in tests and 67 in all matches for the All Blacks between 1984 and 1994. A big winger with great pace and clever footwork, Kirwan could score them from anywhere. But his fortunes started to wane in 1992, in Laurie Mains' first year as All Black coach. Mains kept Kirwan in the side until 1994, after which Kirwan 'retired', stating that Mains had 'lost the plot'.

Mains signed a preliminary commitment to the WRC cause. His major concern was that the Murdoch deal would still not stop players going to league or Japan, whereas the WRC deal would keep them together. A condition of any possible Mains involvement was always that the NZRFU and provincial unions would be involved.

In his book Mains said he 'was naive enough to think that, given the realities of the WRC proposal and the threats to the All Blacks' ranks, the NZRFU would embrace the WRC concept, but the battle for the best interests of rugby increasingly became a battle of personalities.'[6]

Mains was alarmed to read in the *Sydney Morning Herald* of 27 July while the All Blacks were in Sydney preparing for the second Bledisloe Cup game, that, despite the Murdoch-NZRFU agreement, Ken Cowley, head of News Corporation in Australia, was quoted as saying there was no basis for believing Super League (the Murdoch-financed rugby league competition competing with the traditional Australian Rugby League organised competition) had been instructed to lay off poaching rugby players. Soon afterwards, a request from Roberts to one of Murdoch's chiefs in London, Sam Chisholm, that Super League desist, brought an immediate reaction. Super League backed off.

This allowed the NZRFU, with Jock Hobbs and, initially, Brian Lochore doing the donkeywork, to start drawn-out negotiations with players. Mains, through Roberts, continued to have an influence in the matter — he wanted all his players to benefit, not just the elite — and became in danger of being branded a WRC agent. While all the players were exonerated, the NZRFU continued to point the finger at him. He eventually had

WRC's Geoff Levy write a letter which virtually cleared him of any direct involvement with the organisation, especially as a recruiting agent, which he never was.

The NZRFU relented, although, according to Mains, a group of hardliners remained who wanted to pillory him.[7]

The irony is that the NZRFU probably panicked. It needn't have paid out so much to keep its players. As David Kirk said in 1997, if WRC had got started, the players who defected would now be nonentities in striped jerseys playing in Townsville. 'Instead, they are the All Blacks, the finest rugby team in the world, and its players are the stars of world rugby. And they owe it — as we all owe it — to the All Black tradition formed by the 500 or so players since the beginning of the century.'[8]

Mains has paid high tribute to Kevin Roberts, now the world head of advertising agency Saatchi and Saatchi but still an NZRFU councillor. 'He was a tremendous ally of the All Blacks. Together, we professionalised the All Blacks. The All Black Club was just a smoke-screen really,' explained Mains.

'New Zealand rugby is so lucky to have this man. He has the ability to carry the whole thing on his own.

'Any improvement I made as a coach during my All Black era I owe largely to him. In so many ways he opened the door for me, not so much in purely rugby terms, but in giving me direction.'

Mains recalled how, during the World Cup build-up, Roberts had addressed the team and had used a dinner engagement he had recently had with US general Norman Schwartzkopf, leader of the Allied forces in the Gulf War, to illustrate his points about planning a campaign. 'It was sheer brilliance.'

Another unsung hero of Mains is the Hamilton statistician Geoff Miller, who was 'of significant assistance to the All Blacks at the World Cup'.

'Geoff kept the most amazing statistics for us throughout the tournament, and, as planned, we were able to use these to analyse our opponents. He could tell us, for instance, that England's first five-eighth kicked into the box seven times, or used the "wipers" kick across field eight times. It was invaluable information.'[9]

Mains still had one more goal for his All Blacks before he retired. He badly wanted to beat the French, who had made his position less secure when they had scored their historical 2–0 series victory in New Zealand the previous year. The All Blacks looked tired when well beaten in the high winds of Toulouse 15–22, but came back strongly in Paris to dismember the French 37–12.

This was a performance to rank with the All Black ambush of England in the World Cup semifinal in Cape Town.

Mains believes an All Black coach had seldom had to face so many challenges during his term, both from outside forces and from others within the New Zealand game. Here are just a few of them:

- The All Black selection panel of Earle Kirton, Peter Thorburn and Mains had worked closely and well since 1992, with a strategy aimed at the World Cup. But Mains believes it became Auckland's aim to break up the trio, with the ultimate objective of getting John Hart in charge for the 1995 tournament. Thorburn was replaced by Auckland's Lin Colling in December 1993. A year later Colling became expendable when Auckland chairman Rob Fisher phoned him and told him the union would not be supporting his nomination. Its preferred candidate was Hart.
- The loss of John Dowling in 1994 as the NZRFU deputy chairman, replaced by Fisher. Otago's Dowling had been a strong supporter of Mains' All Black goals, and Mains felt the change undermined his position as coach and meant the Hart issue kept simmering away. Mains said Dowling had no reason to suspect he was being challenged by Fisher, who expressed surprise at the result of the ballot, saying he had not sought the position. Dowling soon learned Fisher had in fact done extensive lobbying. Fisher wrote to Dowling a month later, apologising for misleading him.
- Mains' frustration with NZRFU chairman Eddie Tonks. In 1994 he submitted 13 requests to the chairman on behalf of the selectors, only three being approved. Tonks told the council at one stage: 'We've got to let these guys [the selectors] know who is running New Zealand rugby.' Tonks had helped put the 1991 All Blacks on a World Cup 'Mission Impossible' when Alex Wyllie was undermined by Hart becoming a co-coach. He made no secret of the fact he supported Hart in 1994. Mains' gripe was that Tonks made his views public when one would expect any chairman to support his national coach in public. Additionally, after advising Mains early in 1994 that the World Cup squad should be named at the end of August, he later instructed him (on about 20 August) not to name the squad. Mains' conclusion was that Tonks expected the selectors to change. The election came on 15 September. Hart told the *New Zealand Herald* he had received the 'bad news' from Tonks and his deputy, Fisher, and that Tonks 'was pretty disappointed in terms of the outcome'. Tonks, however, gave the All Blacks full support in the final World Cup build-up.
- Being asked to play two successive tests in 1994 on Sundays (ruling out Michael Jones) against the French; then

having only six days before the first of three tests against the All Blacks' traditional rivals, the Springboks; and then the Bledisloe Cup match under lights, midweek, in Sydney. It made Mains wonder whose side the NZRFU was really on.

• The way Rob Fisher, then chairman of Auckland RFU and then deputy chairman of the NZRFU, obstructed the All Blacks' World Cup build-up in early 1995. The series of incidents involved a friendly between North Harbour and Auckland, a goodwill match to help smooth the waters after the fiery NPC grand final a few months earlier. The trouble was the two unions chose a date that was 24 hours before the All Blacks were to assemble for their crucial fourth and final camp, at Christchurch on February 24–27, before the World Cup. The All Black selectors had long ago advised that All Blacks were not to be asked to play in such matches. Harbour's coach, Chas Ferris, was fully co-operative, but Auckland's Graham Henry insisted his All Blacks participate. Mains recalled how Fisher and Mike Banks (today the All Black manager) were 'totally against me' when the NZRFU arranged a telephone hook-up for him to explain his case why the All Blacks shouldn't be involved. Later he rang Fisher, putting his case again and adding that he (Fisher) could end up with egg on his face. 'History records that six players arrived at the camp unable to perform their fitness tests or take part in the first two days' activities,' Mains subsequently revealed. Fisher was 'virtually censured' by the NZRFU a few days later, when the council endorsed its previous decision that Brian Lochore, the All Blacks' campaign manager, was empowered to make binding decisions on the players' activities.[10]

• Early in 1995 the council agreed Mains could take 30 players on the tour of Italy and France at the end of the year. Nearer the time, the council decided, for 'financial reasons', only 26 would tour. Mains arranged sponsorship for the extra players through the All Blacks Club, but the council rejected this. Mains, well informed by friends on the council, alleged Fisher and Banks were driving the opposition 'to make things difficult'.

Mains was influenced by the great Otago coach Vic Cavanagh early in his playing career. After his third game of senior rugby for his club, Southern, he was summoned to Cavanagh's office at Dunedin's now-defunct evening newspaper the *Evening Star*. The advice Cavanagh offered was to have a huge impact on Mains' play, and subsequently his coaching.

'Until then, I had operated instinctively, with only

BEST-LAID PLANS: Laurie Mains masterminded an extraordinary World Cup strategy in 1995, after some mixed results through preceding seasons. His All Blacks 'ambushed' opponents in the tournament, but fell at the final hurdle, losing 12–15 to the Springboks in extra time in the final, after 18 members of his team had been struck down by debilitating food-poisoning.

random thought to what the opposition was scheming,' said Mains.

'That afternoon with Cavanagh was the start for me of a career analysing players and plays. I became known as a sound positional fullback . . . thanks to Vic's sage advice. No first five-eighth ever kicked me out of position.'[11]

Mains was to make a notable All Black debut in 1971 against the British Lions. He had watched the famous Fergie McCormick being outmanoeuvred by Lions first five-eighth Barry John at Carisbrook in the opening test, but felt he was made a scapegoat for the loss. However, this opened the way for Mains himself to play in the second test, at Lancaster Park, Fergie's stamping ground. He recalled receiving generous support from the Canterbury crowd as he helped the All Blacks to a decisive 22–12 victory, made famous by the extraordinary 55-metre solo try late in the game by Ian Kirkpatrick.

It was to be the Lions' only tour loss, however. A Mains try provided the only All Black points in the third test in Wellington, where the rejuvenated Lions won 13–3, while he saved the side from ignominy in the fourth test at Eden Park with a late penalty to tie the scores 14-all.

Mains became one of the casualties as the All Blacks entered a strong rebuilding phase after that series.

LAURIE MAINS

He was not to be called on again until 1976, when he played in the one-off test against the touring Irish at Athletic Park. But his career with Otago had continued through the intervening years and he was to build up a fine career record of 967 points between 1967 and 1976.

Rugby News gave a flattering description of Mains' play in 1975, stating he was 'the safest, surest, winningest fullback in New Zealand rugby — a top-notch player who is operating about 200 per cent better than when he was an All Black in 1971'.[12]

Mains remains the only man ever to play a century of matches for his province and then coach that province in a century of games.

A lover of the outdoors all his life, Mains' favourite recreation is fishing. He trained as a teacher, then turned to real estate after two years to earn enough to finance a farm. But he found farming duties clashed with rugby coaching and travelling, so moved into building. He owned Profile Buildings, one of the leading home builders south of the Waitaki.

In late 1998 Mains signed a three-year contract to coach the Gauteng Lions (formerly Transvaal) in South Africa for the Currie Cup. The vast improvement in 1999 was immediate. The Lions had been a poor-performing side and coaches had not lasted long. 'I wouldn't have it any other way,' said Mains. 'I don't like comfort zones. I have a history of picking up teams not performing to their full potential.'

In 1999 Mains' Lions beat Griqualand West 73-7 in the final of the Vodacom Cup — a vast transformation from the 0-57 hiding they had received from the same team in the 1998 final. Mains was being touted as a likely Super 12 coach and said he was ready to accept a position if offered.

Mains has expressed disappointment that a similar position has not been available for him in New Zealand. He has had no approach from the NZRFU to coach or assist in coaching development since his term as All Black coach. 'I find it distressing I wasn't able to do the same sort of thing in New Zealand,' he said. 'There are half a dozen good coaches, but watching teams right through the divisions there are a lot of coaches who need help.'

REFERENCES

1. Bob Howitt and Robin McConnell, *Laurie Mains*, Rugby Press, 1996.
2-3. Spiro Zavos, *Winter of Revenge*.
4-6. *Laurie Mains*.
7. David Kirk, *Black and Blue*.
8-10. *Laurie Mains*.
11. *Rugby News*.
12. *Laurie Mains*.

BIOGRAPHICAL DETAILS

Laurence William Mains

Born: Dunedin, 16 February 1946

Position: Fullback

Represented NZ: 1971, 1976
15 matches (4 internationals)

Points for NZ: 153

Provincial record: Otago 1967–75 (Southern club) — 115 games; South Island 1970–71, 1975; NZ Juniors 1968

Selector/coach: Otago 1983–91 (164 games)

NZ selector: 1992–95

NZ coach: 1992–95

Occupation: Professional rugby coach, South Africa

NEW ZEALAND COACHING RECORD

1992: lost to World XV 14–28, beat World XV 54–26, 26–15; beat Ireland 24–21, 59–6; lost to Australia 15–16, 17–19, beat Australia 26–23; beat South Africa 27–24

1993: beat Lions 20–18, lost to Lions 7–20, beat Lions 30–13; beat Australia 25–10; beat Western Samoa 35–13; beat Scotland 51–15; lost to England 9–15

1994: lost to France 8–22, 20–23; beat South Africa 22–14, 13–9, drew with South Africa 18 all; lost to Australia 16–20

1995: beat Canada 73–7; beat Australia 28–16, 34–23; beat Italy 51–21; lost to France 15–22, beat France 37–12

World Cup Pool matches: beat Ireland 43–19, beat Wales 34–9, beat Japan 145–17; Quarterfinal: beat Scotland 48–30; Semifinal: beat England 45–29; Final: lost to South Africa 12–15

CHAPTER 34

NEW ZEALAND COACH 1987, co-coach 1991, coach 1996–

JOHN HART

First professional coach survived tumultuous era

ALL BLACK COACH JOHN HART HAD HIS EYES firmly focused on uplifting the Webb Ellis Trophy for Rugby World Cup supremacy in late 1999. It was to be the crowning glory in a tumultuous four years of guiding the team.

The status of near-deity Hart had achieved during the all-conquering 1996 and 1997 seasons, including the All Blacks' historic first series win on South African soil, meant he had a record of victories unsurpassed among his predecessors.

Few would argue he had not proven the near-perfect custodian of the job in the challenging transition from shamateurism to openly professional rugby. As the 1998 test 'season' was about to begin Hart had fashioned a test record of 20 wins, a loss and a draw. No other All Black coach had scored so many victories in such a short period, and the signs pointed to many more.

But his mana crumbled in 1998 when the All Blacks lost five consecutive tests — the worst record in more than a century of All Black history. However, those defeats were almost all narrow and played under extenuating circumstances. Hart looked back on 1998 as a salutary rebuilding year. He survived a vote of confidence by the NZRFU, and his team has carefully managed a programme through 1999 designed to culminate in peak performance for the World Cup.

But the roller coaster ride of Hart as All Black coach strongly reflected the new challenges of international rugby. His period can be divided into three stages: the success of the first two years, disaster in 1998, and a strong recovery to bid for World Cup supremacy.

Hart's obvious enjoyment of the role he played as maestro during 1996–97 was to be savoured all the more after the excruciatingly long wait in the wings. Apart from two short-lived entries and ignominious exits, in 1987 and 1991, and a number of highly publicised challenges to incumbent coaches Alex Wyllie and Laurie Mains, almost a decade had gone by since Hart had last bestrode the national stage as the lead actor.

He had lost the NZRFU vote back in 1987 after taking the All Blacks to Japan when Brian Lochore retired following the World Cup triumphs earlier that year. Wyllie got the job and went nearly three years unbeaten. For the World Cup of 1991 Wyllie and Hart became victims of what was a strange move by the NZRFU to saddle them together as co-coaches. So, with the NZRFU clearly wishing to sweep with a new broom at the end of 1991, Mains got the job. Hart fought his way back into the frame when Mains fumbled through

JOHN HART

HART-FELT TIMES: Josh Kronfeld has the Springboks on the run in the momentous 1996 series in South Africa. John Hart became the first All Black coach to win a series in the republic, after five previous attempts stretching back to 1928 had all failed. Hart's team won nine out of 10 tests in 1996.

three difficult years, and in September 1994 mounted a big challenge.

The New Zealand tabloids used crude statistics in calling for Mains' head — forgetting that by their own criteria one of the darlings of the media, Lochore, who lost three tests out of six leading up to the 1987 World Cup victory, would have got the chop. Some of the All Blacks came out in public in support of Mains. The tabloids also ignored the fact that international rugby had been irreversibly altered by the World Cup cycle.

The defeat at the hands of Mains made it three strikes against Hart — he had been rejected in 1987, 1991 and 1994. That would have finished many ambitious people. He had coached on a very limited basis for a good number of years; younger, proven NPC coaches were coming through; and the game, ever changing, was vastly different from Hart's heady days with the Auckland team of the early 1980s.

That he was able to quickly overcome self-doubt and guide the All Black campaign that swept all before it was to

his great credit. Hart believed he was a better person for the long delay.

'I became wiser for the waiting. I've mellowed a lot,' he told the author. Does he lose his temper? 'Very seldom. I do get upset. But I don't necessarily show it externally. I tend to hold it inside.'

Whether he was a better coach he left for others to judge. But Hart's man-management skills were legendary. Though a coach's leadership role doesn't change, he was sure the requirements of leadership and management had. Players nowadays required 'empowerment' and more 'space' than in previous decades, he said. Create the right environment — by thorough planning, good management people, fair selections and an achievable game plan, building players' courage and involving them in decision-making on and off the field — and you had the winning Hart formula. Or so it seemed . . .

Hart had stood in the middle of a gigantic, empty Loftus Versfeld stadium during the 1995 World Cup, while

THE POWER BEHIND THE ALL BLACKS

COMEBACK KID: Tana Umaga shows the Wallabies how it's done in the 1997 test at Christchurch's Lancaster Park. John Hart's All Blacks blitzed Australia three times and South Africa twice, with only the 26-all draw against England at the end of a grand 10-test year to muddy the waters. Umaga was to make a dynamic return to form in 1999.

comments man for TVNZ, and wondered if he would ever get the opportunity to achieve what many regarded as his destiny. At the time he did not rate his chances too highly. Yet 14 months later that same stadium was to be the scene of perhaps his greatest triumph — where his All Black team became the first to win a full series in South Africa. Although the All Blacks did not achieve a whitewash of the once-mighty Boks, the side won nine out of ten tests in 1996 — the toughest undertaking ever completed by a rugby team in terms of the opposition met.

Privately, Hart believed that seven victories out of 10 would have been 'a really good pass mark'. Playing South Africa five times, Australia twice, Scotland twice and Western Samoa was indeed daunting. The All Blacks had won the first Tri-Nations championship and retained the Bledisloe Cup.

'That record was achieved because of the thorough planning of the management and the skill and character of the players,' Hart said at the time. 'We put a lot of emphasis on planning and organisation. On selecting well and being consistent with selections too. We were able to finish 10 tests using only 18 players in the starting lineup.'

The All Blacks had gained a strong psychological advantage when they outscrummed the Boks at Cape Town in the final Tri-Nations test — probably a key blow in the overall series. Hart believed the South Africans relied too heavily on the scrum and physicality in general.

Reflecting for a moment in June 1999, just as he was about to begin the World Cup build-up, Hart fondly recalled the 1996 achievements as probably the finest moments of his era.

Another 10 tests faced Hart and his team in 1997. But the side had grown in ability, confidence and stature. While other nations, particularly South Africa, were racked with problems, Hart's team was in complete control throughout a long year, excepting the stuttering performance which hinted of extreme tiredness, nothing more, in the draw with England at the end of the arduous campaign.

JOHN HART

The All Blacks blitzed Fiji and Argentina as the entrée, then set about devouring Australia (three times) and South Africa (twice) before undertaking the tour to Britain. Extravagant was the praise of the English critics when the All Blacks destroyed England in the first test at Manchester 25-8. The 26-all second-test draw saw an England team surprise the All Blacks with their more adventurous tactical approach. But New Zealand recovered well from the initial shock. It created and then 'blew' a number of scoring chances that on a 'normal working day' would have been turned to points.

'I had some concerns before that test,' ruminated Hart early in 1998. 'It was the end of a long year and inevitably, despite what you do, the sights of some players start to focus on home. It has to be said that England played the best 30 minutes of test rugby they've probably ever played. They did catch us off-guard. But very few test teams can come back from 3-20 and 9-23 down, like we did. England know they should have won that game!'

In the context of the year's programme, Hart, looking ahead, said that the result also had its favourable elements. 'It was a wake-up call, especially for the public, whose expectations had become enormously unrealistic. It is not possible to win, win, win at this level. Manchester United don't win all the time. Even the TAB gave the All Blacks a 28-point start, when history showed we had never beaten England by more than a 17-point margin.'

Hart took a 36-player squad to Britain, allowing the test players to be rested from midweek fixtures, as occurred in South Africa. 'I understand and recognise we have to play a lot of tests. It's more the spacing of them and making sure we maximise the product instead of playing too many games and minimising the quality. That's what has always concerned me,' he concluded.

A skilful and insightful profile of Hart was penned by British rugby writer Mick Cleary, of the *Daily Telegraph*, during the tour:

'Hart, for all his achievements, was never loved. He was seen as a show pony. He had a sharp patter, a prominent ego and a hunger for power,' wrote Cleary of Hart's pre-1996 days.

'He was not cut from All Black stone: he was urbane, forthright and accessible. He was too out-front and up-front for reticent, conservative New Zealand. He did not conform to the pat notion of good blokeishness. So Hart was given the hand-off. It was a short-sighted, mean-spirited action, one born of provincialism. Who knows how far ahead of the game New Zealand might have been by now if Hart had been in charge sooner?

'Hart ... has made the All Blacks reach out to explore uncharted territory. He plans meticulously, sets up structures and support systems, gauges the needs of each and every individual and tailors his approach accordingly. He scrutinises and probes. Every conceivable detail gets the once-over. He believes in discipline and hard work. It sounds methodical, arid and stifling.

'"It can never be that or it will never work," Hart says. "In fact, it's the absolute reverse of that. Enjoyment is fundamental. It's my belief the last regime was too dictatorial. I've given responsibility back to the players. They own this product called the All Blacks, they create it. They are stakeholders in essence. They have the capacity to enhance their own worth. I simply help create the environment in which this can flourish."' Cleary added that the modern All Black team still prided itself on the traditions of rigour and application. But it had also moved on. There was greater personal pleasure derived not just from each player's own performance, but also from those around them.

'The style of play has little to do with glib notions of entertaining the public,' Cleary claimed. 'They play with the ball in hand simply because, under modern laws, that is the most efficient way of guaranteeing a win.

'These are John Hart's All Blacks. His legacy to the game is priceless.'

In February 1997 the *National Business Review* named Hart its 'New Zealander of the Year'. The All Blacks would have brought back the World Cup from South Africa in 1995 if Hart had been in charge, a rapturous *NBR* writer stated. It was quite some call, considering all the evidence that the All Blacks were poisoned on the eve of the cup final. But it is symptomatic of the unreal expectations that many New Zealanders held for the man and his team. 'Never mind 1995 — we'll be happy if he brings the Cup back in 1999,' might have been a wiser call.

So the All Blacks under Hart had, for many reasons, been more dominant in the world test arena than perhaps ever before. Hart's professional management had moulded the All Black culture into a seemingly equally professional structure. His coaching style had been a revelation, even to his closest supporters. Some of them were surprised by the growth in his leadership skills since the last time he had trod the national stage. His energy and commitment had never been in doubt. But there had been times when he had upset people. It had not always been of his own making, but it had certainly happened.

THE POWER BEHIND THE ALL BLACKS

The shadow of Laurie Mains had, for some critics, hung over the team since 1996. 'The All Blacks were a Mains team coached by Hart,' unkind critics said throughout much of Hart's era, with some justification. The only addition to the front-line All Blacks in 1996 had been fullback Christian Cullen, and he had been on Mains' short list for the tour of France at the end of 1995. Hart even asked that year, unsuccessfully, for the return of Graeme Bachop from Japan.

However, the intimation that few of the modern All Blacks, at least up to 1998, had been 'discovered' by Hart and his panel never bothered him. His dilemma was more when to cast out the older players, with an eye to the World Cup, while still satisfying public demand for victories aplenty in the meantime. It was a subject dear to his heart. And it was fascinating to note the pressure he was under to make changes and how he handled the timing.

For example, in 1996, regarding the older players — men like Frank Bunce, Zinzan Brooke, Michael Jones, Sean Fitzpatrick, even Walter Little — Hart said that talk of replacing them was premature. But he would not shirk from making tough decisions, he added.

'You've got to be careful about that, because I was told this year [1996] that the players were too old. Age is not the issue — it's ability. The big challenge is to know when players are nearly at the end of it. Most of them could play again next year. They've got to see how they want to play — because want is the key thing.'

'There is a tremendous focus on winning the cup, and yes, coaches are judged on that basis,' Hart told the author in 1998. 'I've taken the attitude that it's a big event, but no bigger than events of '96–98. The cup could take your eye off playing the game in the year you're still in, which can lead to trouble. I'm just as happy winning year by year. The World Cup could amount to one game. I don't like to judge my career on one game, but no doubt others will.'

As for the charge he was missing out on opportunities to blood younger players for the cup by staying loyal to the core of hardened veterans he had inherited, Hart saw no parallel with 1991. 'What you saw in 1991 was a very tired team environment,' he said. 'But that was the amateur days and this is very much the professional environment. The squad has the opportunity to train fulltime, to keep injury-free where possible, and to maintain freshness as we come through another busy season in 1999.'

However, to think that Hart and his cohorts had not planned long and hard for replacing ageing key players was seriously to underestimate the man. Modernisation and

GOOD TIMES: John Hart was a halfback, featured here with Waitemata against Ponsonby. He played for Auckland from the Otahuhu club (1967,68) and from Waitemata (1970, 1974-76) and also had a season with Taranaki in 1969.

streamlining of the professional New Zealand game through Super 12 franchises, the New Zealand Academy and NPC teams had produced a blossoming industry of highly skilled young players ready to step into the veterans' boots. This trend had been assisted by the small but very homogeneous nature of the New Zealand rugby scene compared with that of other nations. Together with the liberalising of the international substitution rules, this meant many more young players had had a taste of All Black test rugby.

What Hart and his team were not prepared for in 1998 was the rash of injuries, slippage of form, inexperience at test level and lack of confidence among so many of the young All Black replacements — especially under pressure from the rising Springbok and Wallaby squads.

To maintain the vigour he could sadly recall had been missing from his 1991 World Cup involvement with Wyllie, Hart had also ensured his short-term test and long-term World Cup campaigns stayed fresh. He was instrumental in introducing in 1998 new assistant coaches, Canterbury Crusaders' Wayne Smith and Peter Sloane. His fellow selectors, Ross Cooper and Gordon Hunter, had assisted

JOHN HART

with the coaching in the first two years of his tenure, but he felt the need to reinvigorate the culture with new training, coaching and tactical ideas. Hart described the decision to replace the faithful Hunter and Cooper as 'the most difficult task I've had to make since becoming All Black coach'.

Simply put, Hart had the overview role as head coach, with Smith and Sloane working on development of the picture. But the Hart role required much more — there were the demands from sponsors, public relations and media to fulfil, as well as from the sport's 'stakeholders' — the players and the rugby public.

'It's a far wider role than even the recent past,' said Hart. 'Whether that's a good thing or a bad thing, it doesn't matter, because it is the reality of today's game. But whereas, in the past, every coach worth his salt aspired to be the All Black coach, the management duties now make the job much more difficult. New competitions like the Super 12,

ON THE RECORD: Jeff Wilson stretches England in a 1998 game. Wilson's strike power had taken him to the verge of breaking John Kirwan's all-time All Black try-scoring record as this book went to print. He was just shy of Kirwan's 35-try total. Ahead of him lay the international records of Australia's David Campese (64 tries, 101 tests), England's Rory Underwood (50) and France's Serge Blanco (38).

however, provides the ideal grounding to test the mettle of aspiring coaches.'

Hart also debunked the conspiracy theorists' view that he had little time for his immediate predecessor, Laurie Mains. Apart from the fact that he has retained Mains' test team virtually intact for three years, which is a compliment in itself, Hart describes Mains as 'a great technical coach'.

'I was conscious of the North–South thing when appointed. That's why I went to Dunedin to see Laurie. It was important to talk to him about the team. We found we had a lot of common views about the players.'

A year is a long time in international sport. Hart hit the wall in 1998. He discovered he was not infallible. The All Blacks lost their last five tests on the trot. The black days of 1949 were recalled by the media, when a touring All Black team was whitewashed 0-4 in South Africa while a second team lost 0-2 to the touring Wallabies. Some with even longer memories looked back to the four consecutive losses of 1929–30 — the three tests on the tour of Australia in 1929 followed by the first test loss to the touring Lions in 1930 — to find a precedent. While the two 1998 losses to South Africa had plenty of precedents from series past, the 3-0 loss to the Australians in 1998 was a rarity. The only other time it had happened was in that 1929 series.

But the third year of Hart's tenure was always going to be his most challenging. Much of the team strategy of 1996 and 1997 was determined and implemented by Fitzpatrick, Zinzan Brooke and Bunce (who was the North Harbour back coach). Hart had appeared happy to oversee the exceptional All Black machine he had been left by Mains, allowing the players to take more responsibility and refining the team's ability. It didn't require a lot in technical input from him. He concentrated on supplying the stirring motivational talks he did so well on the Fridays and Saturdays of the big games.

However, by 1998 he had lost Zinzan Brooke, and his great skipper, Fitzpatrick, to chronic knee injury. Bunce was farewelled too. Michael Jones didn't get too far into the test season before injury ended another great All Black career. It was now a time that surely called for stability. But Hart had by then dispensed with Cooper and Hunter, replaced by Smith and Sloane. Players said this had an unsettling effect on the team.

While a number of All Blacks under-performed in 1998 the one to come under most of the spotlight was first five-eighth Andrew Mehrtens, who after a masterful Super 12 championship, when he helped lift the Canterbury

THE POWER BEHIND THE ALL BLACKS

Crusaders from last place to the winner's rostrum, looked out of sorts in the test matches.

He came under a lot of fire after the fifth consecutive loss, Australia's 19-14 win in Sydney, and was substituted 10 minutes from fulltime. Hart, unusually, came out publicly after the first Bledisloe Cup test in Melbourne, saying the five-eighth had made a third of the All Blacks' mistakes and kicked away too much ball. Mehrtens said the public criticism by his coach had been hard to handle, especially as he hadn't had the opportunity to discuss the problems with Hart.

There were calls and public opinion polls for Hart's resignation. Hart offered the NZRFU his resignation if he was not wanted, but in September 1998 the NZRFU gave him a lifeline — to go on and deliver the World Cup in 1999.

Union 'spin doctors' suggested his reappointment was unanimous. And chairman Rob Fisher, perhaps under pressure from fellow NZRFU directors who wanted change, said Hart needed to get back to more hands-on coaching of the team. But Hart's reappointment had not been unanimous — and board member Barry Thomas was one who said publicly he disagreed with it. As an old All Black coach of the 1970s joked after the reappointment: 'I lost two tests and they sacked me. He [Hart] has done well to get away with five.'

On the matter of coaching, some All Blacks, privately, said Fisher's statement that Hart had to get back to coaching was nonsense. The problem had not been too little time and input by Hart, but too much. One to go public was Ian Jones, in his book, *Unlocked*. Jones stated the rot had set in during 1997 on the tour of Britain, when the players had felt they were being over-organised. 'There were too many meetings and they were getting longer, from 30-60, sometimes 90 minutes. Rugby players hate meetings.' Jones described Hart as a most capable coach but said he'd taken on too much and should have learned to delegate.

Norm Berryman, in early 1999, claimed Hart had

SIX MILLION DOLLAR MAN: Jonah Lomu is about to offload against the hapless England tourists of 1998. England had felt the might of the freakish Jonah in the 1995 World Cup, when his four tries virtually single-handedly demolished England in a semi-final. A debilitating kidney disease laid the massive winger low in 1997 but he responded well to treatment to bounce back.

projected an air of negativity and some bad vibes during the centre's brief spell with the All Blacks the previous year.

Rather than Hart doing too little hands-on coaching, it was said that assistants Smith and Sloane had been under-utilised. One player, for example, said Smith had had too little time with the backline and 'it always seemed rushed.'

Hart had seemed critical of the coaching abilities of his fellow selectors and assistant coaches, Cooper and Hunter, during 1997. He told the Listener in August 1997, 'In truth the hands-on coaching of Gordon and Ross had not been great in 1996 and 1997.' At the end of 1997 Hart planned to replace them as selectors also. He told the author in 1999 he had talked with Sloane, Smith and Robbie Deans about the situation, and that Hunter and Cooper were kept in the picture. 'Deans couldn't consider it because he was the Canterbury coach. Contrary to some reports, I spoke to no other coaches about it at all.'

How did Hart survive the NZRFU review and reappointment process? Apart from the fact he is a superb talker and put a strong case to the board, any alternative action by the NZRFU would have been too risky. If it had sacked him, the fallout would have been extreme. Most of Hart's support staff, planning and research would have disappeared. If a successor had then failed during New Zealand's World Cup build-up, where would that have left the board? There was some irony in the fact that these same arguments — that it was too late for change — had been thrown up when Hart had unsuccessfully challenged Laurie Mains in 1994.

It was also Hart's good fortune in 1998 that there did not appear to be a powerful alternative coach in the wings. Graham Henry would have been the obvious candidate, but he had gone to coach Wales. Most of the other aspirants — Robbie Deans, Maurice Trapp, John Boe, Mac McCallion, Frank Oliver, Ross Cooper and Tony Gilbert — were still cutting their teeth at NPC or Super 12 level.

All Black manager and board member Mike Banks had also travelled the length and breadth of New Zealand in early September to canvass the opinions of the All Blacks. According to Banks, the players had their say on various issues in an open, frank and confidential manner, and he was able to refute some of the 'extravagant accusations' about the All Black management problems.

One contention was that Hart, especially compared to his southern hemisphere rivals, Australia's Rod Macqueen and South Africa's Nick Mallett, had left his run to rebuild the All Black team to peak for the World Cup too late.

Significantly, for the last two tests of the 1998 season, for the first time in two and a half years, the All Blacks' starting 15 contained more players from the Hart era than the Mains era.

The questions being asked in early 1999 were: Could Hart allow other experts to reshape a winning team? Or would the prediction of John Graham, former All Black captain and assistant coach to Hart with Auckland in 1980s, come true? Graham had predicted there would be two good years for the All Blacks under Hart and then major problems as his passion for control ran the team down. It certainly seemed bizarre that all the 1998 criticisms of 'too many voices' in management had led to the situation of an even larger group of assistants and advisers for the World Cup.

In spite of the 1998 All Black record the selectors believed they were well on track to building a side capable of taking the World Cup. 'Although the basis of the side is there, there are still a number of players who have been injured who will come back strongly,' said Cooper. A lot of progress had recently been made, he added, particularly in the introduction of young players to the forwards. He pointed out how the young All Blacks had led both South Africa and Australia for 80 per cent of their last games of 1998. 'Only the mental toughness to finish it off was missing,' Cooper said.

New All Blacks in 1998 were the backs Joeli Vidiri, Mark Mayerhofler, Caleb Ralph and Norm Berryman, and forwards Xavier Rush, Isitolo Maka, Scott Robertson, Kees Meeuws, Royce Willis and Carl Hoeft. Hart used 32 players in seven tests.

But the selectors' quiet confidence did not alter the fact that opportunities to blood young players or give them more than a handful of test experience had been lost during the Hart era. It is contended that if changes had been made in late 1997, on the tour of Britain for instance, much of the trauma of 1998 might have been avoided. A group of exceptionally promising young All Blacks, including possibly the entire front row, would now go into the World Cup with a fraction of the experience of their major opponents. The vital balance of skill and nous may not have been reached by the team.

Questions asked were why Michael Jones and Mark Carter were persevered with, blocking the chances for players who would have been at peak for the World Cup but would now lack experience. Why were Meeuws, Hoeft, Willis, Maka, Rush, Mayerhofler and Ralph not selected for the 1997 tour of Britain?

When these questions were run past Hart in June 1999, he did not feel it was a fair contention. 'Some of these

RUGBY RENAISSANCE: John Hart brought about an instant revival to Auckland's fortunes in 1982, his first year as provincial coach, when Auckland won the NPC. He did it two more times during his five-year tenure. But his greatest legacy was that he laid the foundations for a 15-year dominance by the Auks of New Zealand rugby. (Above) Andy Haden (behind Hart) and team hear the coach's halftime directions.

players were unavailable and others, only just emerging, were not ready for the All Blacks.'

Why did Hart state publicly he'd choose the 1998 test teams on Super 12 form and then, rather conservatively, stay with tried and trusted players, many of whom had not shone at all in Super 12? Why did Hart claim the 1997 tour, which meant the All Blacks had little summer break, was the major reason for later poor form, when the Wallabies and Springboks also toured late in 1997? Why did he stick with 11 Auckland players, the largest contingent in the 1998-99 summer training squad, when Auckland had had its worst season since 1976? The poor 1999 Super 12 form of the Auckland Blues just reinforced this view. Choosing unfit players, as in 1998, was also not an option in the future.

Hart's management system underwent subtle change for 1999. Peter Sloane remained as assistant coach, with Smith now a 'technical adviser'. Smith, previously the strongest contender to replace Hart as All Black coach in the year 2000, had to battle to regain his credibility but was assisted by the way his Crusaders retained their Super 12 title in 1999. Cooper disappeared off the national selection panel, where Sloane and Hunter were Hart's co-selectors. Hart told the author in June 1999 that Fitzpatrick, who'd been offered an assistant coaching position in 1997 but declined, would not join the World Cup party in an official capacity, but would probably be 'called in to talk to the team'.

The obvious shift in player strength to the South Island — visible since 1997 when Canterbury won the NPC, underlined when the Canterbury Crusaders won the Super 12 and Otago the NPC in 1998 and reinforced when the Crusaders retained their title in 1999 — was finally recognised in the All Black selections in 1999. All Black leadership was an all-Otago affair, with Taine Randell retaining the captaincy, Jeff Wilson becoming the vice-captain and Anton Oliver the other forward leader.

Players to force their way into the first All Black squad of 1999 included newcomers Daryl Gibson, Pita Alantini, Tony Brown, Byron Kelleher, Dylan Mika, Kupu Vanisi, Norm Maxwell and Greg Feek, while Tana Umaga, Todd Blackadder, Alama Ieremia, Carlos Spencer and Andrew Blowers returned after absences. Others included Wilson, Christian Cullen, Jonah Lomu, Andrew Mehrtens, Justin Marshall, Josh Kronfeld, Ian Jones, Robin Brooke, Oliver, Randell and Mark Hammett.

The All Blacks were installed as early favourites to win the World Cup, though logically they ranked no better than third. Bookmakers had learned through history never to write off a New Zealand side. But sensible punters knew the Springboks and Wallabies possessed a big psychological advantage.

'Any of four or five countries could win the cup this time, given the timing, the conditions and other factors,' said Hart. 'England had advantages of home crowds and familiar conditions. I rate the French. The Scots and the Welsh have made enormous strides and could easily upset the favourites.

'I have watched Rod Macqueen growing the Australian team in the lead-up to the cup, when they will have settled on certain players. And Nick Mallett, South Africa's coach, has been great for their game. We mustn't under estimate the Springboks' ability to come out and defend their title.'

In *Change of Hart*, the coach looked ahead to the World Cup. 'In 1999, New Zealand rugby's focus has to be on winning the cup. We'll need everyone pulling in the same direction and the key will be to work co-operatively so that

JOHN HART

THE POWER BEHIND THE ALL BLACKS

COMING OF AGE: John Hart's young captain, Taine Randell, had a difficult baptism of fire in 1998, after replacing the durable and successful Sean Fitzpatrick as All Black leader. The new Hart-Randell combination lost five tests in succession in 1998. But it was clear in early 1999 that Randell's leadership skills had matured immeasurably as he helped push the All Blacks into likely World Cup favouritism.

DEADLY STRIKER: John Hart's choice of fullback Christian Cullen – seen here scoring during the All Blacks' record 28-0 victory over South Africa at Carisbrook, Dunedin in July, 1999 – as a wing three-quarter proved inspirational. Cullen's strike rate was 31 tries in 31 All Black appearances, the first 29 at fullback.

JOHN HART

things happen by agreement rather than by dictate.' Hart was referring to the likelihood few of the All Black World Cup squad members would participate in the 1999 national championship.

So it would prove. A great advantage for the All Blacks over rivals would be that they were spared an overseas tour in late-1988, unlike Australia and South Africa. The players became refreshed. On 30 August, 1999, after tests against Samoa, France, South Africa and Australia, Hart and his team chose their World Cup squad. If they made the final of the World Cup on 7 November, the All Blacks would have been in test mode since 1 June. It seemed a big programme after the almost-as-tough Super 12 competition from February until late May. But it was developed in response to requests from players, who wanted more space in the programme to focus on the match buildup.

The 1999 Tri-Nations series showed New Zealand had the players to make it supreme at the World Cup. Everything was in its favour. All that was required was for Hart and his team to put it altogether. Victory would surely uplift Hart's era back to a pedestal to match the best of the great coaches who had come before him.

Several other negatives needed to be overcome by the team. The loss of scrum cornerstone tight-head prop Olo Brown to neck injury was a huge blow. The vexing question of captaincy was another after the traumatising 1998 experiences of Fitzpatrick's replacement, Taine Randell. The midfield was a third unknown quantity, with four players tried at centre in 1998 as replacements for the retired 55-test veteran Bunce. The inside backs had also disappointed. And the gifted 'back three' of Christian Cullen, Jeff Wilson and Jonah Lomu had operated on a starvation diet (two tries between them in the entire 1998 season). The secret to All Black magic at the World Cup would be activating this trio plus Tana Umaga.

However, the record breaking victory by the All Blacks over the Springboks in the Tri-Nations served to suggest New Zealand had overcome most of its problems. Randell's leadership had grown immensely, the positional questions seemed answered and many of the young players had shown they were ready to match the achievements of their All Black predecessors.

REFERENCES

1. *Daily Telegraph.*
2. *National Business Review.*
3. Ian Jones, *Unlocked.*
4. John Hart, *A Change of Hart.*

BIOGRAPHICAL DETAILS

John Bernard Hart

Born: Auckland

Position: Halfback

Provincial record: Auckland 1967–70, 1973–76 — 26 games; Taranaki 1969

Selector/coach: Auckland 1982–86 (3 championship titles, a second and a third place)

NZ selector: 1987, 1989–91, 1996–99

NZ coach: 1987, 1991, 1996–99

Other: ONZM for services to rugby 1997

Occupation: Professional rugby coach; previously 30 years in personnel management with Fletchers, and later as a consultant

NEW ZEALAND COACHING RECORD

1987: beat Japan 74-0, 106-4

1991: World Cup Pool matches: beat England 18-12, beat USA 46-6, beat Italy 31-21. Quarterfinal: beat Canada 29-13. Semifinal: lost to Australia 6-16. Play-off for third place: beat Scotland 13-6

1996: beat Western Samoa 51-10; beat Scotland 62-31, 36-12; beat Australia 43-6; beat South Africa 15-11; beat Australia 32-25; beat South Africa 29-18; beat South Africa 23-19, 33-25, lost to South Africa 22-32

1997: beat Fiji 71-5; beat Argentina 93-8, 62-10; beat South Africa 35-32, 55-35; beat Australia 30-13, 33-18, 36-24; beat Ireland 63-15; beat Wales 42-7; beat England 25-8, drew with England 26-26

1998: beat England 64-22, 40-10; lost to Australia 16-24; lost to South Africa 3-13; lost to Australia 23-27; lost to South Africa 23-24; lost to Australia 14-19

CONCLUSION

HIGH STANDARDS SET EARLY AND SELDOM DIMINISHED

WHAT CONCLUSIONS CAN BE GAINED FROM this study of the evolution of the All Black coaches? We have been able to learn much about the methods, the character, the challenges, the times and the strictures under which these often exceptional men operated.

We know that almost all the All Black coaches were former players of at least representative standard. The majority had been All Blacks.

We know too that the success rate of these All Black coaches has usually been high. Exceptional standards were set virtually from the very first All Black team in the 19th Century and they have seldom fallen from that august level. No other rugby nation has a comparable record of such remarkable consistency, although South Africa did hold supremacy for a very long period.

The youngest All Black coaches were Vince Meredith, only 33 when he took the All Blacks to Australia in 1910, and Jim Burrows, 33 when he battled with the 1937 Springboks. Jimmy Duncan was 35 when he coached the New Zealand team which beat Great Britain in 1904, a year after he retired as New Zealand captain. Bob Stuart was 35 when he assisted Tom Morrison, conqueror of the Springboks for the first time in 1956, who had been only 36 when he became the All Black coach in 1950. Ivan Vodanovich was 39.

The oldest coach was Alex McDonald, 66 when he completed his third stint as the national coach in 1949. Bryce Rope was 60 when he began his two years as the coach in the early 1980s.

JUST WHO IS THE GREATEST?

By August 1997, after the Tri-Nations series, some critics were calling for John Hart to be hailed the most successful coach in All Black history. While there was little doubt Hart would soon record more test victories than any other All Black coach, he had not reached that point then.

All Black coaches have accumulated some fabulous records over the years. Fred Allen, Alex Wyllie, Neil McPhail and Tom Morrison could have been ranked ahead of Hart, on some 'scales', at least, at that stage.

As sole coach, Hart had taken the All Blacks to 17 wins and one loss in 18 tests by August 1997. If the six matches of the 1991 World Cup (where Hart was the 'co-coach' with Wyllie) were included, Hart had 22 wins from 24 tests.

Hart's dismal 1998 season meant that his era did not compare well with coaches such as:

- Allen, who was the 'perfect' coach. His record is 'unbeatable' — 14 tests for 14 victories during 1966-68. Hart, in comparison, lost to the Springboks soon after he began his stint as sole coach and had lost the semi-final of the 1991 World Cup as 'co-coach'. He would have had to have won his first 15 tests to better Allen.
- Wyllie, who went almost three years unbeaten and finished his stint with 24 test victories, three losses and a draw. On another measurement scale, for all games played, Wyllie finished with 64 games played for 58 wins, five losses and a draw.
- McPhail, All Black coach 1961-65, who also had an arguably better record than Hart's early years. It wasn't until the great McPhail reached his fourth year as coach that he lost his first test, after winning the series, against Australia, in 1964. McPhail lost only two tests in five years!
- Morrison, convener of selectors (1950-56), and coach of the first New Zealand team to beat the Springboks in a series, who never lost a series in those seven years.

CONCLUSION

In all games (including non-tests) coached by the 'best' of the All Black coaches before Hart, Allen heads the list with a 97.3 per cent success rate, followed by Jack Gleeson (92.3), McPhail (90.7), Wyllie (90.6pc), Bryce Rope (87.9), Brian Lochore (86.2), Eric Watson (82.9), Ivan Vodanovich (81.3), Bob Duff (80), JJ Stewart (78.8), Peter Burke (77.8) and Morrison, whose teams played tests only (73).

Let us not forget that Allen beat every nation except South Africa, whom he helped beat as assistant coach to McPhail in 1965, the year before he succeeded McPhail. McPhail bowed to no-one, at home or abroad. Gleeson was the first All Black coach to win the Grand Slam, in 1978, although four previous All Black teams had been unbeaten in the tests they played on tour there. Lochore remains the only coach to win a World Cup. Mains beat every major country away from home, including the 'Grand Slam' during the 1995 World Cup and went into extra time in the final, with a food-poisoned side, before letting the cup slip.

There are other factors in any search for 'greatness'. Hart inherited a professional team that ran largely unchanged for another two years. It was highly questionable whether some of the players, forwards in particular, could maintain the standards necessary to win the 1999 World Cup. Conversely, opportunities to provide experience for more of the younger All Blacks were being lost with each succeeding test.

Perhaps Hart would need to add the World Cup to his impressive record before he could reasonably be hailed as fit to join this illustrious band?

ARE COMPARISONS FUTILE?

But true comparisons between coaches, teams and players are impossible. For instance, the man who guided South Africa to the 1995 World Cup and the most successful Springbok coach of all time, the late Kitch Christie, believed the best modern test teams would destroy their predecessors. 'If the current test teams played the South African lineups of 30 or 40 years ago, they would give them 40 points,' said Christie. 'The tempo, the intensity and the game plan have all changed.'

Christie's contention is hard to deny. But this author does not fully concur. If we turned the scenario around and had today's All Blacks or Springboks go back in time — if they had to play the 1924 Invincibles, for instance, under the rules of that era, the score would be closer, because of the differing skills required.

Other sports, by their nature, seem more able to compare champions through the eras. Cricket is one. The authoritative *Wisden's* publication recently chose its all-time 100 greats. The list was topped by W.G. Grace, Don Bradman and Gary Sobers, in that order. Grace scored 55,000 runs, hit 126 centuries, took 2800 wickets and held 900 catches in a remarkable career of almost 40 years. His record makes a good case.

The subject, for rugby, provides an interesting, endless and inevitably inconclusive debate. But some champions of one era would surely be champions in another. The author believes that Colin Meads and Maurice Brownlie, for example, would be All Black locks or siderowers superior in many ways to players like Robin Brooke and Ian Jones. Meads and Brownlie had the size, mobility, strength, athleticism, ball skills, and mental and physical toughness to succeed and indeed thrive, with some adaptations necessary, in the modern, professional game.

Similarly would Jarden, Nepia, Tiny White, Peter Jones, Going, McCormick, Scott, Skinner, Gray, Cooke, McLeod, Nicholls and dozens of others still be at the top of their game in the 1990s? The answer is yes. But conversely, how would a bulky, less mobile player like the great Don Clarke have coped at fullback compared to the Cullens of the new game? Probably, his incredible match-winning skills, concentration and instincts would still make his presence in the team invaluable, even in another position.

IS THIS MEASUREMENT FAIR?

While the success of each All Black coach is usually measured by the number of victories his sides achieved, there are other methods that can be used to analyse his reign. Major points are likely to be the style of rugby played by his All Blacks; whether he had to develop a team from largely youthful or inexperienced material; and the age, experience and remaining potential of the players in the squad when the coach retired.

A recent illustration of these cyclical features would be the advanced average age of the All Black squad when Alex Wyllie quit after the 1991 World Cup; the way his successor, Laurie Mains, experimented with many players in the aftermath but developed a great depth through to the 1995 World Cup; the total acceptance and deployment by Hart of Mains' test squad in 1996; the powerful temptation for Hart to stay with these tried and trusted players and keep winning tests; and the need for a balance to ensure that 1999 World Cup requirements were not ignored in the quest to satisfy the rugby public's thirst for immediacy in winning tests.

The All Black coaches and player-coaches in this book have each had their own style of coaching and man management. Hart's powerful and persuasive methods and 'professional' approach did not in fact emerge with him. His predecessor, Mains, though clearly hamstrung by the attitudes of an amateur hierarchy at official level, sought and gained many improvements for the players and the public. Mains had gained some of his insights from his own experiences as an All Black under coaches such as Ivan Vodanovich and JJ Stewart.

The point is that All Black coaches are part of the evolution of the game, just as much as the players. Frustrations suffered by Mains, for example, were felt equally by earlier coaches and many of these frustrations are aired in this book. Tour reports that were filed away in the bowels of the NZRFU headquarters, coaches who had no management support or even no manager at all, recommendations that were ignored — the list is long.

It is also impossible to rate the performance of Hart alongside that of Dave Gallaher, for instance. Gallaher undoubtedly was a 'man ahead of his time', unfettered in his originality by the hierarchical and historical layers that would pull and push at future coaches. Hart, as the incumbent, should likewise leave his mark on the game. Whether that mark is as a creator or caretaker remains to be seen.

The NZRFU has come under criticism through the years, from media, players, coaches and anyone else who thought its structure and methods outdated. Perhaps so. But how does one explain the level of success on international scoreboards if the NZRFU systems were so faulty? Was it a case of sheer talent overcoming all? That is doubtful.

No, while the system undoubtedly left out some talented men, who couldn't afford to join the long 'waiting list' of the inter-island and national selection 'apprenticeships', it did serve to expose a stream of dedicated, wise and often gifted coaches through this tried and trusted democratic process. Coaches and selectors 'lived and died' by their records. Those not up to it could run, but they could not hide. Incompetency was usually rooted out within a season or two, as was bias. The power of Otago at the end of the last century, or of Auckland at the end of this century, for instance, was kept under control by a method of geographical balance. No All Black selectors could afford to choose a team they did not believe could win!

WINNING IS NOT NECESSARILY ENOUGH

The inculcating of a tradition of excellence by All Black coaches, selectors and captains meant that, unlike most New Zealanders, the All Blacks are used to winning in the international arena. But there is more. Such is their record that in many tests the All Blacks have felt they need to do more than win. Their psyche and pride requires them to win by a handsome margin and, if possible, to do it in style. They have won so often they know New Zealanders will not accept a close or fortuitous victory. The New Zealand public expectation of them is far higher than for any other sporting endeavour and while it may hope for victory from other teams or individuals, it demands that the All Blacks 'bring home the bacon'.

The All Blacks of the late 1980s demonstrated a compulsion with excellence, consistency and the worthy but impossible goal of attempting to play the perfect game. This level of performance, higher even than most of the greatest deeds of earlier All Black teams, was epitomised in the obsessional drive of the first five-eighth and world-record-setting goalkicker, Grant Fox.

Such perfectionism developed further on during the Mains and Hart eras with the teams adopting new systems that reflected the management theories of the new technological age. In 1991 a book called *Upgrading New Zealand's Competitive Advantage*, by Grahame Crocombe, Michael Enright and Michael Porter, showed how the All Blacks' consistent position near or at the top of world rugby was the result of the advantages the game enjoys in New Zealand through the dynamic processes of improvement, innovation and upgrading.

'Why, for over a century, have the All Blacks been the team to beat in international competition?' the authors asked. Factors mentioned included the relatively mild winters, the proliferation of sports fields and the fact New Zealanders were physically larger than average.

But other factors were more important, the authors argued. Rugby knowledge was unparalleled, with innovative ideas readily accepted. Such was the 'passion' for the game that spectators represented a highly informed sector, which, in turn, could be a 'harsh judge of performance and a warm rewarder of excellence'. An All Black was still very much a national hero. A host of

CONCLUSION

'support' industries surrounded the game, in media, tourism, sports medicine and training.

'There are clear incentives for rugby teams and individuals in New Zealand to excel,' the authors concluded. 'It is this specialised, interdependent system that is most difficult for other nationals to replicate and therefore provides the basis for sustained international success.'

CONDEMNATION

Coaching was long a contentious issue in rugby, particularly at the international level. New Zealand and South Africa early adopted 'the man outside the game' but in Britain he was for far too long very doubtfully regarded. A coach's activities, it appeared to conservative minds, reeked of professionalism. Rugby had to remain wholly amateur.

The coaching of New Zealand and All Black rugby was condemned for generations, especially in Britain and, even into the 1970s, it was said to produce an unwelcome kind of 'sameness' in New Zealand's national game.

While there is no doubt that some All Black coaches did stifle the talent of All Black backs and backlines in the 1950s and 1960s, in the quest for error-free rugby, it was wrong for critics, particularly the British, to assume that All Black coaches were all in the same, unimaginative mould. Rugby methods, like fashions, have come and gone in the ebb and flow that is New Zealand rugby. It is remarkable how the 'brains trusts' of the game at club, provincial and international levels could, decade after decade, invent, perfect, nullify and reinvent systems, or 'units' of a 'winning' method of rugby.

Ironically, today, in an era of strong dominance by the All Blacks, it is New Zealand's provincial style of game which is in more danger than ever of losing its distinctive regional characteristics. The five Super 12 teams have superseded the 26 traditional provinces. Additionally, all is not rosy in the New Zealand rugby garden. Club rugby continues to wither, in spite of 'weasel word' calls from top administrators about its importance. The steady nibbling away of coaches and players just below the level of those under national contracts to poaching British and Japanese clubs is creating an as yet uncharted vacuum in the New Zealand game.

'WORTH HIS WEIGHT IN GOLD'

Times have changed, and with them the style and delivery of the All Black coaches. The ranters and rah-rah coaches have been replaced by the quieter, more analytical coaches. An autocratic disciplinarian of the Fred Allen mould would not succeed with the young men of today, we are told. Nor would the mind and limb-numbing training sessions of an Ivan Vodanovich be acceptable in the more liberal climate of the 1990s. But such views are over-simplified. Allen, for instance, a product of the war years, would surely modify and successfully adapt his approach if coaching today.

To be a successful All Black coach has always required certain qualities. He must have the ability to help choose the best team, and work with other selectors as panel convener; he needs an excellent technical knowledge and an ability to impart that knowledge to younger players; he needs to be a shrewd analyst of the opposition's strengths and weaknesses, as much as his own team's; and most importantly, he needs to obtain the maximum performance from the players during a test match or on tour.

The great All Black fullback of the 1940s and early 1950s, Bob Scott, was to write in *The Bob Scott Story*, with Terry McLean, that he was completely convinced of the need for a coach:

'"The man outside the game" who can take a good long look at you, who can tell you what went wrong and why, who has such a mastery of the fundamentals that he can turn you back from the wrong path on to the right, and who himself has such a cool, courageous, determined and withal humorous temperament that you can feel his strength and be comforted by it, that man is worth his weight in gold.'

MULTI-FACETED COACHES

The most recent All Black coaches have been even more multi-faceted individuals. The steady growth of programmes at test match level through the 1970s and 1980s means today's All Blacks face a dozen tests each year, whereas even in the 1960s the annual test programme was small. This placed new pressures on players and coach. The times they were called on to perform were far more numerous. Media, administrative and other off-field demands grew.

The All Black coach has long been and remains constantly under the public microscope. It is not just black humour when the former Prime Minister of New Zealand, Jim Bolger, a former rugby player who took every opportunity at home and abroad to watch the All Blacks, said he'd rather be the All Black coach when they win but the Prime Minister when the All Blacks lose.

The All Black coach is a highly visible person and his behaviour and win-loss record is studied both objectively and subjectively, sometimes depending on which part of the country the member of the public resides in.

But the embracement of the fully professional era has altered the demands on the All Black coach. He can now call on a massive support network of coaches, medical and media experts. Hart, for instance, does not have the technical expertise of a Wyllie, Mains, Lochore or Graham Henry. But with fellow coaches at his call, he does not need to have. His position is more like the role of a professional sports team 'manager' than a traditional All Black coach.

THE PLAYERS' EXPECTATIONS

What do the players expect of their coach? The All Blacks told Robin McConnell, an author and senior lecturer in sport management and coaching at Massey University, Albany, who followed the All Blacks during the Mains era while researching for his doctorate, what they expected: honesty, integrity, good organisation, an ability to relate well with them, an excellent technical knowledge, a harmonious relationship with the manager, keeping player interests as a high priority, a clear sense of direction, and, preferably, experience as a test player.

The All Black coach's most difficult role perhaps is the ability to get close enough to his players to know and understand them well. Psychology plays a huge part in any sports coach's success but, at the same time, coaching the All Blacks requires hard decisions. When a player is 'over the hill' or his play inferior to another or less suitable for a particular game or circumstance, the coach must have the strength to act appropriately.

This book has told how some All Black coaches received criticism for being too close to particular players and for taking notice of the views of senior players when making test selections. But the ability to take on board the views of other equally knowledgeable people in selections and tactics more often reflects a strength of character than a weakness. An All Black coach needs, on a long or arduous tour, for instance, to be able to say: "This is the way I want it done!"

DO THE ALL BLACKS COACH THEMSELVES?

Some critics, through the decades, have claimed the All Black coach does not actually coach his players. The theory is the players are somehow technically 'perfect' on selection, or after a season or two in the international arena, and do not require coaching. The truth is, over the last century, many players have needed individual and group coaching, in skills, positional play and the All Black pattern.

The key coaching skills, however, are as organiser and motivator. The coach, especially before the advent of professionalism and especially for a home test series, has not had the time to individually hone the skills of a young test newcomer, for instance. He rightfully could expect a high level of fitness and skill from his squad. His job on assembly was therefore to mould the players quickly together as a team and ensure they were in the best frame of mind as individuals and as a group when they took the field.

Confidence is vital — the coach's confidence in the squad to play and win with the tactical plan he has laid down, and the players' confidence that the coach has done everything possible to ensure victory. Such confidence has always been a feature of successful All Black teams. Once established and recognised by both parties, the team's direction is smooth, often machine-like, in its negotiation of obstacles such as opposition test sides.

SADLY UNDERESTIMATED

But the media, spectators and followers, officials and even some All Blacks have sometimes totally underestimated the contribution of the All Black coaches. This shortsighted and unrealistic view comes through in newspaper coverage and biographies from time to time. But, as every senior grade rugby coach knows only too well, some players, even All Blacks, do not possess the breadth of vision to appreciate how and why certain tactics are planned. They cannot see much further than the demands of their own particular small 'unit' within the game.

They would seldom have begun to consider the planning that a coach, the All Black coach in particular, puts into the annual, monthly, weekly or daily schedules for training, fitness and playing, or the patterns and tactics, the individual technical knowledge required, and the tough but fair selections needed.

The media too have sometimes been guilty of failing to understand the influence of the rules on the All Black coaches' approach. In times past, they have wanted the coach to play open, entertaining rugby, but ignored the fact he can only play the way the opposition allows, and that he must temper onfield ambitions with the need to

CONCLUSION

maintain a good record. The 1950s and early 1960s provided the classic period for such views.

THE AFRICAN CONNECTION

It has been stated that only the higher level rugby player can really understand the attraction to an All Black of touring South Africa, especially up to 1996, when the All Blacks had never won a full test series in the republic since the first All Blacks tried in 1928.

The Springboks had been beaten on New Zealand soil in series a number of times (though it took until 1956, after first failing in 1921, for that to be first achieved). Each time an All Black team toured South Africa, New Zealand had the highest expectations. On five great treks, the All Blacks returned, battered, bruised and empty-handed. It stuck in the craw of the old players and the public. It was to take until 1992, with victory in the only test, and 1996, winning the series 3-1 (or 2-1, depending on how the series was interpreted), before the All Blacks could expunge the previous humiliations.

So in placing the All Blacks and their coaches at the head of the world's rugby playing nations, one should never discount the Springboks. By the end of 1996, the great rivals were poised at 22 tests wins each. But New Zealand had edged ahead of its rival, 24 to 22, after 1997. At the end of 1998 it was level-pegging — 24 tests each again.

South African critics could convincingly mount a counter to the claim of All Black superiority, pointing out the superiority of the Springboks over the All Blacks through the first half of the 20th Century and the equally imposing record of four Grand Slams in Britain before New Zealand had accomplished its first! But All Black teams had toured Britain unbeaten (in the tests) four times before their 1978 Grand Slam. Due to circumstances beyond their control, they did not always get the opportunity to play all four Home Unions.

South Africa's racial policies also prevented the finest possible All Black teams being sent on tour until 1970. Outstanding Maori players had been left behind in 1928, 1949 and 1960. In 1967, an All Black tour of South Africa was cancelled because of the colour bar. The All Blacks, under Fred Allen, who would retire undefeated, instead made a triumphant tour of Britain and France. They were at their peak in 1967, whereas by 1970, when a softened South African government policy allowed a tour, they had lost Allen and were a much less disciplined team.

South Africa's immense size and its altitude were other touring problems which lessened in importance as the decades wore on. But perhaps the most influential factor in the difficulties experienced by All Black touring sides in South Africa was the referees.

Up to and including 1976, the All Blacks, under South African referees, had played 20 tests in South Africa, for five wins, 14 losses and one draw. From 1992 to 1997, under neutral referees, the All Blacks had played seven tests in South Africa, winning five and losing two (including the World Cup final).

The Springboks had played 14 tests in New Zealand under New Zealand referees during four tours, for five wins, eight losses and a draw. But since 1981, when neutral referees handled the series, there had been eight tests between the two countries played in New Zealand. The All Blacks had won six, lost one and drawn one.

Since the advent of neutral referees, therefore, there had been 15 tests. The All Blacks had won 11, the Boks three and one had been drawn. It has become very one-sided. To be fair, these tests had also coincided with the re-emergence of post-apartheid South Africa from sporting isolation.

THE INEXACT SCIENCE

According to Lindsay Knight, coaching, while important, might also be overrated and certainly is not an exact science. 'A country's player base still seems critical,' wrote Knight in the *Dominion* newspaper in mid-1997.

Knight alluded to the possibility, in July 1997, that the successful Auckland coach, Graham Henry, might be lured overseas. This scenario was seen in some quarters, though not by Knight, as being potentially tragic for New Zealand rugby. But Knight pointed out that there had already been a large, recent 'braindrain' of top New Zealand coaches, including former All Black coach Alex Wyllie, and Andy Leslie, John Phillips, John Mitchell, Mike Brewer, Murray Kidd, Noel McQuilken and Brad Johnstone. All were coaching overseas. Brad Meurant, Wayne Shelford, Glenn Ross and Wayne Smith are others who had returned to New Zealand after coaching overseas.

Knight asked how much impact this trend had had on the balance of world rugby and concluded that it was difficult to assess. But its effect on New Zealand appeared minimal by 1997, while countries such as Japan, Argentina or Ireland, who had embraced New Zealand coaches, had 'not been transformed overnight into superstars'.

In August 1997, New Zealand rugby underwent changes to the national coaching and selection systems. These changes took cognisance of the need for compatibility among the coaching panel, that some are happier than others in an assistant's role, and tried to ensure that gifted coaches remained in New Zealand to coach Super 12 and National Provincial Championship (NPC) teams, without necessarily jeopardising their national prospects. To protect its assets the NZRFU did not recognise the qualifications of any coach or player, for national duties, while they were based overseas.

In 1998 the NZRFU even placed a 'lifetime' ban on any New Zealand coach of a national team from coaching the All Blacks. Graham Henry, by then coach of Wales, was the obvious target. Henry has said he wants to coach the All Blacks from 2003.

Until this time, New Zealand had operated, since the mid-1960s, under a three-man selection panel, the convener of which is the coach of the All Blacks. Before then, though the panel was more often than not a trio, it had varied between a sole selector (on one occasion) and a seven-man panel, the larger panels being deemed necessary because of the limitations on travel and communications earlier in the century.

A PEEP INTO THE FUTURE

But what of the future for the All Black coaches? They will be an integral part of an expanding world game. New Zealand, as it has done since the game became international, will continue as a world leader and innovator.

The advent of the professional era has seen New Zealand quickly build on its superior game style of the 1995 World Cup. A small, united country's homogeneity has helped. The new Southern Hemisphere competitions, Tri-Nations and the Super 12 series, also involving South Africa and Australia, provided New Zealand administrators with a new challenge. New Zealand's 26 provinces were grouped into five teams for the Super 12, promoting the best 150 players as professionals.

The input of the NZRFU in controlling the five teams, including who coached them, and the involvement of the national coaching panel to gain consistency in approach between the five teams and the All Blacks, were crucial moves ensuring a high but even standard among the five and an All Black performance that built momentum during 1996 and 1997, stuttered in 1998 but recovered powerfully towards World Cup time.

But for how long can this nation of three million people maintain an advantage, or even keep pace, with more populous and financially advantaged rivals such as England, France, South Africa and Australia, or those who may emerge early in the next millennium such as Japan, Canada, the United States and European countries?

The last Rugby World Cup was said to have had the third-largest world sporting audience on record, after the Olympics and the leading soccer events. But rugby has reached only part of its true global potential.

If the right options are taken to build rugby into a truly worldwide sport, at or near the top of the branded entertainment options available in the next century, there is going to be much soul-searching among traditionalists in New Zealand and the other IRB countries. To quote an NZRFU councillor, Kevin Roberts, who previously headed Lion Breweries in New Zealand, sponsor of the All Blacks, the game is 'going to go through the roof' on the world stage if it positions itself correctly. Now based in New York as the worldwide head of the advertising group Saatchi and Saatchi, Roberts believes rugby 'must work to become a serious competitor with the Brazils, the Manchester Uniteds and the Chicago Bulls of this world'.

'They are some of the great sporting dynasties — the branded entertainments which have moved out of the traditional sporting area, to compete with all the other major forms of entertainment,' said Roberts.

To keep pace, New Zealand, with one of the smallest markets, would need to form alliances with other countries and media and commercial entities, he said. New Zealand had already made a strong beginning in this direction and was well placed, in comparison with other rugby nations, to maintain control of the destiny of its most marketable product, the All Blacks.

Among Roberts' ideas for the future of world rugby are that the game be played in one international season each year (eg. the Northern Hemisphere summer), a world club championship (eg. the European champion versus the Super 12 winner), an annual international championship (eg. winner of the Five Nations versus the Tri Nations champion) and a world-wide Sevens circuit. Big games should be played in 'hot television markets' like Japan and Hong Kong and a clearly defined calendar of world events should be put in place.

SELECTORS AND MANAGERS

THE EVOLUTIONARY NATURE OF the All Black coaching role means, in all probability, some selectors and managers also played a part in coaching their teams.

Apart from the selectors and managers documented as All Black coaches in this book, the evidence that others contributed with coaching input has largely been lost through time and the archiving methods (some would say lack of them) adopted by the national union.

All Black selectors, for instance, often had strong provincial and club coaching backgrounds and could well have contributed to the coaching, especially in home series. Some team managers were also well qualified to coach.

These men played a large part in building the records of the All Blacks through their specialist contributions as selectors and managers. But in the development of the All Blacks' schedules through the decades, team management and personnel styles varied.

As detailed earlier in this book, coaching was frowned on as 'professional' by the home unions and the IRB. While enthusiastically adopted from the outset at all levels in New Zealand, coaching at international level required a 'smokescreen' to be applied by the NZRFU.

Some sides toured with manager only. Sometimes he was also coach. Sometimes the captain did the coaching, particularly in the early 20th century through to the 1930s, while at other times the job was shared. Much later an assistant manager (this was in fact the code word for coach) was appointed.

Research for this book, especially of NZRFU archives, was frustrated by the lack of surviving detailed records on such matters, which tended to suggest a deliberate policy of obscuring coaching appointments.

A glance through the potted biographies below of prominent selectors and managers makes fascinating reading for those who might believe, like the author, they had much to contribute.

Among the early selectors, George Fache, Frank Evans, Don Stuart, Alan Adams (who had played for England) and Harold Strang had strong playing backgrounds. Many others with All Black backgrounds were to follow.

Among the early managers, Samuel Sleigh, George Campbell, Edgar Wylie, Bob Isaacs, Ernest Little and 1924 Invincible Stan Dean, who appears to have possessed the man-management skills of the modern coach, had also played to a high standard.

SELECTORS

The more prominent selectors include:

George Fache (Wellington), NZ selector 1896–97, 1901, 1903–05 — born Clyde 1870, died Gore 1948; represented Wellington 1890 (Wellington club), later leading referee; Wellington RFU committee, selector; NZRFU management committee 1902–06, 1915–18; Commissioner of Prisons when retired 1929.

Frank 'Dutchy' Evans (Canterbury), NZ selector 1896, 1903, 1905, 1907 — born Christchurch 1868, died Christchurch 1949; represented Canterbury 1888–93 (Merivale club), South Island v. British team 1888; refereed NZ v. Great Britain 1904; Canterbury RFU committee 1892–1904, selector, life member; NZRFU president 1919; school inspector.

Henry Harris (Otago), NZ selector 1903–05, 1907–08, 1910, 1914 — born Dunedin 1869, died Dunedin 1949; represented Otago as halfback (Union club), representative referee; Otago RFU committee, selector, treasurer, president, life member; NZRFU president 1918, life member 1939; worked at *Otago Daily Times* for 66 years, retiring as manager of compositing department.

Don Stuart (Otago), NZ selector 1920–23 — born Dunedin 1880, died Dunedin 1936; represented Otago as forward 1904–05 (Pirates club), South Island 1904; Otago RFU committee 1909–13, president 1926–28; NZRFU president 1935 (died in office); founded D. Stuart Ltd, tea importers and merchants.

Arthur Geddes (Southland), NZ selector 1924–30 — born Balclutha 1876, died Invercargill 1942; NZRFU president 1922; manager of All Blacks in Australia 1934; father of Bert Geddes, All Black winger 1929; master tailor.

Alan Adams (West Coast), NZ selector 1927, 1934–37 — born Greymouth 1880, died Greymouth 1963; represented Otago 1902–03, 1905–06 (University club), South Island 1906, NZ Universities in Australia en route to England to study medicine 1908, London University; England against France as centre three-quarter 1910, Barbarians 1909, 1912; West Coast RFU chairman; NZRFU president 1929, council 1937–43, life member 1945; doctor.

Harold Strang (Southland), NZ selector 1945–49 — born Invercargill 1890, died Invercargill 1962; represented Southland as lock forward 1921–22 (Star club); Southland RFU president, life member; NZRFU council 1946, 1949–50, president 1947, life member 1952; manager of All Blacks in Australia 1947; director of David Strang Ltd, coffee and spice merchants.

Merv Corner (Auckland), NZ selector 1950–53 — born Auckland 1908, died 2 February 1992; represented Auckland as halfback 1929–35, All Blacks 1930–32, 1934–36 (25 matches, six tests), 25 points (one try, 11 conversions); 5ft 5in, 9st 7lb; Auckland RFU president 1959–61, selector; general manager Auckland Savings Bank 1968–73, chairman Fishing Industry Board 1974.

Ron King (West Coast), NZ selector 1957–60 — born Waiuta 1909, died 10 January 1988; represented West Coast 1928–39 (Hokitika Excelsior), 1940–45 (Cobden), South Island 1934, 1936–39; All Blacks lock forward 1934–38 (42 matches; 13 tests; seven tries); described as 'best of the forwards' on tour of Britain 1935–36, led NZ against touring Springboks 1937; represented West Coast as winger in final year at school, before becoming specialist lock in provincial career lasting 18 years; West Coast selector-coach; proprietor King's Hotel, Greymouth.

Les George (Southland), NZ selector 1964–70 — born Invercargill 1908, died 10 August 1996; represented Southland as front-row forward 1929–30, 1932–39 (Invercargill club), South Island 1933, 1935, 1938–39, All Blacks in Australia 1938 (seven matches; three tests); likely prospect for All Blacks denied tour of South Africa 1940; Southland RFU executive 1947–75, coach 1946–54, selector 1952–60; NZRFU council 1966–72; farmer, storeman.

Stan 'Tiny' Hill (Canterbury), NZ selector 1981–86 — born New Plymouth 1927; represented Canterbury as lock or loose forward 1951–53, 1958–59 (Christchurch club), 1954–57 (Burnham Army), Counties 1961–62 (Papakura Army), South Island 1954, 1956–60, NZ Maoris 1956, NZ Combined Services 1952–53, 1955–57, 1959–61, All Blacks 1955–59 (19 matches; 11 tests); three winning tests against touring Springboks 1956, four against touring Lions 1959; Canterbury RFU president 1996–97; warrant officer NZ Army; retired.

THE POWER BEHIND THE ALL BLACKS

Earle Kirton (Wellington), NZ selector 1988, 1992–95 — born Taumarunui 1940; represented Otago as first five-eighths 1960–69 (University club), South Island 1963, 1965, 1968–69, All Blacks 1963–64, 1967–70 (48 matches; 13 tests; 13 tries; one dropped goal); renowned as part of combination with halfback Chris Laidlaw at club, provincial and international levels; left NZ to do postgraduate work in dentistry in England 1971; played for Harlequins and Barbarians, selector-coach of Harlequins and Middlesex; after returning to NZ, coached Wellington to NPC title 1986; dentist.

Ross Cooper (Counties), NZ selector and assistant coach 1996–98 — born Te Kuiti 11 December 1951; represented Wairarapa-Bush 1978–79 (Tahirangi club), Thames Valley 1980–83 (Paeroa West club); coached NZ Universities age-grade teams, Thames Valley 1988–90, Counties 1992–94; co-coach Romania 1991 World Cup, NZ staff coach since 1988; IRB technical advisory committee 1996–97; chairman NZ coaching committee for Hillary Commission 1997; former primary-school principal, now professional rugby coach, Chiefs, Super 12, 1998–99.

Gordon Hunter (Otago), NZ selector (1996–99) and assistant coach (1996–97) — born Invercargill 7 November 1949; represented Otago 1969 (Zingari-Richmond club), NZ Combined Services 1974–78, Zingari-Richmond club 1969–79, Ravensbourne club 1979–74; coach NZ Combined Services 1990–92, Otago 1992–95, Otago Highlanders Super 12 1996; former police detective.

MANAGERS

The more prominent managers include:

Samuel Sleigh (Otago), manager NZ team to Australia 1884, first NZ side to tour overseas — born November 1855, died England 1909; toured NZ with Dunedin club 1877, two years later played for Otago Clubs, forerunner to Otago representative team; Otago RFU first secretary 1881; with Canterbury RFU secretary William Milton, organised Australia tour 1884, selecting players from Auckland, Wellington, Canterbury, Otago only; manager of this unbeaten team; edited *NZ Rugby Football Annual* 1885, believed earliest book published on NZ rugby; returned to England, Rugby Football Union (England) committee 1888–91.

George Campbell (Wellington), NZ selector 1893–94 and manager first NZRFU team to Australia, captained by Tom Ellison, 1893 — born Nelson 1858, died Stoke 1937; represented Wellington 1875–76 (Wellington club), 1877, 1879–80, 1882–84 (Athletic club); one of outstanding forwards of era, original choice to lead first NZ team to Australia 1884 but unable to accept; Wellington RFU president 1924, 1936, life member, selector; helped found NZRFU 1892, president 1893, 1903, 1908; auditor general 1922–37.

Isaac Hyams (Wellington), manager NZ team to Australia 1897 — born Auckland 1862, died Wellington 1927; Wellington RFU management committee, treasurer, NZRFU management committee 1895, 1907, 1914, treasurer 1896–1903; tailor.

Alfred Charles 'Jack' Norris (Wellington), manager NZ team to Australia 1903 — born Lyttelton 1862, died Paki Paki 1923; prominent referee; NZRFU secretary 1902–04; 1903 NZ side captained by Jimmy Duncan (Otago), thrashed Australia 22-3 in only test of tour, for many years claimed stronger than 1905–06 All Black Originals.

George Dixon (Wellington), manager All Black Originals, which lost only one controversial tour match, to Wales 0-3, on first tour of Britain and France 1905–06 — born Huddersfield, England, 1859, died Auckland 1940; arrived NZ 1879, played for Albert club as halfback; Auckland RFU secretary 1887–1900; NZRFU management committee 1901–10, 1913–18, chairman 1904–10, 1915–18, president 1911–12, first life member 1921; author *The Triumphant Tour of the New Zealand Footballers* (Geddes and Blomfield, 1906); accountant, manager *NZ Observer* and *NZ Times,* founder *NZ Free Lance.*

Edgar Wylie (Wellington), manager All Blacks to Australia 1907 aged 28, youngest person to manage NZ team — born Wellington 1878, died Wellington 1946; represented Wellington as a forward 1899–1904 (Oriental club), Manawatu 1902; Wellington RFU management committee 1905, selector 1905, 1906, 1908; NZRFU secretary 1905–06, management committee 1907–08, treasurer 1912–18, 1921–30, life member 1931.

Bob Isaacs (Wellington), manager All Blacks to Australia 1914 — born Dunedin 1869, died 1938; represented Otago 1887, 1889–92 (Montecillo and Dunedin clubs); Otago RFU management committee 1895–98, 1900–01; NZRFU management committee 1902–14; Invercargill district manager NZ Railways; retired.

Thomas Jones (Wellington), manager All Blacks to Australia 1920 — born Rununga c. 1888, died Auckland 1960; prominent referee in Wellington; NZRFU treasurer 1919–20; journalist *Auckland Star,* sports columns by 'Ponty' 1926–43.

Ernest Little (Wellington), manager All Blacks to Australia 1924 — born Wellington 1885, died Wellington 1959; coached Oriental to Wellington championship 1910; Wellington RFU management committee 1911–14, treasurer 1915, president 1947; NZRFU management committee 1921–24; clerk.

Stan Dean (Wellington), manager All Blacks to Australia 1922, All Black Invincibles to Britain 1924–25 — born Auckland 1887, died Wellington 1971; played for Grafton club, Auckland, Mines club, Johannesburg; Poverty Bay selector 1914; Wellington RFU 1922, 1924, 1927–37 (Poneke club delegate); Wellington RFU president 1953; NZRFU management committee 1920–21, chairman 1922–47, president 1931, life member 1947, delegate Imperial Rugby Conferences, London, 1924, 1935; largely responsible for NZ's admission to IRFB 1947; manager South British Insurance Co. 1919–49.

Henry Samuel Leith (Wellington), manager All Blacks to Australia 1926 — born Dunedin 1889, died Wellington 1959; played for Southern club, Dunedin; refereed Ranfurly Shield and international tour matches; Otago RFU management committee 1919; NZRFU management committee 1925–30, treasurer 1931–36; clerk.

Bill Hornig (Wellington), manager All Blacks first tour of South Africa 1928 — born Havelock 1879, died Wellington 1963; played for Prince Albert, Waimea and Oriental clubs; coached Oriental senior team, served club for many years in various positions; Wellington RFU management committee 1911–15, 1919–20, treasurer 1916–19, selector 1917; NZRFU management committee 1923–28; men's outfitter.

James McLeod (Taranaki), manager 1929 All Blacks to Australia — born Dunedin 1878, died New Plymouth 1944; Taranaki RFU chairman 1912–42; NZRFU president 1920–21, life member 1940; managing director New Plymouth printing company McLeod and Slade Ltd; member of Legislative Council.

Arthur Geddes (Southland), manager All Blacks to Australia 1934 — see under Selectors.

Harold Strang (Southland), manager All Blacks to Australia 1947 — see Selectors

SELECTORS AND MANAGERS

Jim Parker (Wellington), manager All Blacks to South Africa 1949 — born Lyttelton 1897, died Auckland 1980; represented Canterbury 1920, 1923, All Blacks 1924–25 (21 matches; 3 tests; 18 tries) as attacking wing forward; considered fastest man in Invincibles, kept captain Cliff Porter out of three tests in Britain, outstanding contributor to side's unbeaten record; retired after tour with record of only 35 first-class games; NZRFU executive 1939–56, life member 1959; orchardist, chairman NZ Apple & Pear Marketing Board 1954–64.

Norm Millard (Wellington), manager All Blacks to Britain and France 1953–54 — born Fortrose, Southland, 1890, died Wellington 1978; represented Otago 1911 (University club); Wellington sole selector 1927–33, selector 1952–53; Wellington RFU management committee 1916–44, chairman 1937–64; NZRFU executive 1953–66, president 1942, life member 1967; Millard Stand, Athletic Park, named after him; principal Hutt Valley High School.

Lou Carmine (Wellington), manager All Blacks who defeated South Africa for first time, in home series 1956 — born Lyell 1891, died Wellington 1959; represented Buller 1914 (White Star club); Buller RFU secretary-treasurer 1914–23, selector 1922–23; Wanganui selector 1925–30; King Country president 1935–38; NZRFU executive 1944–59, president 1940; worked for NZ Railways, managed Wellington's Waterloo Hotel 1951–59.

Bill Craddock (Buller), manager All Blacks to Australia 1957 — born Westport 1907, died Westport 1979; Buller RFU management committee, secretary-treasurer, selector, president, life member 1948; NZRFU president (youngest, aged 34) 1941, council 1945–73, life member 1974; mayor of Westport; company manager.

Tom Pearce (Auckland), manager All Blacks to South Africa 1960 — born Auckland 1913, died Auckland 1976; represented Auckland as prop 1934, 1936–39, 1942, 1945–46 (Grafton and Manukau clubs), North Island 1937–38, NZ Trials 1937; reserve against touring Springboks 1937; Auckland selector 1951–53; Auckland RFU management committee 1947–61, chairman 1955–61, president 1964–66; NZRFU management committee 1955–65, president 1965, life member 1966; qualified lawyer, proprietor of haulage company, chairman Auckland Regional Authority 1968–76.

John David King (Wellington), manager All Blacks to Australia 1962 — born Hampden 1900, died Wellington 1966; represented Wellington 1921–24 (Oriental and Petone clubs); Wellington RFU management committee 1931–52, life member 1953; NZRFU executive 1948–52, 1956–65.

Frank Kilby (Wellington), manager All Blacks to Britain and France 1963–64 — born Invercargill 1906, died 3 September 1985; represented Southland as halfback 1925 (aged 19), South Island 1926, North Island 1927 (moved to Wellington), played for Wellington 1927, 30–36; All Blacks 1928, 1932, 1934 (18 matches; four tests), touring South Africa and captaining two tours to Australia; Wairarapa RFU management committee 1944–45; Auckland selector 1951–52; NZRFU executive 1955–74, life member 1976; bank manager.

Charlie Saxton (Otago), manager All Blacks to Britain 1967 — born Kurow 1913; represented Otago 1935–36 (Pirates club), South Canterbury 1937–38 (Timaru HSOB), Southland 1939 (Pirates club), Canterbury 1940 (Army), South Island 1938–39, NZEF 1945–46; halfback for All Blacks to Australia 1938 (three tests; four tries); captained Kiwis on successful European tour 1946; Otago selector 1947–49, coach 1950–57; NZRFU council 1956–71, president 1974, life member 1976; author *The ABC of Rugby* 1960; traveller, men's outfitter.

Duncan Ross (Northland), manager All Blacks to Australia 1968 — born Dargaville 1915, died 21 May 1981; played for HSOB club, Whangarei; North Auckland RFU chairman 1947–76; NZRFU council 1954–79, president 1979, life member 1980; solicitor.

Ron Burk (Auckland), manager All Blacks to South Africa 1970 — born Auckland 1916, died Auckland 1981; played for College Rifles club; prominent referee; Auckland RFU management committee 1955–68, chairman 1962–68; NZRFU council 1963–70; brewery executive.

Ernie Todd (Wellington), manager All Blacks to Britain and France 1972–73, embroiled in Keith Murdoch banishment controversy — born Wellington 1917, died Wellington 1974; represented Wellington as No. 8 1936–41, 1946 (St Pat's club); All Black trialist 1939, strong prospect for cancelled tour of South Africa 1940; Wellington RFU management committee 1958–66; NZRFU executive 1966–73; real estate agent.

Les Byars (King Country), manager All Blacks to Australia 1974 — born Oamaru 1925, died April 1994; played for Athletic in Taumarunui 1939–53; King Country RFU management committee 1957–74, president 1963–74; NZRFU president 1973; NZ representative on IRB 1973; undertaker's company director.

Noel Stanley (Taranaki), manager All Blacks to Britain 1974, South Africa 1976 — born New Plymouth 1919, died 11 August 1994; played for Rahotu and Opunake clubs; Taranaki RFU management committee 1954–80, chairman 1959–77, president 1958; NZRFU council 1966–80; manager NZ Juniors 1972, All Blacks 1973 on internal tours; dairy farmer, Opunake.

Ron Don (Auckland), manager All Blacks to Argentina 1976, v. touring Lions, and to France 1977 — born Auckland 1925; played for Grammar club; Auckland RFU management committee 1953–80, chairman 1969–80; NZRFU council 1971–80; fabric wholesaler.

Russ Thomas (Canterbury), manager All Blacks to Britain 1978, first to achieve grand slam, to Australia and to England and Scotland 1979 — born Christchurch 1926; played for HSOB club; Canterbury RFU management committee 1959–80; NZRFU council 1974–80; manager of grocery retail and wholesale company.

Ray Harper (Southland), manager All Blacks to Australia, and Fiji, N America and Wales 1980 — born Invercargill 19 July 1927; represented Southland (Pirates club) 1948–54, All Black trialist 1951; Pirates club coach, committee, president, life member; Southland RFU management committee for 22 years; NZRFU 13 years; master builder, president Invercargill Licensing Trust 1995–97; retired.

Peter Gill (Wellington), manager All Blacks v. touring Springboks 1981, to Romania and France 1982 — born Wellington 3 December 1936; Marist Old Boys club executive 1958–66, president 1967–69; Marist St Pat's club management committee 1971–77, president 1997; Hutt Old Boys Marist chairman 1985–86; Wellington RFU executive 1969–74; NZRFU executive 1969–74; actively involved in promotion of the Springbok tour 1981 — spoke in Parliament, met regularly with Prime Minister Robert Muldoon, debated issues with protesters, etc.; awarded QSM for services to sport 1997; managing director Hutt Valley Cartage Ltd.

Paul Mitchell (Wanganui), manager All Blacks v. touring British Isles, to Australia and to England and Scotland 1983, to Australia and Fiji 1984, to Argentina 1985 —

THE POWER BEHIND THE ALL BLACKS

born Palmerston North 24 February 1931; played for Technical OB, Wanganui 1958–67; Technical OB committee for 25 years, president 1970–71; Wanganui RFU management committee 1968–97, chairman 1974–83; Wanganui city councillor 1968–89, deputy mayor 1974–80, chairman Wanganui Harbour Board 1977–80; real estate agent, auctioneer, valuer, company director.

Dick Littlejohn (Bay of Plenty), manager All Blacks at home and in Australia 1984, v. touring Argentina, and to South Africa (cancelled) 1985 — born Hamilton 24 February 1931; played for Whakatane United and Bay of Plenty; elected NZRFU council 1981; NZ director on board of Rugby World Cup Ltd, which organised first World Cup 1987.

Ritchie Guy (Northland), manager All Blacks to France 1986, at World Cup in NZ 1987, to Australia 1987 — born Lower Hutt 6 April 1941; represented North Auckland as prop forward 1966–74, All Blacks 1971–72; North Auckland RFU management committee 1978–97, chairman 1981–86; NZRFU council board 1984–97, chairman 1995–96; father played for Wellington; farmer.

Malcolm Dick (Auckland) manager All Blacks to Japan 1987 — born Auckland 3 January 1941; represented Auckland as wing three-quarter 1962–70 (Ponsonby club), All Blacks 1963–70 (55 games, 15 tests); Te Atatu president/chairman 1974–77; Auckland president 1981–83, chairman 1984–89, life member 1991; NZRFU council 1986–90, deputy chairman 1989–90; father John Dick was All Black 1937–38; chartered accountant.

John Sturgeon (West Coast), manager All Blacks 1987–95 (longest-serving); term included World Cup 1991, 1995, unbeaten run with coach Alex Wyllie 1988–90 — born Motueka 12 December 1935; played for Star United club, longtime West Coast representative; NZRFU council 1987–95.

Neil Gray (Waikato), manager All Blacks at home and overseas 1992–93, with coach Laurie Mains, at time of resumption of play with South Africa — born 13 April 1943; Waikato management committee 1977–89, chairman 1985–89; NZRFU council 1989–95.

Colin Meads (King Country), manager All Blacks 1994–95, with coach Laurie Mains; term included World Cup 1995 — born Cambridge 3 June 1936; played for King Country 1955–72, All Blacks 1957–71 (133 matches; 55 tests; 86 points); 361 first-class matches (NZ record); NZ selector 1986; NZRFU council 1992–96.

Mike Banks (Manawatu), manager All Blacks 1996–99; term included 1st series win in South Africa 1996, Bledisloe Cup victories, Tri-Nations series wins 1996, 1997, undefeated UK tour 1997 — born Hamilton 30 January 1948; represented Manawatu 1976–79 (Queen Elizabeth COB club); administrator QECOB club 1974–94, chairman 10 years, life member; Manawatu RFU 12 years, deputy chairman 7 years; NZRFU since 1994; hotelier.

SELECTORS, 1893–1999
The New Zealand selectors from the first official test match to the present day have been:
1883: G. F. C. Campbell (Wellington), T. Henderson (Auckland) and F. Logan (Hawke's Bay).
1894: F. Logan (Hawke's Bay), T. Henderson (Auckland), G. F. C. Campbell (Wellington), J. P. Firth (Nelson) and W. J. Cotterill (Canterbury).
1896: A. D. Downes (Otago), F. T. Evans (Canterbury) and G. C. Fache (Wellington).
1897: H. J. Coutts (Wanganui), G. C. Fache (Wellington) and W. G. Garrard (Canterbury).
1901: A. Bayly (Taranaki), G. C. Fache (Wellington) and J. S. Hutchison (Otago).
1903: F. T. Evans (Canterbury), G. S. Fache (Wellington), H. F. Harris (Otago) and F. S. M. Murray (Auckland).
1904: G. C. Fache (Wellington), W. G. Garrard (Canterbury), H. F. Harris (Otago) and F. S. M. Murray (Auckland).
1905: A. Bayly (Taranaki), F. T. Evans (Canterbury), G. C. Fache (Wellington) and H. F. Harris (Otago).
1907: F. T. Evans (Canterbury), D. Gallaher (Auckland), H. F. Harris (Otago) and H. W. Kelly (Wellington).
1908: D. Gallaher (Auckland), H. F. Harris (Otago), H. W. Kelly (Wellington) and S. F. Wilson (Canterbury).
1910: D. Gallaher (Auckland), H. F. Harris (Otago), V. R. S. Meredith (Wellington) and S. F. Wilson (Canterbury).
1913: V. G. Cavanagh (Otago), D. Gallaher (Auckland), H. J. Mynott (Taranaki) and S. F. Wilson (Canterbury).
1914: D. Gallaher (Auckland), H. F. Harris (Otago), J. H. Lynskey (Wellington) and S. F. Wilson (Canterbury).
1920: A. J. Griffiths (Wellington), G. W. Nicholson (Auckland) and D. M. Stuart (Otago).
1921: A. J. Griffiths (Wellington), G. W. Nicholson (Auckland) and D. M. Stuart (Otago).

1922: A. J. Griffiths (Wellington) and D. M. Stuart (Otago).
1923: W. A. Drake (Canterbury), A. J. Griffiths (Wellington), E. Parata (Horowhenua) and D. M. Stuart (Otago).
1924: L. V. Carmine (Buller), H. E. Davis (Canterbury), A. J. Geddes (Southland), W. A. Guy (Taranaki), E. McKenzie (Wairarapa), N. A. McKenzie (Hawke's Bay) and N. Z. Wilson (Wellington).
1925: H. E. Davis (Canterbury), A. J. Geddes (Southland), E. McKenzie (Wairarapa), N. A. McKenzie (Hawke's Bay) and N. A. Wilson (Wellington).
1926: A. J. Geddes (Southland) and E. McKenzie (Wairarapa).
1927–28: A. A. Adams (West Coast), A. J. Geddes (Southland), W. A. Guy (Taranaki), E. McKenzie (Wairarapa), N. A. McKenzie (Hawke's Bay) and T. Milliken (Auckland).
1929–30: A. J. Geddes (Southland), W. E. J. Maxwell (Canterbury), A. McDonald (Otago), E. McKenzie (Wairarapa), N. A. McKenzie (Hawke's Bay) and G. W. Nicholson (Auckland).
1931–32: A. McDonald (Otago) and E. McKenzie (Wairarapa).
1934–35: A. A. Adams (West Coast), E. McKenzie (Wairarapa), V. R. S. Meredith (Auckland) and W. J. Pearson (Otago), with S. S. M. Dean (chairman, NZRFU management committee, arbiter) co-opted.
1936–37: A. A. Adams (West Coast), J. T. Burrows (Canterbury), E. McKenzie (Wairarapa), M. F. Nicholls (Wellington), G. W. Nicholson (Auckland) and W. J. Pearson (Otago), with F. H. Masters (Taranaki) co-opted.
1938–39: E. McKenzie (Wairarapa).
1944: P. W. Storey (Canterbury and Services), C. Brown (Taranaki) and A. McDonald (Wellington).
1945: A. McDonald (Wellington), F. W. Lucas (Auckland) and H. S. Strang (Southland).
1946: F. W. Lucas (Auckland), A. McDonald (Wellington) and H. S. Strang (Southland).
1947–48: A. McDonald (Wellington), N. A. McKenzie (Hawke's Bay) and H. S. Strang (Southland).
1949: R. R. Masters (Canterbury), N. A. McKenzie (Hawke's Bay) and H. S. Strang (Southland).
1950–53: M. M. N. Corner (Auckland); A. E. Marslin (Otago) and T. C. Morrison (Wellington).

SELECTORS AND MANAGERS

1954–56: A. E. Marslin (Otago), T. C. Morrison (Wellington) and J. L. Sullivan (Taranaki).

1957–60: R. A. Everest (Waikato), R. R. King (West Coast) and J. L. Sullivan (Taranaki).

1961–63: N. J. McPhail (Canterbury), J. Finlay (Manawatu) and R. G. Bush (Auckland).

1964: N. J. McPhail (Canterbury), F. R. Allen (Auckland), R. G. Bush (Auckland), D. L. Christian (Horowhenua) and V. L. George (Southland).

1965: N. J. McPhail (Canterbury), F. R. Allen (Auckland) and V. L. George (Southland).

1966: F. R. Allen (Auckland), D. L. Christian (Horowhenua) and V. L. George (Southland).

1967–68: F. R. Allen (Auckland), V. L. George (Southland) and I. M. H. Vodanovich (Wellington).

1969–70: I. M. H. Vodanovich (Wellington), V. L. George (Southland) and P. T. Walsh (Counties).

1971: I. M. H. Vodanovich (Wellington), R. H. Duff (Canterbury) and P. T. Walsh (Counties).

1972: I. M. H. Vodanovich (Wellington), R. H. Duff (Canterbury) and J. Gleeson (Manawatu).

1973: J. J. Stewart (Wanganui), R. H. Duff (Canterbury) and J. Gleeson (Manawatu).

1974–77: J. J. Stewart (Wanganui), E. A. Watson (Otago) and J. Gleeson (Manawatu).

1978–79: P. S. Burke (Taranaki), E. A. Watson (Otago) and J. Gleeson (Manawatu).

1980: P. S. Burke (Taranaki), E. A. Watson (Otago, convenor) and D. B. Rope (Auckland).

1981–82: P. S. Burke (Taranaki, convenor), S. F. Hill (Canterbury) and D. B. Rope (Auckland).

1983–84: S. F. Hill (Canterbury), B. J. Lochore (Wairarapa) and D. B. Rope (Auckland, convenor).

1985: S. F. Hill (Canterbury), B. J. Lochore (Wairarapa, convenor) and D. B. Rope (Auckland).

1986: S. F. Hill (Canterbury), B. J. Lochore (Wairarapa, convenor) and C. E. Meads (King Country).

1987: J. B. Hart (Auckland), B. J. Lochore (Wairarapa, convenor) and A. J. Wyllie (Canterbury).

1988: E. W. Kirton (Wellington), P. L. Penn (Wairarapa Bush) and A. J. Wyllie (Canterbury, convenor).

1989–91: J. B. Hart (Auckland), P. L. Penn (Wairarapa Bush) and A. J. Wyllie (Canterbury, convenor).

1992–93: L. W. Mains (Otago, convenor), P. T. Thorburn (North Harbour) and E. W. Kirton (Wellington).

1994: L. W. Mains (Otago, convenor), E. W. Kirton (Wellington) and L. Colling (Auckland).

1995: L. W. Mains (Otago, convenor), E. W. Kirton (Wellington) and R. Cooper (Counties).

1996–98: J. B. Hart (Auckland, convenor), R. Cooper (Counties) and G. Hunter (Otago).

1999: J. B. Hart (Auckland, convenor) and G. Hunter (Otago).

BIBLIOGRAPHY

After the Final Whistle, Spiro Zavos, Whitcoulls, 1979.

A Long Brief, Sir Vincent Meredith, Collins, 1996.

All Black Magic, Terry McLean, Reed, 1968.

All Black Magic: The Triumphant Tour of the 1967 All Blacks, Terry McLean, Reed, 1968.

All Black Power, Terry McLean, Reed, 1968.

All Blacks in Chains, J. M. Mackenzie, Truth, 1960.

All Blacks Retreat from Glory, Don Cameron, Hodder and Stoughton, 1980.

All Blacks Tour 1963–64, Andrew Mulligan, Whitcombe and Tombs, 1964.

All Blacks Versus Springboks, Graeme Barrow, Heinemann, 1981.

The Art of Rugby Football, Tom Ellison, Geddis and Blomfield, 1902.

The Battle for the Rugby Crown, Terry McLean, Reed, 1956.

Battle of the Giants, C. O. Medworth, Reed, 1960.

Battling the Boks, Terry McLean, Reed, 1970.

Beaten by the Boks, Terry McLean, Reed, 1960.

Beegee: The Bryan Williams Story, Bob Howitt, Rugby Press, 1981.

The Best of McLean, Terry McLean, Hodder and Stoughton, 1984.

Between the Posts: A New Zealand Rugby Anthology, Ron Palenski (ed.), Hodder and Stoughton, 1989.

Black, Black, Black, J. M. Mackenzie, Minerva, 1969.

Black Magic, Graham Hutchins, Moa, 1988.

The Bob Scott Story, Bob Scott and Terry McLean, Herbert Jenkins, 1956.

The Bok Busters, Terry McLean, Reed, 1965.

The Boot, Don Clarke and Path Booth, Reed, 1966.

Boots 'n' All, Andy Haden, Rugby Press, 1984.

Brothers in Arms: The Alan and Gary Whetton Story, Paul Lewis, Moa, 1991.

Buck: The Wayne Shelford Story, Wynne Gray, Moa, 1990.

The Canterbury Rugby History, Larry Saunders, C.R.F.U., 1979.

Centenary: 100 Years of All Black Rugby, R. H. Chester and N. A. C. McMillan, Moa, 1984.

Cock of the Rugby Roost: France–New Zealand 1961, Terry McLean, Reed, 1961.

Colin Meads All Black, Alex Veysey, Collins, 1974.

The Complete Rugby Footballer, D. Gallaher and W. J. Stead, Methuen, 1906.

Danie Craven on Rugby, Danie Craven, Beerman Publishers, 1952.

Ebony and Ivory, Alex Veysey, Moa, 1984.

The Encyclopaedia of New Zealand Rugby, R. H. Chester and N. A. C. McMillan, Moa 1981.

The Encyclopaedia of World Rugby, Keith Quinn, Shoal Bay Press, 1991.

BIBLIOGRAPHY

Famous Fullbacks, Joseph Romanos, Rugby Press, 1989.
Fergie, Alex Veysey, Whitcoulls, 1976.
Football Is 15, Gordon Slatter, Whitcombe and Tombs, 1970.
For the Record: The Allan Hewson Story, Ian Gault, Rugby Press, 1984.
Forerunners of the All Blacks, Greg Ryan, Canterbury University Press, 1993.
The Fourth All Blacks, 1953–54, John Hayhurst, Longmans, 1954.
The Fourth Springbok Tour of New Zealand, R. J. Urbahn and D. B. Clarke, Hicks, Smith and Sons, 1965.
Fred Allen on Rugby, Fred Allen and Terry McLean, Casswell, 1970.
Fronting Up: The Sean Fitzpatrick Story, Stephen O'Meagher, Moa Beckett, 1994.
The Game, the Goal: The Grant Fox Story, Alex Veysey, Rugby Press, 1992.
The Geriatrics, Lindsay Knight, Moa, 1986.
Goodbye to Glory: The 1976 All Black Tour to South Africa, Terry McLean, Reed, 1976.
Graham Mourie Captain, Ron Palenski, Moa, 1982.
Grant Batty, Bob Howitt, Rugby Press, 1977.
Great Days in New Zealand Rugby, Terry McLean, Reed, 1959.
Great Men of New Zealand Rugby, Tillman.
Great Rugby Players, David Norrie, Hamlyn, 1980.
Grizz: The Legend, Phil Gifford, Rugby Press, 1991.
Haka! The All Blacks' Story, Winston McCarthy, Pelham Books, 1968.
High Flying Kiwis, Mark Taylor, Rugby Press, 1988.
History of New Zealand Rugby Football, vols. 1 (Reeds, 1948) and 2 (Whitcombe & Tombs, 1958), A. C. Swan.
History of New Zealand Rugby Football, vols. 3 and 4, R. H. Chester and N. A. C. McMillan, Moa.
I, George Nepia, George Nepia and Terry McLean, Reed, 1963.
Iceman: The Michael Jones Story, Robin McConnell, Rugby Press, 1994.
Inga the Winger, Bob Howitt, Rugby Press, 1993.
Kings of Rugby: The British Lions 1959 New Zealand Tour, Terry McLean, Reed, 1960.
Kirky, Lindsay Knight, Rugby Press, 1979.
Kirwan: Running on Instinct, Paul Thomas, Moa, 1992.
Laurie Mains, Bob Howitt and Robin McConnell, Rugby Press, 1996.
The Lions' Share, Gabriel David and David Frost, Hicks, Smith and Sons, 1971.
Listen, It's a Goal, Winston McCarthy, Pelham Books, 1973.
Lochore: An Authorised Biography, Alex Veysey, Gary Caffell and Ron Palenski, Hodder Moa Beckett, 1996.
Loveridge: Master Halfback, Ron Palenski, Moa, 1985.
Magic Matches: Great Days of New Zealand Rugby, Graham Hutchins, Moa, 1991.
Makers of Champions: Great New Zealand Coaches, Joseph Romanos, Mills Publications, 1987.
McKechnie: Double All Black, Lynn McConnell, Craigs Publishers, 1983.
Men in Black, R. H. Chester and N. A. C. McMillan, Moa, 1978.
Mexted: Pieces of Eight, Alex Veysey, Rugby Press, 1986.
The Mighty Lions, John Reason, Whitcombe and Tombs, 1971.
Mud in Your Eye, Chris Laidlaw, Reed, 1973.
New Zealand Rugby Almanack, Arthur Carman, Arthur Swan and Read Masters, Sporting Publications, various editions.
New Zealand Rugby Almanack, R. H. Chester and N. A. C. McMillan, Moa.
New Zealand Rugby Football Union Archive Interviews, 1990, various.
New Zealand Rugby Legends, Terry McLean, Moa, 1987.
New Zealand Rugby Museum Newsletter, Bob Luxford, various.
New Zealand Rugby Skills and Tactics, Ivan Vodanovich (tech. ed.), Lansdowne Press, 1982.
Now Is the Hour: The 1965 Springboks in New Zealand, A. C. Parker, Whitcombe and Tombs, 1965.
Old Heroes: The 1956 Springbok Tour and the Lives Beyond, Warwick Roger, Hodder and Stoughton, 1991.
On the Ball, Gordon Slatter, Whitcombe and Tombs, 1970.
On with the Game, Norman McKenzie, Reed, 1960.
One Hundred Great Rugby Characters, Joseph Romanos and Grant Harding, Rugby Press, 1991.
Otago Rugby Football Union Annual 1956, Otago Daily Times & Witness.
Out of the Ruck: A Selection of Rugby Writing, David Parry-Jones (ed.), Pelham Books, 1986.
Pathway among Men, Jim Burrows, Whitcombe and Tombs, 1974.
The Pride of Southern Rebels, Sean O'Hagan, Pilgrims South Press, 1981.
Record of Otago Rugby 1882–1940, A. C. Swan.
Red Dragons of Rugby, Terry McLean, Reed, 1969.
Round the World with the All Blacks 1953–54, Winston McCarthy, Sporting Publications, 1954.
Rugby Annual, Bob Howitt, Moa, various editions.
Rugby and Be Damned: All Blacks' Tour of South Africa 1970, Gabriel David, Hicks, Smith and Sons, 1970.
Rugby Greats, vols. 1 and 2, Bob Howitt, Moa, 1975 and 1982.
Rugby in Blue and Gold, Dave McLaren.
Rugby in My Time, Winston McCarthy, Reed, 1958.
Rugby on Attack, Ron Jarden, Whitcombe and Tombs, 1961.
Rugby Players That Made New Zealand Famous, R. A. Stone, Scott & Scott Ltd.
Rugger: The Man's Game, E. H. D. Sewell and O. L. Owen, Hollis and Carter, 1950.
Rugby Triumphant, Don Cameron, Hodder and Stoughton, 1981.
Shield Fever, Lindsay Knight, Rugby Press, 1986.
Smokin' Joe, Phil Gifford, Rugby Press, 1990.
Springbok and Silver Fern, Reg Sweet, Reed, 1960.
Springboks at Bay, Maxwell Price, Longmans, 1956.
Springboks down the Years, Danie Craven, Howard Timmins, 1956.
Straight from the Hart, Paul Thomas, Moa Beckett, 1993.
Super Sid, Bob Howitt, Rugby Press, 1978.
They Led the All Blacks, Lindsay Knight, Rugby Press, 1991.
They Missed the Bus: Kirkpatrick's All Blacks of 1972–73, Terry McLean, Reed, 1973.
Tour of the Century: The All Blacks in Wales 1980, Keith Quinn, Methuen, 1981.
The Tour of the Third All Blacks, 1935, Charlie Oliver and Eric Tindill, Sporting Publications, 1936.
Trek Out of Trouble, Noel Holmes, Whitcombe and Tombs, 1960.
Up Front: The Story of the All Black Scrum, Graeme Barrow, Heinemann, 1985.
Willie Away, Terry McLean, Reed, 1964.
Winter of Discontent: The 1977 Lions in New Zealand, Terry McLean, Reed, 1977.
Winters of Revenge, Spiro Zavos, Penguin, 1997.
With the All Blacks in Great Britain, France, Canada and Australia 1924-1925, Read Masters, Christchurch Press, 1928.
With the All Blacks in Springbokland 1928, M. F. Nicholls, L. F. Watkins, 1928.

INDEX

Aarvold, Carl — 49, 69
Abercrombie, David — 198
Abott, 'Bunny' — 41
Adams, Alan — 87, 232
Adkins, G.T. — 77
Aitken, George — 36
Alatini, Pita — 221
Allen, Fred — 9, 62, 65, 94, 97, 135, 138, 139, 144-149, 151, 152, 184, 194, 196, 206, 225, 226, 230
Allen, Nicky — 173
Alley, Geoff — 84, 85, 90
Anderson, Albert — 191, 198
Antelme, J. G. M. — 126
Archer, Robin — 102, 117, 123, 183
Archer, Watson — 183
Armitt, 'Barney' — 81
Arnold, Keith — 62
Asher, Opai — 22, 125
Ashworth, John — 170, 182, 185, 186

Babrow, Louis — 83, 128, 130
Bachop, Graeme —198, 217
Badeley, Ces — 46
Bagley, Keith — 114
Ball, Nelson ('Kelly') — 77, 78, 136
Banks, Mike — 211, 220, 236
Barclay, Wattie — 63
Barry, Kevin — 134
Barry, Ned —62
Bastard, W.T. — 84
Batty, Grant — 154, 156, 161, 164, 165, 169
Baxter, James ('Bim') — 68, 69
Bayley, Alf — 16, 21, 81
Beamish, Graham — 55
Beatty, George — 103
Bedell-Sivright, 'Darkie' — 37
Bekker, Daan — 158
Bekker, Jaap — 117, 157, 158
Belcher, A. St A. ('Slip') — 92
Bell, Ray — 108, 109
Belliss, Moke — 49
Bennett, Phil — 171
Berghan, Trevor — 92, 106
Berryman, Norm — 219, 220
Best, J.J. — 77
Bevan, Vince — 65, 103, 108, 114, 145
Bezuidenhout, Gert — 163
Birtwhistle, Bill — 140
Blackadder, Todd — 221
Blair, Jim — 192
Blake, Jack — 62
Blanco, Serge — 218
Blazey, Ces — 132, 150, 184
Boe, John — 220
Blowers, Andrew — 221
Bolger, Jim — 228
Bond, Garth — 120
Bonis, Eddie— 49
Boon, Roger — 183
Booth, Ernest ('General') — 29
Boroevich, Kevin — 186, 198
Boshier, Fred — 103
Botica, Frano — 188, 190, 191, 198
Botting, R.W.S. — 92, 94
Bowen, Mike — 208
Bowers, Guy — 102, 114
Bradman, Don — 226
Brand, Gerry — 61, 74, 83, 130
Bremner, 'Mick' — 128
Brewer, Mike — 190, 197, 198, 204, 230
Briscoe, Kevin — 126, 127, 129, 134, 183
Brooke, Robin — 205, 208, 221, 226
Brooke, Zinzan — 188, 191, 198, 204, 208, 217, 218

Brooke-Cowden, Mark — 188, 191
Brooks, John — 136
Brown, Charlie — 54
Brown, Handley — 77
Brown, Olo — 224
Brown, Ross — 117, 123, 134, 183
Brown, Tony — 221
Brownlie, Cyril — 45, 57, 58, 61, 148
Brownlie, James — 57
Brownlie, Laurence — 57
Brownlie, Maurice — 9, 34, 51, 53-59, 61, 63 66, 80 , 85, 87, 158, 226
Bruce, Doug — 165, 169
Brynard, Gert— 140
Bunce, Frank — 79, 217, 218, 224
Burger, Freek — 207
Burgess, Bob — 168
Burgoyne, Mike — 173
Burk, Ron — 152, 235
Burke, Peter — 102, 123, 176, 178-183, 184, 185, 187, 188, 226
Burmeister, R.D. — 127
Burns, Paddy — 30
Burrows, Jim — 24, 74, 76, 82-90, 225
Bush, Bill — 161, 165, 169, 197
Bush, Percy — 24, 40
Bush, Ron — 134-136, 138
Buttery, J.A. —31
Buxton, John — 117
Byars, Les — 162, 235

Cameron, Bill — 183
Cameron, Don — 150, 153
Cameron, Lachie —182
Campbell, George — 232
Campese, David — 218
Carman, Arthur —59, 60, 65, 70
Carmine, Lou — 117, 235
Carrington, Ken — 168
Carter, Mark — 220
Catchpole, Ken — 134
Catley, Haswell ('Has') — 96, 123, 124
Caughey, 'Pat' — 77, 79
Caulton, Ralph — 127, 131, 138
Cavanagh, Dick — 97
Cavanagh, Vic jnr ('Young Vic') — 11, 91, 92, 94, 96, 97 ,98, 111, 114, 115, 119, 123, 124, 125, 146, 188, 211
Cavanagh, Vic snr ('Old Vic') — 30, 96, 97, 119
Cerutti, Bill — 49, 73
Cherrington, 'Brownie' — 103
Chester, Rod — 26, 78, 81, 133
Chisholm, Sam — 209
Cholley, Gerard — 170
Christian, Des — 194
Christian, Ken — 135
Christie, Kitch — 226
Claassen, Johan — 129
Claassen, Wynand — 179
Clamp, Mike — 188
Clark, Bill — 101, 102, 114, 117, 118, 159
Clark, Frank — 84, 90
Clarke, Adrian — 127
Clarke, Don — 71, 101, 117, 118, 123, 124, 125, 126, 127, 28, 129, 131, 134, 138, 157, 159
Clarke, Ian — 102, 113, 114, 117, 123, 124, 125, 127, 129, 134, 137, 138, 157, 158, 159, 226
Cleary, Mike — 216
Cleaver, Billy — 102
Clode, Len — 108-110, 188
Coates, Gordon — 68
Coates, Peter — 153
Cockerill, Maurice ('Snow') — 108, 109

Colling, Lin — 155, 161, 168, 210
Collins, W.R. — 77
Connor, Des — 134, 138
Conrad, Bill — 124
Conway, Dick ('Red') 127, 128, 140
Cooke, Bert — 46, 49, 51, 53, 54, 58, 62, 66, 70, 73, 80, 136, 226
Cooper, Greg — 190
Cooper, Ross — 217, 218, 220, 221, 233
Corkill, Tom — 62
Corner, Merv — 43, 73, 77, 78, 102, 108, 115, 233
Cottrell, 'Beau' — 87
Cottrell, Wayne — 200
Couch, Ben — 65, 145
Cowley, Ken — 209
Craddock, Bill — 123, 235
Craven, Danie — 60, 74, 82, 83, 84, 86, 92, 94, 145, 146, 152
Creighton, John — 134
Cromb, Ian — 90
Crowe, Kevin — 148
Crowley, Kieran — 191, 198
Crowley, Pat — 96, 103
Cullen, Christian — 205, 217, 221, 223, 224
Cundy, Rawi — 62
Cunningham, Bill — 24, 72
Cunningham, Gary — 173

Dallas, John — 30
Dalley, Bill — 33, 49, 84
Dalton, Andy — 11, 170, 173, 178, 179, 182, 184, 185, 186, 187, 190, 191, 192, 194
Dalton, Ray — 62, 77, 94
Dalzell, Nelson — 102, 114
Davies, Gerald — 151
Davies, Mervyn — 151
Davis, Bill — 139
Davis, Keith — 114, 117, 119
Davis, Lyn — 169, 199, 200
Dawson, Ronnie — 128
Dean, Stan — 9, 43, 44, 45, 46, 51, 63, 69, 232
Deans, Bob — 29, 30, 37, 44, 73
Deans, Bruce —191, 198
Deans, Robbie — 186, 220
Devenish, George — 54
Diack, 'Tuppy' — 127
Dick, Johnny — 82
Dick, Malcolm — 148, 236
Dixon, George — 24, 29, 234
Dixon, Morrie — 114, 117, 123
Don, Ron — 169, 170, 235
Donald, Andrew — 185, 186
Donald, Quentin — 58, 63
Donaldson, Mark — 170, 173, 182
Donoghue, Paul — 133
Dougan, John — 161, 168
Dowd, Craig — 205, 208
Dowling, John — 210
Drake, John — 191
Duff, Bob — 103, 109, 113, 114, 117, 142, 154-159, 161, 162, 164, 174, 176, 179, 182, 200, 226
Duncan, James/Jimmy — 11, 22-27, 28, 29, 31, 37, 38, 40, 71, 76, 81, 225
Duncan, Mick —153
Dunn, Eddie — 173
Dunn, Ian — 185
du Toit, Piet — 129
Dwyer, Pat — 149

Earl, Andy — 191, 198
Eastgate, Peter — 117, 119
Edwards, Brent — 177
Edwards, Gareth — 151

Eliason, Ian — 168
Ellison, Tom — 14, 18-21
Elsom, Alan — 102, 114
Elvidge, Ron — 94, 96, 97, 102, 103
Ercerg, Percy — 108
Evans, Frank — 232
Eveleigh, Kevin — 165, 169
Everest, Dick — 9, 97, 122-125, 126, 127, 129
Eyton, Thomas — 13

Fache, George — 232
Falwasser, Albert — 62
Familton, N.D. — 191
Fanning, Bernie — 22
Farrell, Colin — 169
Fawcett, Kit — 166
Feek, Greg — 221
Ferris, Chas — 211
Finlay, Jack — 134, 138
Finlayson, 'Bunny' — 51, 66, 73, 136
Fisher, Rob — 210, 211, 219
Fitzgerald, Jim — 114
Fitzpatrick, Brian — 102, 109, 110, 110, 114
Fitzpatrick, Sean — 11, 191, 198, 207, 208, 217, 218, 221, 223, 224
Fleming, John — 173
Ford, Brian — 173
Ford, Jocky' — 84
Fox, Grant — 185, 191, 196, 198, 202
Fraser, Bernie — 173, 182, 185, 186
Freebairn, Stu — 114
Fright, Bill — 158
Fuller, Fred — 61, 62

Gage, Davey — 14, 16, 21, 81
Gainsford, John — 140
Gallagher, John — 191, 198, 199
Gallaher, Dave — 11, 22, 24, 27, 28-31, 33, 38, 72, 73, 232
Gard, Phil — 153, 168
Gatland, Warren — 198
Geddes, Arthur — 232, 234
Geffin, 'Oakey' — 145
Gemmell, Sam — 61
George, Les —135, 139, 194, 233
Gibbons, Clarrie — 109, 110
Gibson, Darryl —221
Gibson, Mike — 176
Gifford, Phil — 199, 203
Gilbert, Mike — 77, 79
Gilbert, Tony — 220
Gill, Peter — 182, 235
Gillespie, Bill — 123, 127
Gledhill, K. J. — 161, 166
Gleeson, Jack — 9, 156, 161, 162, 167-171, 173, 174, 176, 177, 196, 226
Goddard, Morrie — 62, 96
Going, Sid — 148, 154, 155, 156, 161, 166, 168, 169, 194, 200, 201, 226
Goldsmith, Jasin — 198
Gould, Arthur — 75
Grace, W.G. — 226
Graham, Jim — 124
Graham, John — 128, 134, 138, 193, 200, 220
Grant, Lachie — 62, 96, 108, 109
Gray, Bill — 117, 123
Gray, 'Doddy' — 30, 33
Gray, Ken — 138, 139, 147, 148, 194, 226
Gray, Neil — 236
Gray, Wynne — 203
Green, Craig — 185, 191
Grenside, Bert — 56, 61
Griffiths, A.J. — 35
Griffiths, Jack — 77, 78
Guy, Richie — 168, 191, 236

THE POWER BEHIND THE ALL BLACKS

Haden, Andy — 156, 165, 166, 169, 170, 171, 173, 174, 176, 177, 179, 182, 183, 186, 187, 199
Hadley, Bill — 77, 78
Haig, Jimmy — 114
Haig, Laurie — 102, 108, 109, 110, 114
Hales, Duncan —168
Hamilton, Doug — 114
Hammett, Mark — 221
Hammond, Ian Arthur — 109
Hansen, Horace — 132
Harding, Arthur — 72
Harper, Ray — 235
Harris, Henry — 232
Harris, Perry — 165
Harris, Tony — 74, 83, 84, 86, 130
Hart, George — 77, 78, 87
Hart, Gus — 45, 49
Hart, John — 145, 156, 178, 185, 191, 192, 196, 198, 199, 201, 203, 205, 210, 213-224, 225, 226, 227
Harvey, Lester — 103, 114
Hasell, 'Nuts' — 143
Hayhurst, John — 111, 115
Hazlehurst, 'Buck' — 87
Hazlett, Bill — 80
Hazlett, Jack — 147, 200
Heeps, Rod — 134
Hemi, Ron — 102, 114, 117, 123, 127, 128, 159
Henderson, Peter — 96, 102, 103
Henry, Graham — 97, 202, 211, 220, 229, 230, 231
Herewini, Mac — 138, 139
Herman, Doug — 119
Hewson, Alan — 173, 178, 179, 182, 185, 186, 187
Higginson, Graeme — 173, 182
Hill, Rowland — 20
Hill, 'Tiny' — 101, 117, 123, 127, 157, 182, 187, 189, 190, 233
Hobbs, Jock — 185, 186, 190, 192, 209
Hoeft, Carl — 220
Hogg, Cuth — 106
Holmes, Bevan — 168
Hook, Lew — 49
Hooper, Jack — 84
Hopkinson, Alister — 147, 200
Hore, John — 77
Hornig, Bill — 53, 234
Horsley, Ron — 138
House, Roger — 176
Howitt, Bob — 152, 153, 159, 166, 171, 177, 212
Hughes, Arthur — 62, 65, 103
Hunter, Gordon — 217, 218, 220, 221, 233
Hunter, Jimmy — 30, 38
Hurst, Ian —156, 161

Ieremia, Alama — 221
Ifwersen, Karl — 36, 80
Ingpen, Morrie — 132
Innes, Craig — 207
Innnes, Gordon — 87
Irvine, 'Bull' — 51, 58, 61, 62, 66, 73, 136
Irwin, Mark — 102, 157
Isaacs, Bob — 232

James, Carwyn — 98, 151
Jarden, Ron — 102, 103, 108, 110, 113, 114, 115, 117, 125, 226
Jardine, Douglas — 97
Jefferd, Andy — 182
Jessep, E. M. — 136
John, Barry — 151, 152, 171, 211
Johnson, Lance — 62
Johnstone, Brad — 166, 169, 170, 173, 230
Johnstone, Peter — 96, 108, 114, 115, 179
Jones, Alan — 188, 190

Jones, Ivow — 49
Jones, Ken — 102
Jones, Lewis — 102
Jones, Michael — 191, 198, 217, 218, 220
Jones, Murray — 161
Jones, Peter — 101, 102, 117, 118, 119, 128, 157, 159, 226
Jones, Thomas — 234
Joseph, Howard — 153

Karam, Joe — 156, 165
Keane, Kieran — 173
Kearney, Jim — 62, 114
Kelleher, Byron — 221
Kelly, Jack — 114, 121
Keogh, Pat — 14
Ketels, Rod — 173, 182
Kidd, Murray — 230
Kilby, Frank — 55, 73, 74, 76, 235
King, John — 235
King, Ron — 77, 87, 127, 129, 233
Kirk, David — 185, 188, 190, 191, 192, 194, 210, 212
Kirkpatrick, Alex —61
Kirkpatrick, Ian — 33, 147, 148, 152, 155, 156, 161, 163, 164, 168, 169, 200, 211
Kirton, Earle — 139, 208, 210, 233
Kirwan, John — 185, 188, 190, 191, 196, 198, 202, 209, 218
Knight, Gary — 170, 173, 179, 182, 186
Knight, Laurie — 169, 170
Knight, Lindsay — 121, 149, 171, 183, 188, 195, 230
Koch, Chris — 117, 157, 158
Kronfeld, Josh — 205, 214, 221
Kyle, Jackie — 83, 102

Laidlaw, Chris — 138, 139, 142, 147, 148, 188, 194
Laidlaw, Kevin — 126, 129, 183
Laing, D. R. — 191
Lam, Pat — 202
Lambert, Kent — 156, 161, 169
Lambourne, Artie — 77
Lawton, Tommy — 49, 73, 74
Le Lievre, Jules — 134
Leith, Henry — 234
Lendrum, Bob — 161
Leslie, Andy — 11, 156, 162, 163, 164, 230
Levien, Howard — 123
Levy, Geoff — 210
Lilburne, Herb — 49, 84
Lineen, Terry — 123, 125, 126, 127
Little, Ernest — 232
Little, Walter — 217
Littlejohn, Dick — 236
Llewellyn, Willie — 72
Loader, Colin — 102, 114
Lochner, G.P. — 84
Lochore, Sir Brian — 138, 139, 147, 148, 151, 174, 184, 185, 187, 189-195, 196, 200, 201, 207, 208, 213, 214, 226, 229
Lockyear, Dick — 129
Loe, Richard — 191, 198, 202, 208
Lomas, Micky — 66
Lomu, Jonah — 205, 206, 207, 219, 221, 224
Lotz, Jan — 74, 83
Louw, 'Boy' — 74, 83, 84
Louw, 'Fanie' — 74
Loveridge, Dave — 169, 173, 176, 182, 184, 186, 187
Lucas, Fred — 42, 45, 49, 51, 66, 73, 80, 136
Lynch, Tom — 108, 109
Lynskey, Jimmy — 30

McAtamney, Frank — 123, 157
McCahill, Bernie — 191, 202
McCallion, Mac — 220
McCarthy, Winston — 61, 65, 70, 129, 145, 149
McCaw, Bill — 102, 108, 109, 110, 114
McCleary, Brian — 58
McCormick, Fergie — 148, 151, 152, 194, 200, 211, 226
McConnell, Robin — 153, 166, 212, 229
McCullough, John — 127, 131, 183
McDonald, Alex — 11, 33, 35, 39, 41, 91-98, 103, 125, 146, 225
McDonald, Malcolm — 123
McDowell, Steve — 191, 198, 202
MacEwan, Nev — 117, 123
McGregor, Duncan — 22, 24
McGregor, Neil — 55, 84
McIntosh, Don — 103, 117, 123
McKay, Don — 138
McKechnie, Brian — 170, 182
McKenzie, Bert — 58, 60, 61, 63, 67, 68
McKenzie, Jack — 60, 61
McKenzie, Norman — 53, 57, 58, 59, 60-65, 66, 67, 68, 70, 80, 95, 142
McKenzie, Rod — 77
McKenzie, Ted — 53, 57, 58, 59, 60-65, 66, 67, 68, 70, 80, 95
McKenzie, William ('Offside Mac') — 16, 25, 26, 60, 61, 64, 81
McLaren, Hugh — 124,
McLean, Hugh — 9, 46, 51, 77, 78
McLean, Sir Terry — 9, 18, 35, 42, 46, 55, 59, 65, 76, 78, 79, 81, 91, 92, 98, 111, 113, 115, 116, 121, 128, 132, 133, 149, 228
McLeod, Bruce — 140, 147, 226
McLeod, James — 234
McMillan, Neville — 26, 78, 81, 133
McMullen, Frank — 123, 125, 126, 129
McNab, Jack — 62, 96, 103, 114
McNaughton, Alan — 168
McPhail, Alex — 143
McPhail, Bruce — 143
McPhail, Clem — 143
McPhail, Hamish — 143
McPhail, Neil — 9, 97, 118, 134, 135, 137-143, 145, 146, 156, 178, 191, 193, 194, 196, 225, 226
McQuilken, Noel — 230
McRae, Ian — 98, 139
Macdonald, Hamish — 156, 161, 168
Mackenzie, Morrie — 9, 24, 25, 27, 51, 73, 75, 123, 124, 125
Mackereth, Jim — 124
Macqueen, Rod — 220, 221
Mahoney, Athol — 77
Mains, Laurie — 97, 152, 156, 166, 167, 176, 178, 191, 192, 202, 205-212, 213, 214, 217, 218, 220, 226, 227, 229
Maka, Isitolo — 220
Malan, Abe — 140
Malcolm, Sid — 49
Mallett, Nick — 220, 221
Manchester, Jack — 76, 77, 87
Manu, Daniel — 202
Markotter, A. F. ('Oubaas') — 86
Marshall, Sir John — 132
Marshall, Justin — 205, 221
Marslin, Arthur — 99, 101, 102, 108, 111-115, 116, 117, 188
Marter, Charles — 21
Mason, George — 32-34
Masters, Harold — 87
Masters, Read — 34, 46, 66, 84
Max, Donald — 136
Maxwell, Norm — 221
Mayerhofler, Mark — 220
Mayhew, R. J. — 198, 199
Meads, Colin — 57, 123, 125, 126, 127, 128, 134, 135, 137, 138, 140, 147, 148, 153, 187, 190, 191, 192, 194, 195, 208, 226, 236
Meads, Stan — 134, 137, 147
Meates, Bill — 103
Meeuws, Kees — 220
Mehrtens, Andrew — 193, 205, 208, 218, 219, 221
Meredith, Bill — 80
Meredith, Sir Vincent — 9, 24, 30, 34, 76-81, 136, 225
Metcalfe, T.C. — 136
Meurant, Brad — 230
Mexted, Graham — 103
Mexted, Murray — 173, 174, 176, 179, 182, 186, 187
Mika, Dylan — 221
Mill, Jimmy — 43, 49, 51, 55, 58, 61, 62, 66, 73, 123, 136
Millar, Billy — 57
Millard, Norman — 110, 111, 113, 114, 234
Miller, Geoff —210
Milliken, Tom — 84
Mitchell, 'Brushy' — 77, 82, 92, 106
Mitchell, Paul — 186, 230, 236
Mitchinson, Frank — 30, 33
Moffitt, Jim — 62
Molloy, Brian — 123
Moreton, Ray — 134
Morgan, Teddy — 44, 72, 73
Morley, Jack — 49
Morris, Trevor — 168
Morrison, Terry — 161
Morrison, Tom — 70, 76, 92, 99-107, 108, 115, 117, 118, 126, 149, 150, 153, 178, 225, 226
Mortlock, George — 120
Mourie, Graham — 11, 167, 168, 170, 173, 174, 179, 185, 187
Muldoon, Sir Robert — 132
Muller, Henie — 96, 97, 101, 127, 142, 145, 146
Muller, 'Jazz' — 147, 195
Murdoch, Keith — 154, 155, 156, 162, 168, 176
Murdoch, Rupert — 208, 209
Mynott, 'Simon' — 37, 79

Nathan, Waka — 134, 138, 140, 147
Naude, 'Tiny' — 140
Nel, 'Lofty' — 140
Nel, Philip — 61, 74, 83, 159
Nelson, Keith — 138
Nepia, George — 9, 43, 46, 49, 51, 53, 54, 55, 58, 61, 62, 63, 66, 73, 136
Nesbit, Steve — 126
Neser, 'Knoppie' — 55
New Zealand Natives team — 13-16, 18-21
New Zealand Rugby Football Union (NZRFU) – 18, 24, 33, 60, 66, 68, 69, 70, 74, 91, 92, 93, 96, 99, 101, 106, 108, 118, 123, 130, 132, 133, 143, 149, 150, 155, 161, 162, 163, 165, 166, 184, 189, 194, 197, 199, 202, 209, 210, 211, 212, 213, 227, 231, 232, 233, 234, 235, 236.
Nicholls, 'Doc' — 52
Nicholls, 'Ginger' — 52, 62
Nicholls, Gwynne — 72, 73
Nicholls, Mark — 46, 49, 51, 54, 55, 57, 59, 62, 66, 73, 84, 87, 92, 125, 136, 226
Nicholls, Syd — 55, 75
Nicholson, George — 16, 30, 35, 38, 39-42, 73, 87, 91
Nola, George — 124
Norling, Clive — 179
Norris, Alfred —234
Norton, Tane — 153, 156, 161, 168, 169, 171

INDEX

Obolensky, Prince Alexander — 78
O'Dea, R.J. — 114
Old, Geoff — 182, 186
Oliver, Anton — 221
Oliver, Charlie — 77, 78, 87, 136
Oliver, Des — 102, 114
Oliver, Don — 49
Oliver, Frank — 169, 171, 220
Ormand, Jack — 58, 61
Osborne, Bill — 169, 170, 173
Osler, Bennie — 53
O'Sullivan, Terry — 183
Owen, Dicky — 72
Oxlee, Keith — 129, 140

Packer, Kerry — 208
Paewai, Lui — 58, 61, 62
Page, 'Curly' — 34, 84, 90
Page, 'Rusty' — 77, 136
Palenski, Ron — 156, 159, 167, 171, 173, 177
Parker, Jim — 44, 45, 58, 84, 92, 93, 146, 234
Parkinson, Mike — 161
Pearce, Tom — 117, 127, 128, 129, 235
Pearson, William — 87
Pelser, Martin — 129
Penn, Lane — 198
Pepper, C. S. — 77
Pescini, Dave — 161
Peterson, Lew — 84
Phillips, Bill — 92
Phillips, John — 230
Philpott, Shane — 198
Pickering, Rex — 123, 124
Pienaar, Theo — 57
Pierce, Murray — 191, 198, 202
Poidevin, Simon — 188
Pokere, Stephen — 185, 186
Porter, Cliff — 9, 34, 43-52, 58, 62, 66, 69, 70, 73, 85, 92, 136, 142
Powers, Brian — 208
Price, Max — 158
Pritchard, Charlie — 72
Purdue, George — 136

Quinn, Keith — 52, 168
Quittenton, Roger — 171

Ralph, Caleb — 220
Randell, Taine — 205, 221, 223, 224
Ranfurly Shield — 30, 74, 94
Rangi, Ron — 140
Rankin, Jack — 84, 119, 142, 156
Reid, Hika — 173, 178, 186, 187
Reid, John — 176
Reid, 'Ponty' — 101, 109, 117, 123, 124, 157
Reid, S.T. ('Tori') — 77
Retief, Daan — 103
Rhind, Pat — 142
Richardson, Jock — 44, 45, 58, 66
Ridge, Matthew — 198
Rippin, Bert — 132
Roberts, Freddy — 24, 30, 37, 38, 72, 79
Roberts, Kevin — 208, 209, 210, 231
Robertson, Bruce — 156, 163, 168, 169, 173
Robertson, Duncan — 161, 166, 169
Robertson, Ian — 163
Robertson, Scott — 220
Robilliard, Alan — 45, 66, 84
Robinson, Eddie — 108, 109
Rodriguez, Laurent — 202
Rollerson, Doug — 173, 182
Roos, Paul — 57
Rope, Bryce — 182, 184-188, 189, 225, 226
Roper, Roy — 103
Ross, Alex — 49, 73

Ross, Duncan — 138, 235
Ross, Glenn — 230
Rush, Xavier — 220
Ryan, Greg — 13

Sadler, Joey — 77, 78, 83
Saunders, Larry — 34
Savage, Larry — 119
Saxton, Charlie — 9, 26, 70, 92, 95, 96, 106, 142, 144, 235
Schuler, Kevin ('Herb') — 207
Schuster, John — 198, 207
Schwartzkopf, Norman — 210
Scott, Bob — 94, 95, 96, 102, 103, 108, 111, 113, 114, 121, 128, 145, 226, 228
Scrimshaw, George — 84
Seddon, Richard — 37
Seear, Gary — 165, 169
Sewell, E.H.D. — 75, 77, 81
Shaw, Mark — 173, 179, 182, 186
Shelford, Wayne ('Buck') —11, 188, 190, 198, 210, 202, 203, 204, 206, 230
Simon, Harry — 83, 92
Simpson, Johnny — 62, 96, 102, 103, 117, 146
Skinner, Kevin — 58, 96, 101, 108, 109, 110, 114, 117, 157, 158, 159, 226
Sleigh, Samuel — 232
Sloane, Peter — 169, 173, 217, 218, 220, 221
Smith, Bruce — 185
Smith, George — 40, 72
Smith, Johnny —62, 65, 118, 145
Smith, Max — 34, 40, 42
Smith, Ross — 102
Smith, Wayne — 185, 186, 188, 217, 218, 220, 221, 230
Sobers, Gary — 226
Solomon, Dave — 77
Solomon, Frank — 136
Soper, Alistair — 123
Spencer, Carlos — 221
Spiers, John — 173
Stanley, Jeremy — 207
Stanley, Joe — 79, 190, 191, 198, 207
Stanley, Noel — 235
Stead, Billy — 24, 28, 30, 35-38, 39, 42, 72, 91
Steel, Jack — 45, 84
Steel, Tony — 148
Steele, Brian — 109
Stewart, Alan — 138, 140
Stewart, Jim — 200, 201
Stewart, John ('J.J.') — 9, 156, 160-166, 169, 174, 176, 226, 227
Stewart, Ken — 156, 161, 173, 182
Stewart, Ron — 51, 55, 73, 136
Stewart, Vance — 173
Stoddard, Andrew — 11
Stohr, Jack' — 33
Stokes, Peter — 186
Stone, Arthur — 185, 186
Stone, R. A. — 38
Strachan, Ant — 202
Strahan, Sam — 147, 161
Strang, Archie — 84, 136
Strang, Harold — 95, 232, 234
Stransky, Joel — 207
Stuart, Bob — 9, 19, 65, 76, 97, 99, 100, 101, 102, 111, 113, 114, 115, 116-121, 156, 157, 178
Stuart, Don — 35, 232
Stuart, Kevin — 102, 121
Sturgeon, John — 197, 198, 199, 202, 236
Sullivan, Jack — 9, 34, 74, 82, 83, 92, 99, 101, 102, 106, 115, 116, 117, 125, 126-133, 150, 155, 156, 163, 232
Sullivan, Mary — 132
Sutcliffe, Bert — 176, 177
Sutherland, Alan — 161, 168, 173, 182
Svenson, 'Snowy' — 44, 45, 62, 66

Tairoa, Jack — 21
Tanner, John — 108, 110, 114
Tanner, Kerry — 166
Taylor, Jack — 82, 84, 92, 110
Taylor, Mark — 169
Taylor, Murray — 173
Taylor, Warwick — 185, 186, 191, 198
Tetzlaff, Percy — 62
Thomas, Barry (All Black) — 138
Thomas, Barry (NZRFU member) — 219
Thomas, Les — 62
Thomas, Paul — 203
Thomas, Russell — 156, 170, 173, 235
Thompson, Barry — 173
Thompson, Hec ('Moana') —72
Thorburn, Peter — 210
Thornett, Dick — 134
Thornett, John — 135
Thornton, Neville — 62
Timu, John — 198, 207
Tindall, Eric — 77, 78
Todd, Ernie — 155, 156, 235
Tonks, Eddie — 196, 210
Townsend, Lindsay — 102
Trapp, Maurice — 201, 220
Tremain, Kel — 127, 128, 134, 137, 138, 140, 147, 148, 166, 191, 194
Trevathan, Dave — 83, 84
Tuigamala, Inga — 207
Turner, Freddy — 84
Twigden, Tim — 173

Umaga, Tana — 215, 221, 224
Underwood, Rory — 218
Urbahn, Roger — 127, 183
Urlich, Ron — 168
Uttley, Ian — 138, 188

van Zyl, Hennie — 129
van Zyl, Hugo — 129
Vanisi, Kupu — 221
Veysey, Alex — 171, 177, 195
Vidiri, Joeli — 220
Villepreux, Pierre — 194
Vincent, Pat — 103, 142, 157
Vodanovich, Ivan — 102, 107, 145, 149, 150-153, 189, 194, 195, 225, 226, 227, 228
Vorrath, Fred ('Did') — 77, 79

Wakefield, Wavell — 58, 59
Wallace, Billy — 25, 41, 44, 69, 71-74, 81, 82
Walsh, Pat — 102, 117, 123, 125, 138
Ward, Ron — 183
Watson, Albie — 176
Watson, Eric — 97, 162, 167, 168, 169, 172-177, 184, 185, 187, 226
Watson, Ernie — 176
Watson, Len — 176
Watt, Bruce — 134, 138, 139
Watt, Russell — 123, 125, 129, 134
Webb, Des — 127
Webster, Tom — 62
West, Alf — 47
Wheel, Geoff — 171
Whetton, Alan — 191, 198, 202
Whetton, Gary — 186, 191, 198, 202, 204
Whineray, Wilson — 11, 123, 125, 126, 127, 128, 129, 134, 135, 138, 139, 140, 142, 147, 193, 194
White, H.L. ('Snow') — 114
White, Roy — 62
White, 'Tiny' — 102, 109, 110, 117, 119, 155, 157, 159, 226
Whiting, Graham — 168
Whiting, Peter — 153, 156, 165, 195
Wightman, Dave — 108
Williams, Bryan — 154, 156, 161, 165, 166, 168, 169, 201

Williams, Dai — 83, 130
Williams, J.P.R. — 151, 170
Williams, Ron — 198
Williment, Mick — 188
Willis, Royce — 220
Willocks, Charlie — 62, 114, 146
Wilson, Bevan — 170
Wilson, Doug — 114
Wilson, Hec — 109
Wilson, Jeff — 193, 205, 208, 218, 221, 224
Wilson, Len — 109
Wilson, Lionel — 140
Wilson, Norm — 108
Wilson, Richard — 173
Wilson, Stu — 169, 170, 173, 174, 182, 184, 185, 186, 187
Winfield, Bert — 72
Wintle, 'Bo' — 94
Wolfe, Neil — 134, 138
Wood, Morrie — 16, 40
Woodman, Fred — 182
Woods, Arthur — 114, 119
Wright, Don — 68
Wright, Terry — 191, 198, 202
Wylie, Edgar — 232
Wylie, Jim — 33
Wyllie, Alex — 145, 151, 154, 161, 185, 191, 192, 196-204, 205, 206, 210, 213, 225, 226, 229, 230
Wynyard, J.G. — 77

Young, Dennis — 103, 117, 123, 128, 134, 135, 137, 138

Zavos, Spiro — 107, 208, 212